CHAPTER 16

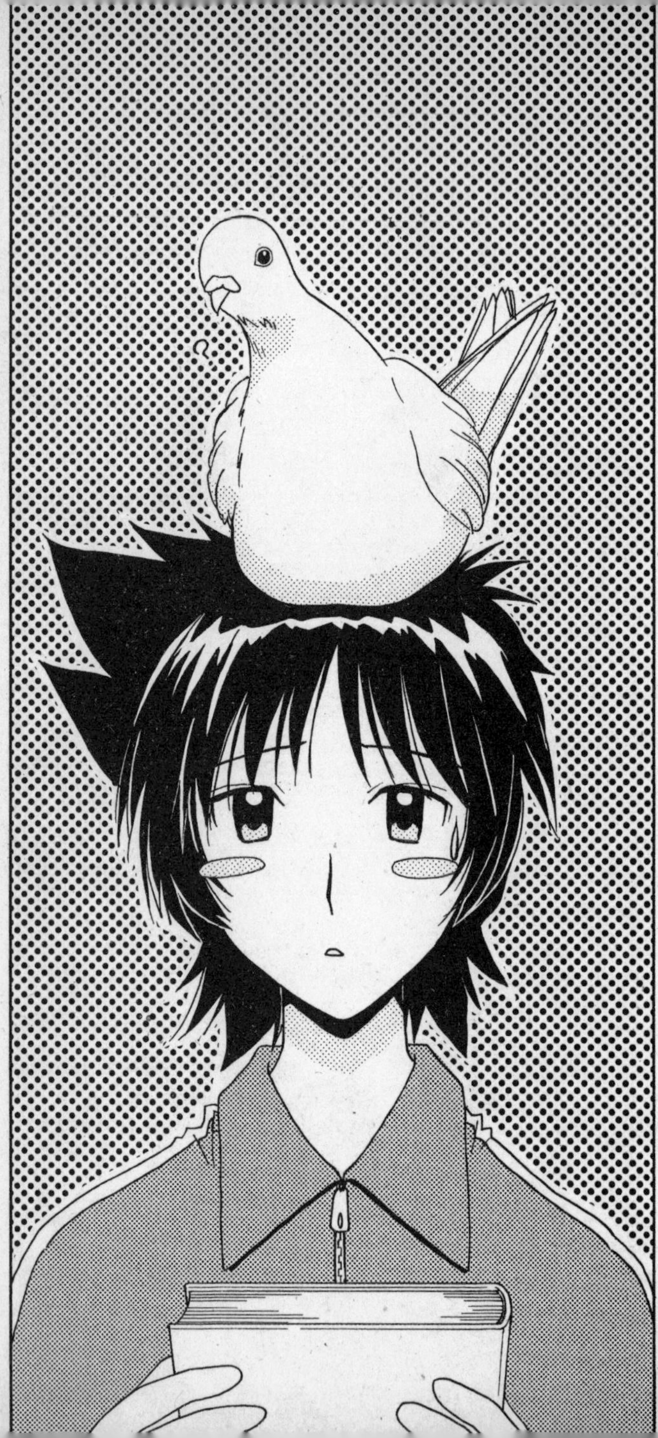

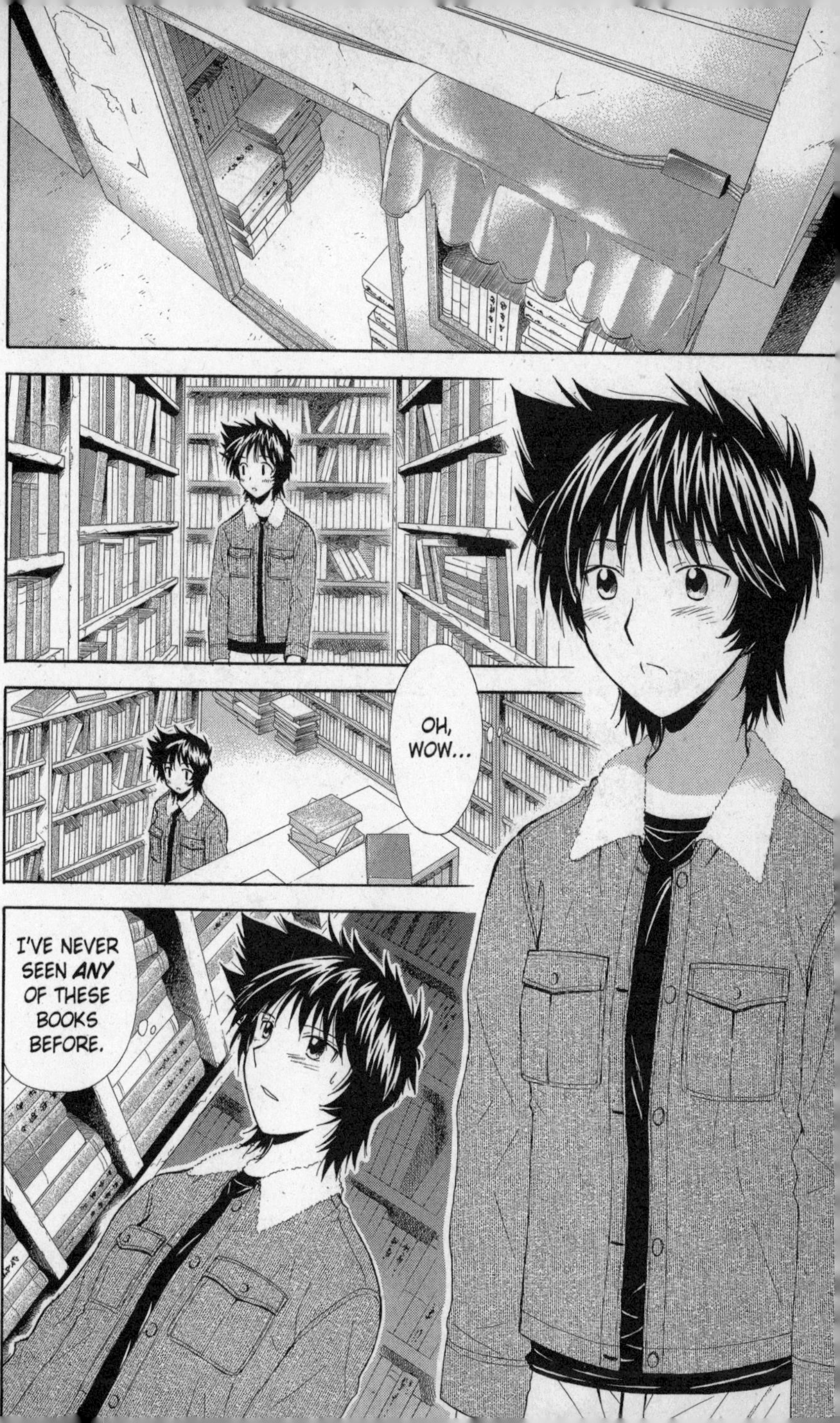
OH, WOW...
I'VE NEVER SEEN *ANY* OF THESE BOOKS BEFORE.

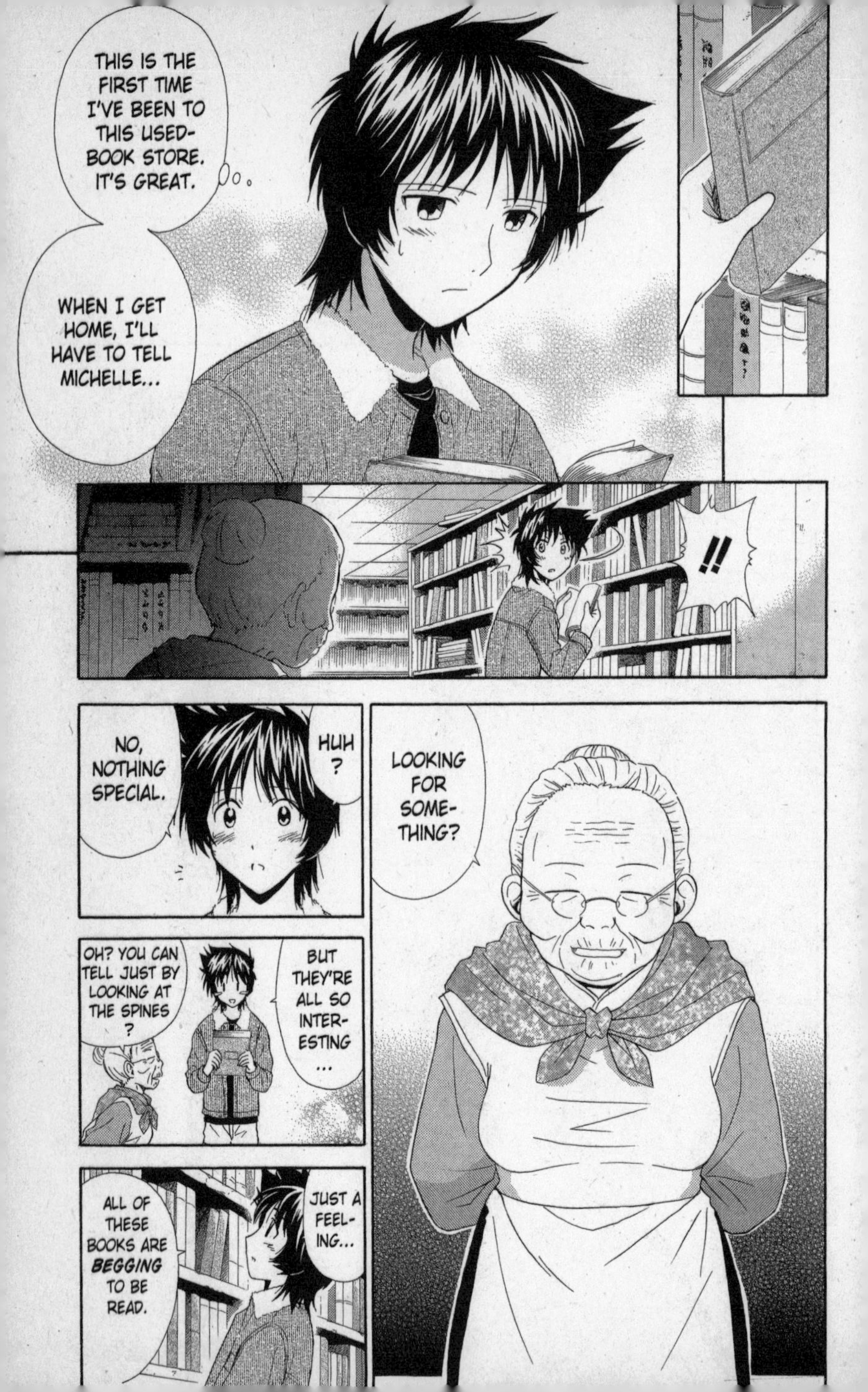
THIS IS THE FIRST TIME I'VE BEEN TO THIS USED-BOOK STORE. IT'S GREAT.
WHEN I GET HOME, I'LL HAVE TO TELL MICHELLE...
!!
LOOKING FOR SOME-THING?
HUH?
NO, NOTHING SPECIAL.
BUT THEY'RE ALL SO INTER-ESTING...
OH? YOU CAN TELL JUST BY LOOKING AT THE SPINES?
JUST A FEEL-ING...
ALL OF THESE BOOKS ARE *BEGGING* TO BE READ.

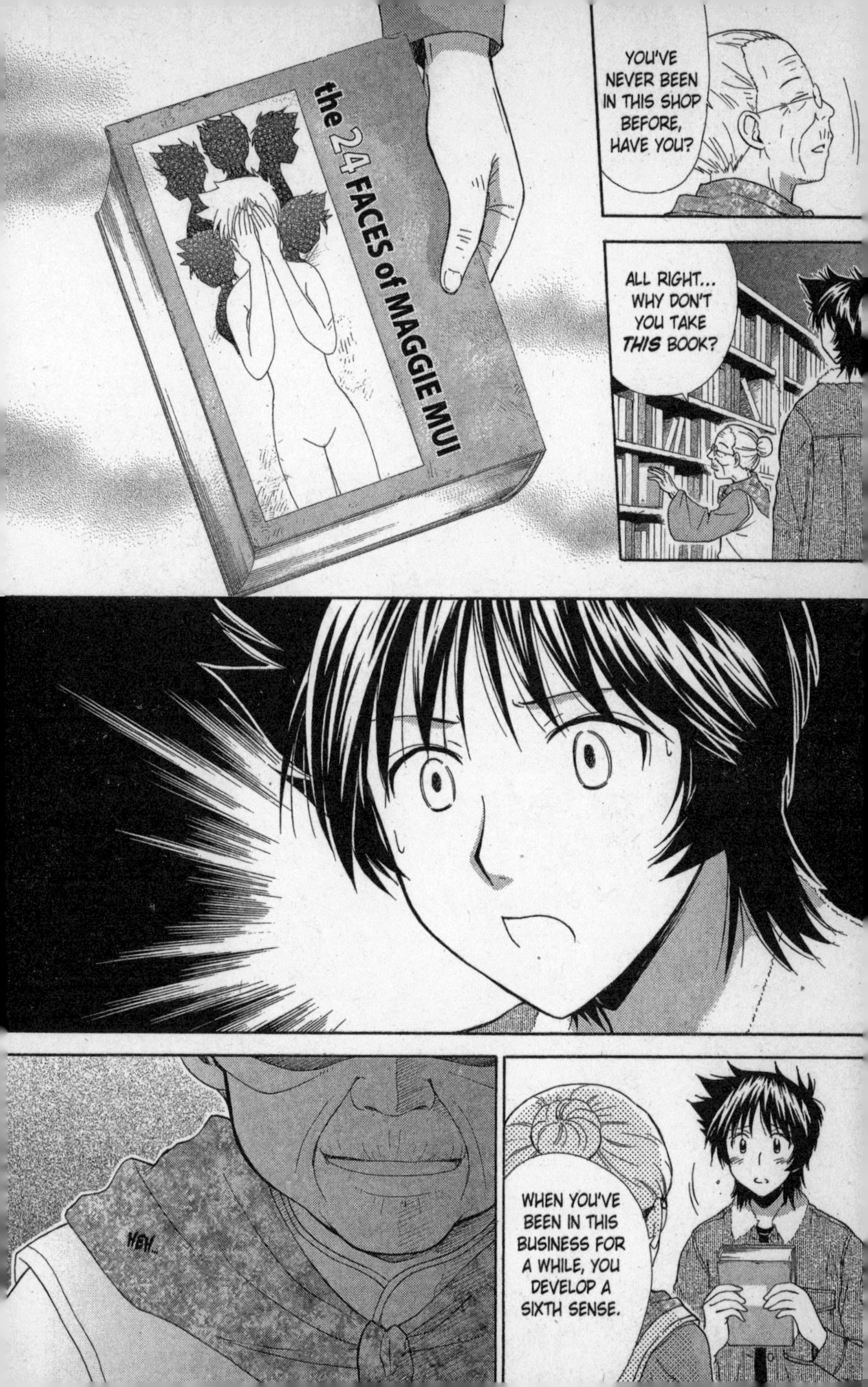
YOU'VE NEVER BEEN IN THIS SHOP BEFORE, HAVE YOU?
ALL RIGHT... WHY DON'T YOU TAKE *THIS* BOOK?
the 24 FACES of MAGGIE MUI
WHEN YOU'VE BEEN IN THIS BUSINESS FOR A WHILE, YOU DEVELOP A SIXTH SENSE.
HEH..

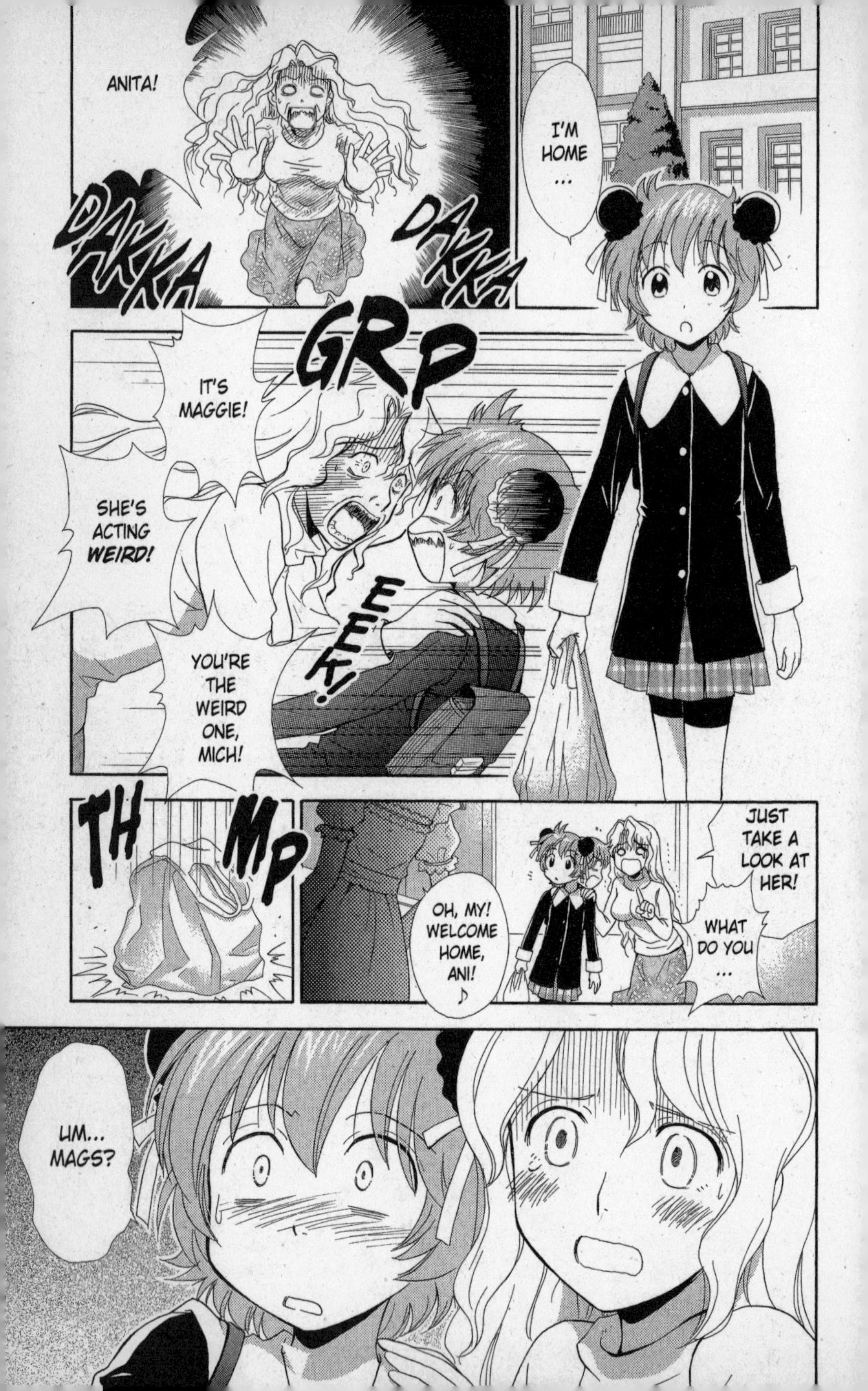
I'M HOME ...
DAKKA
ANITA!
DAKKA
GRP
IT'S MAGGIE!
SHE'S ACTING *WEIRD!*
EEEK!
YOU'RE THE WEIRD ONE, MICH!
JUST TAKE A LOOK AT HER!
WHAT DO YOU ...
OH, MY! WELCOME HOME, ANI! ♪
THMP
UM... MAGS?

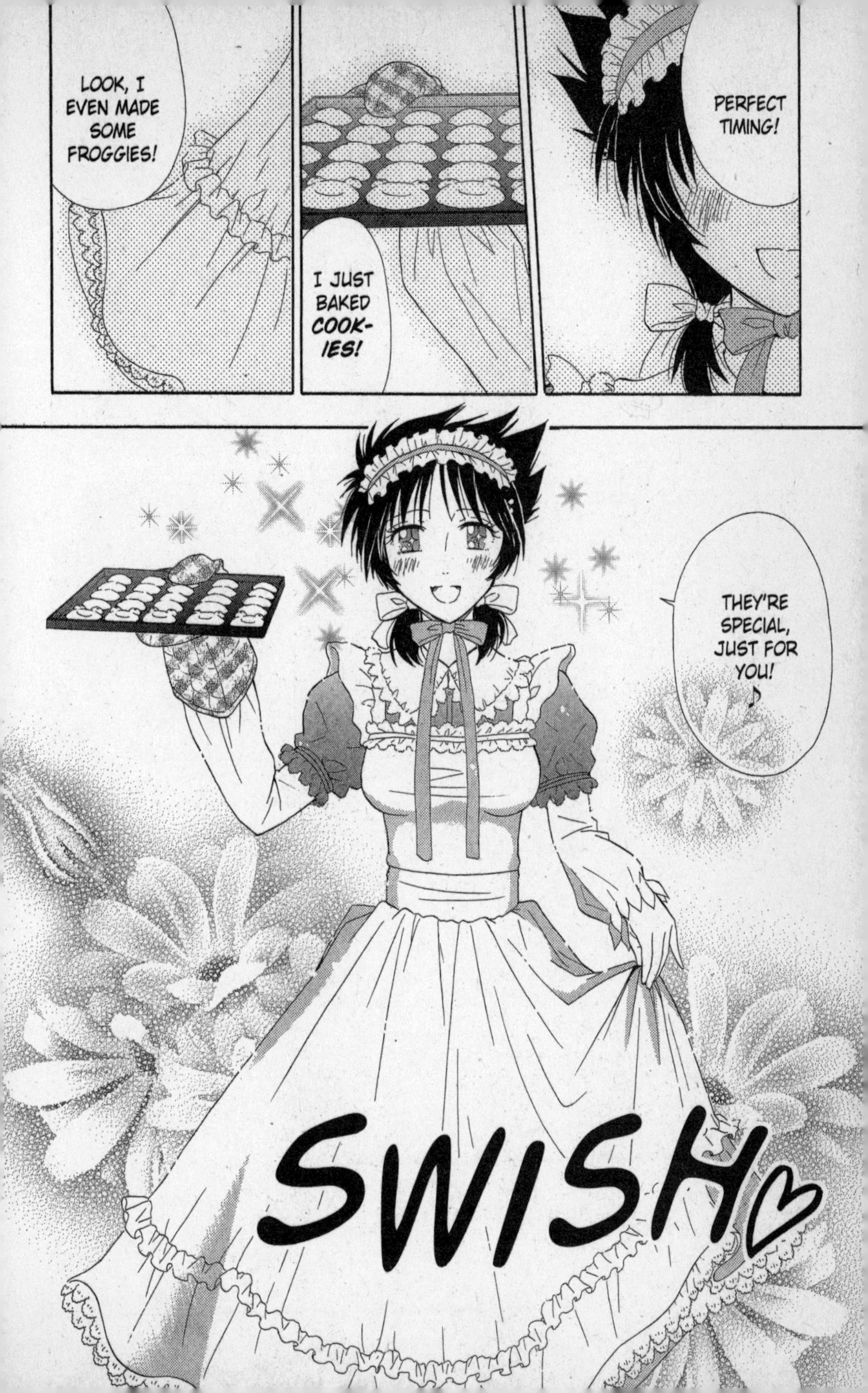
PERFECT TIMING!
I JUST BAKED COOK-IES!
LOOK, I EVEN MADE SOME FROGGIES!
THEY'RE SPECIAL, JUST FOR YOU! ♪
SWISH♡

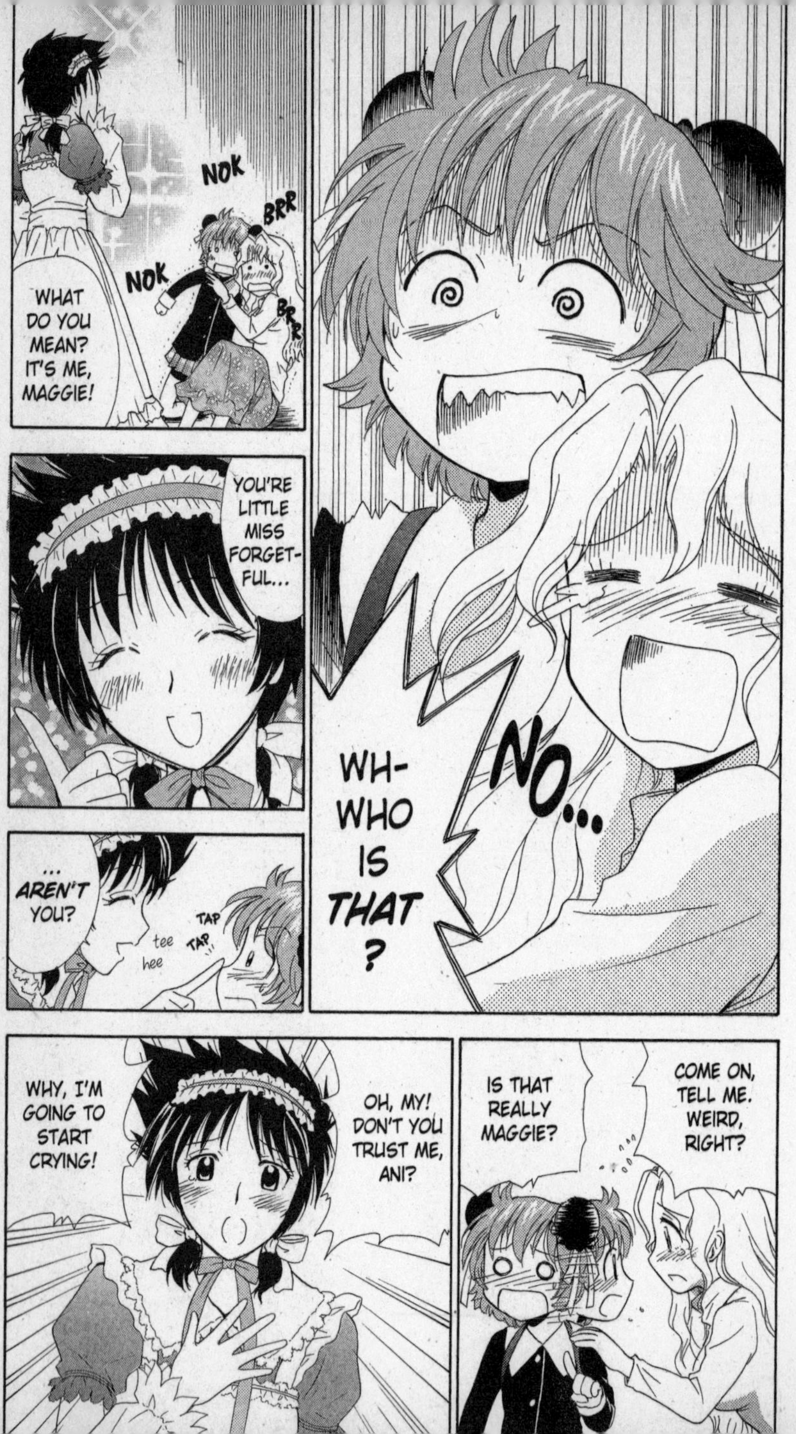
NO...
WH-WHO IS THAT?
NOK
BRR
NOK
BRR
WHAT DO YOU MEAN? IT'S ME, MAGGIE!
YOU'RE LITTLE MISS FORGET-FUL...
... AREN'T YOU?
TAP TAP
tee hee
COME ON, TELL ME. WEIRD, RIGHT?
IS THAT REALLY MAGGIE?
OH, MY! DON'T YOU TRUST ME, ANI?
WHY, I'M GOING TO START CRYING!

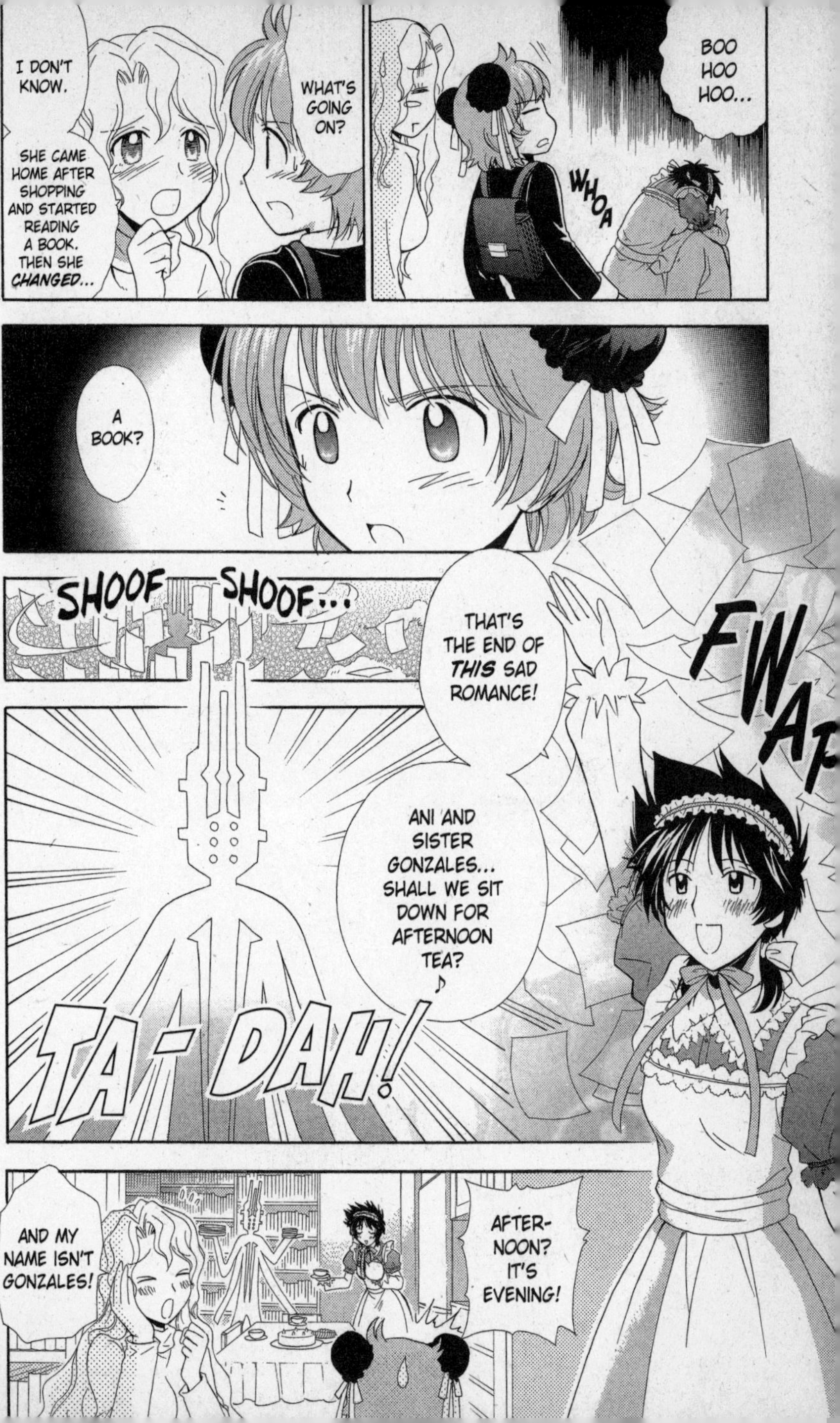
BOO HOO HOO...
WHOA
WHAT'S GOING ON?
I DON'T KNOW.
SHE CAME HOME AFTER SHOPPING AND STARTED READING A BOOK. THEN SHE *CHANGED*...
A BOOK?
FWAP
THAT'S THE END OF *THIS* SAD ROMANCE!
SHOOF SHOOF...
ANI AND SISTER GONZALES... SHALL WE SIT DOWN FOR AFTERNOON TEA? ♪
TA-DAH!
AFTER-NOON? IT'S EVENING!
AND MY NAME ISN'T GONZALES!

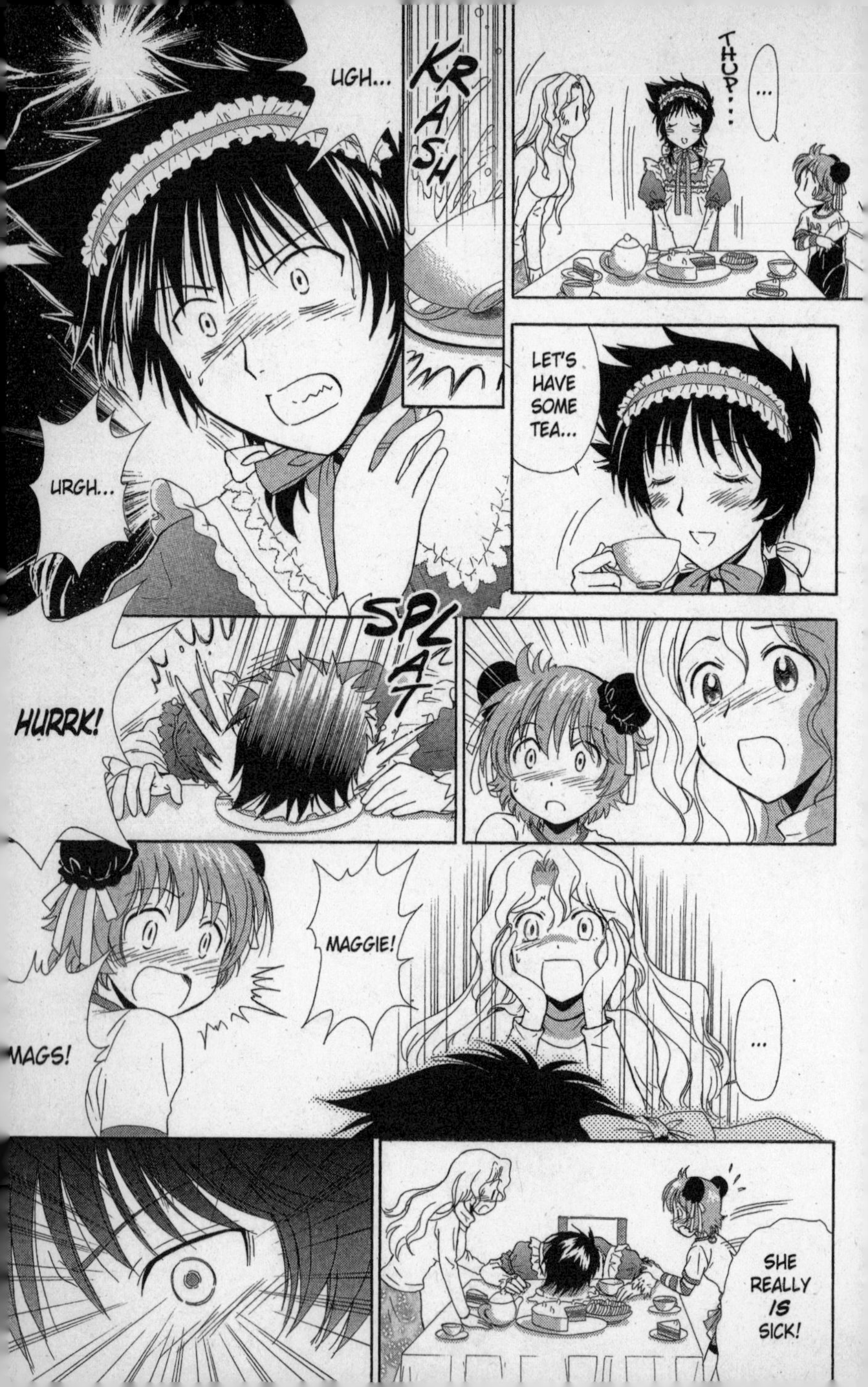
THUP...
...
LET'S HAVE SOME TEA...
KRASH
UGH...
URGH...
SPLAT
HURRK!
...
MAGGIE!
MAGS!
SHE REALLY IS SICK!

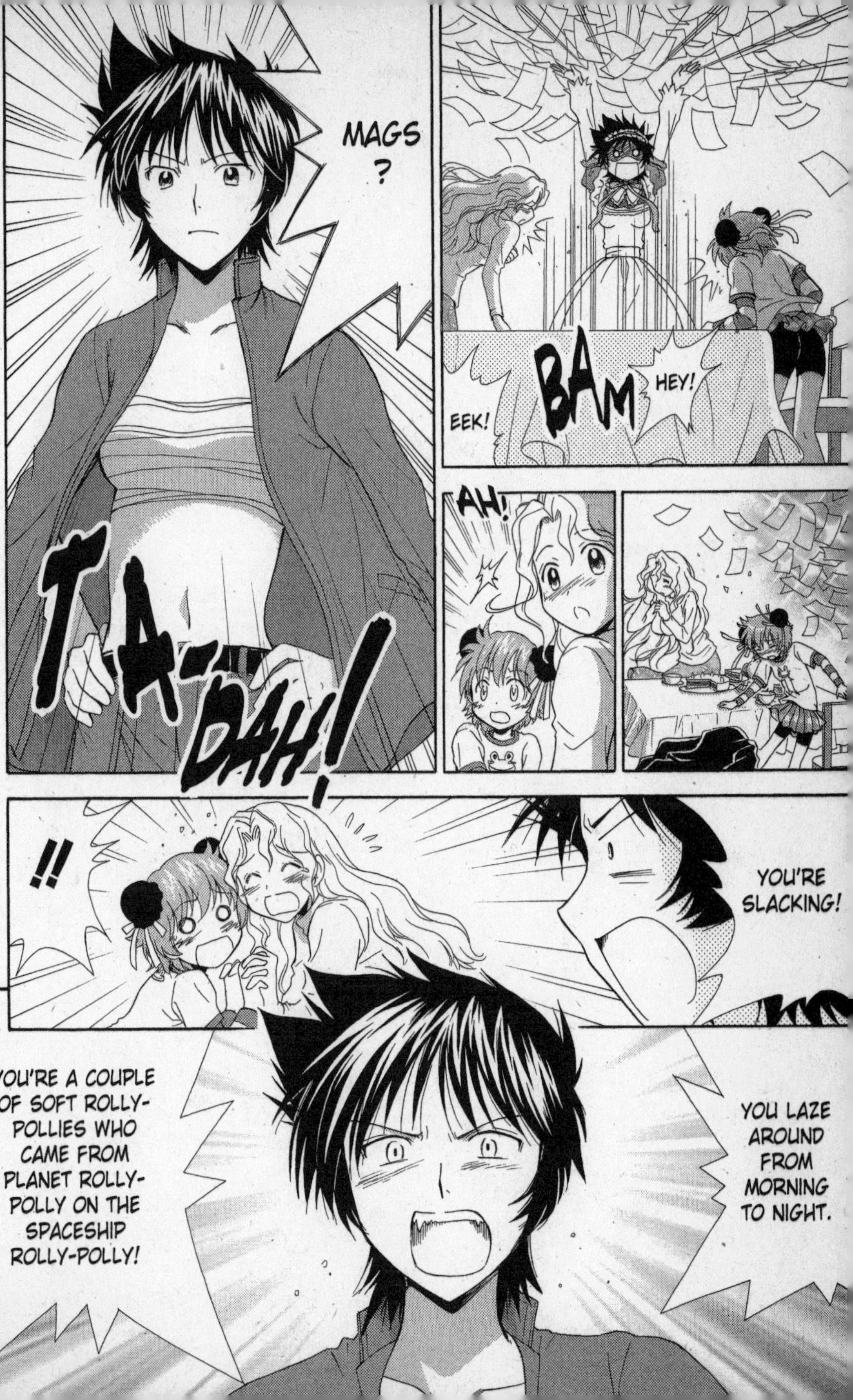
HEY!
BAM
EEK!
AH!
MAGS ?
TA-DAH!
YOU'RE SLACKING!
!!
YOU LAZE AROUND FROM MORNING TO NIGHT.
YOU'RE A COUPLE OF SOFT ROLLY-POLLIES WHO CAME FROM PLANET ROLLY-POLLY ON THE SPACESHIP ROLLY-POLLY!

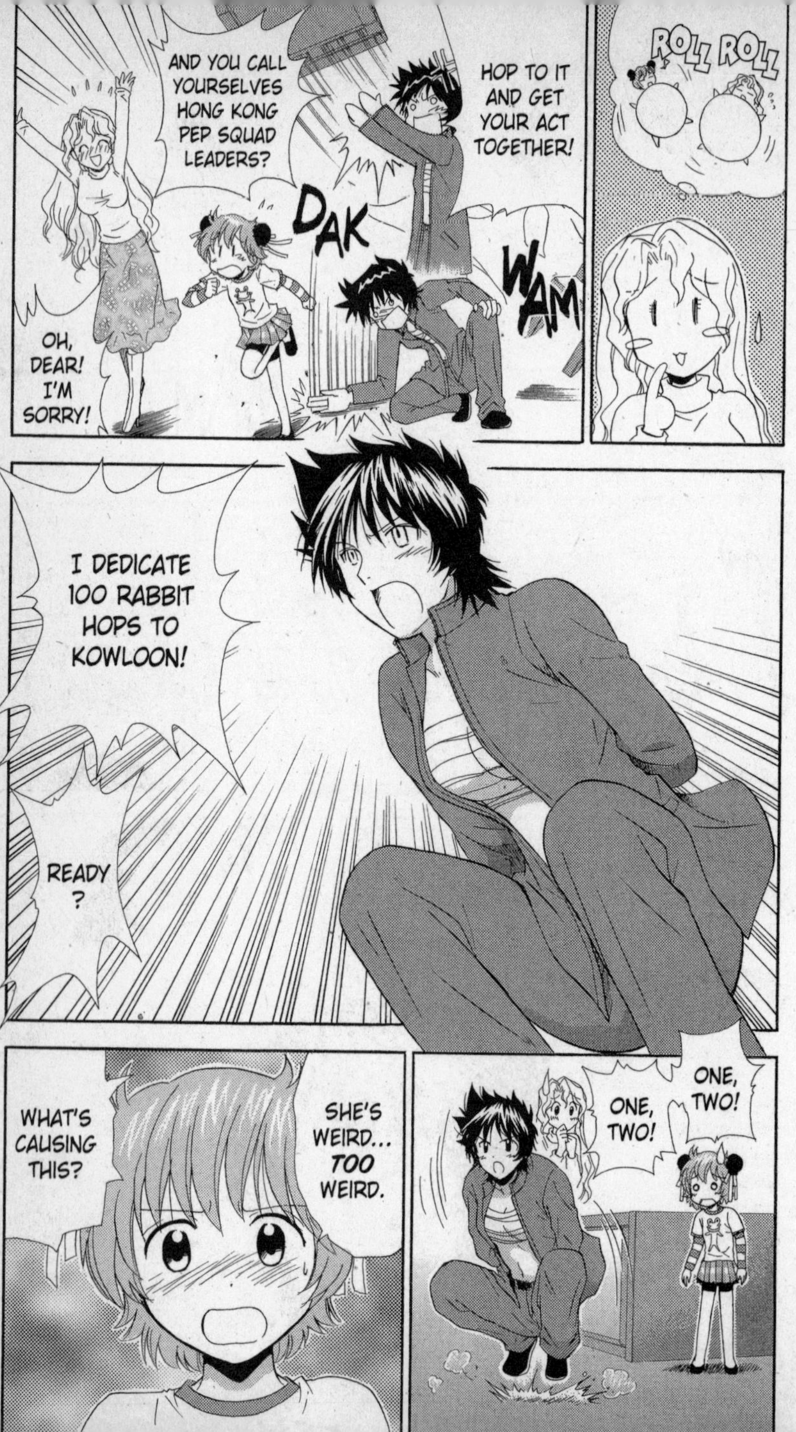
ROLL ROLL
HOP TO IT AND GET YOUR ACT TOGETHER!
AND YOU CALL YOURSELVES HONG KONG PEP SQUAD LEADERS?
WAM
DAK
OH, DEAR! I'M SORRY!
I DEDICATE 100 RABBIT HOPS TO KOWLOON!
READY?
ONE, TWO!
ONE, TWO!
SHE'S WEIRD... *TOO* WEIRD.
WHAT'S CAUSING THIS?

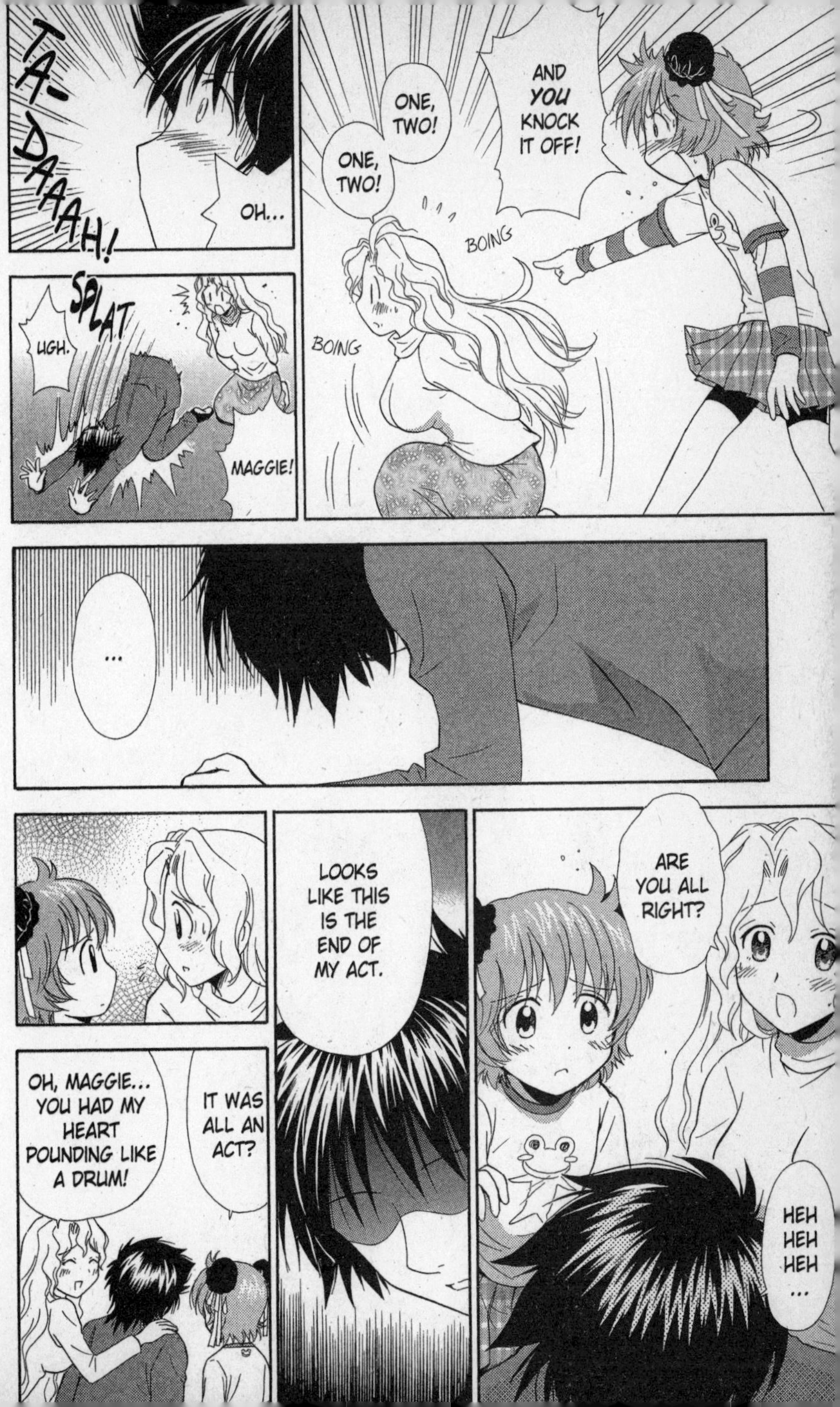
AND YOU KNOCK IT OFF!
ONE, TWO!
ONE, TWO!
BOING
BOING
TA-DAAAAH!
OH...
SPLAT
UGH.
MAGGIE!
...
ARE YOU ALL RIGHT?
HEH HEH HEH ...
LOOKS LIKE THIS IS THE END OF MY ACT.
IT WAS ALL AN ACT?
OH, MAGGIE... YOU HAD MY HEART POUNDING LIKE A DRUM!

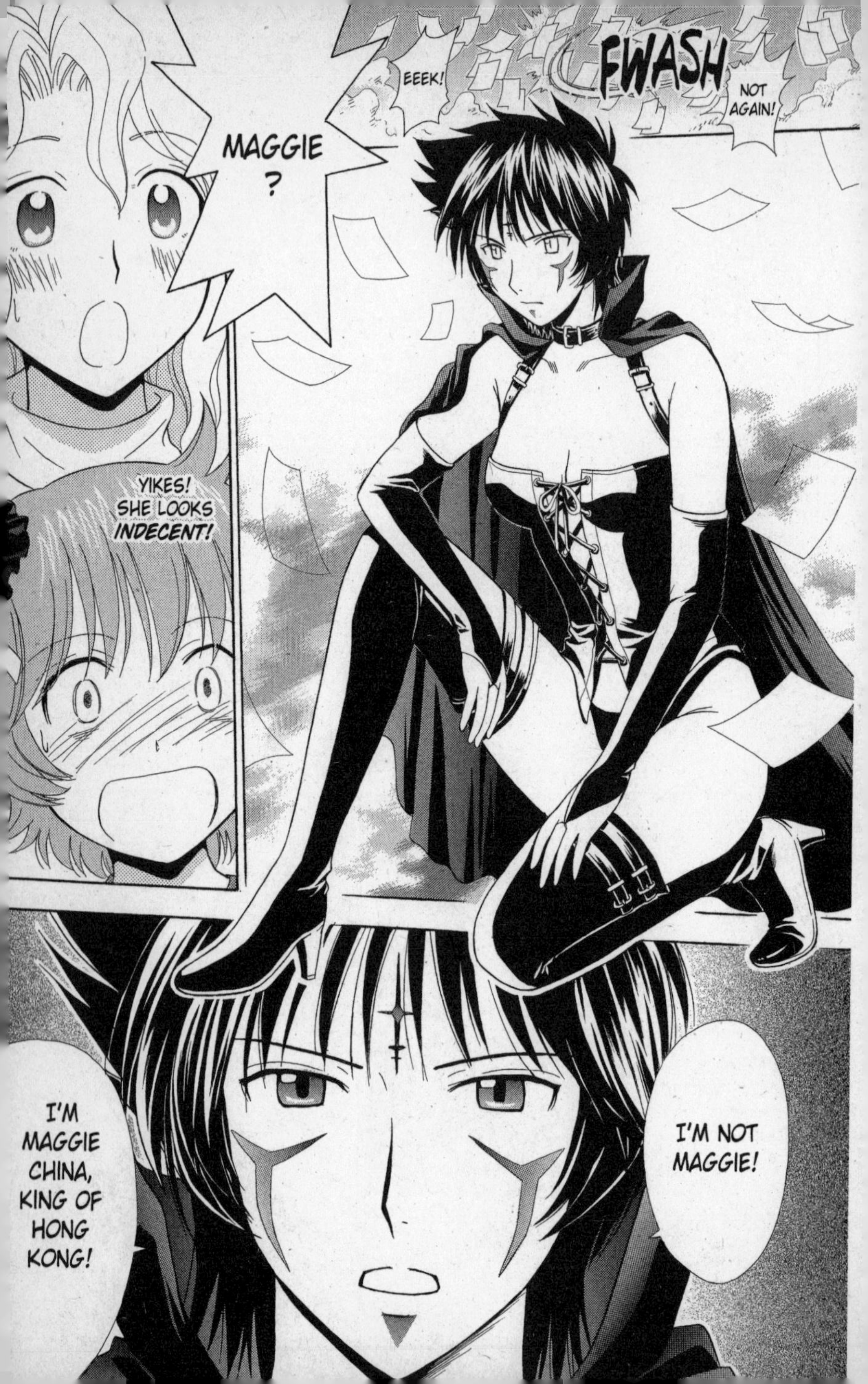
NOT AGAIN!
FWASH
EEEK!
MAGGIE ?
YIKES! SHE LOOKS INDECENT!
I'M NOT MAGGIE!
I'M MAGGIE CHINA, KING OF HONG KONG!

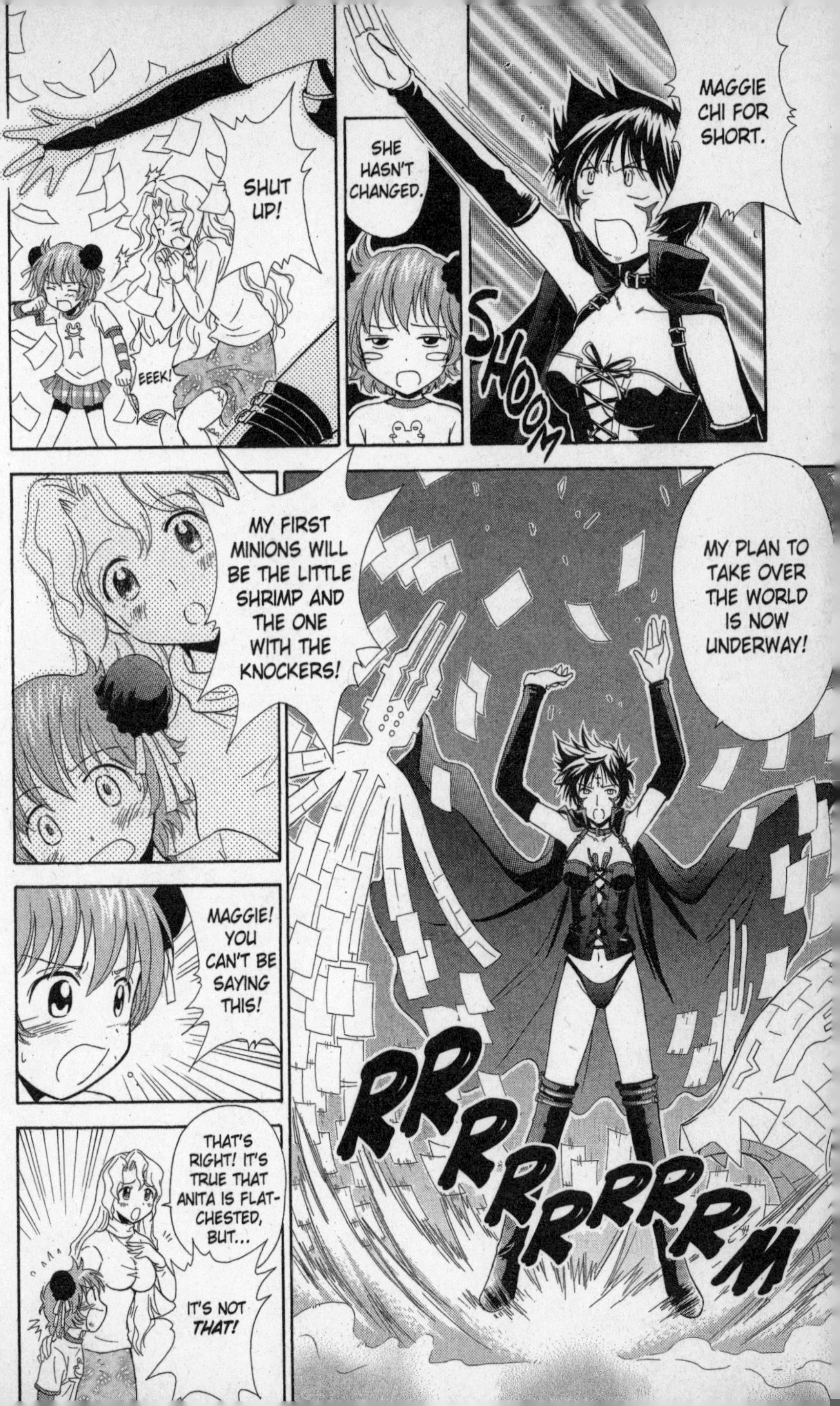
MAGGIE CHI FOR SHORT.
SHOOM
SHE HASN'T CHANGED.
SHUT UP!
EEEK!
MY PLAN TO TAKE OVER THE WORLD IS NOW UNDERWAY!
MY FIRST MINIONS WILL BE THE LITTLE SHRIMP AND THE ONE WITH THE KNOCKERS!
RRRRRRRRM
MAGGIE! YOU CAN'T BE SAYING THIS!
THAT'S RIGHT! IT'S TRUE THAT ANITA IS FLAT-CHESTED, BUT...
IT'S NOT *THAT*!

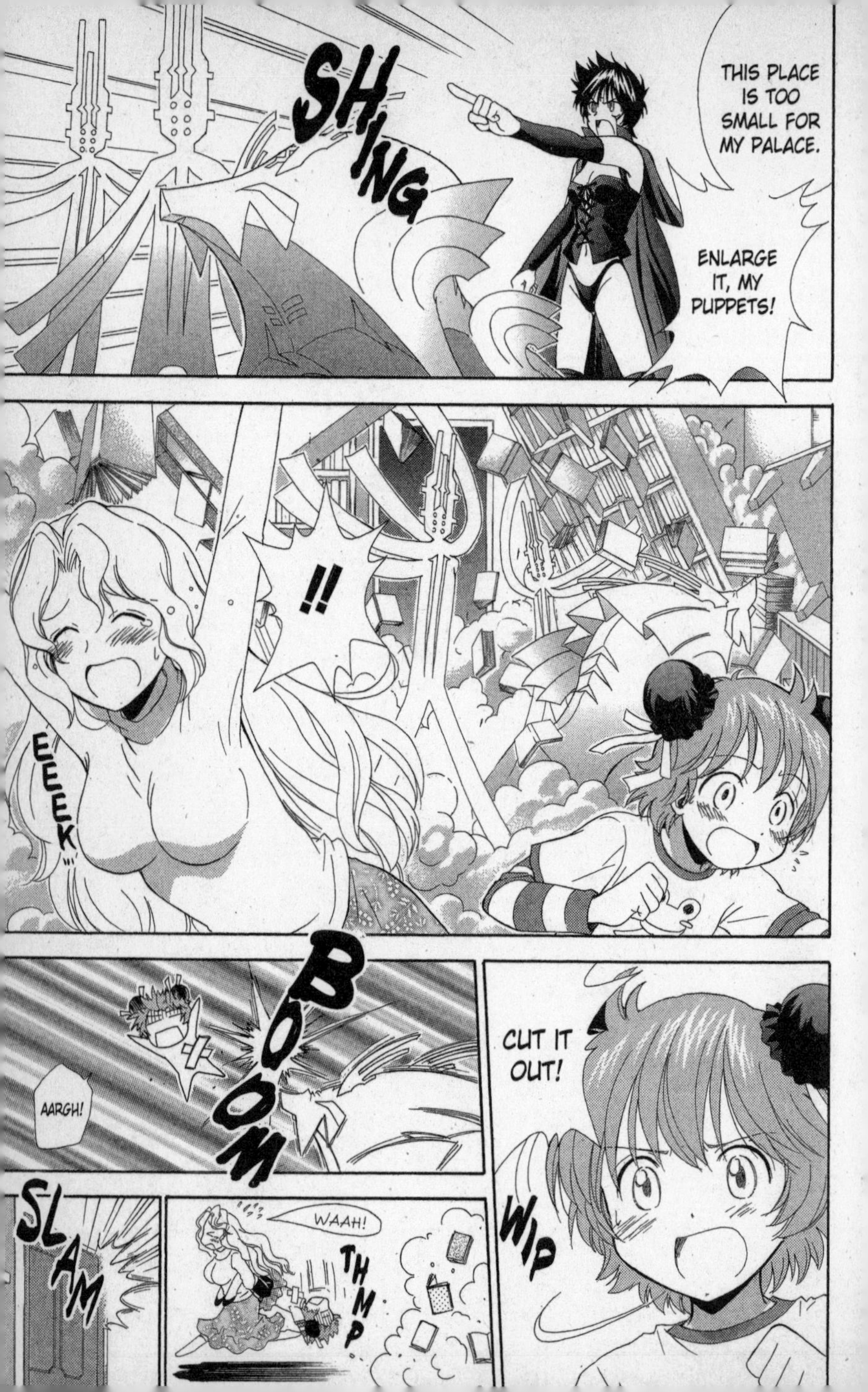
THIS PLACE IS TOO SMALL FOR MY PALACE.
ENLARGE IT, MY PUPPETS!
SHING
!!
EEEEK!!!
BOOM
CUT IT OUT!
WIP
AARGH!
WAAH!
THMP
SLAM

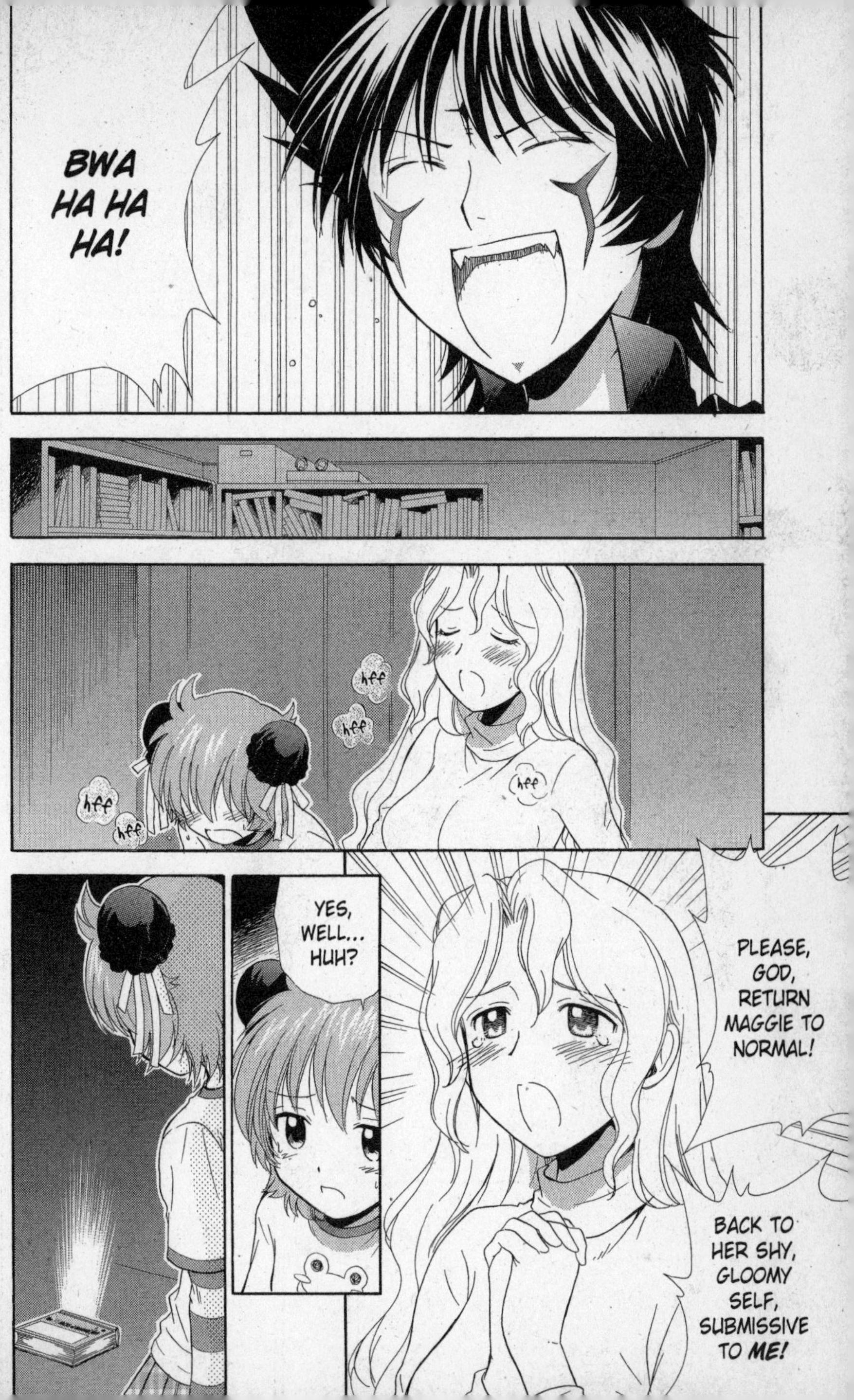
BWA HA HA HA!
hff
hff
hff
hff
hff
PLEASE, GOD, RETURN MAGGIE TO NORMAL!
BACK TO HER SHY, GLOOMY SELF, SUBMISSIVE TO *ME!*
YES, WELL... HUH?

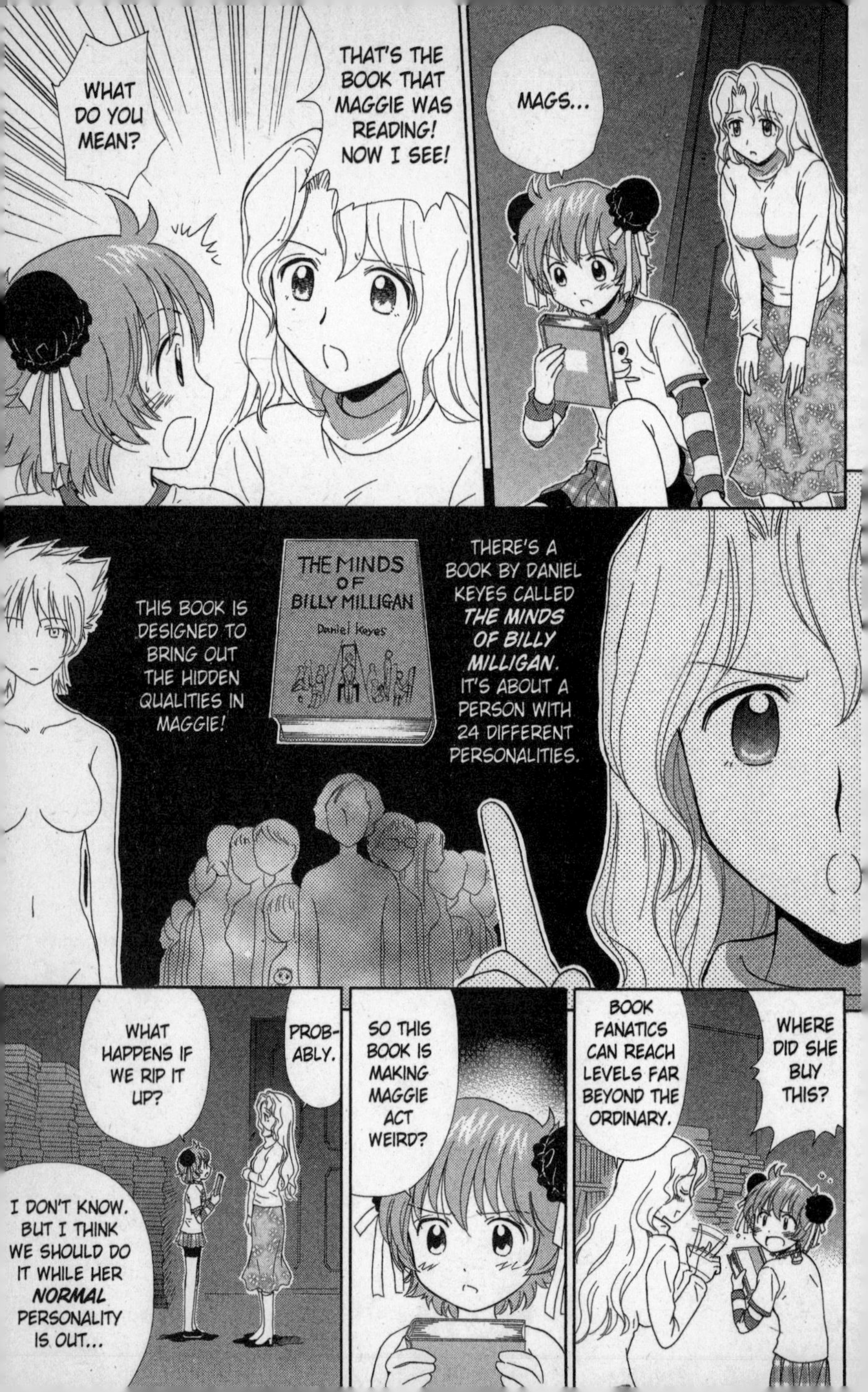
MAGS...
THAT'S THE BOOK THAT MAGGIE WAS READING! NOW I SEE!
WHAT DO YOU MEAN?
THERE'S A BOOK BY DANIEL KEYES CALLED *THE MINDS OF BILLY MILLIGAN*. IT'S ABOUT A PERSON WITH 24 DIFFERENT PERSONALITIES.
THE MINDS OF BILLY MILLIGAN
Daniel Keyes
THIS BOOK IS DESIGNED TO BRING OUT THE HIDDEN QUALITIES IN MAGGIE!
WHERE DID SHE BUY THIS?
BOOK FANATICS CAN REACH LEVELS FAR BEYOND THE ORDINARY.
SO THIS BOOK IS MAKING MAGGIE ACT WEIRD?
PROB-ABLY.
WHAT HAPPENS IF WE RIP IT UP?
I DON'T KNOW. BUT I THINK WE SHOULD DO IT WHILE HER *NORMAL* PERSONALITY IS OUT...

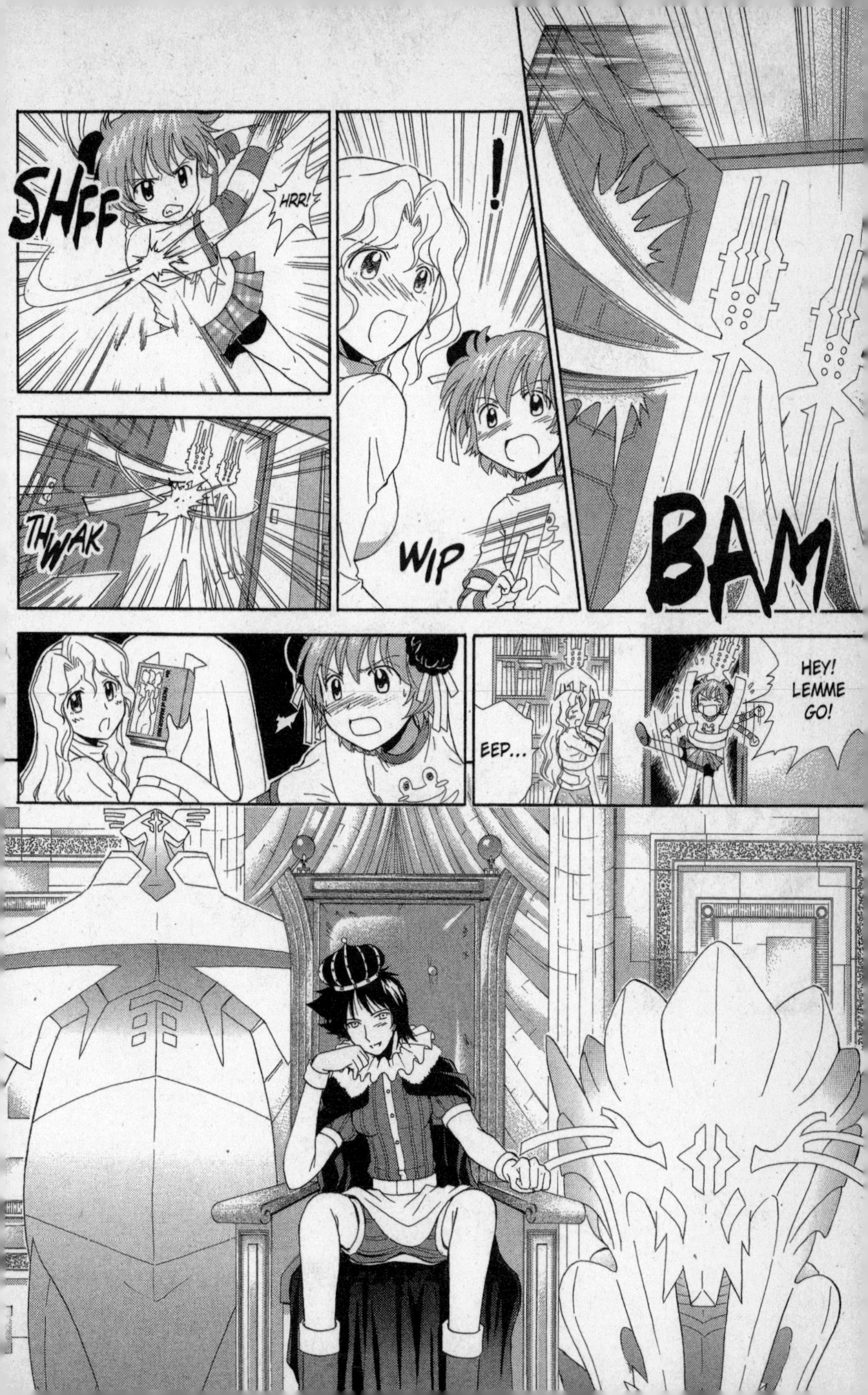
BAM
!
WIP
HRR!
SHFF
THWAK
HEY! LEMME GO!
EEP...

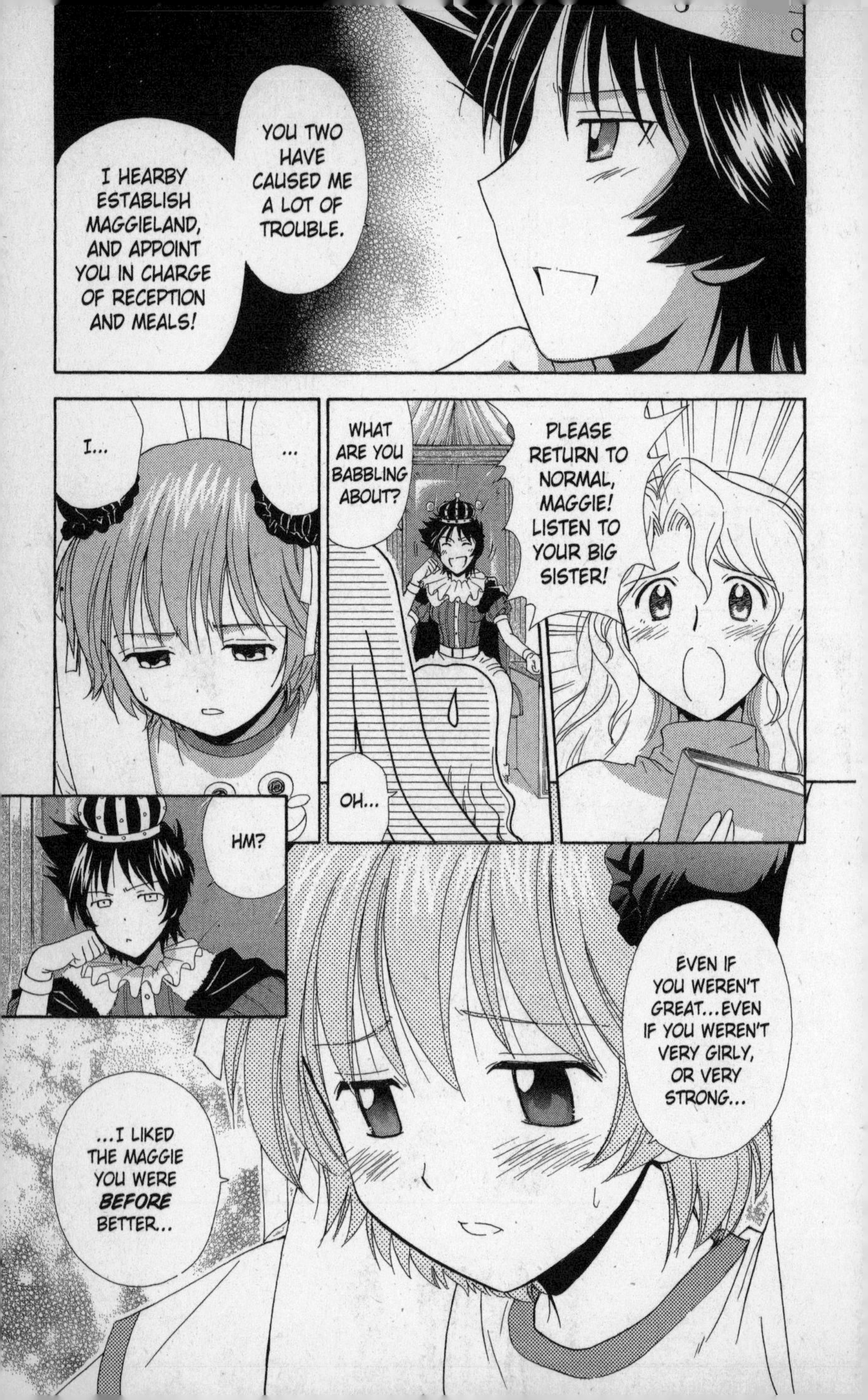
YOU TWO HAVE CAUSED ME A LOT OF TROUBLE.
I HEARBY ESTABLISH MAGGIELAND, AND APPOINT YOU IN CHARGE OF RECEPTION AND MEALS!
PLEASE RETURN TO NORMAL, MAGGIE! LISTEN TO YOUR BIG SISTER!
WHAT ARE YOU BABBLING ABOUT?
OH...
...
I...
HM?
EVEN IF YOU WEREN'T GREAT...EVEN IF YOU WEREN'T VERY GIRLY, OR VERY STRONG...
...I LIKED THE MAGGIE YOU WERE *BEFORE* BETTER...

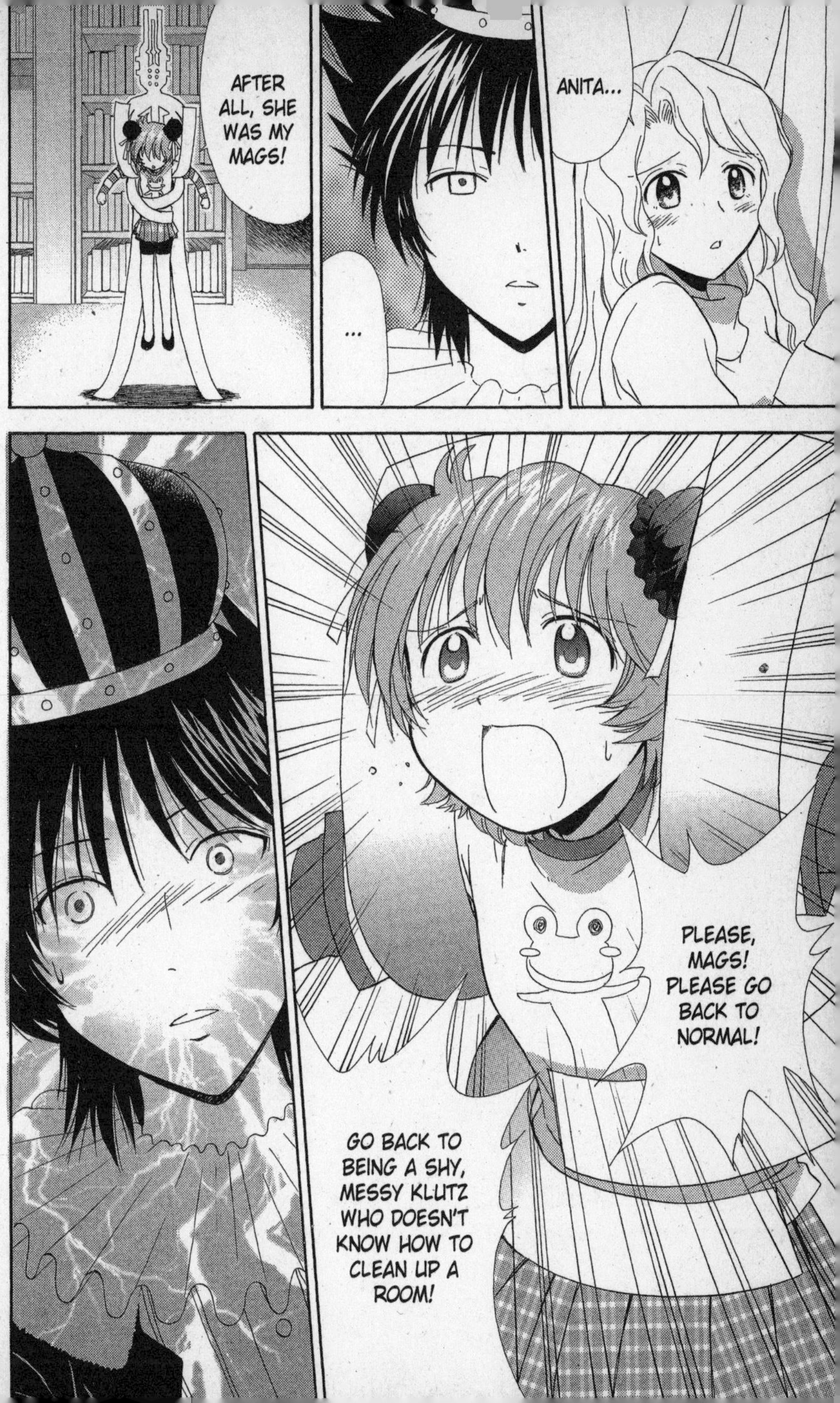
ANITA...
...
AFTER ALL, SHE WAS MY MAGS!
PLEASE, MAGS! PLEASE GO BACK TO NORMAL!
GO BACK TO BEING A SHY, MESSY KLUTZ WHO DOESN'T KNOW HOW TO CLEAN UP A ROOM!

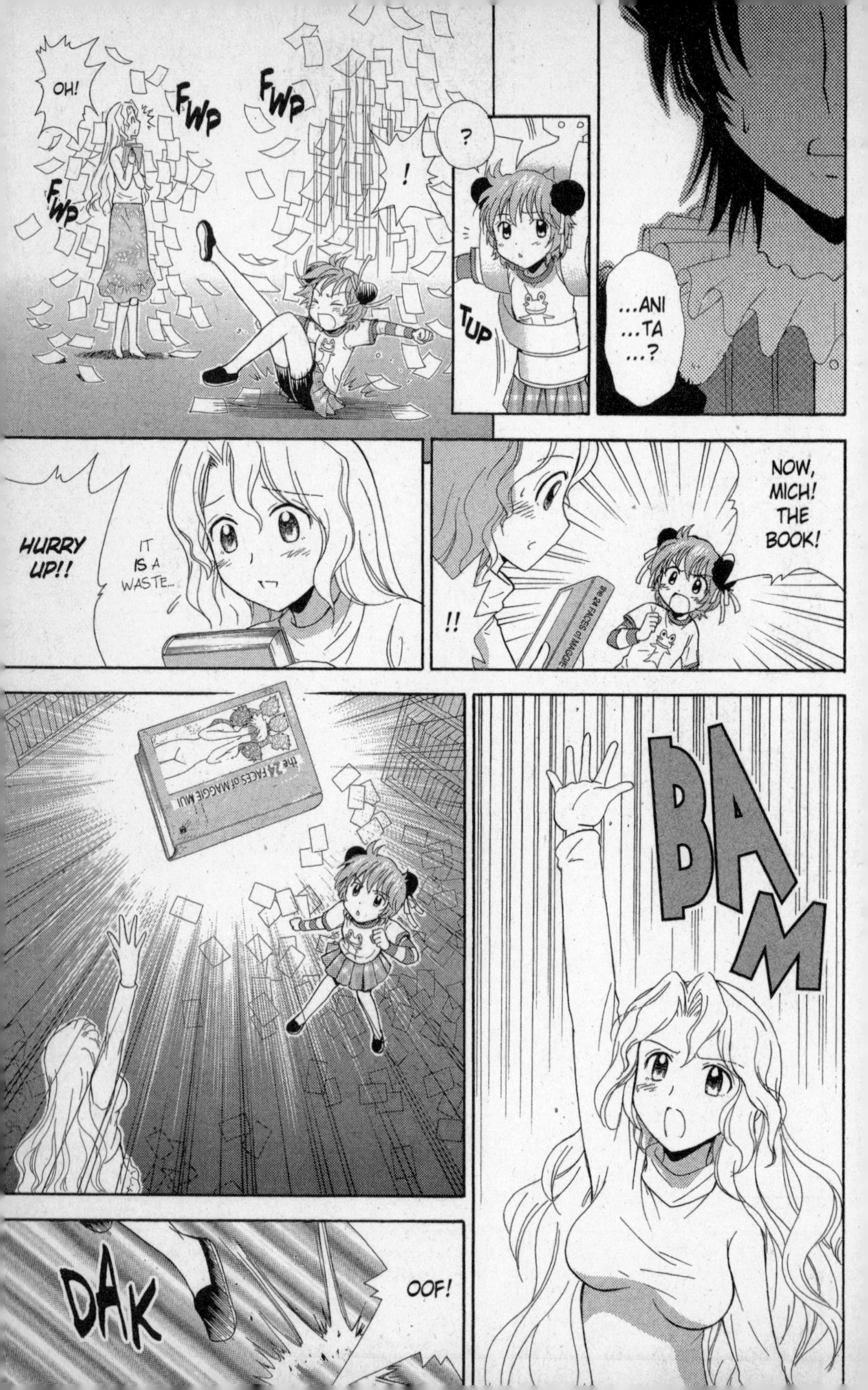
...ANI ...TA ...?
?
TUP
OH!
FWP
FWP
FWP
!
NOW, MICH! THE BOOK!
!!
the 24 FACES of MAGGIE
HURRY UP!!
IT IS A WASTE...
BAM
the 24 FACES of MAGGIE MUI
DAK
OOF!

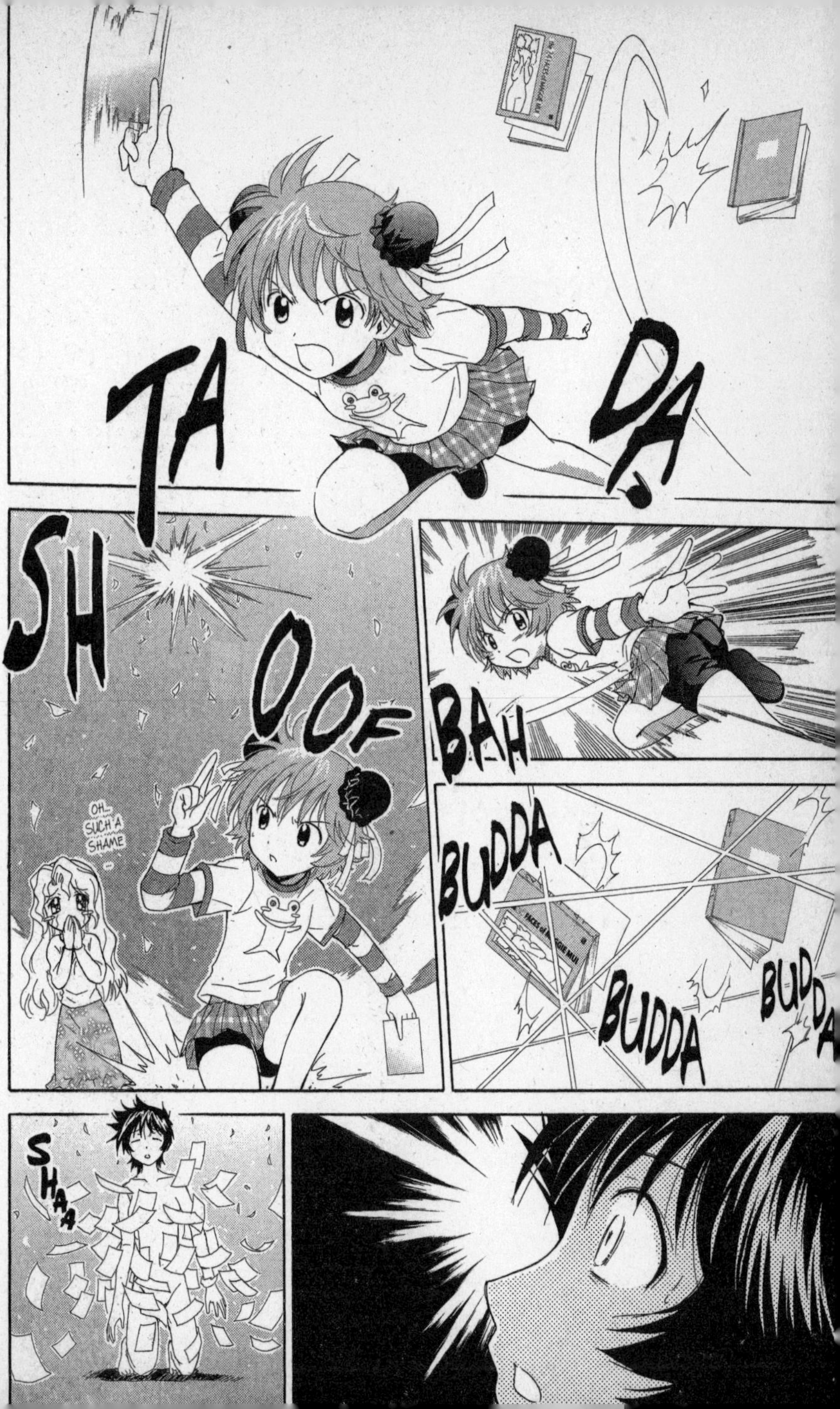
TA DA
BAH
BUDDA
FACES of MAGGIE MUI
BUDDA
BUDDA
SH OOF
OH... SUCH A SHAME ...
SHAA

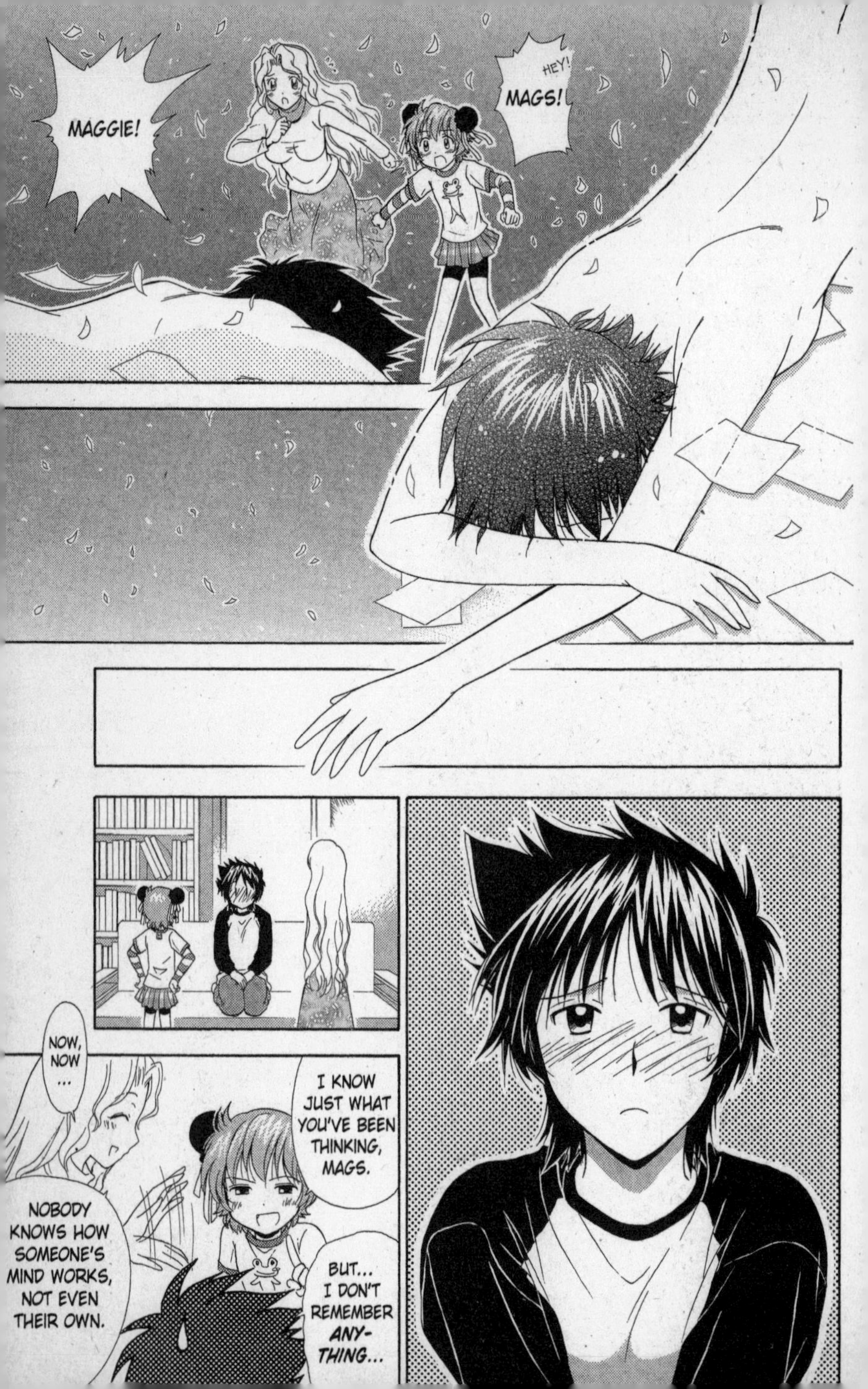
HEY!
MAGS!
MAGGIE!
I KNOW JUST WHAT YOU'VE BEEN THINKING, MAGS.
NOW, NOW ...
NOBODY KNOWS HOW SOMEONE'S MIND WORKS, NOT EVEN THEIR OWN.
BUT... I DON'T REMEMBER ANYTHING...

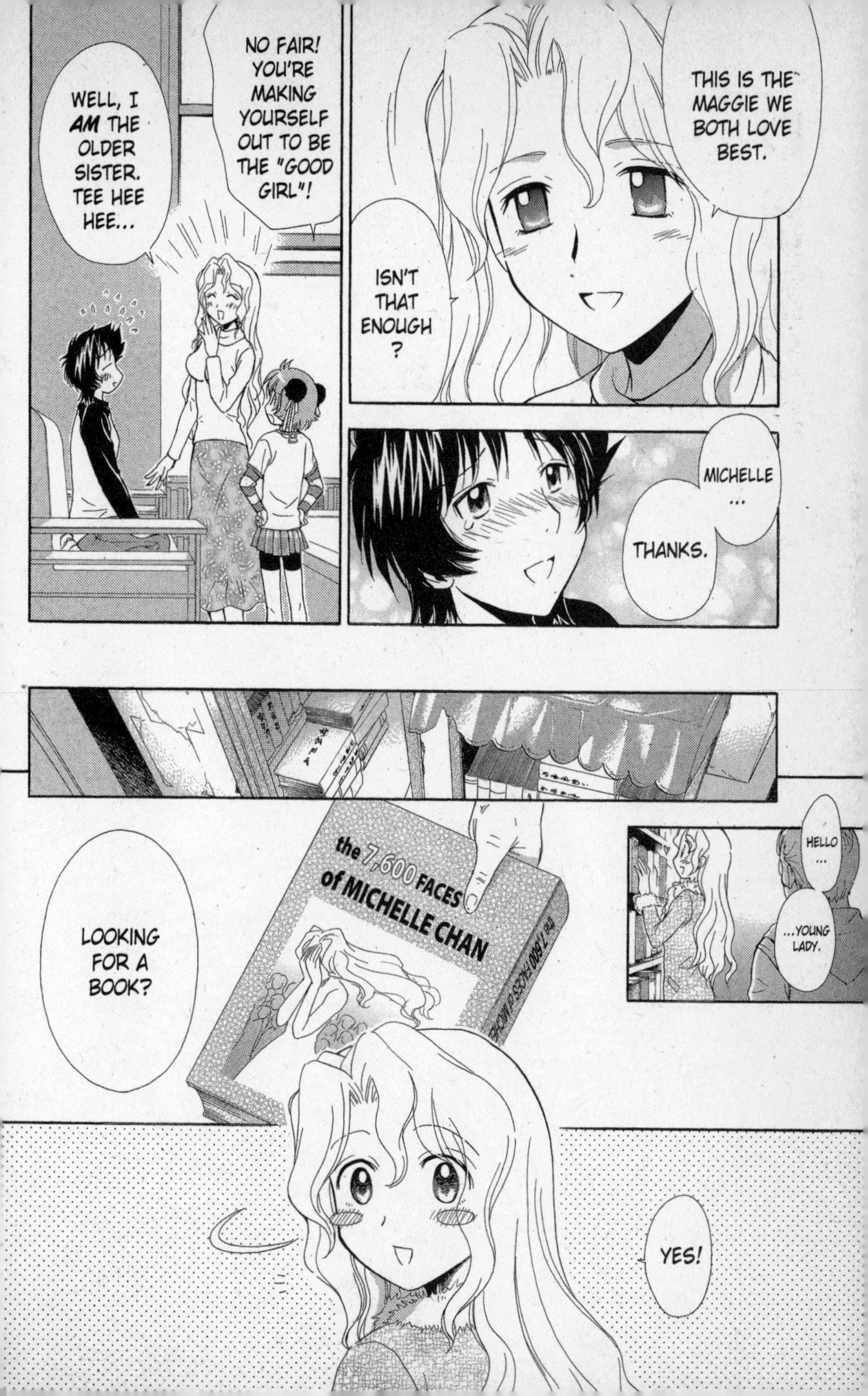
THIS IS THE MAGGIE WE BOTH LOVE BEST.
ISN'T THAT ENOUGH?
MICHELLE...
THANKS.
NO FAIR! YOU'RE MAKING YOURSELF OUT TO BE THE "GOOD GIRL"!
WELL, I **AM** THE OLDER SISTER. TEE HEE HEE...
HELLO...
...YOUNG LADY.
the 7,600 FACES of MICHELLE CHAN
LOOKING FOR A BOOK?
YES!

CHAPTER 17

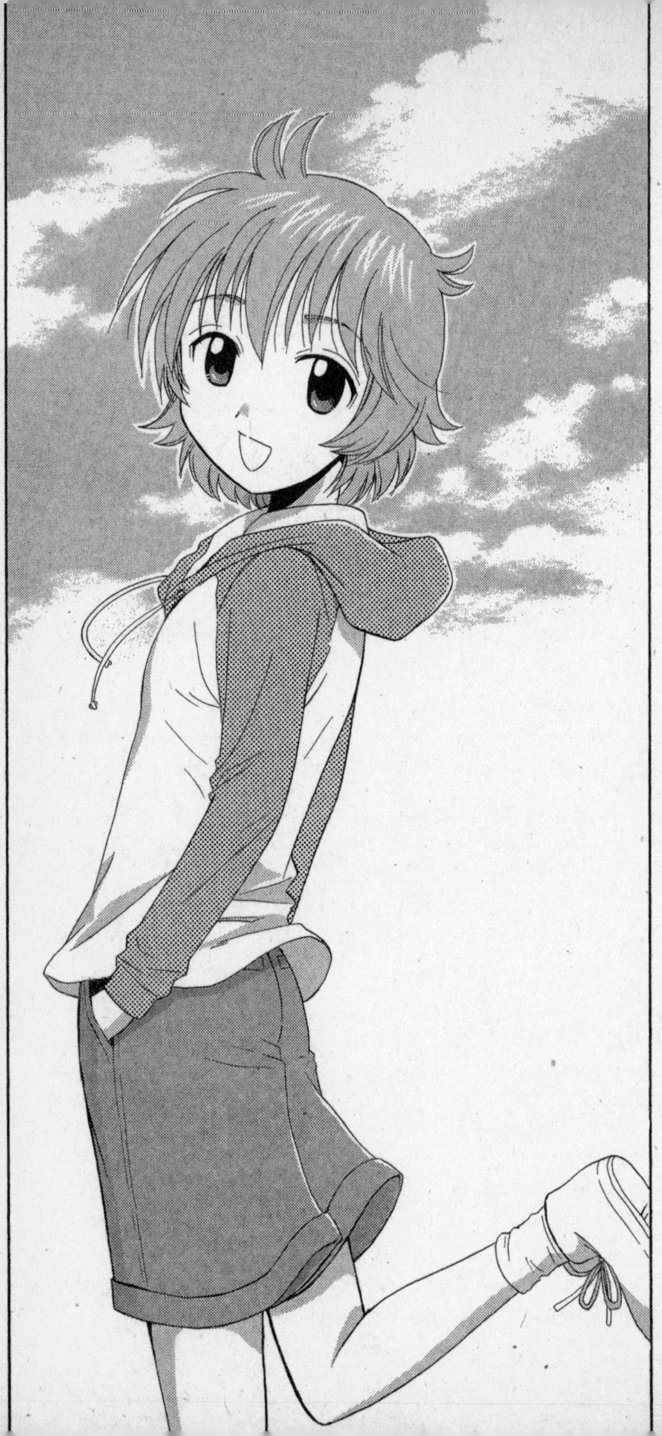

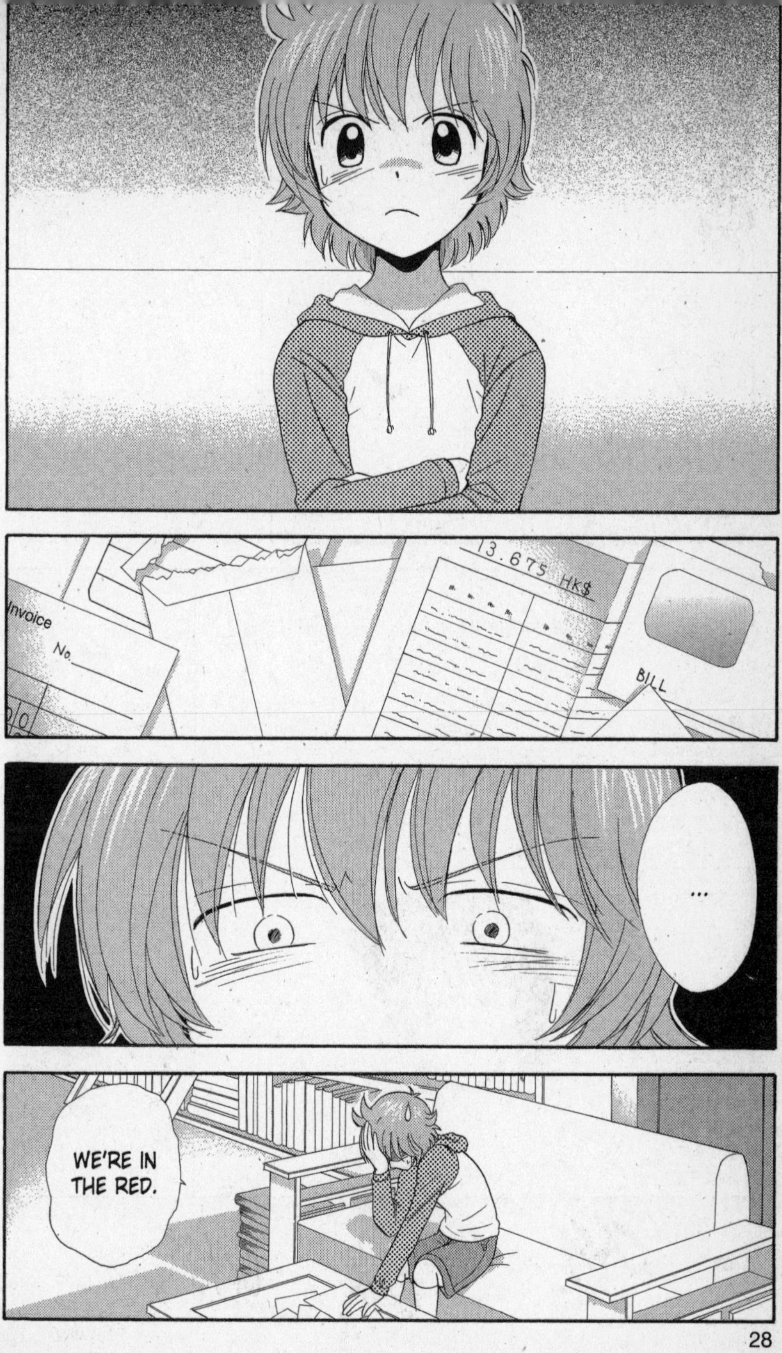
13.675 HK$
BILL
Invoice
No.
...
WE'RE IN THE RED.

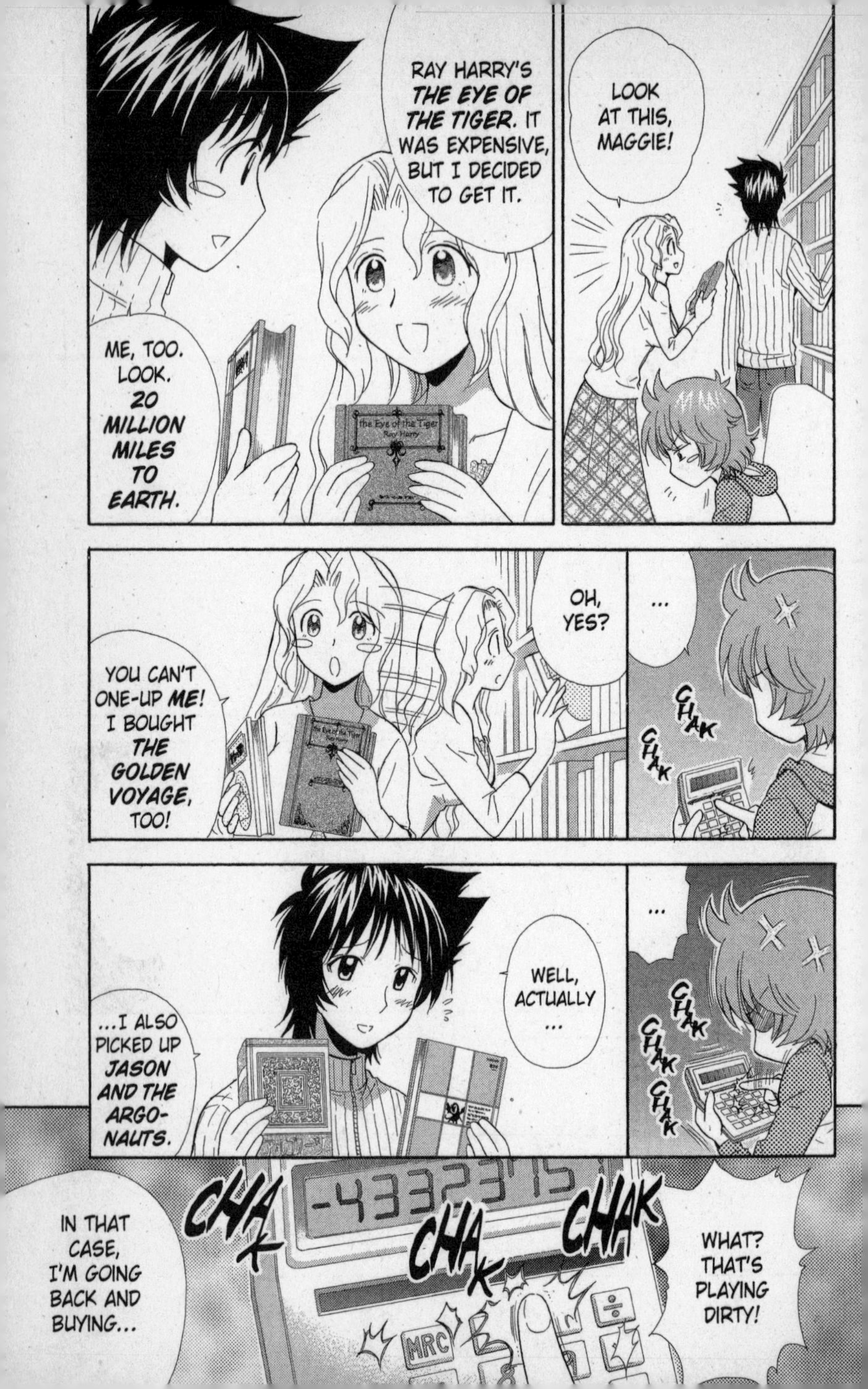
LOOK AT THIS, MAGGIE!
RAY HARRY'S *THE EYE OF THE TIGER*. IT WAS EXPENSIVE, BUT I DECIDED TO GET IT.
the Eye of the Tiger
Ray Harry
ME, TOO. LOOK. ***20 MILLION MILES TO EARTH***.
...
CHAK
CHAK
OH, YES?
YOU CAN'T ONE-UP *ME*! I BOUGHT ***THE GOLDEN VOYAGE***, TOO!
...
CHAK
CHAK
CHAK
CHAK
WELL, ACTUALLY ...
...I ALSO PICKED UP ***JASON AND THE ARGONAUTS***.
WHAT? THAT'S PLAYING DIRTY!
CHAK
CHAK
CHAK
-4332315
MRC
IN THAT CASE, I'M GOING BACK AND BUYING...

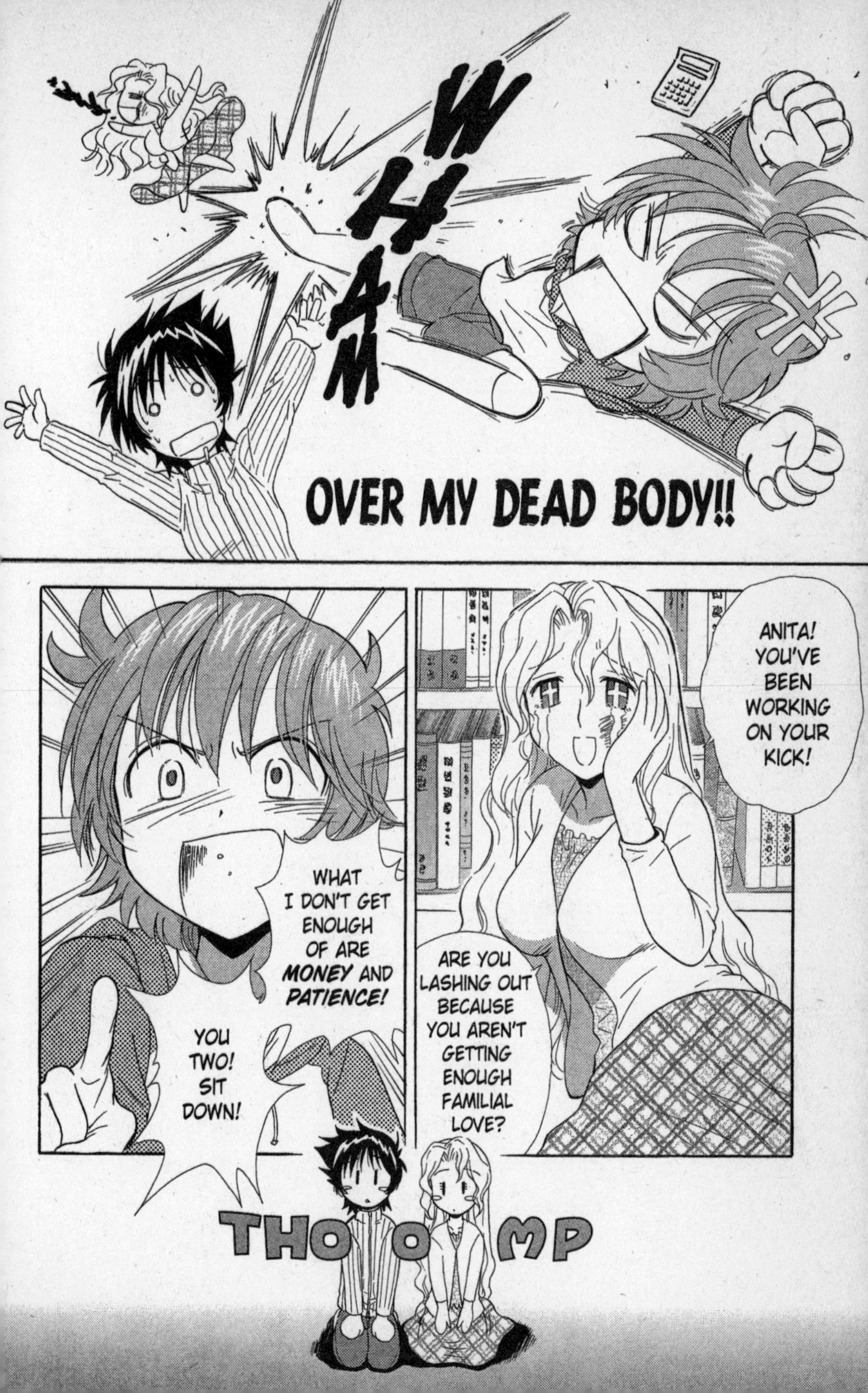
WHAM
OVER MY DEAD BODY!!
ANITA! YOU'VE BEEN WORKING ON YOUR KICK!
ARE YOU LASHING OUT BECAUSE YOU AREN'T GETTING ENOUGH FAMILIAL LOVE?
WHAT I DON'T GET ENOUGH OF ARE MONEY AND PATIENCE!
YOU TWO! SIT DOWN!
THOOMP

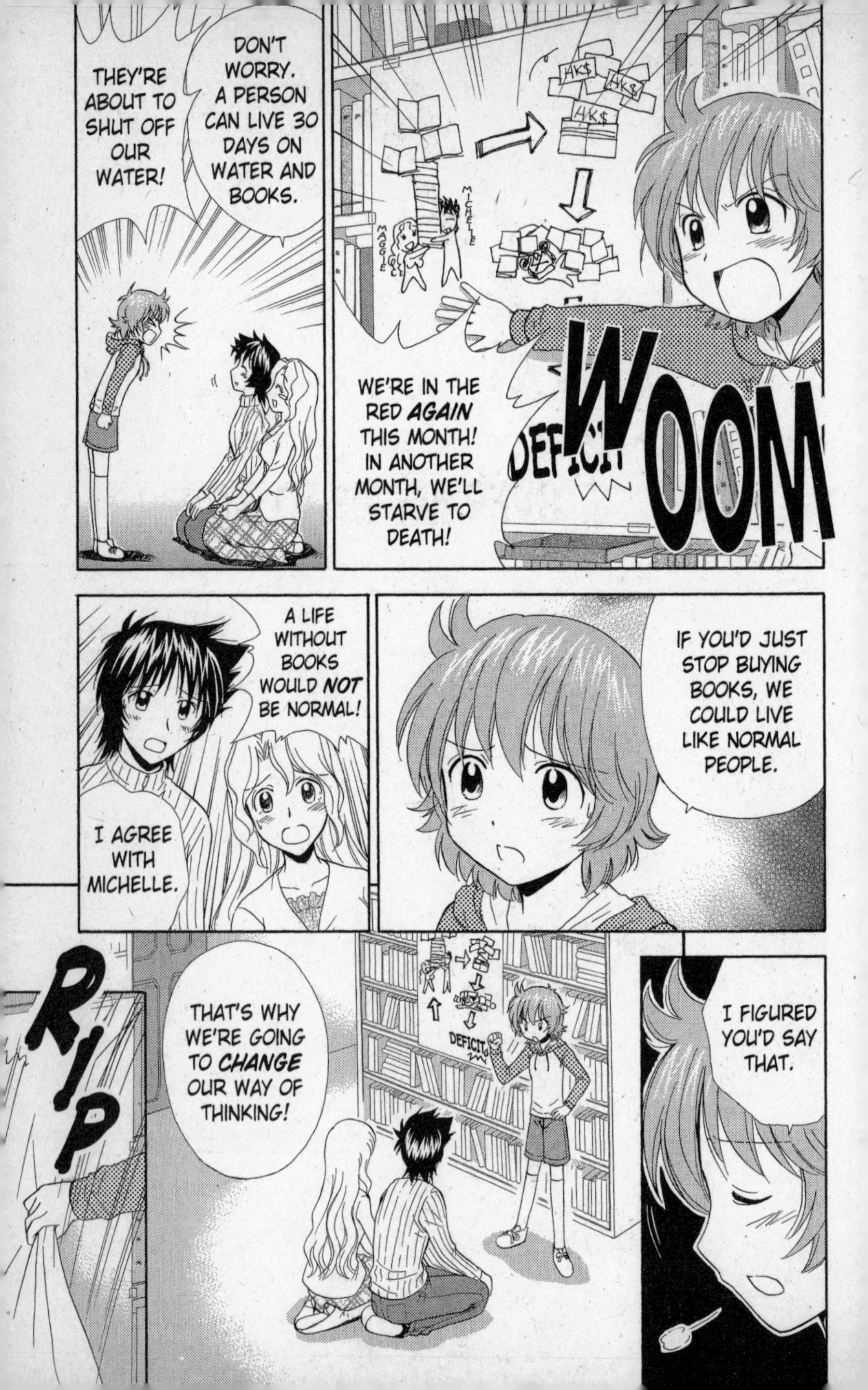
HK$
HK$
HK$
MICHELLE
MAGGIE
WE'RE IN THE RED *AGAIN* THIS MONTH! IN ANOTHER MONTH, WE'LL STARVE TO DEATH!
WOOM
THEY'RE ABOUT TO SHUT OFF OUR WATER!
DON'T WORRY. A PERSON CAN LIVE 30 DAYS ON WATER AND BOOKS.
IF YOU'D JUST STOP BUYING BOOKS, WE COULD LIVE LIKE NORMAL PEOPLE.
A LIFE WITHOUT BOOKS WOULD *NOT* BE NORMAL!
I AGREE WITH MICHELLE.
I FIGURED YOU'D SAY THAT.
DEFICIT
THAT'S WHY WE'RE GOING TO *CHANGE* OUR WAY OF THINKING!
RIP

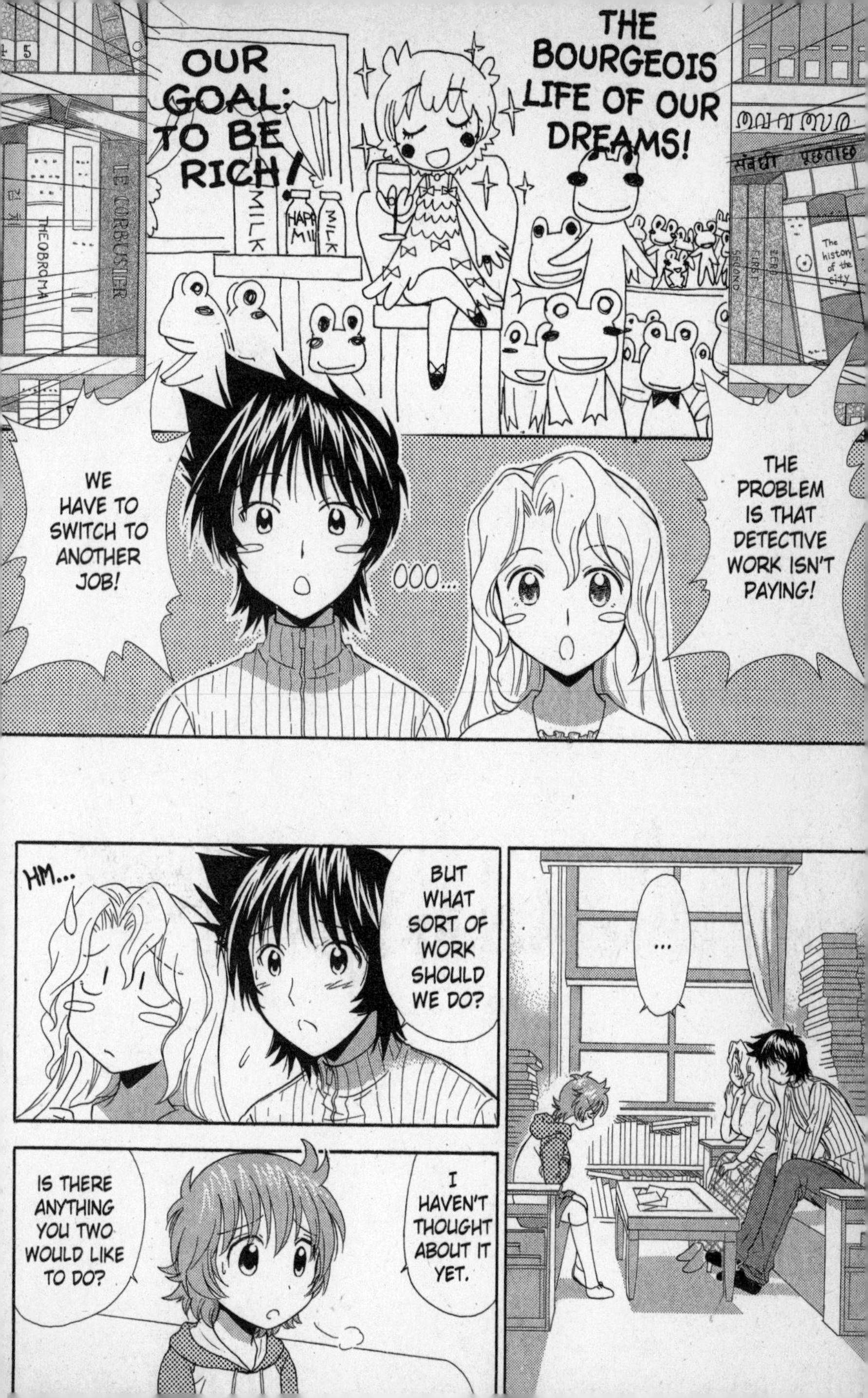
THE BOURGEOIS LIFE OF OUR DREAMS!
OUR GOAL: TO BE RICH!
MILK
LE CORBUSIER
THEOBROMA
The history of the city
THE PROBLEM IS THAT DETECTIVE WORK ISN'T PAYING!
OOO...
WE HAVE TO SWITCH TO ANOTHER JOB!
...
BUT WHAT SORT OF WORK SHOULD WE DO?
HM...
I HAVEN'T THOUGHT ABOUT IT YET.
IS THERE ANYTHING YOU TWO WOULD LIKE TO DO?

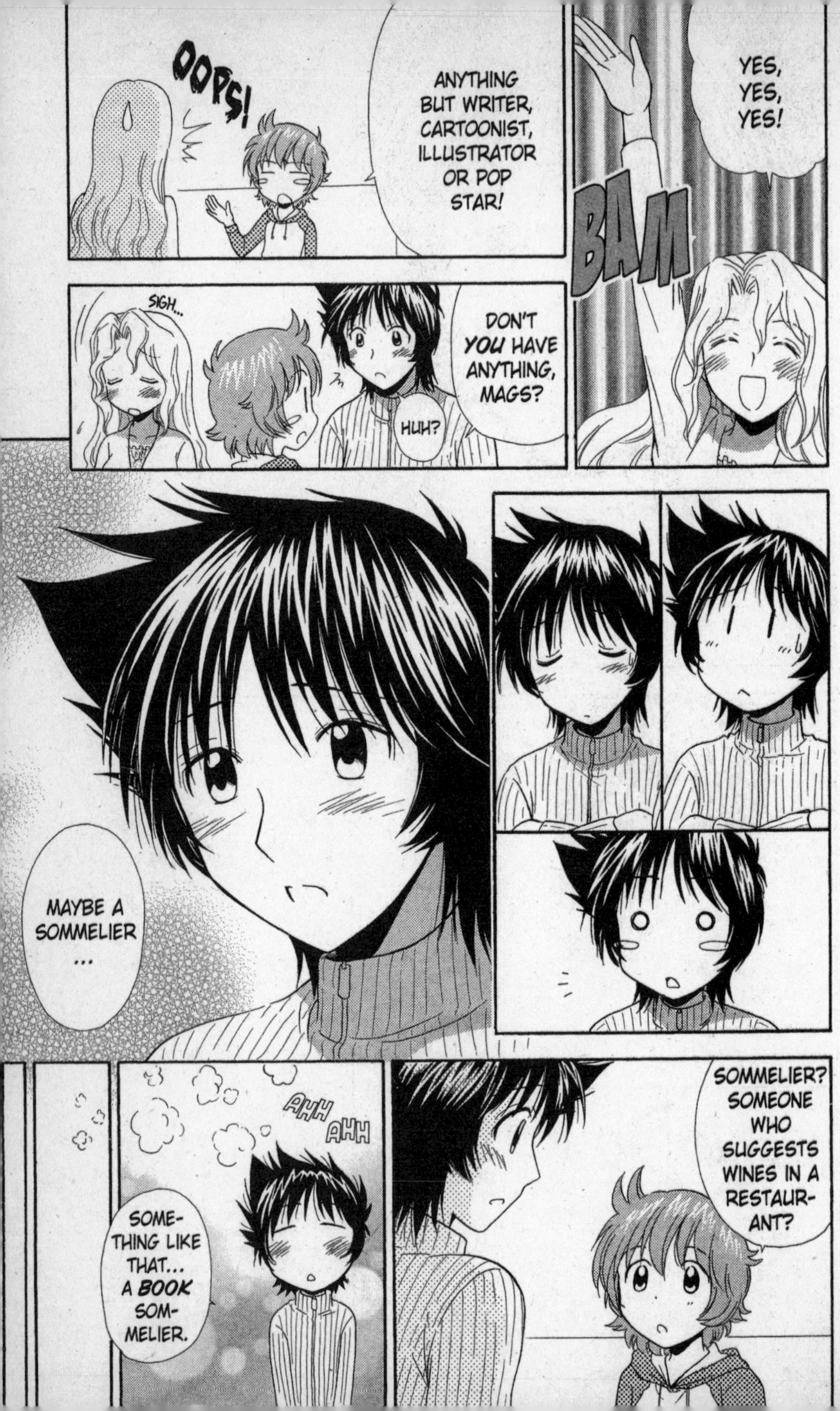
YES, YES, YES!
BAM
OOPS!
ANYTHING BUT WRITER, CARTOONIST, ILLUSTRATOR OR POP STAR!
DON'T *YOU* HAVE ANYTHING, MAGS?
HUH?
SIGH...
MAYBE A SOMMELIER ...
SOMMELIER? SOMEONE WHO SUGGESTS WINES IN A RESTAUR-ANT?
AHH AHH
SOME-THING LIKE THAT... A *BOOK* SOM-MELIER.

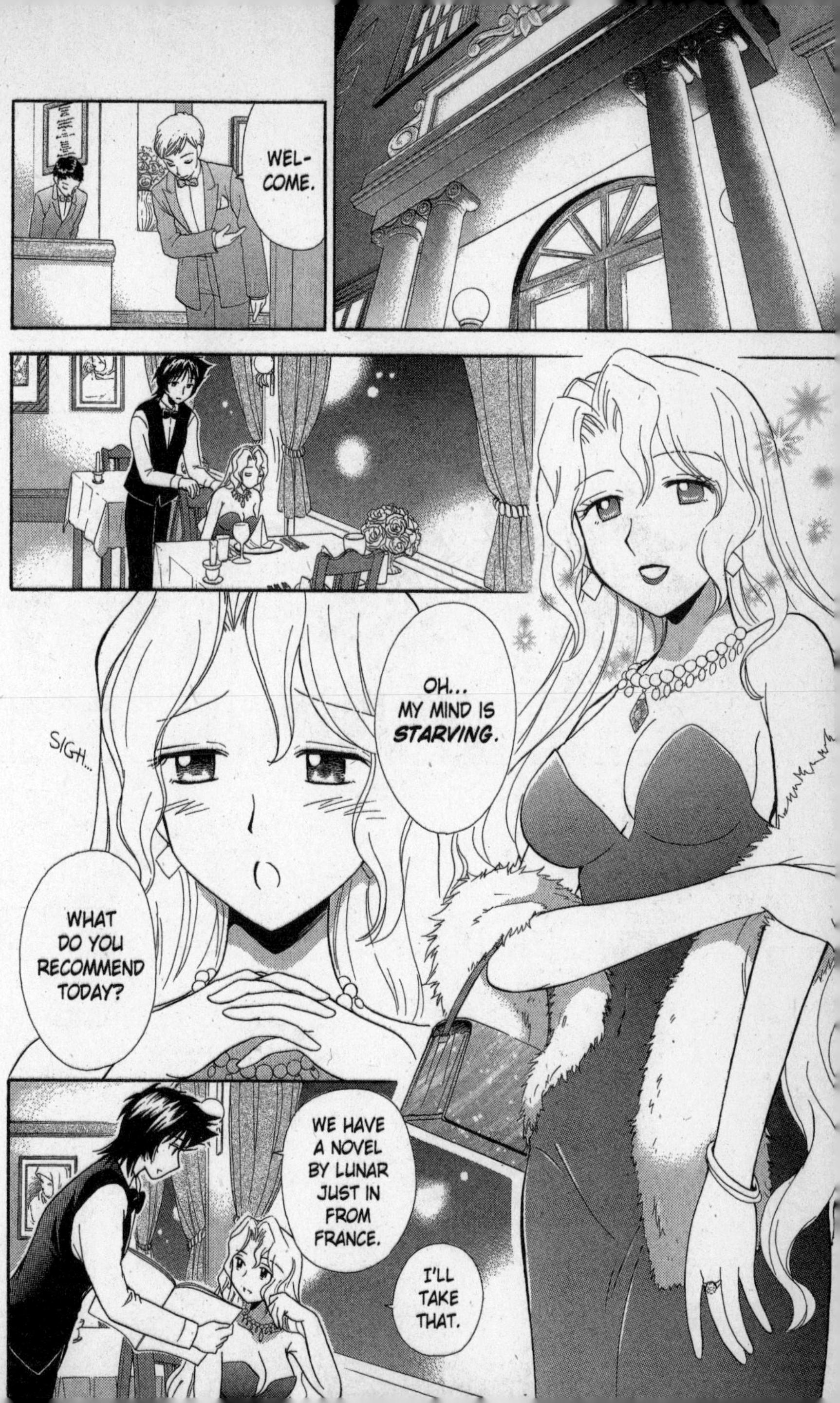
WEL-
COME.
OH... MY MIND IS **STARVING**.
SIGH...
WHAT DO YOU RECOMMEND TODAY?
WE HAVE A NOVEL BY LUNAR JUST IN FROM FRANCE.
I'LL TAKE THAT.

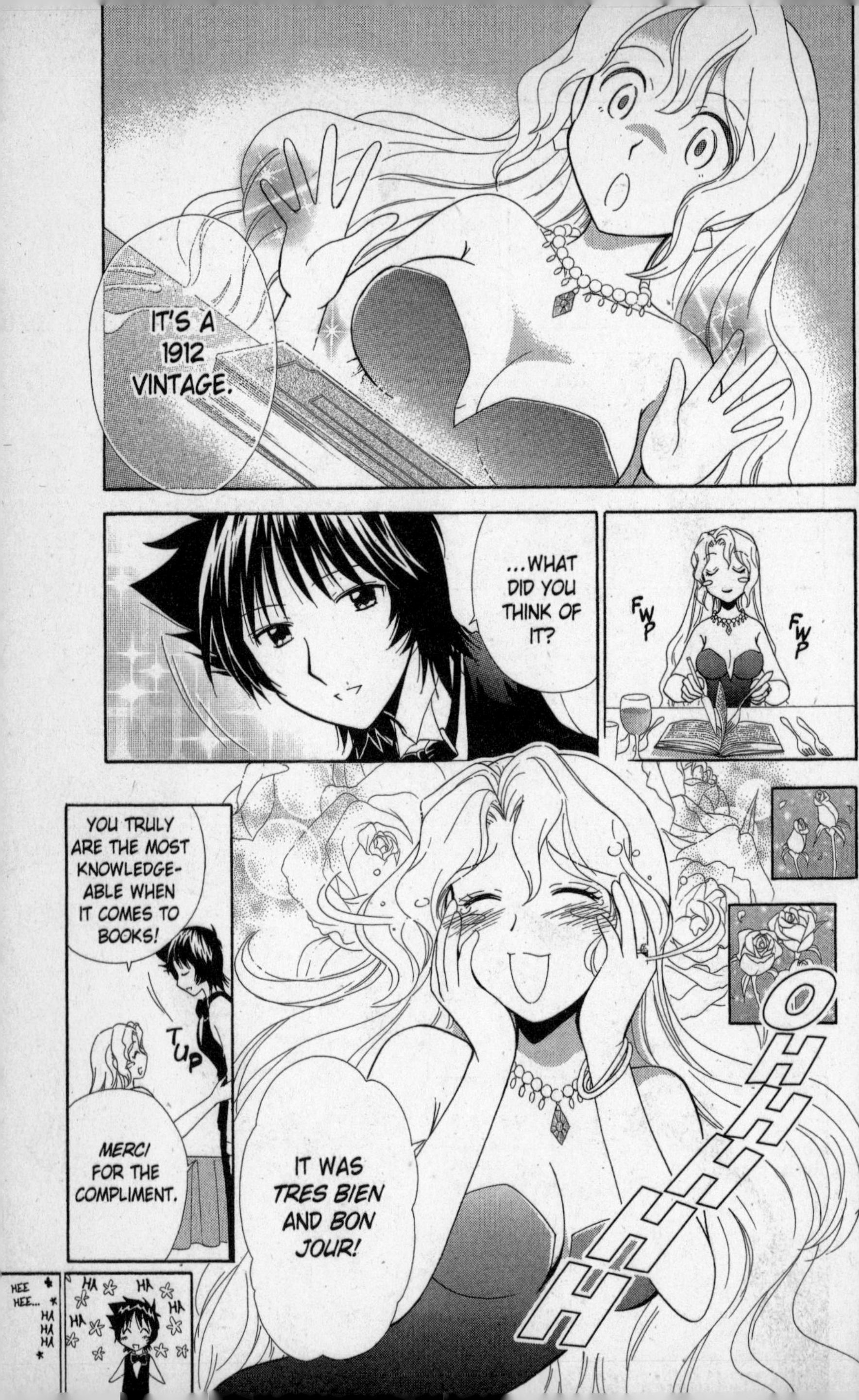
IT'S A 1912 VINTAGE.
FWP
FWP
...WHAT DID YOU THINK OF IT?
OHHHHHHH
IT WAS TRES BIEN AND BON JOUR!
YOU TRULY ARE THE MOST KNOWLEDGE-ABLE WHEN IT COMES TO BOOKS!
TUP
MERCI FOR THE COMPLIMENT.
HA HA HA HA
HEE HEE... HA HA HA

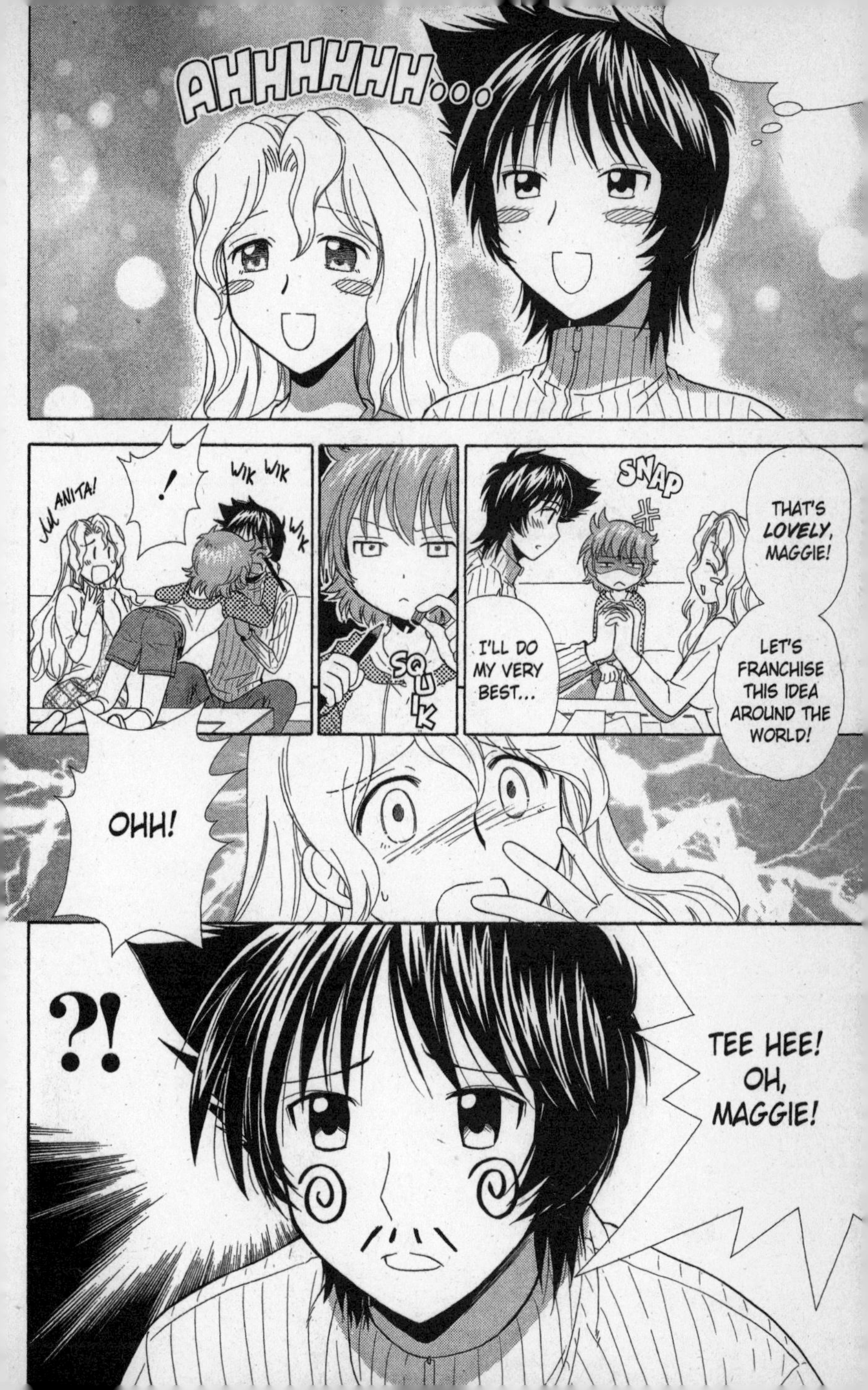
AHHHHHH...
THAT'S *LOVELY,* MAGGIE!
LET'S FRANCHISE THIS IDEA AROUND THE WORLD!
SNAP
I'LL DO MY VERY BEST...
SQUIK
!
WIK WIK WIK
ANITA!
OHH!
TEE HEE! OH, MAGGIE!
?!

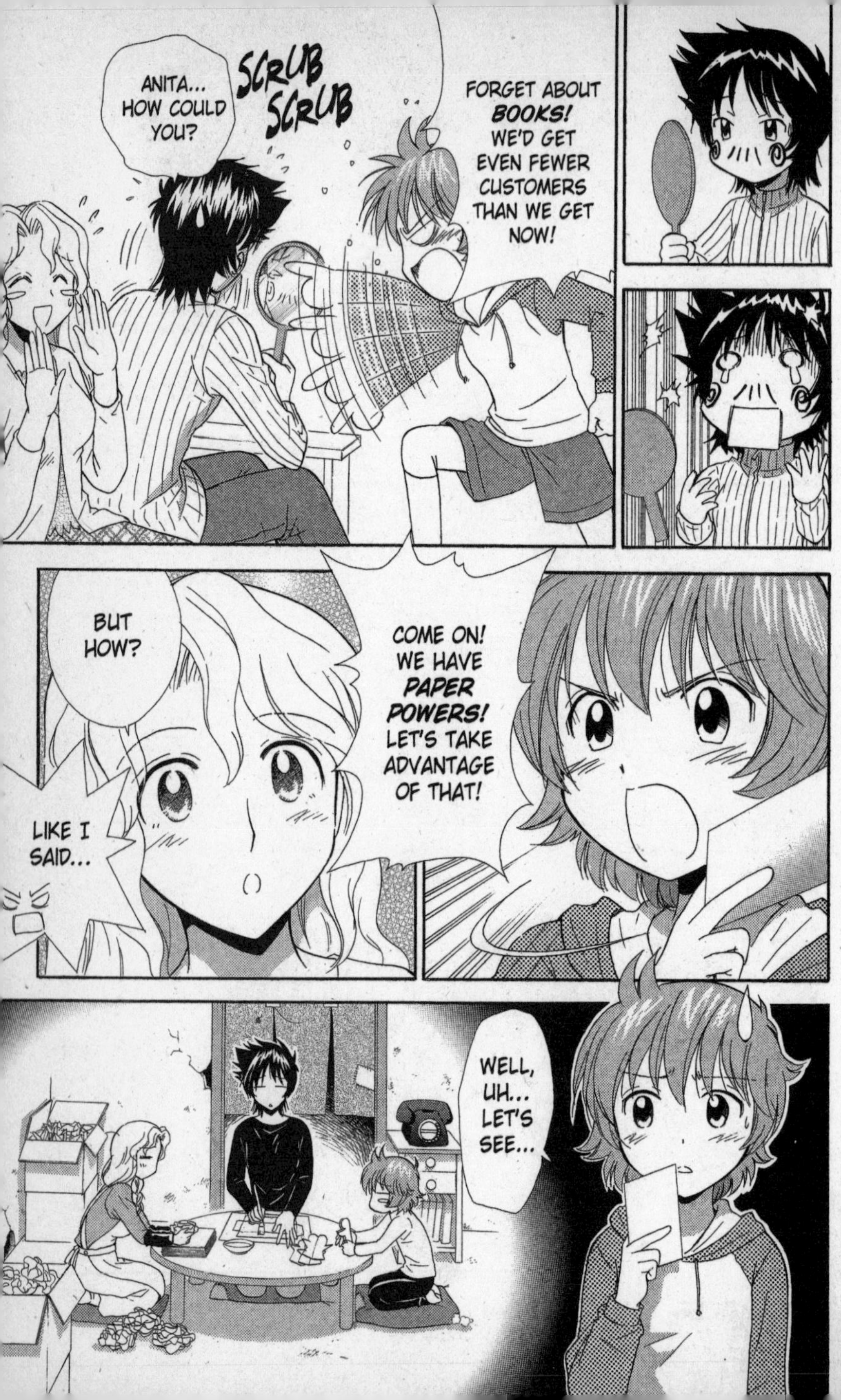
FORGET ABOUT BOOKS! WE'D GET EVEN FEWER CUSTOMERS THAN WE GET NOW!
SCRUB SCRUB
ANITA... HOW COULD YOU?
COME ON! WE HAVE PAPER POWERS! LET'S TAKE ADVANTAGE OF THAT!
BUT HOW?
LIKE I SAID...
WELL, UH... LET'S SEE...

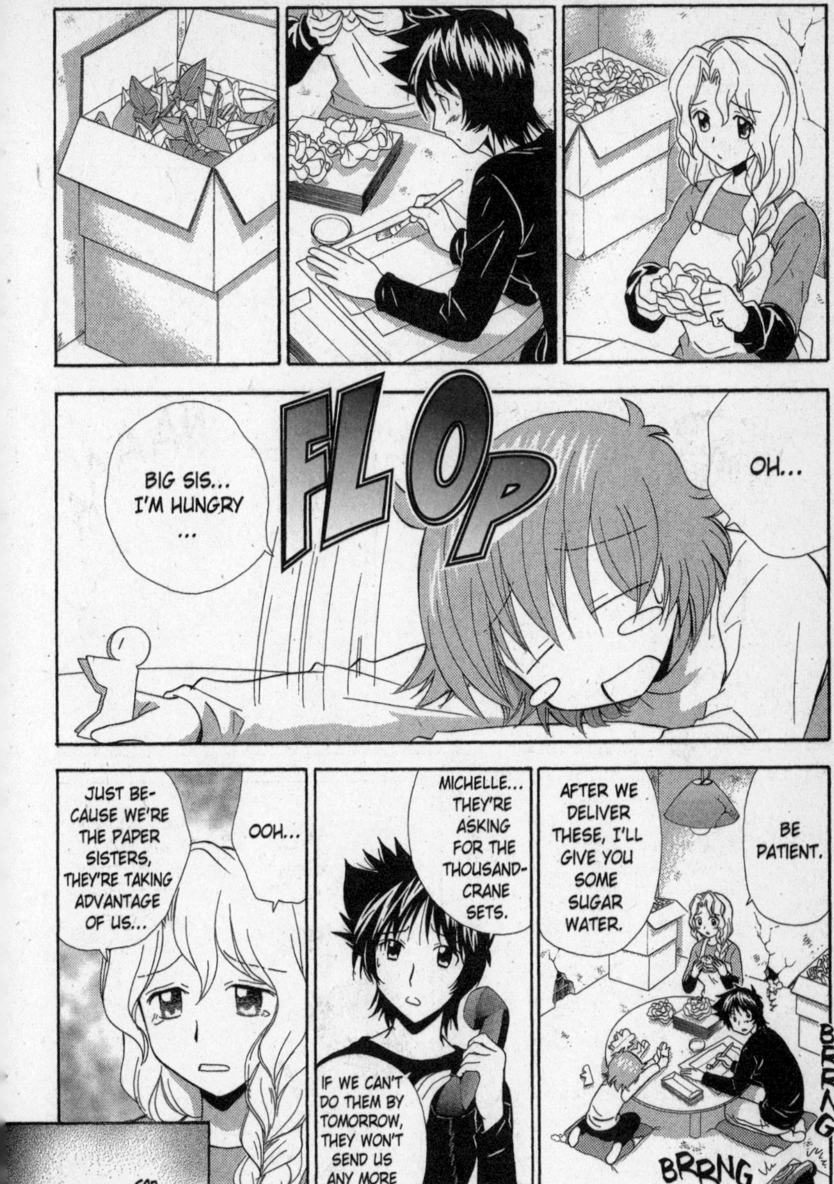
OH...
FLOP
BIG SIS... I'M HUNGRY ...
BE PATIENT.
AFTER WE DELIVER THESE, I'LL GIVE YOU SOME SUGAR WATER.
BRRNG
BRRNG
MICHELLE... THEY'RE ASKING FOR THE THOUSAND-CRANE SETS.
IF WE CAN'T DO THEM BY TOMORROW, THEY WON'T SEND US ANY MORE WORK...
OOH...
JUST BE-CAUSE WE'RE THE PAPER SISTERS, THEY'RE TAKING ADVANTAGE OF US...
sniff... SOB SOB

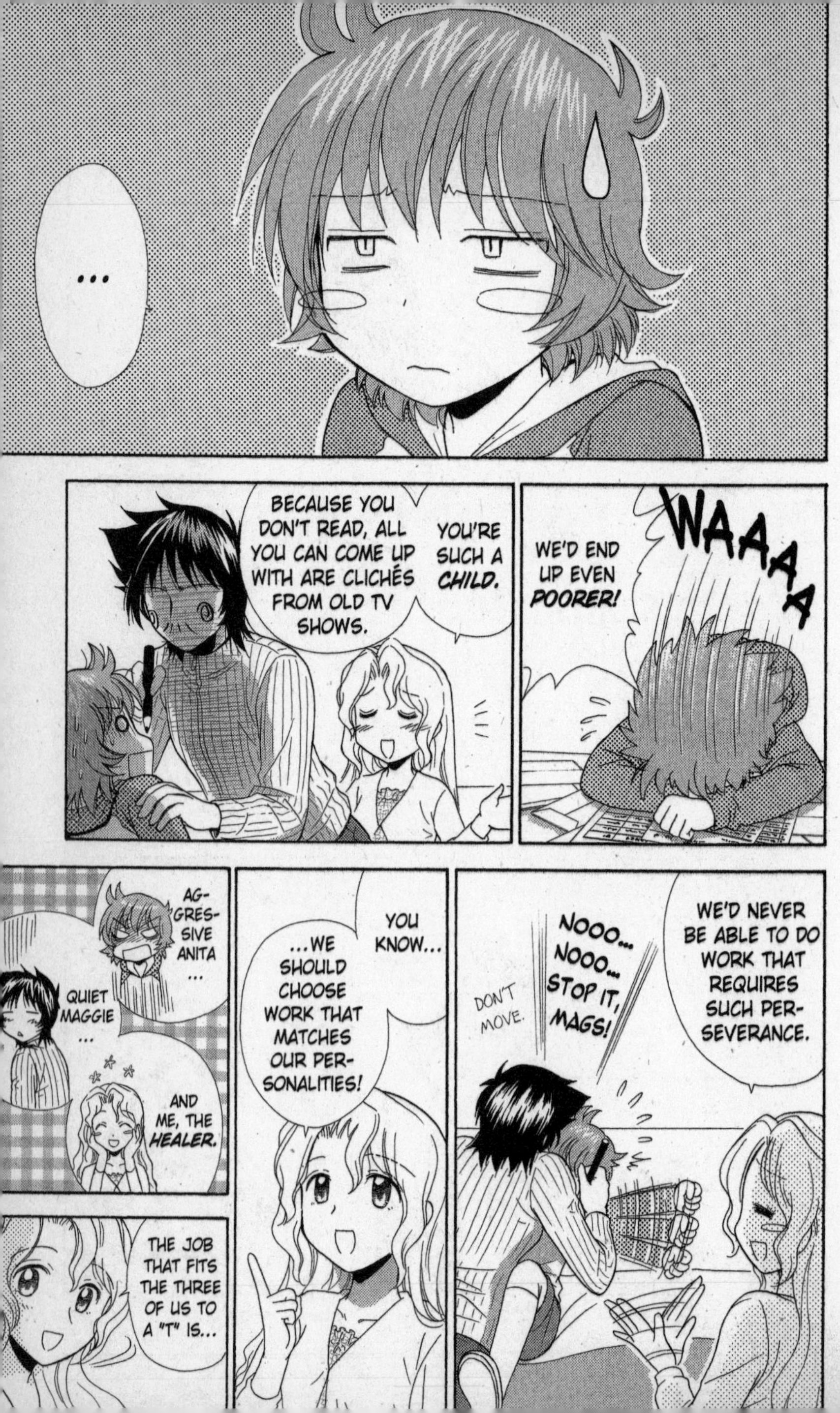
...
WAAAA
WE'D END UP EVEN POORER!
BECAUSE YOU DON'T READ, ALL YOU CAN COME UP WITH ARE CLICHÉS FROM OLD TV SHOWS.
YOU'RE SUCH A CHILD.
WE'D NEVER BE ABLE TO DO WORK THAT REQUIRES SUCH PER-SEVERANCE.
NOOO... NOOO... STOP IT, MAGS!
DON'T MOVE.
YOU KNOW...
...WE SHOULD CHOOSE WORK THAT MATCHES OUR PER-SONALITIES!
AG-GRES-SIVE ANITA ...
QUIET MAGGIE ...
AND ME, THE HEALER.
THE JOB THAT FITS THE THREE OF US TO A "T" IS...

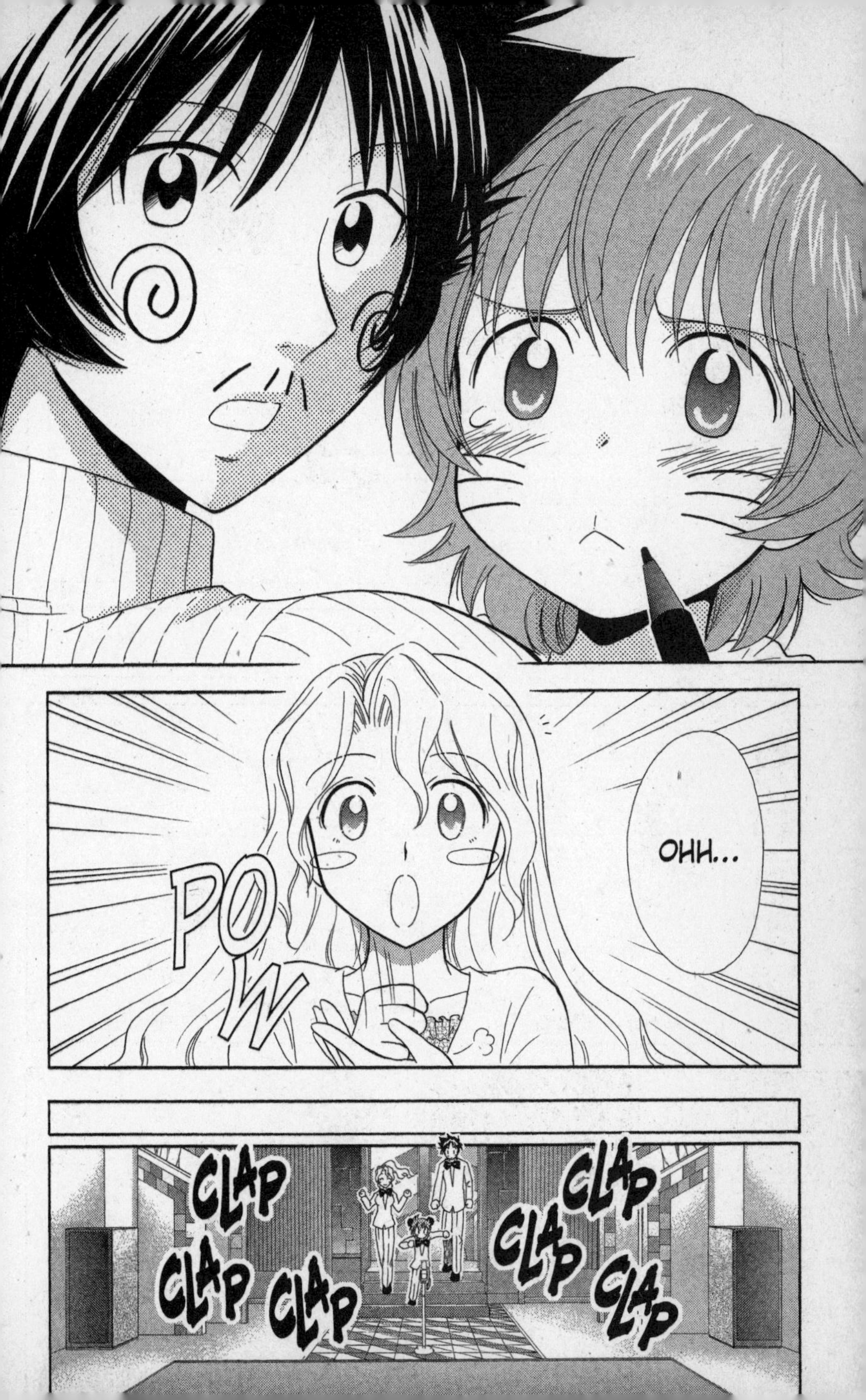
OHH...
POW
CLAP
CLAP
CLAP
CLAP
CLAP
CLAP

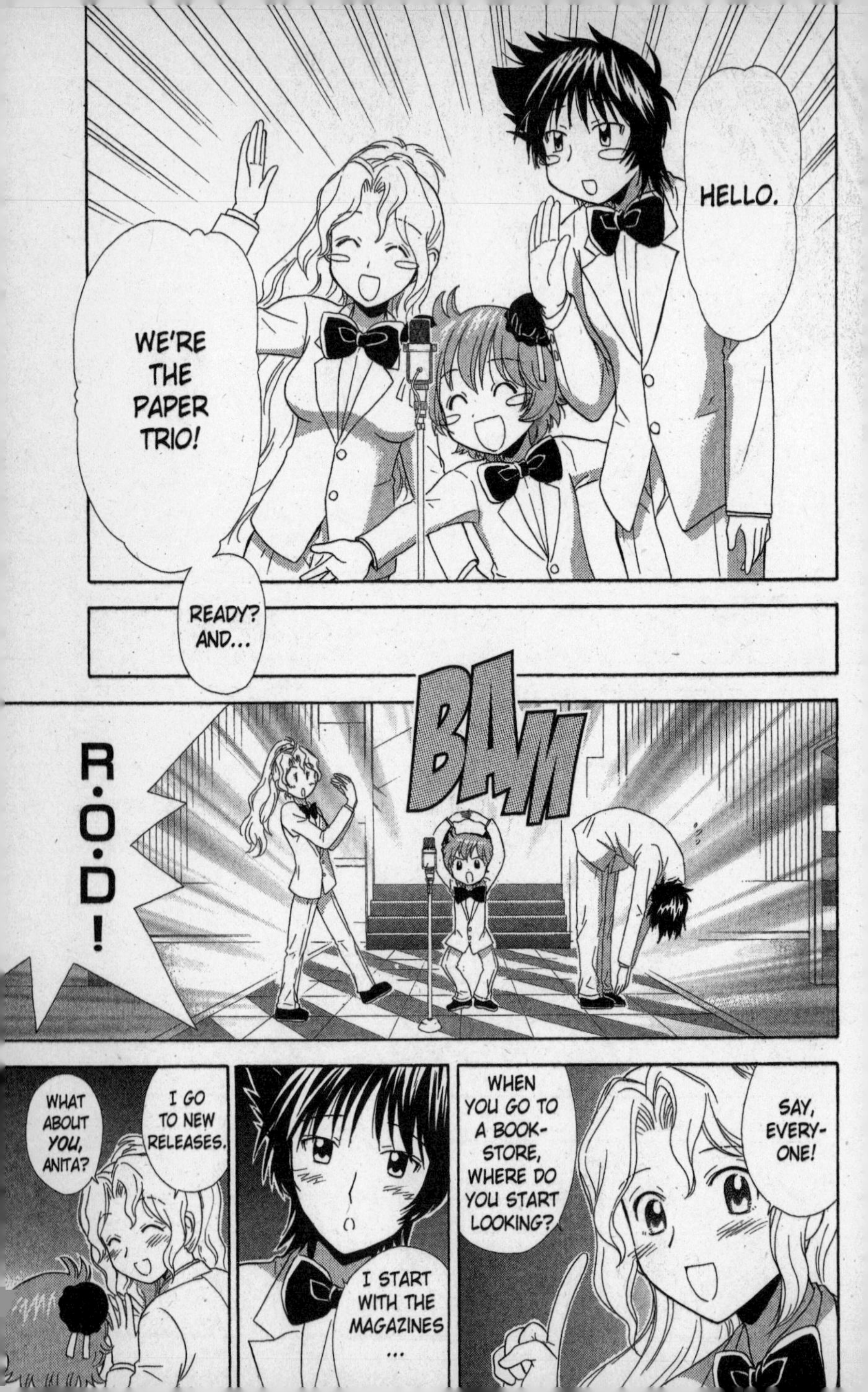
HELLO.
WE'RE THE PAPER TRIO!
READY? AND...
BAM
R·O·D!
SAY, EVERY-ONE!
WHEN YOU GO TO A BOOK-STORE, WHERE DO YOU START LOOKING?
I START WITH THE MAGAZINES ...
I GO TO NEW RELEASES.
WHAT ABOUT *YOU*, ANITA?

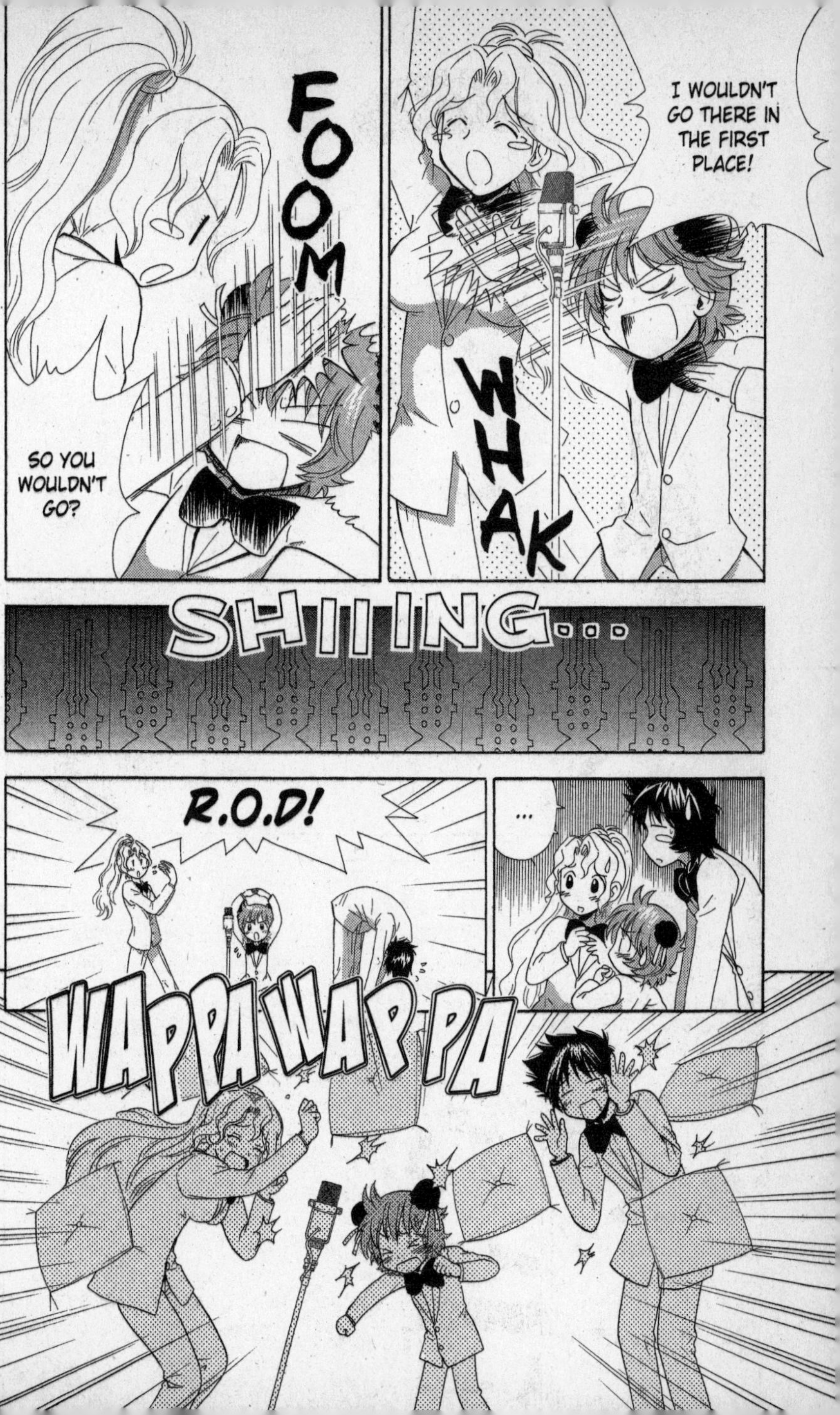

I WOULDN'T GO THERE IN THE FIRST PLACE!
WHAK
FOOM
SO YOU WOULDN'T GO?
SHIIING...
...
R.O.D!
WAPPAWAPPA

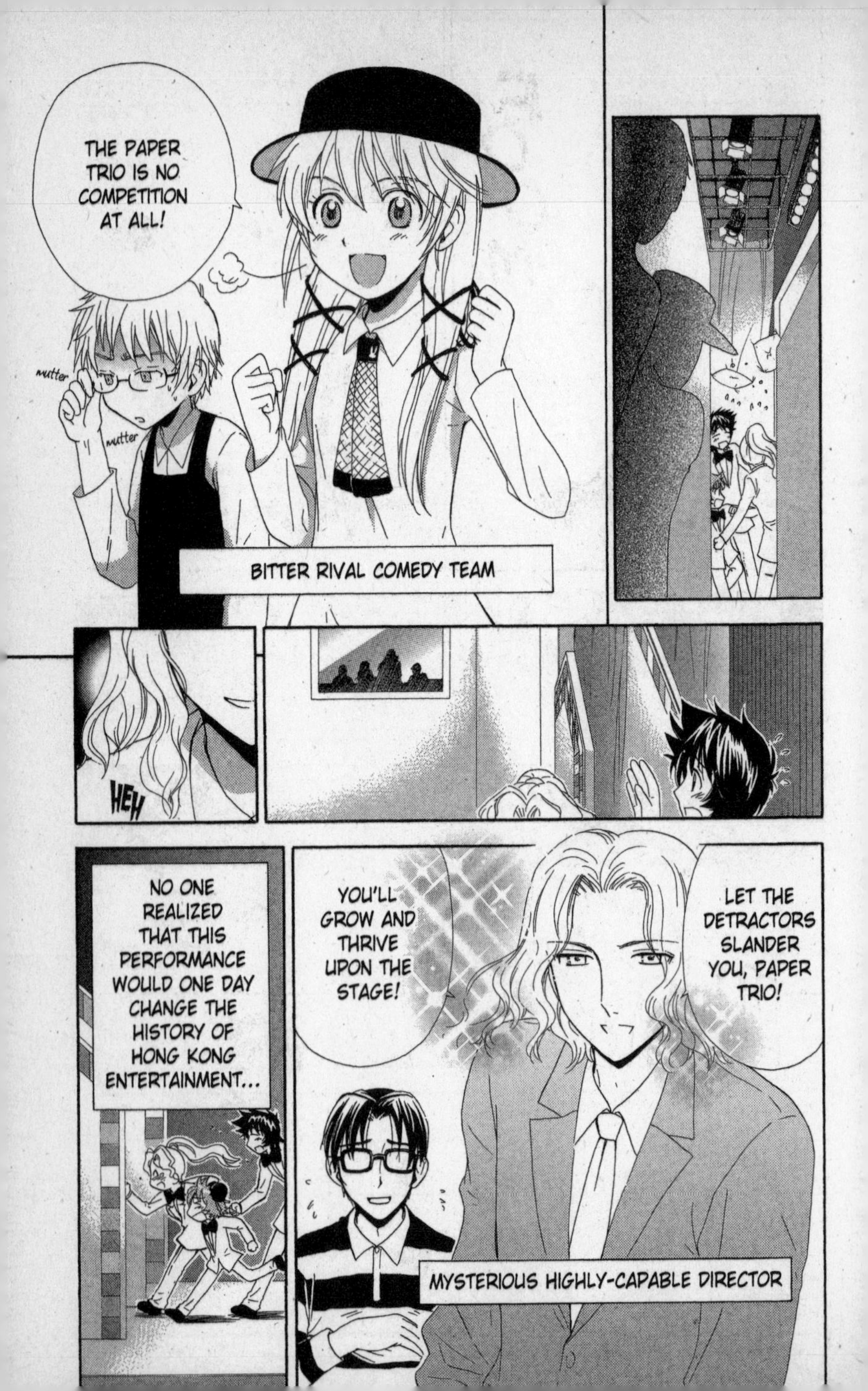
THE PAPER TRIO IS NO COMPETITION AT ALL!
mutter
mutter
BITTER RIVAL COMEDY TEAM
HEH
LET THE DETRACTORS SLANDER YOU, PAPER TRIO!
YOU'LL GROW AND THRIVE UPON THE STAGE!
MYSTERIOUS HIGHLY-CAPABLE DIRECTOR
NO ONE REALIZED THAT THIS PERFORMANCE WOULD ONE DAY CHANGE THE HISTORY OF HONG KONG ENTERTAINMENT...

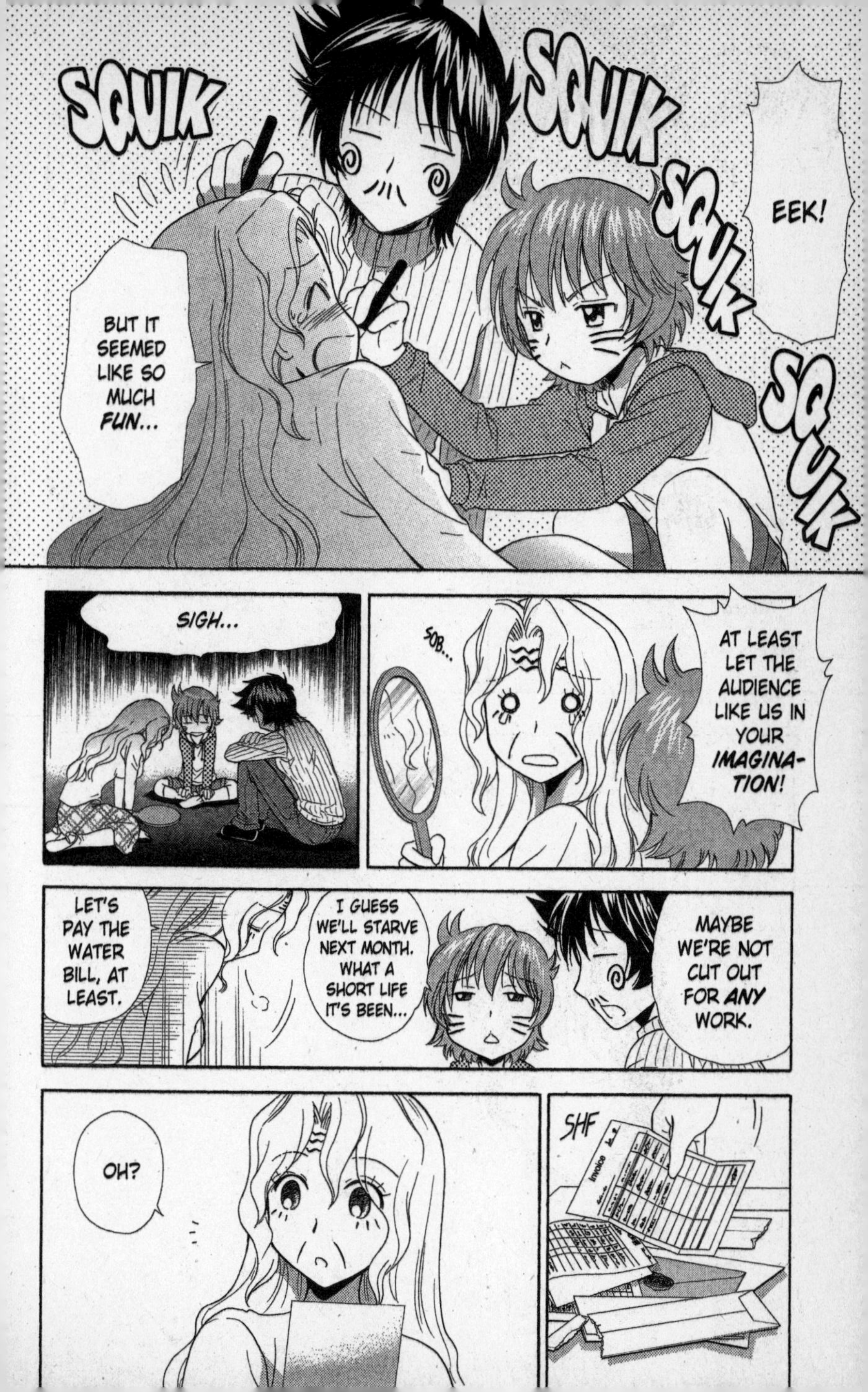

EEK!
SQUIK SQUIK SQUIK SQUIK
SQUIK
BUT IT SEEMED LIKE SO MUCH *FUN*...
AT LEAST LET THE AUDIENCE LIKE US IN YOUR *IMAGINATION!*
SOB...
SIGH...
MAYBE WE'RE NOT CUT OUT FOR *ANY* WORK.
I GUESS WE'LL STARVE NEXT MONTH. WHAT A SHORT LIFE IT'S BEEN...
LET'S PAY THE WATER BILL, AT LEAST.
SHF
Invoice
OH?

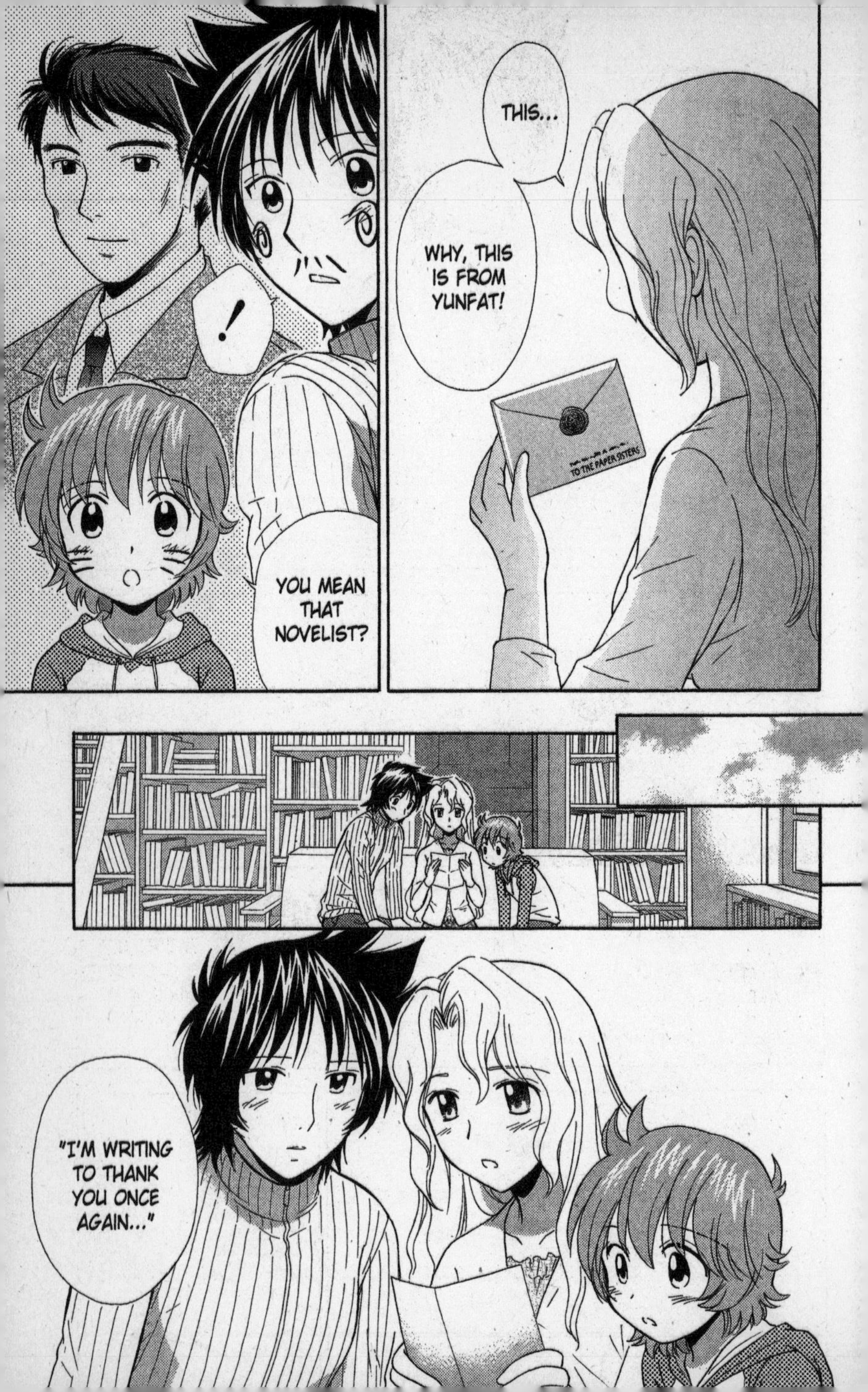
THIS...
WHY, THIS IS FROM YUNFAT!
TO THE PAPER SISTERS
!
YOU MEAN THAT NOVELIST?
"I'M WRITING TO THANK YOU ONCE AGAIN..."

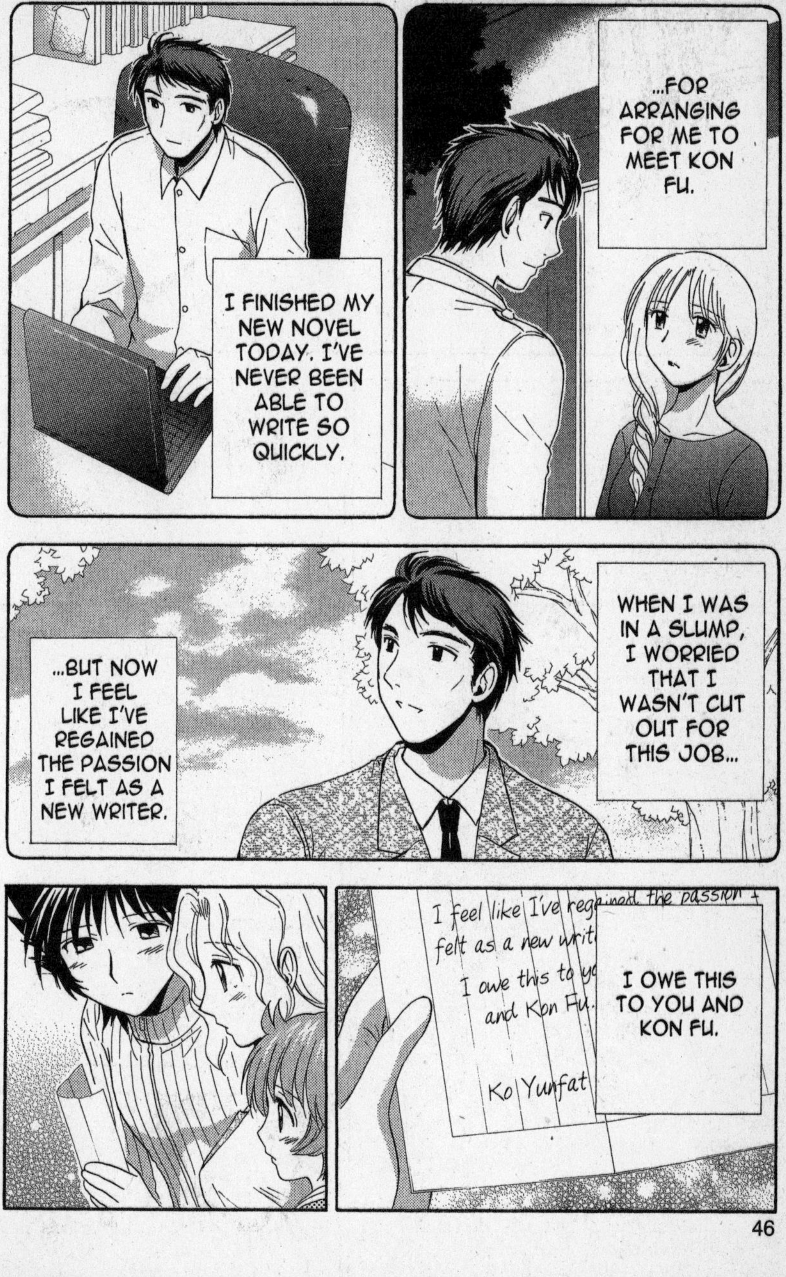
...FOR ARRANGING FOR ME TO MEET KON FU.
I FINISHED MY NEW NOVEL TODAY. I'VE NEVER BEEN ABLE TO WRITE SO QUICKLY.
WHEN I WAS IN A SLUMP, I WORRIED THAT I WASN'T CUT OUT FOR THIS JOB...
...BUT NOW I FEEL LIKE I'VE REGAINED THE PASSION I FELT AS A NEW WRITER.
I feel like I've regained the passion
felt as a new writ
I owe this to y
and Kon Fu.
Ko Yunfat
I OWE THIS TO YOU AND KON FU.

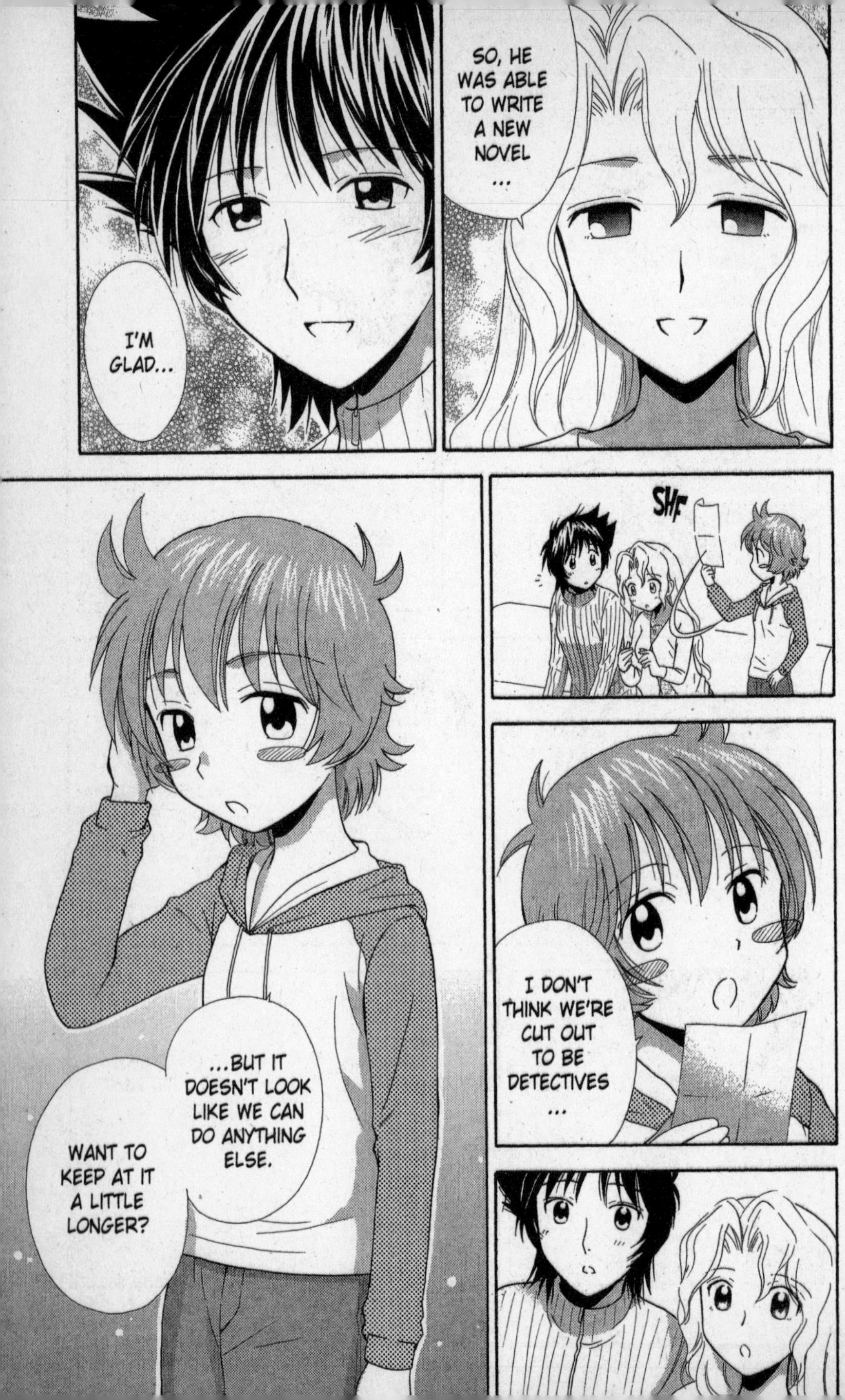
SO, HE WAS ABLE TO WRITE A NEW NOVEL ...
I'M GLAD...
SHF
I DON'T THINK WE'RE CUT OUT TO BE DETECTIVES ...
...BUT IT DOESN'T LOOK LIKE WE CAN DO ANYTHING ELSE.
WANT TO KEEP AT IT A LITTLE LONGER?

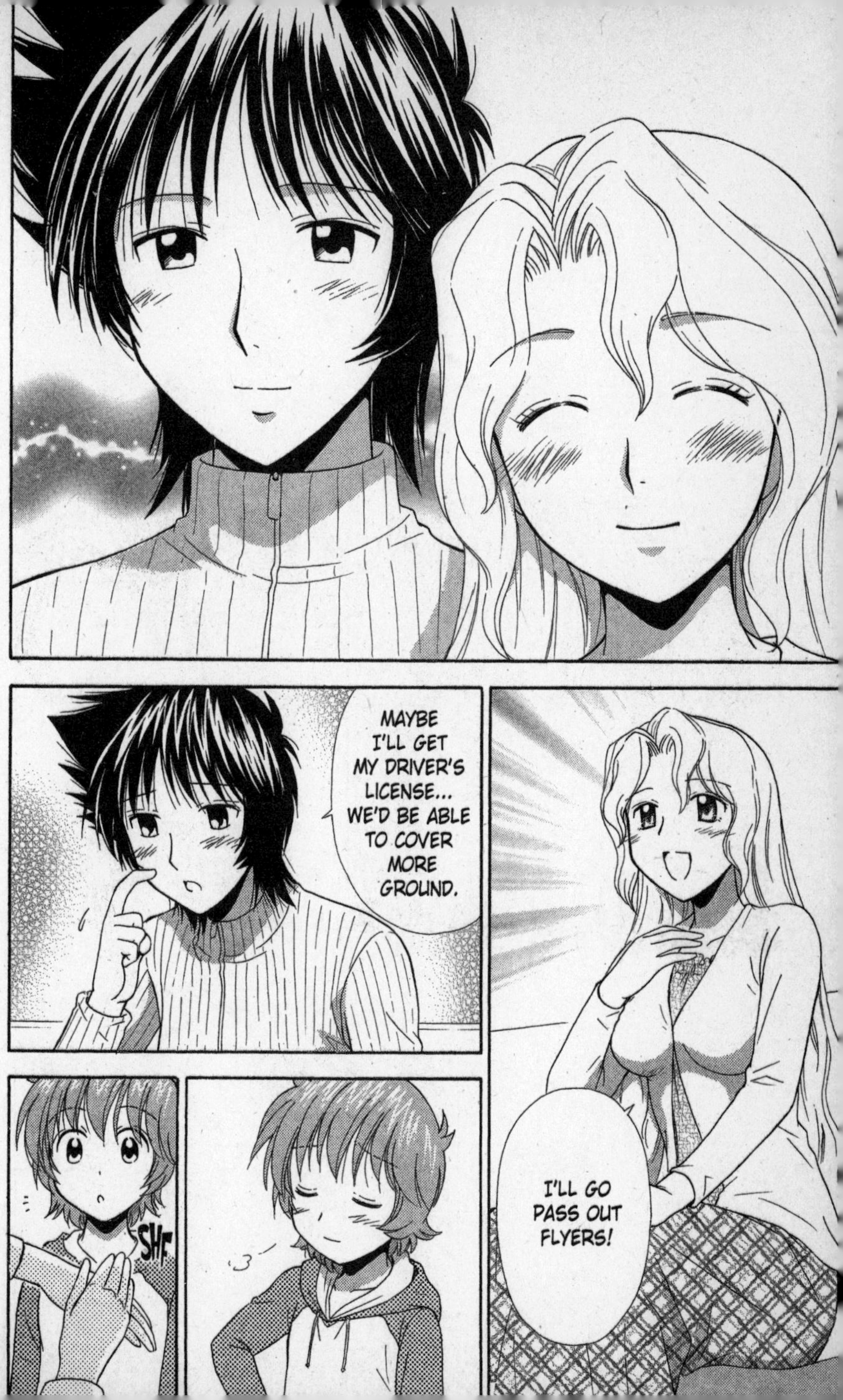
MAYBE I'LL GET MY DRIVER'S LICENSE... WE'D BE ABLE TO COVER MORE GROUND.
I'LL GO PASS OUT FLYERS!
SHF

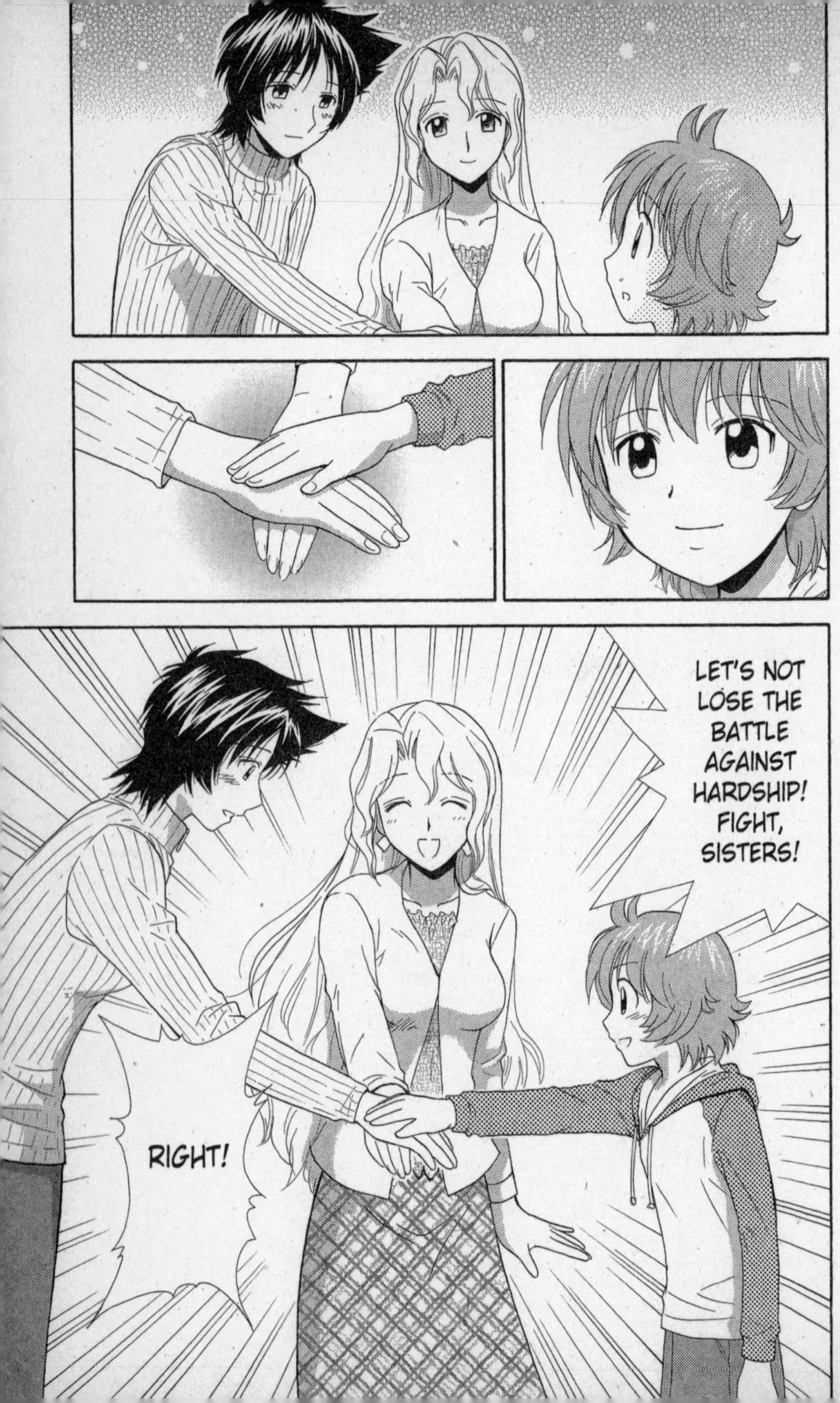
LET'S NOT LOSE THE BATTLE AGAINST HARDSHIP! FIGHT, SISTERS!
RIGHT!

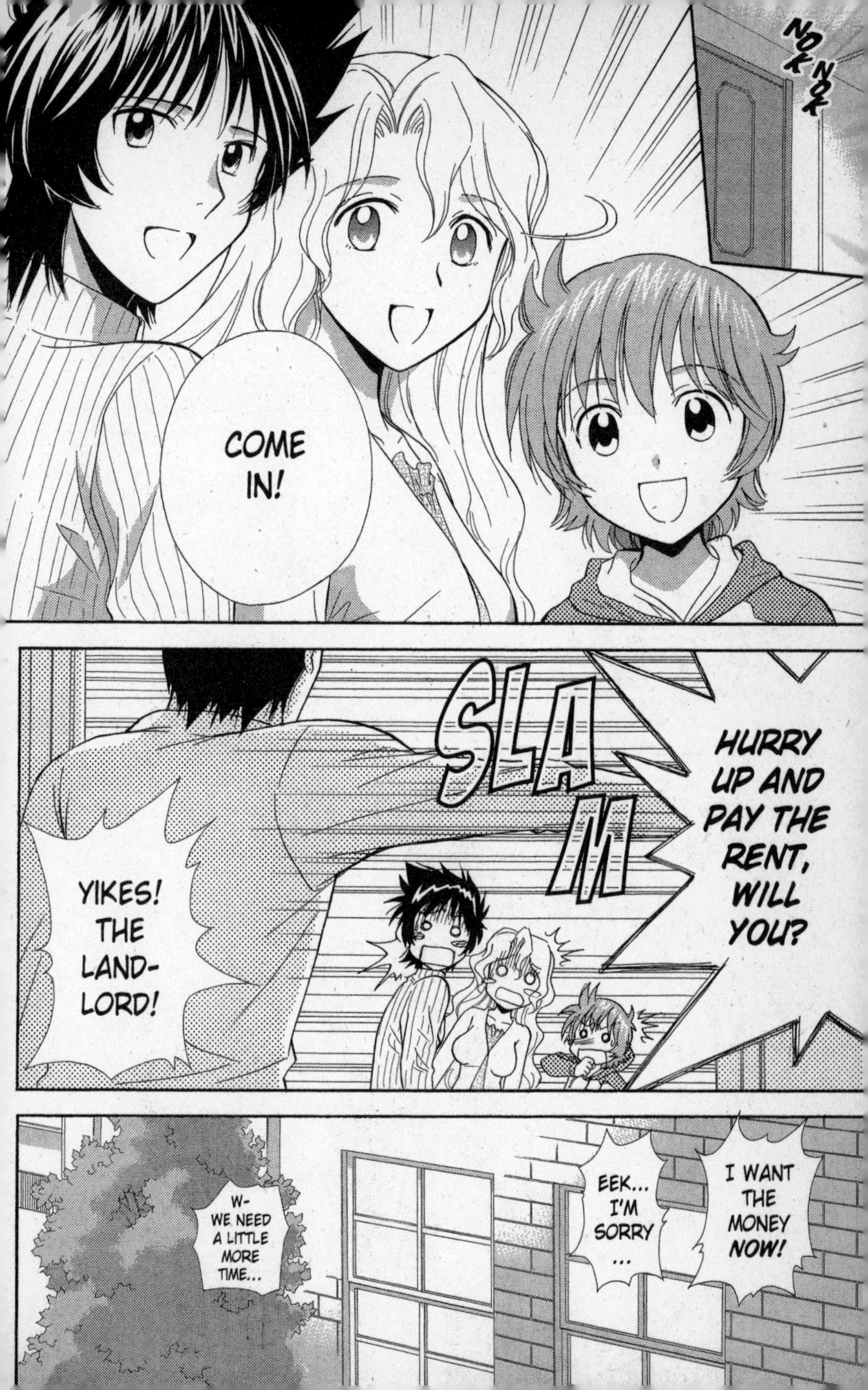
NOK NOK
COME IN!
SLAM
HURRY UP AND PAY THE RENT, WILL YOU?
YIKES! THE LAND-LORD!
I WANT THE MONEY NOW!
EEK... I'M SORRY...
W-WE NEED A LITTLE MORE TIME...

CHAPTER 18

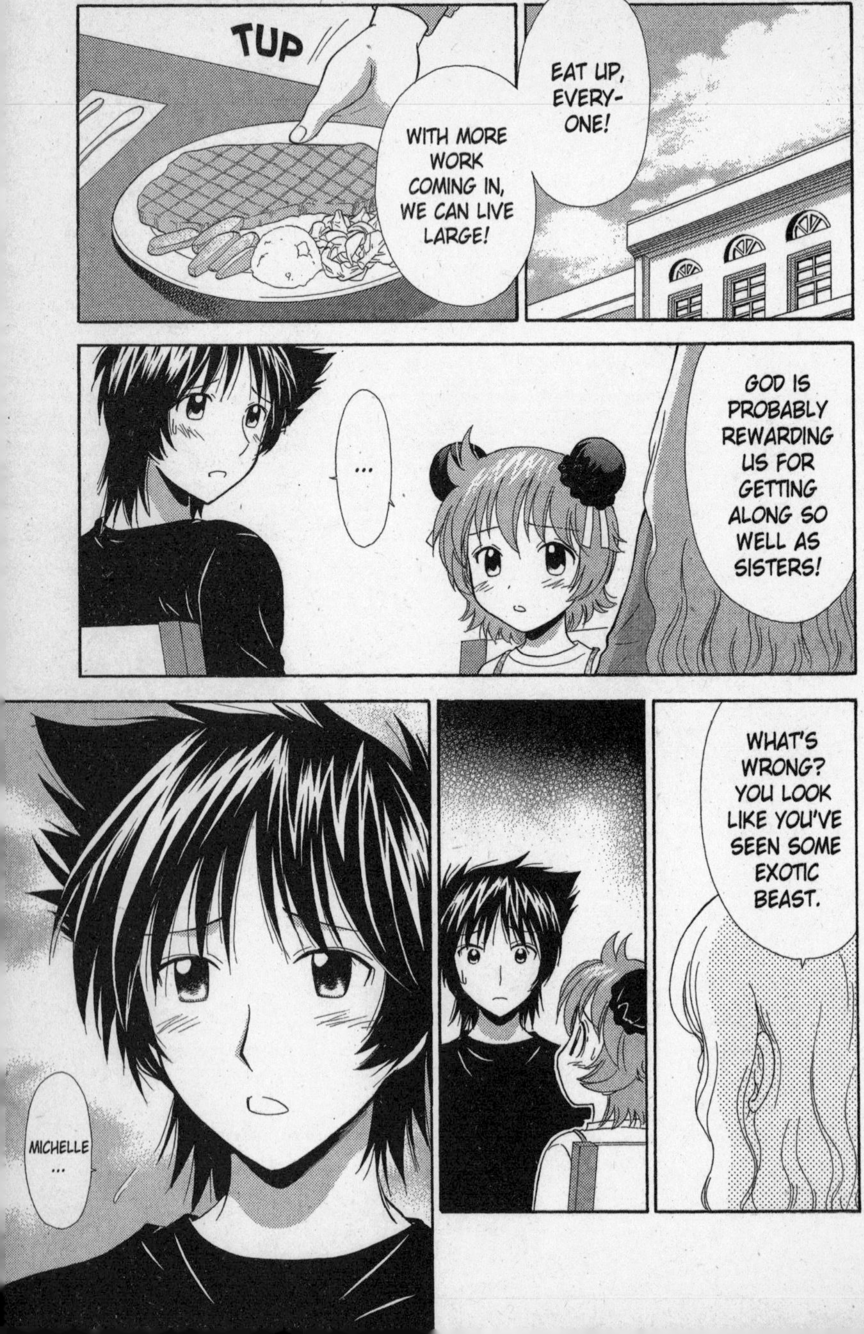
EAT UP, EVERY-ONE!
WITH MORE WORK COMING IN, WE CAN LIVE LARGE!
TUP
GOD IS PROBABLY REWARDING US FOR GETTING ALONG SO WELL AS SISTERS!
...
WHAT'S WRONG? YOU LOOK LIKE YOU'VE SEEN SOME EXOTIC BEAST.
MICHELLE ...

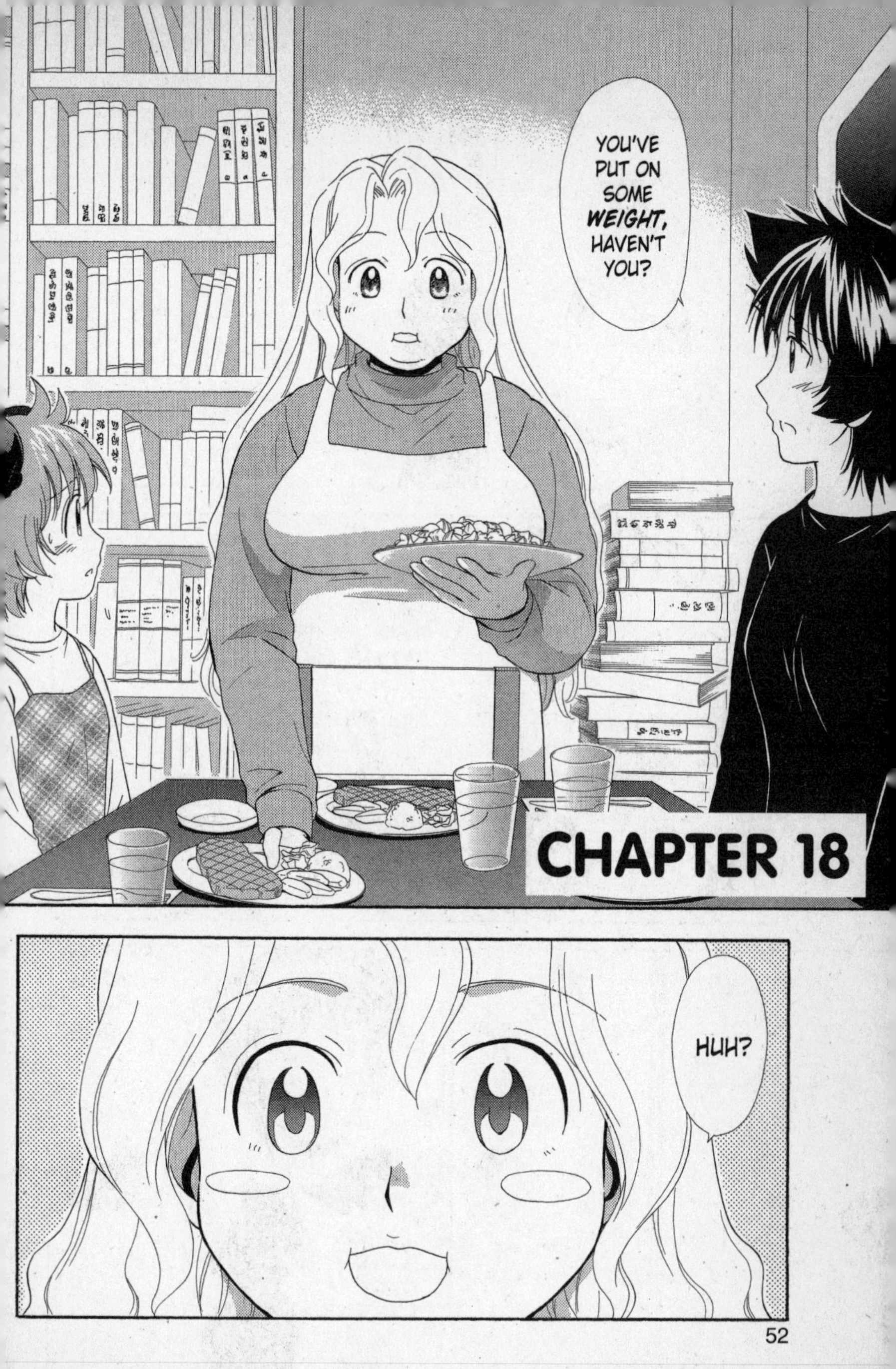
YOU'VE PUT ON SOME *WEIGHT*, HAVEN'T YOU?
CHAPTER 18
HUH?

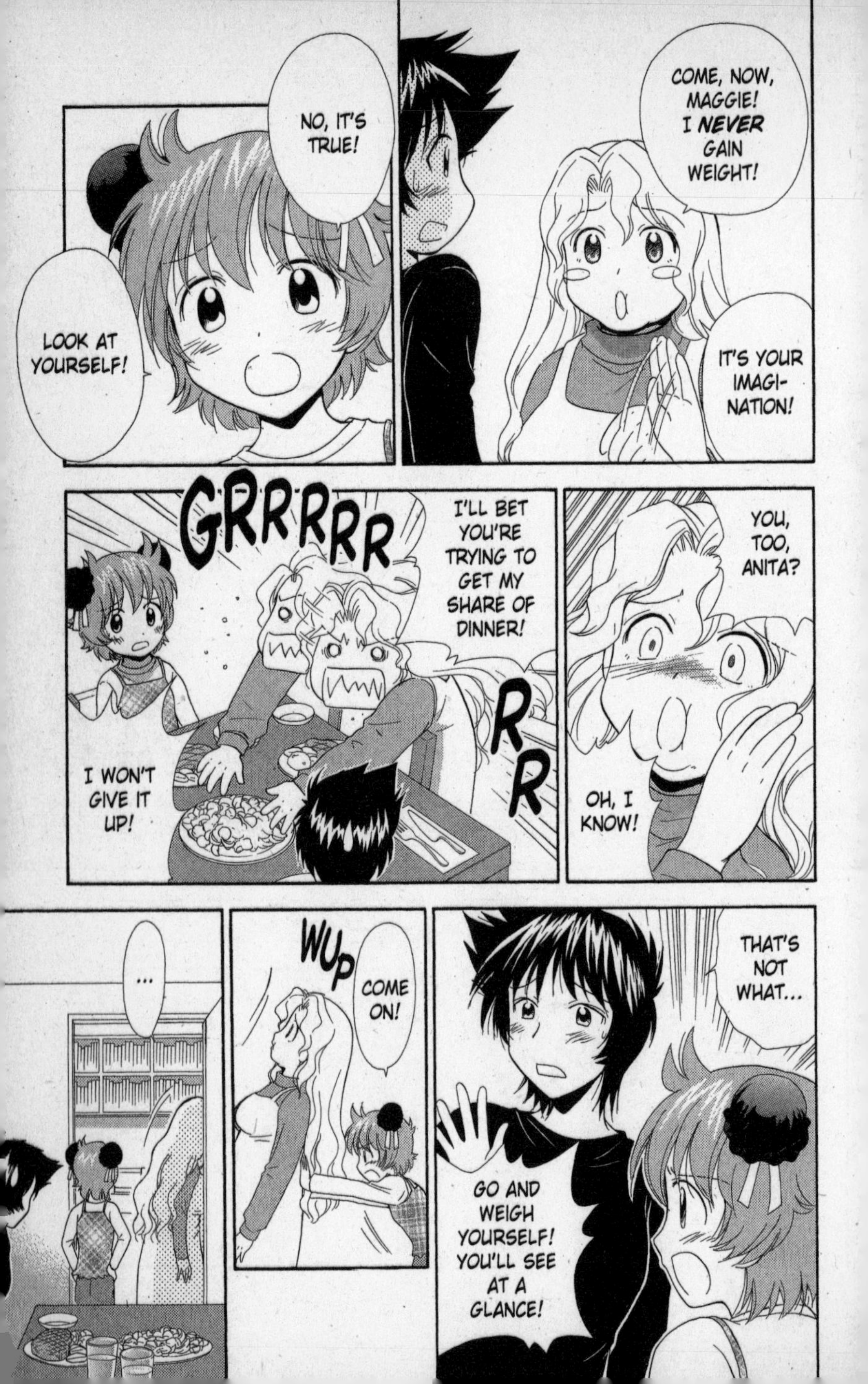
COME, NOW, MAGGIE! I **NEVER** GAIN WEIGHT!
IT'S YOUR IMAGI-NATION!
NO, IT'S TRUE!
LOOK AT YOURSELF!
YOU, TOO, ANITA?
OH, I KNOW!
GRRRRRR
I'LL BET YOU'RE TRYING TO GET MY SHARE OF DINNER!
RR
I WON'T GIVE IT UP!
THAT'S NOT WHAT...
GO AND WEIGH YOURSELF! YOU'LL SEE AT A GLANCE!
WUP
COME ON!
...

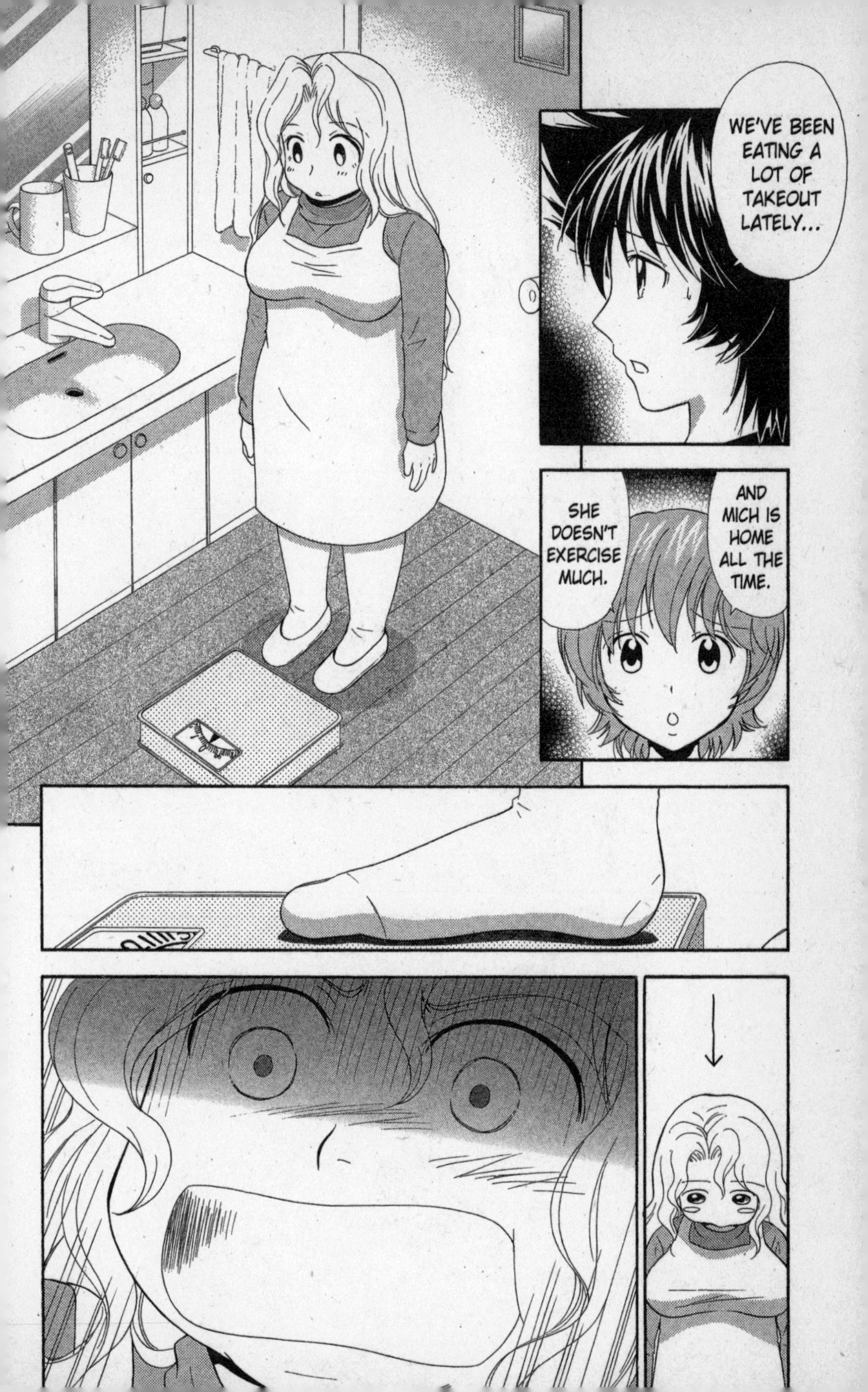
WE'VE BEEN EATING A LOT OF TAKEOUT LATELY...
AND MICH IS HOME ALL THE TIME.
SHE DOESN'T EXERCISE MUCH.

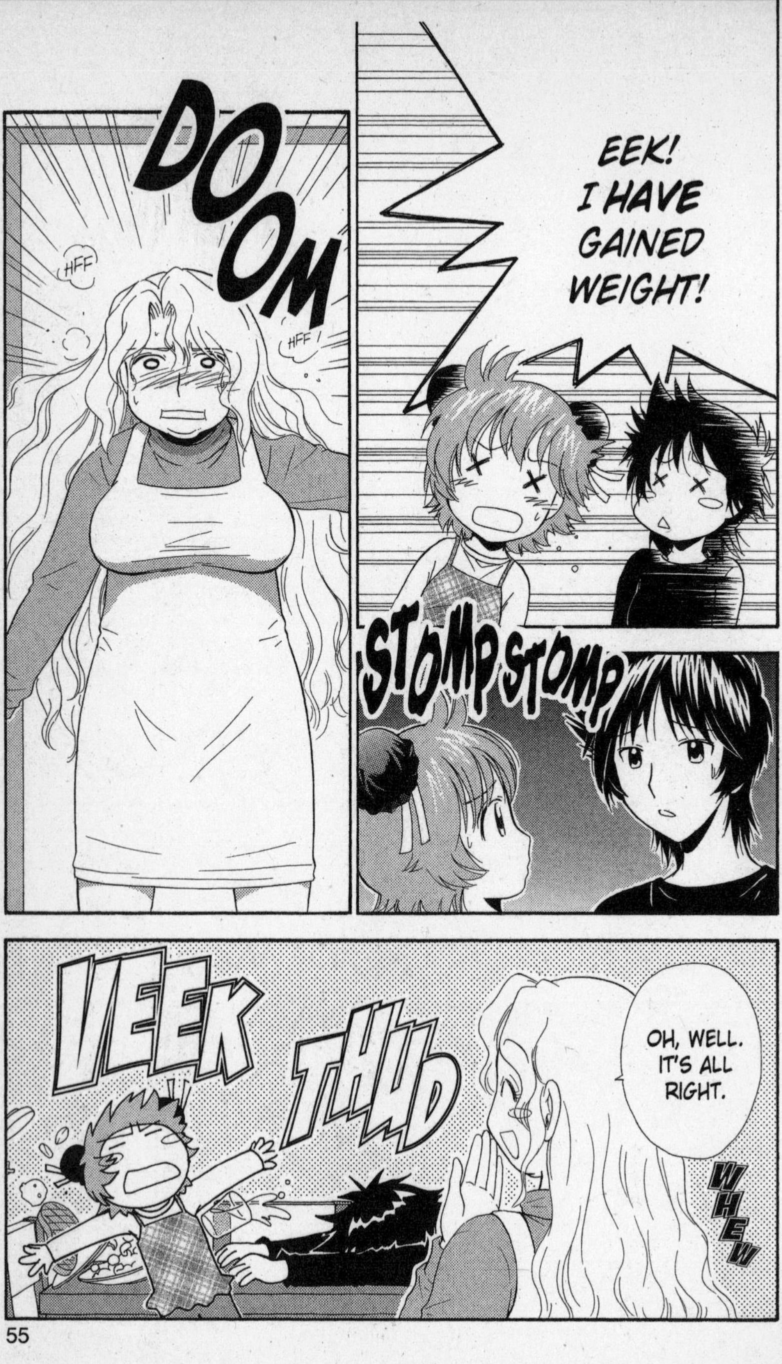
EEK! I HAVE GAINED WEIGHT!
STOMP STOMP
DOOM
HFF
HFF
OH, WELL. IT'S ALL RIGHT.
WHEW
THUD
VEEK

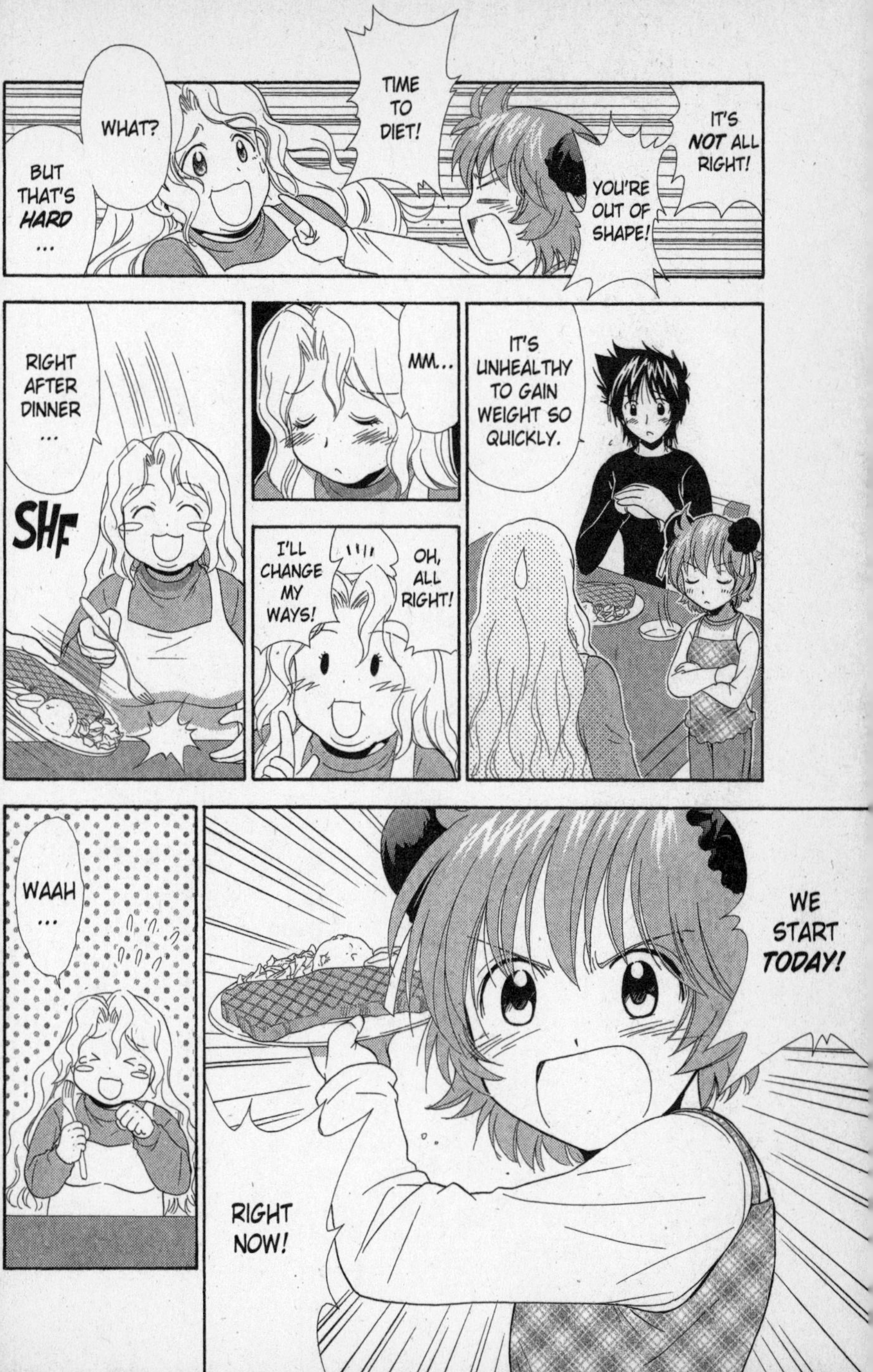
IT'S NOT ALL RIGHT!
YOU'RE OUT OF SHAPE!
TIME TO DIET!
WHAT?
BUT THAT'S HARD ...
IT'S UNHEALTHY TO GAIN WEIGHT SO QUICKLY.
MM...
OH, ALL RIGHT!
I'LL CHANGE MY WAYS!
RIGHT AFTER DINNER ...
SHF
WE START TODAY!
RIGHT NOW!
WAAH ...

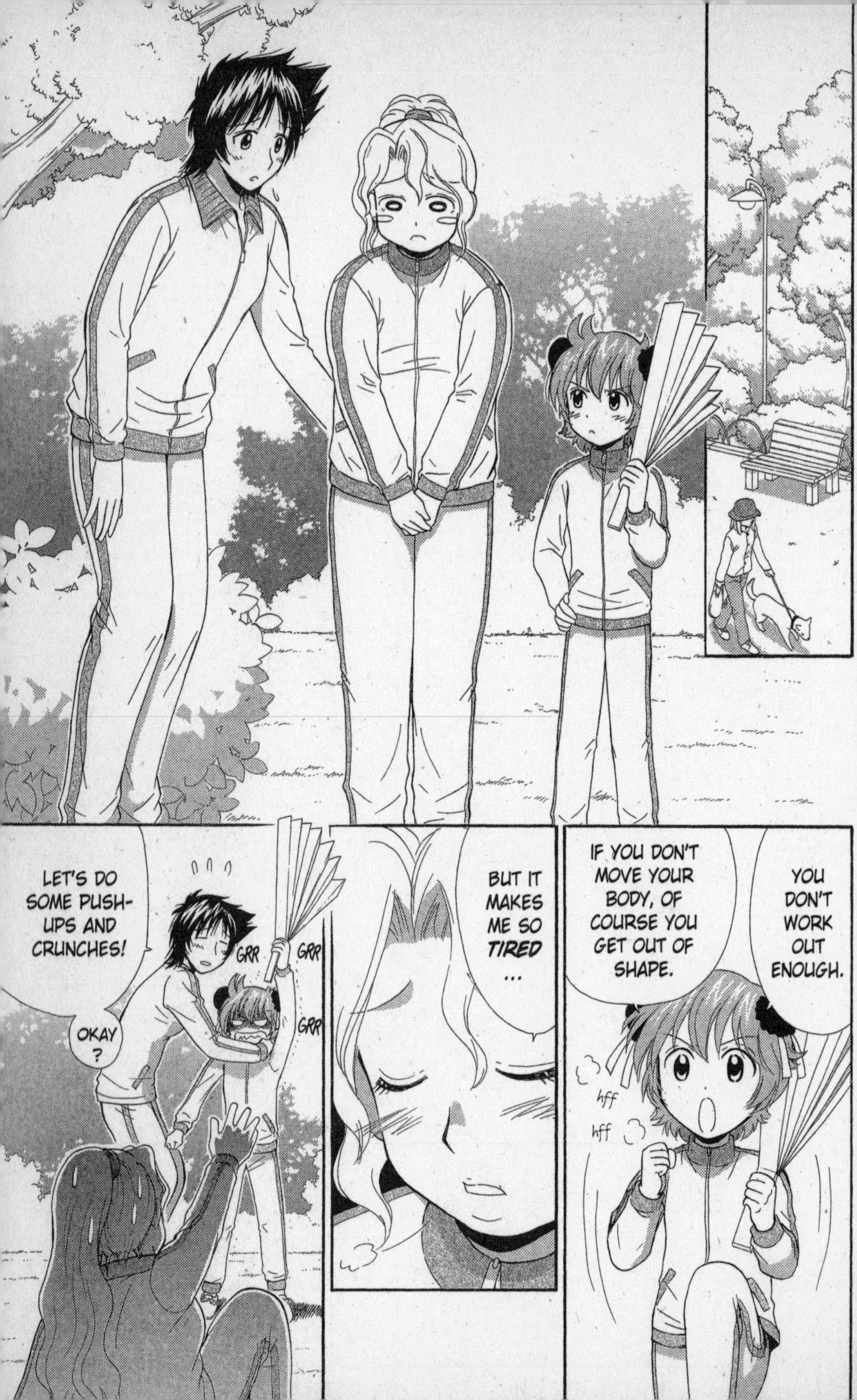
YOU DON'T WORK OUT ENOUGH.
IF YOU DON'T MOVE YOUR BODY, OF COURSE YOU GET OUT OF SHAPE.
hff
hff
BUT IT MAKES ME SO *TIRED* ...
LET'S DO SOME PUSH-UPS AND CRUNCHES!
GRR
GRR
GRR
OKAY?

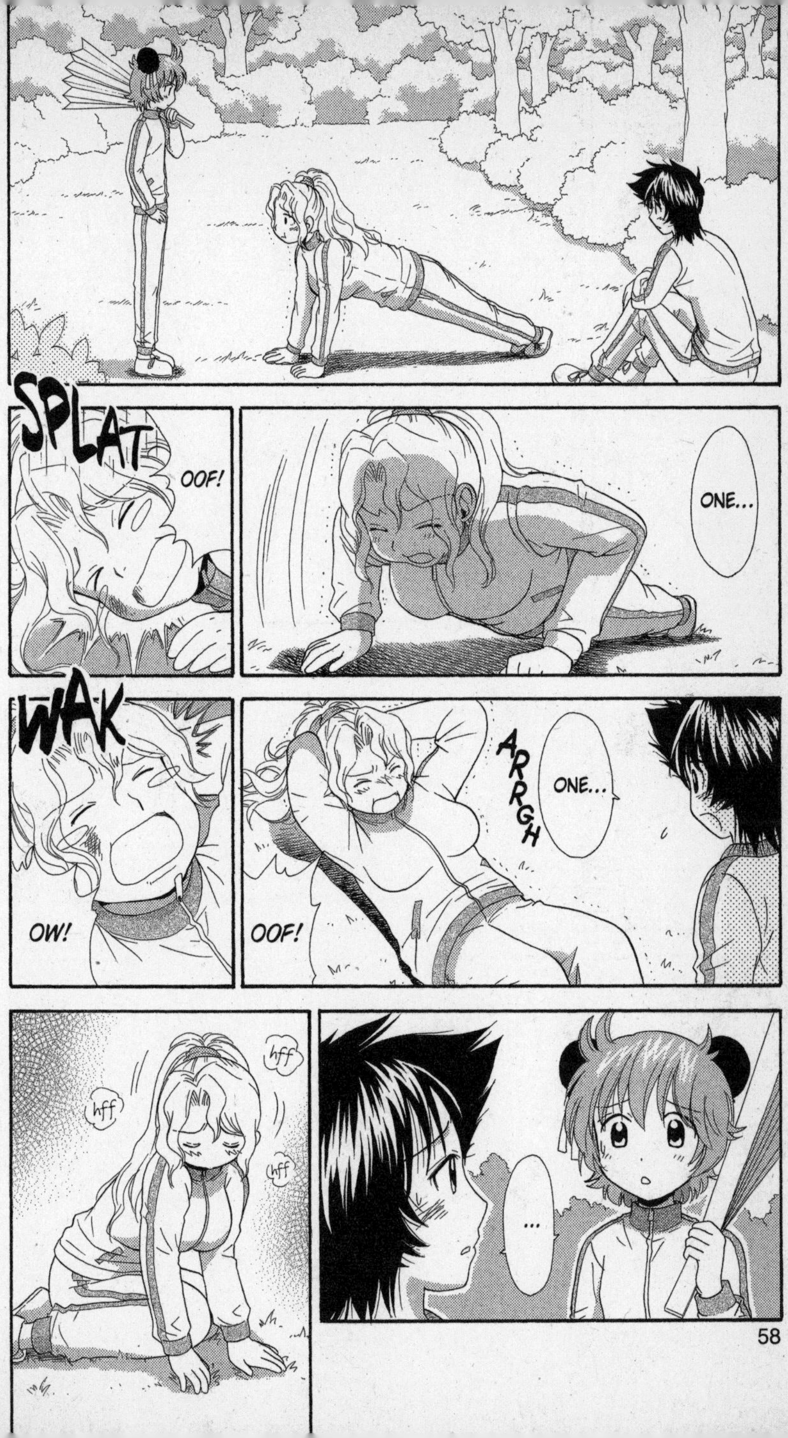
ONE...
SPLAT
OOF!
ONE...
ARRGH
OOF!
WAK
OW!
...
hff
hff
hff

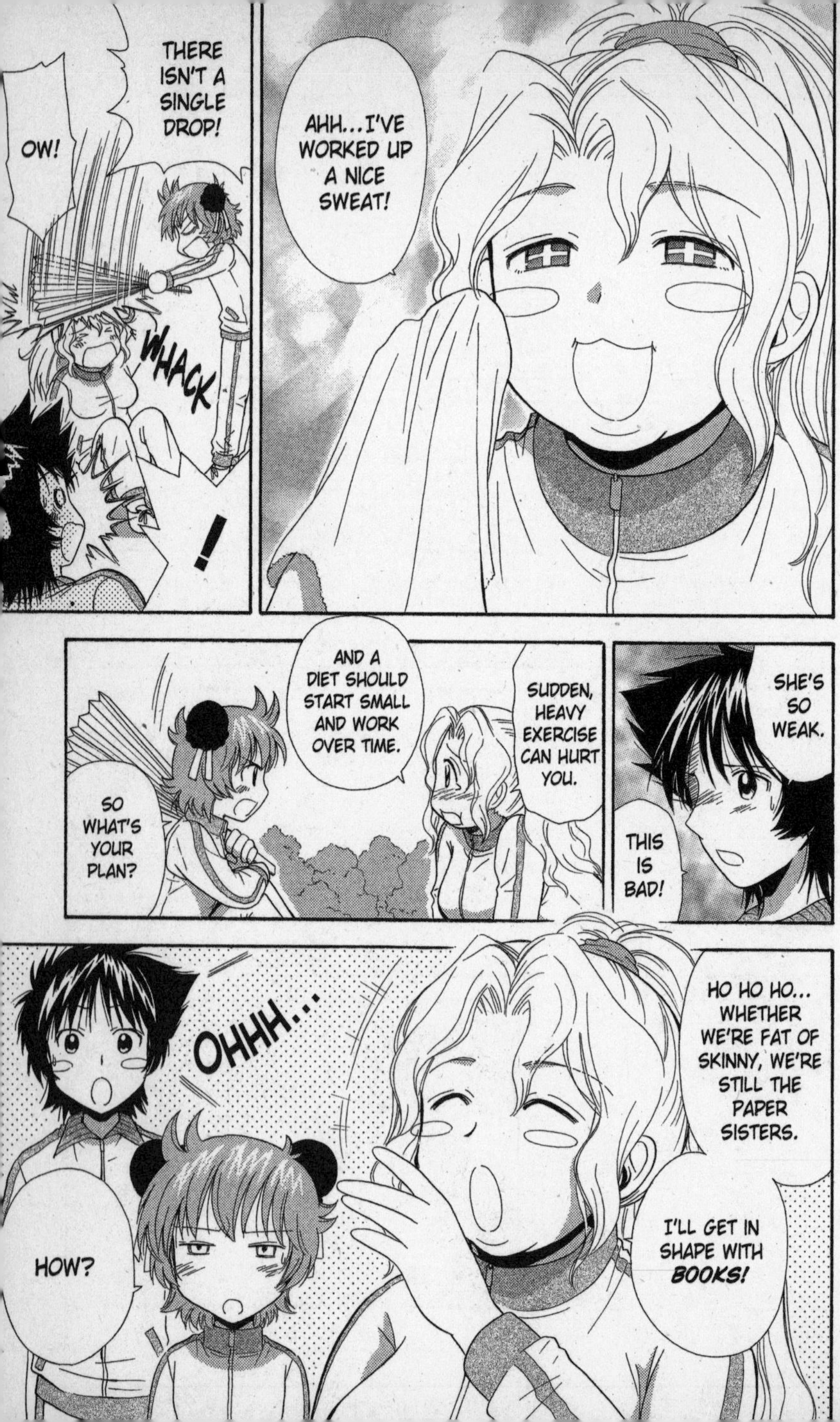
AHH...I'VE WORKED UP A NICE SWEAT!
THERE ISN'T A SINGLE DROP!
OW!
WHACK
!
SHE'S SO WEAK.
THIS IS BAD!
SUDDEN, HEAVY EXERCISE CAN HURT YOU.
AND A DIET SHOULD START SMALL AND WORK OVER TIME.
SO WHAT'S YOUR PLAN?
HO HO HO... WHETHER WE'RE FAT OF SKINNY, WE'RE STILL THE PAPER SISTERS.
I'LL GET IN SHAPE WITH *BOOKS!*
OHHH...
HOW?

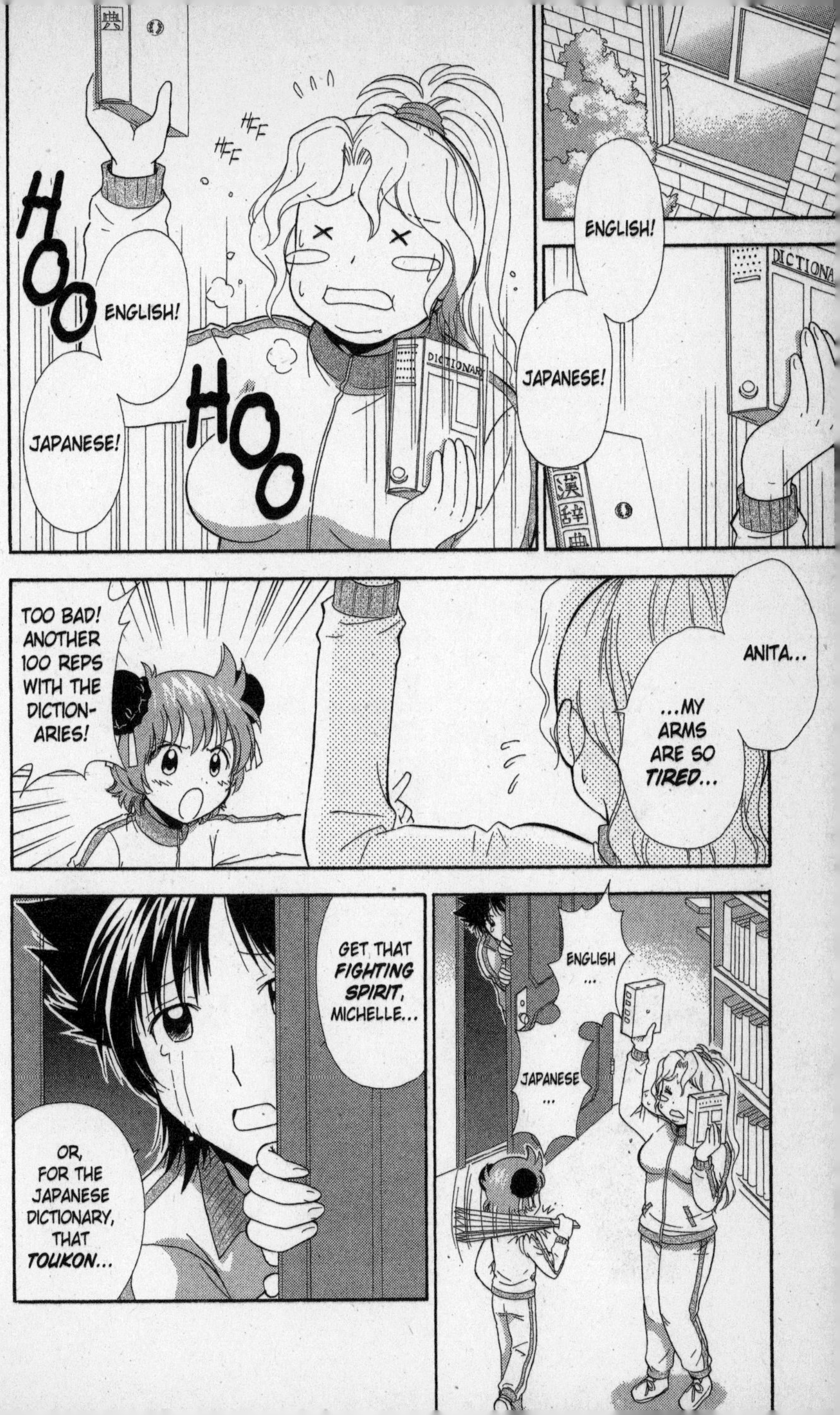
ENGLISH!
JAPANESE!
HFF
HFF
HOO
ENGLISH!
JAPANESE!
HOO
ANITA...
...MY ARMS ARE SO TIRED...
TOO BAD! ANOTHER 100 REPS WITH THE DICTION-ARIES!
ENGLISH...
JAPANESE...
GET THAT FIGHTING SPIRIT, MICHELLE...
OR, FOR THE JAPANESE DICTIONARY, THAT TOUKON...

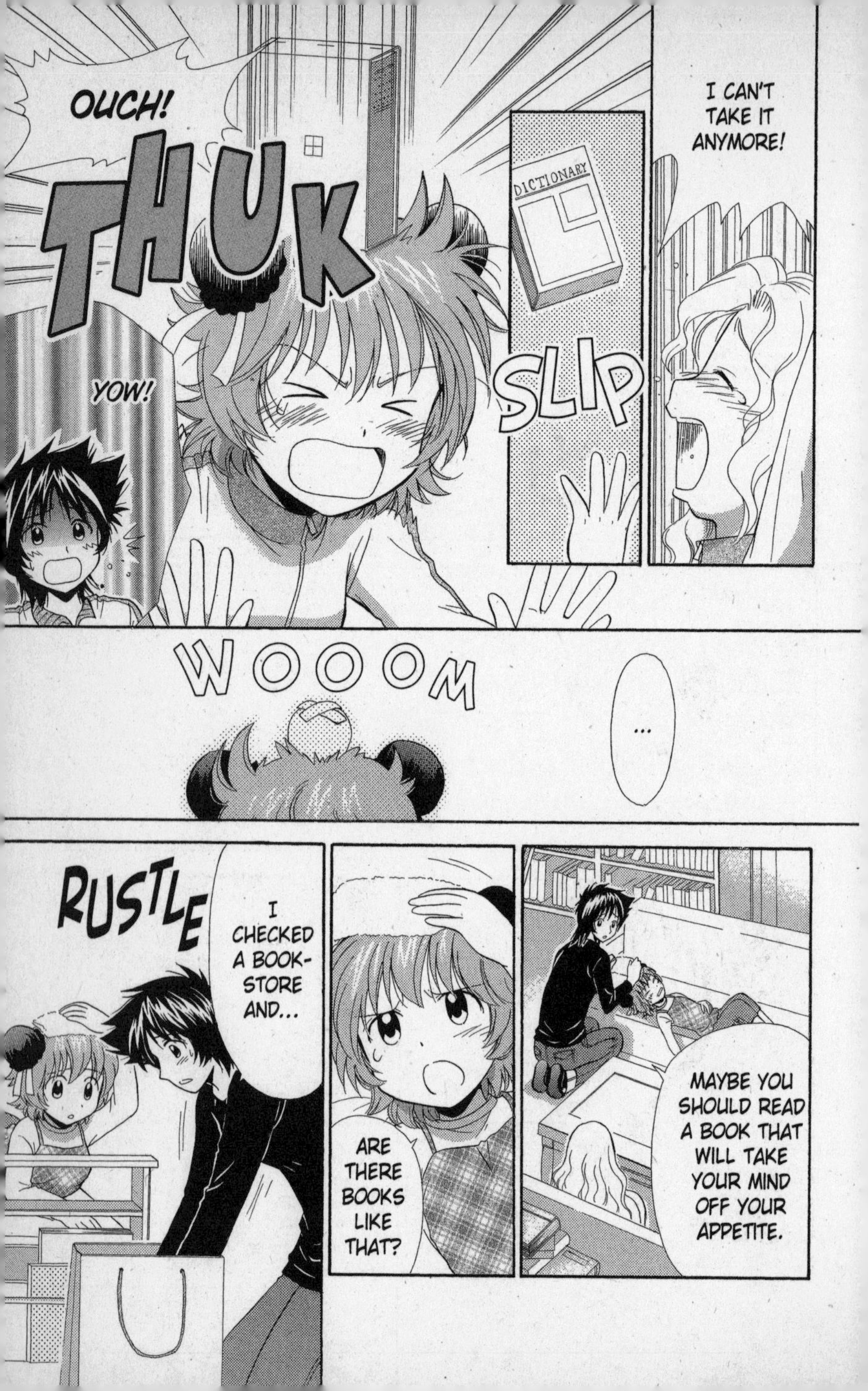
I CAN'T TAKE IT ANYMORE!
DICTIONARY
SLIP
OUCH!
THUK
YOW!
...
WOOOM
MAYBE YOU SHOULD READ A BOOK THAT WILL TAKE YOUR MIND OFF YOUR APPETITE.
ARE THERE BOOKS LIKE THAT?
I CHECKED A BOOK-STORE AND...
RUSTLE

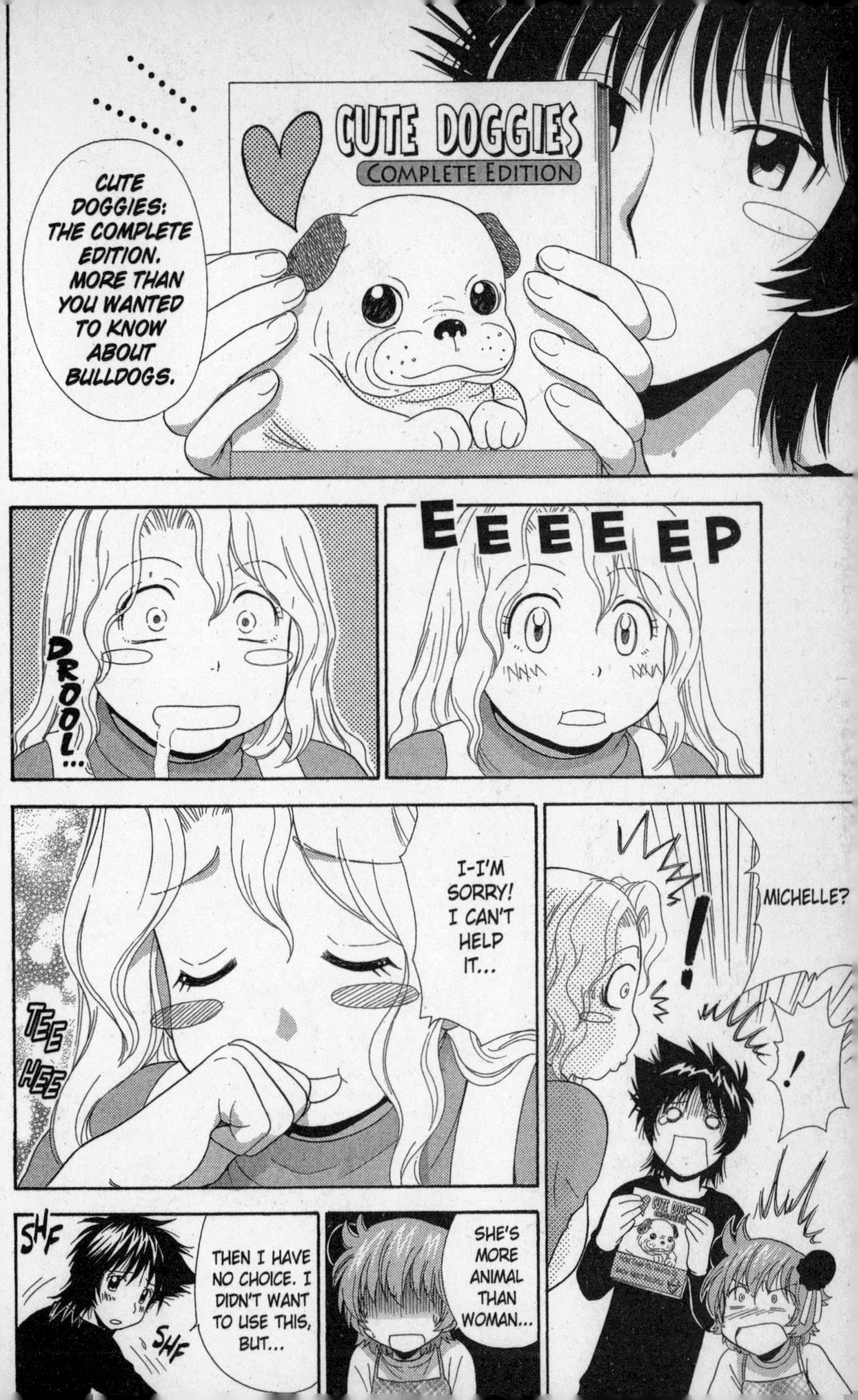
CUTE DOGGIES
COMPLETE EDITION
CUTE DOGGIES: THE COMPLETE EDITION. MORE THAN YOU WANTED TO KNOW ABOUT BULLDOGS.
EEEE EP
DROOL...
MICHELLE?
I-I'M SORRY! I CAN'T HELP IT...
TEE HEE
SHE'S MORE ANIMAL THAN WOMAN...
THEN I HAVE NO CHOICE. I DIDN'T WANT TO USE THIS, BUT...
SHF
SHF

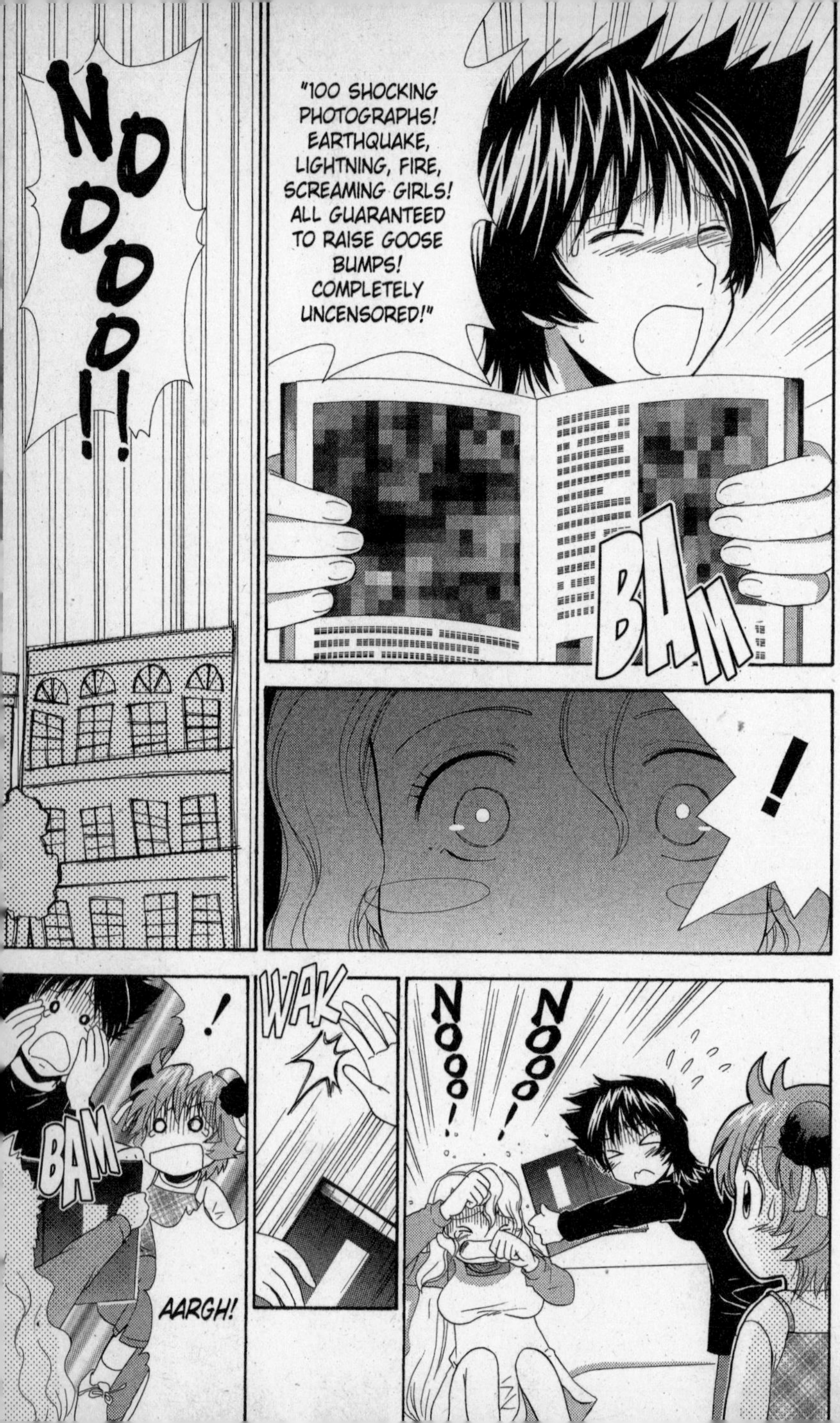
"100 SHOCKING PHOTOGRAPHS! EARTHQUAKE, LIGHTNING, FIRE, SCREAMING GIRLS! ALL GUARANTEED TO RAISE GOOSE BUMPS! COMPLETELY UNCENSORED!"
BAM
!
NOOOO!!
NOOOO!
NOOOO!
WAK
!
BAM
AARGH!

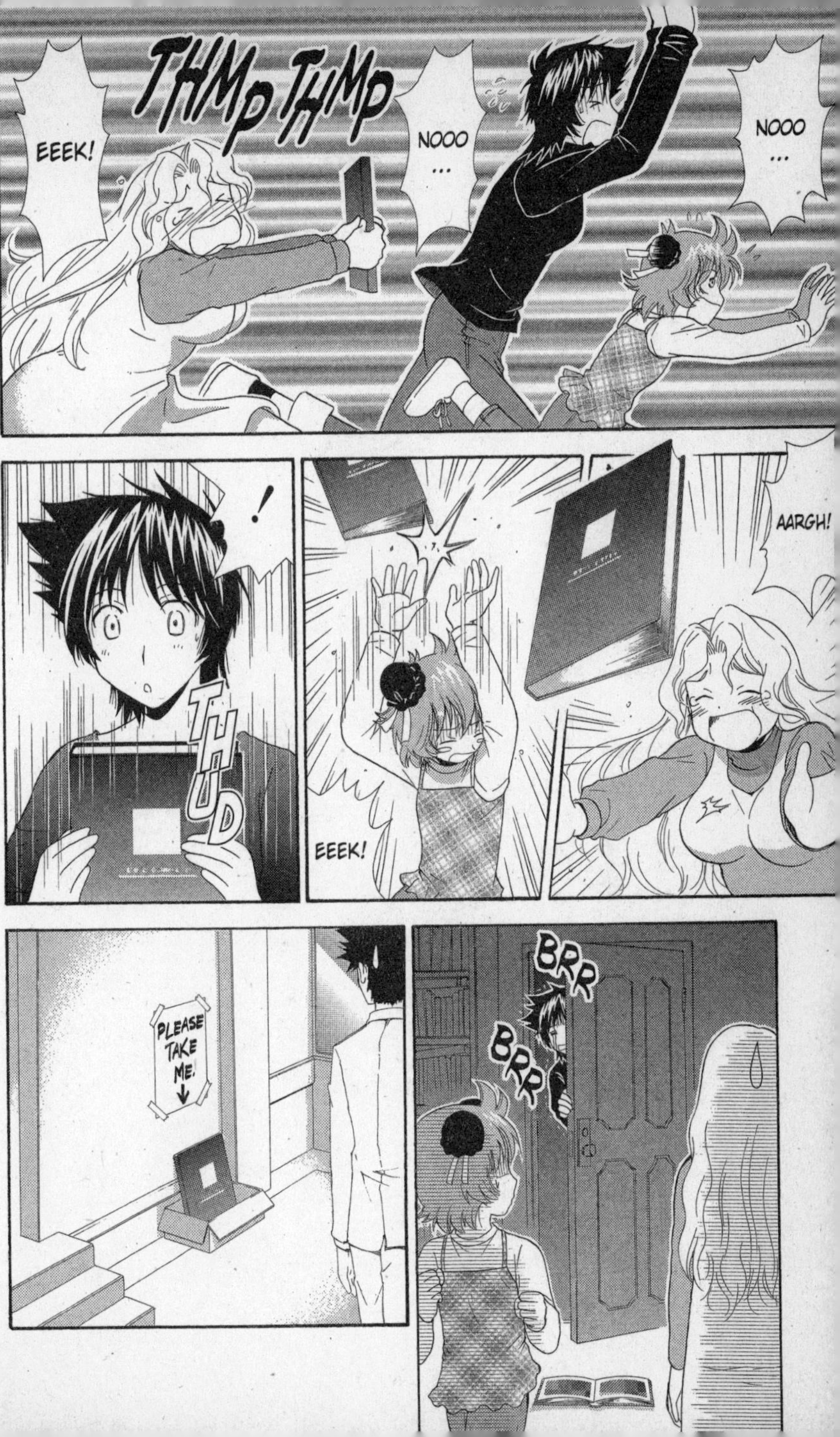
NOOO ...
NOOO ...
THMP THMP
EEEK!
AARGH!
EEEK!
!
THUD
BRR BRR
PLEASE TAKE ME!

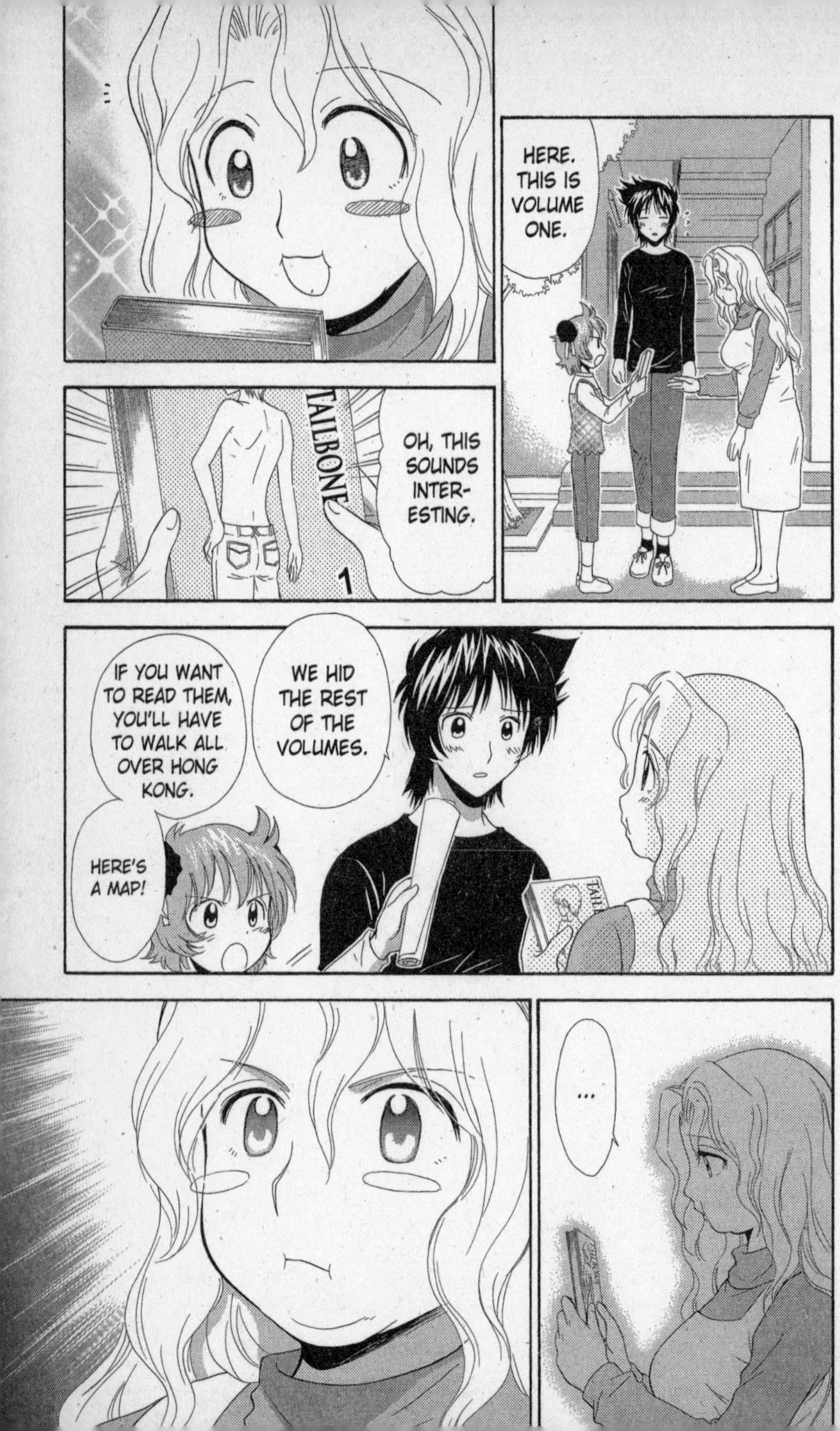
HERE. THIS IS VOLUME ONE.
TAILBONE
1
OH, THIS SOUNDS INTER-ESTING.
WE HID THE REST OF THE VOLUMES.
IF YOU WANT TO READ THEM, YOU'LL HAVE TO WALK ALL OVER HONG KONG.
HERE'S A MAP!
...

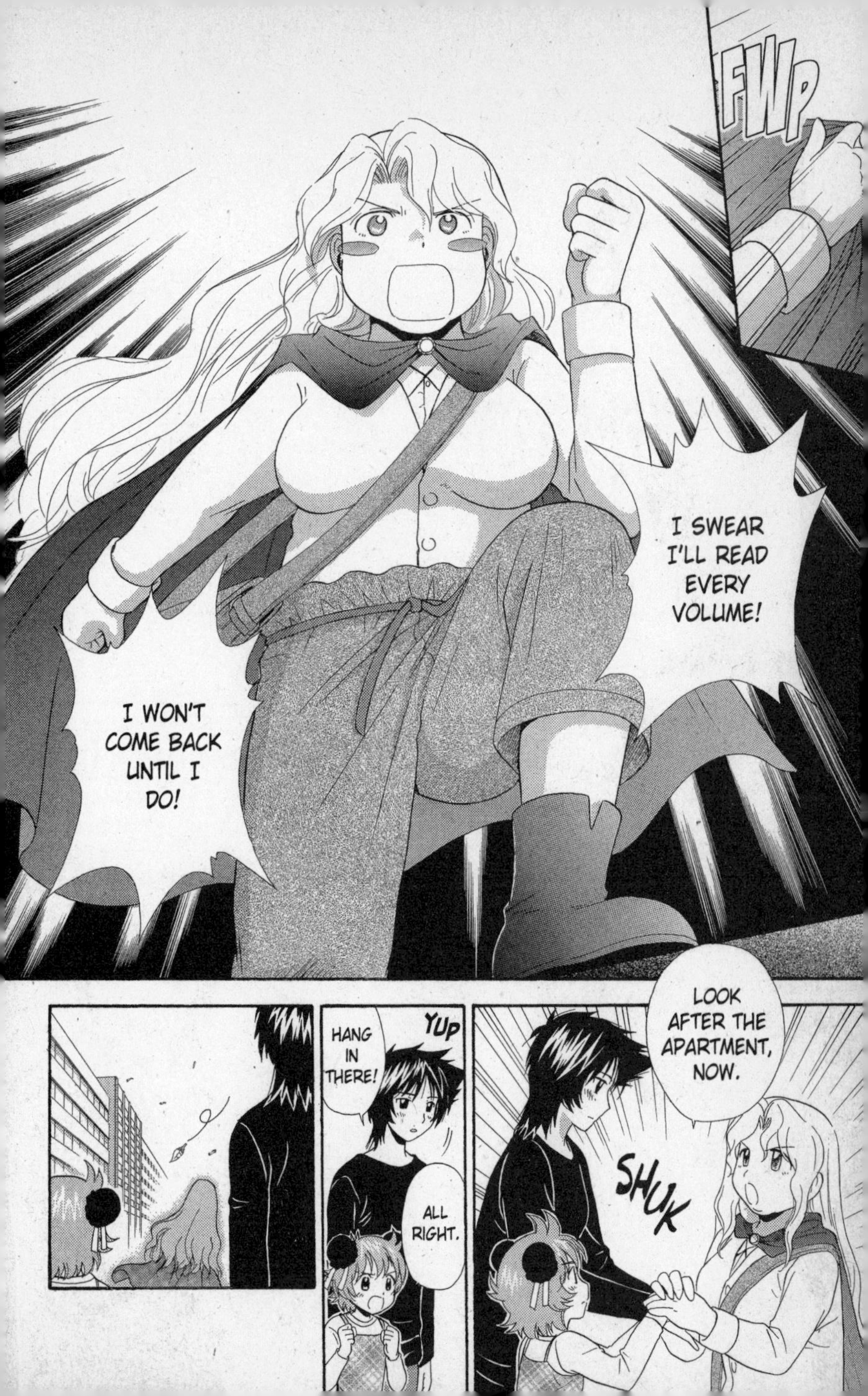
FWP
I SWEAR I'LL READ EVERY VOLUME!
I WON'T COME BACK UNTIL I DO!
LOOK AFTER THE APARTMENT, NOW.
SHUK
YUP
HANG IN THERE!
ALL RIGHT.

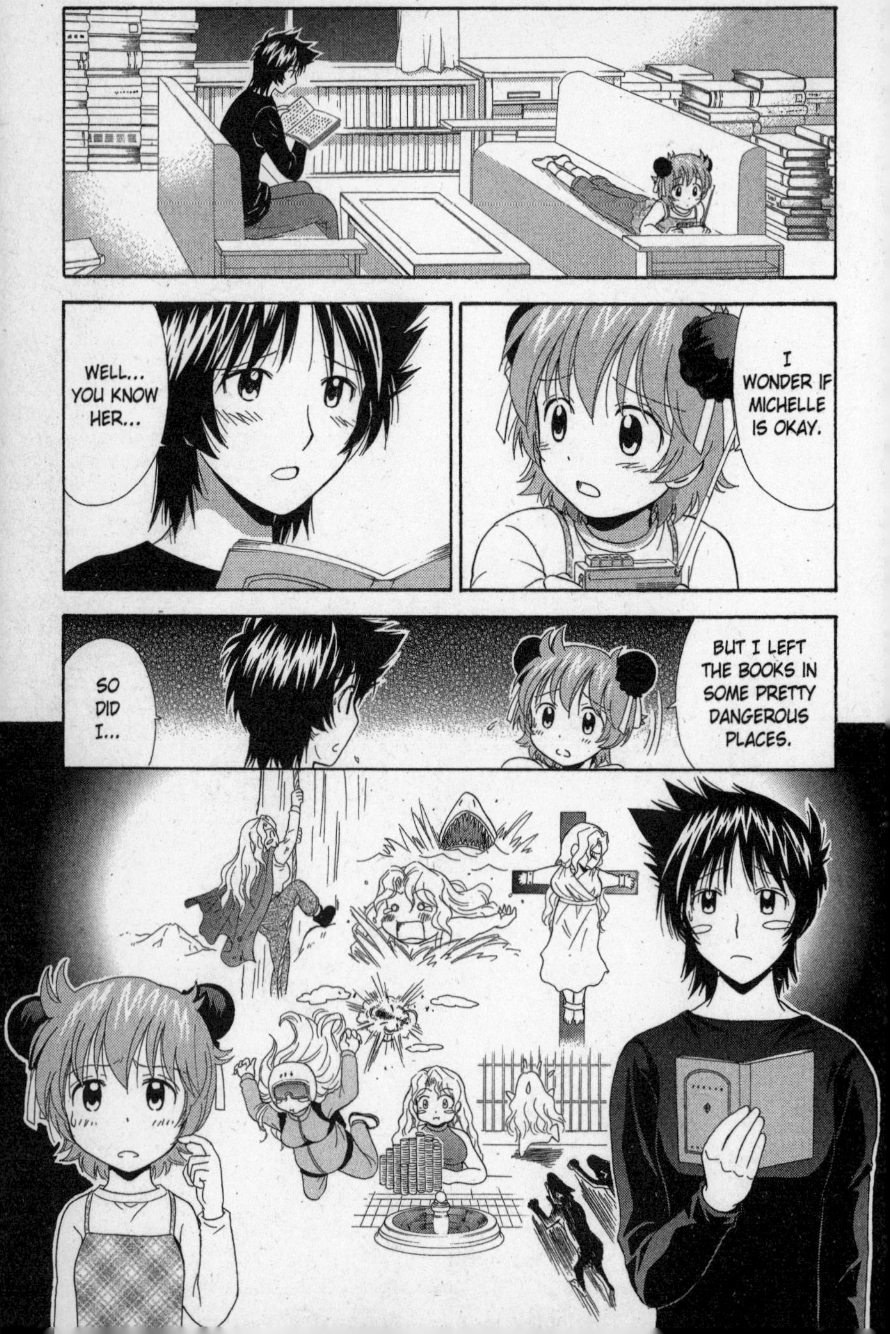
I WONDER IF MICHELLE IS OKAY.
WELL... YOU KNOW HER...
BUT I LEFT THE BOOKS IN SOME PRETTY DANGEROUS PLACES.
SO DID I...

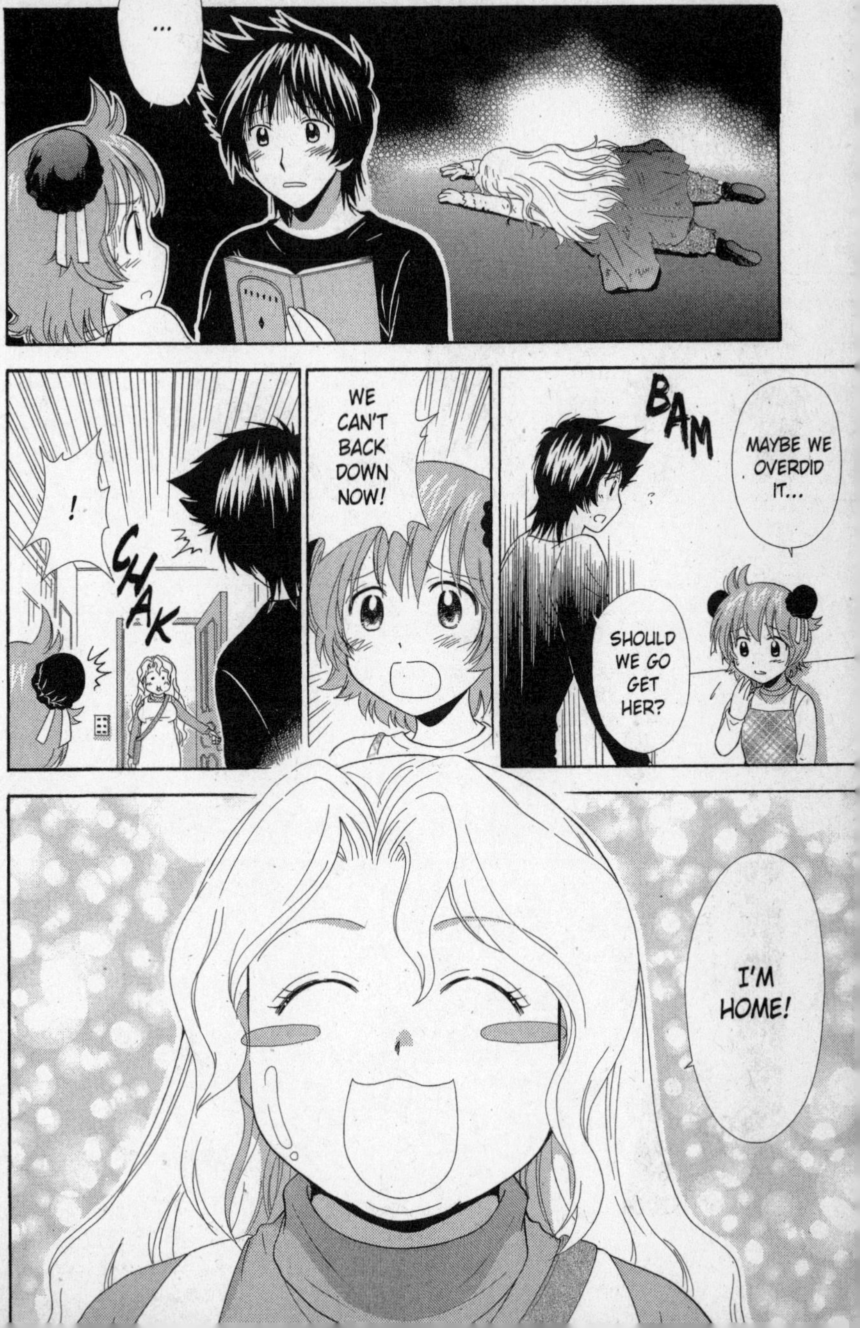
...
BAM
MAYBE WE OVERDID IT...
SHOULD WE GO GET HER?
WE CAN'T BACK DOWN NOW!
CHAK
!
I'M HOME!

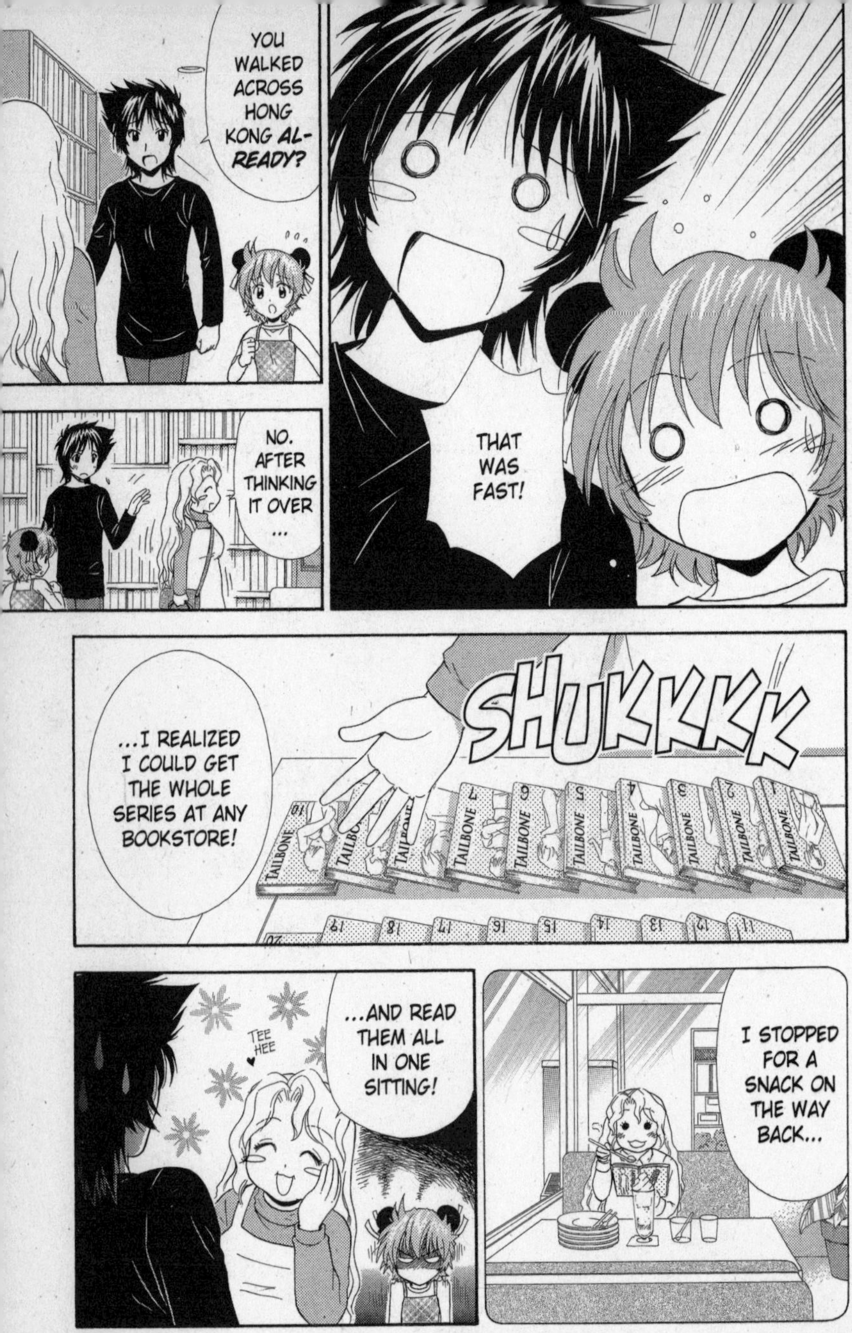
THAT WAS FAST!
YOU WALKED ACROSS HONG KONG ALREADY?
NO. AFTER THINKING IT OVER ...
SHUKKKK
...I REALIZED I COULD GET THE WHOLE SERIES AT ANY BOOKSTORE!
TAILBONE
I STOPPED FOR A SNACK ON THE WAY BACK...
...AND READ THEM ALL IN ONE SITTING!
TEE HEE

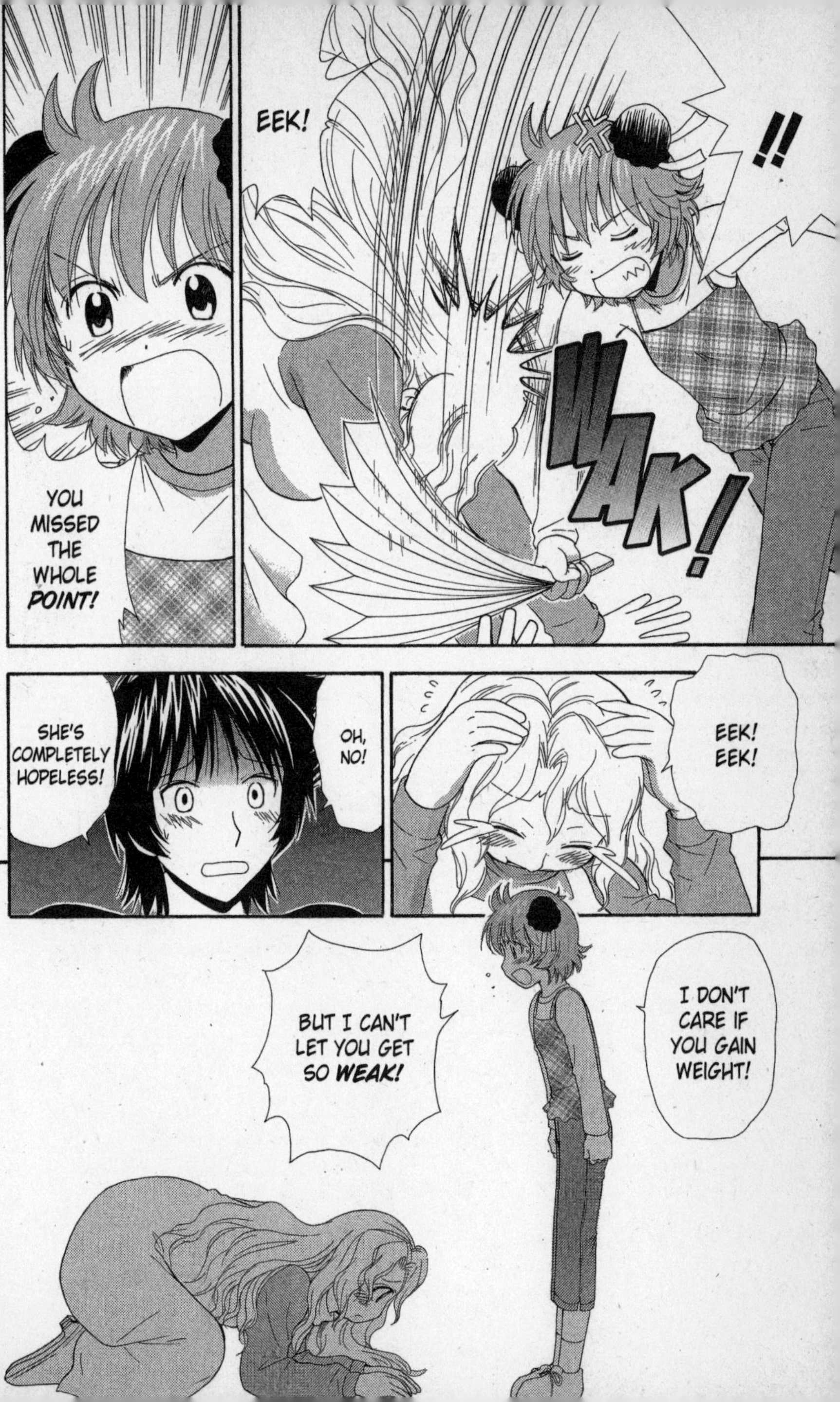
!!
EEK!
WHAK!
YOU MISSED THE WHOLE POINT!
EEK! EEK!
OH, NO!
SHE'S COMPLETELY HOPELESS!
I DON'T CARE IF YOU GAIN WEIGHT!
BUT I CAN'T LET YOU GET SO WEAK!

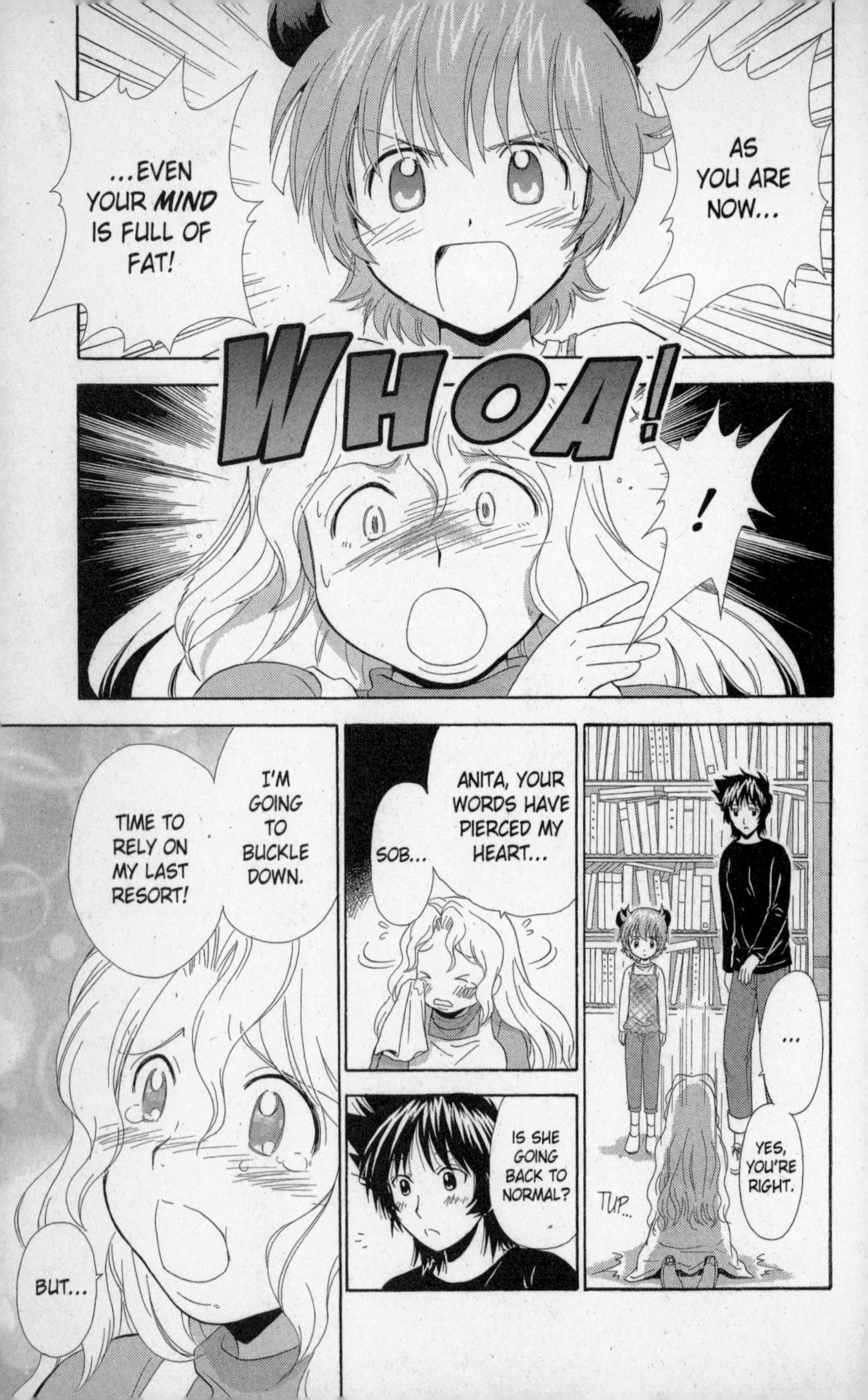
AS YOU ARE NOW...
...EVEN YOUR MIND IS FULL OF FAT!
WHOA!
!
...
YES, YOU'RE RIGHT.
TUP...
ANITA, YOUR WORDS HAVE PIERCED MY HEART...
SOB...
IS SHE GOING BACK TO NORMAL?
I'M GOING TO BUCKLE DOWN.
TIME TO RELY ON MY LAST RESORT!
BUT...

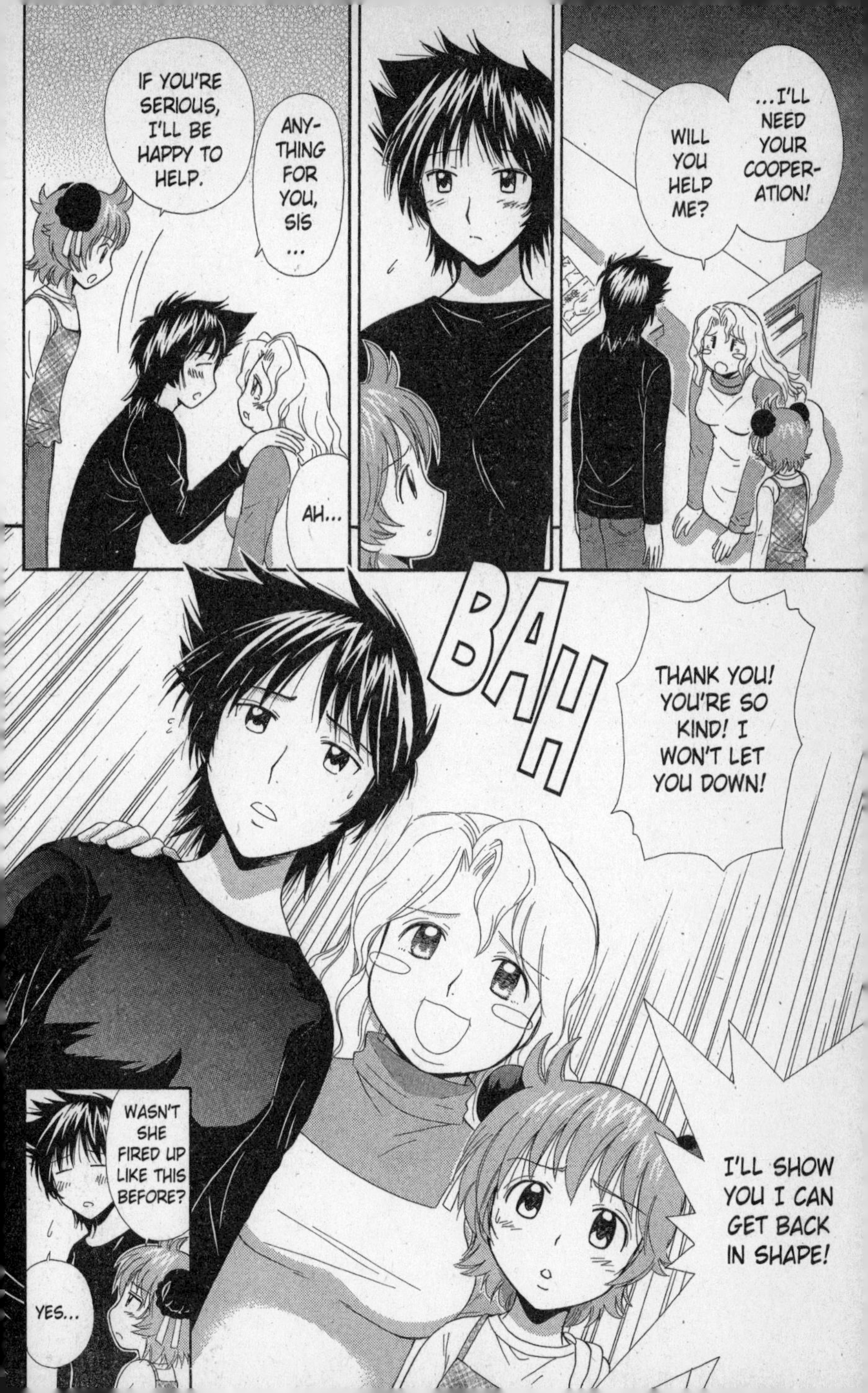
...I'LL NEED YOUR COOPERATION!
WILL YOU HELP ME?
ANYTHING FOR YOU, SIS...
IF YOU'RE SERIOUS, I'LL BE HAPPY TO HELP.
AH...
BAH
THANK YOU! YOU'RE SO KIND! I WON'T LET YOU DOWN!
I'LL SHOW YOU I CAN GET BACK IN SHAPE!
WASN'T SHE FIRED UP LIKE THIS BEFORE?
YES...

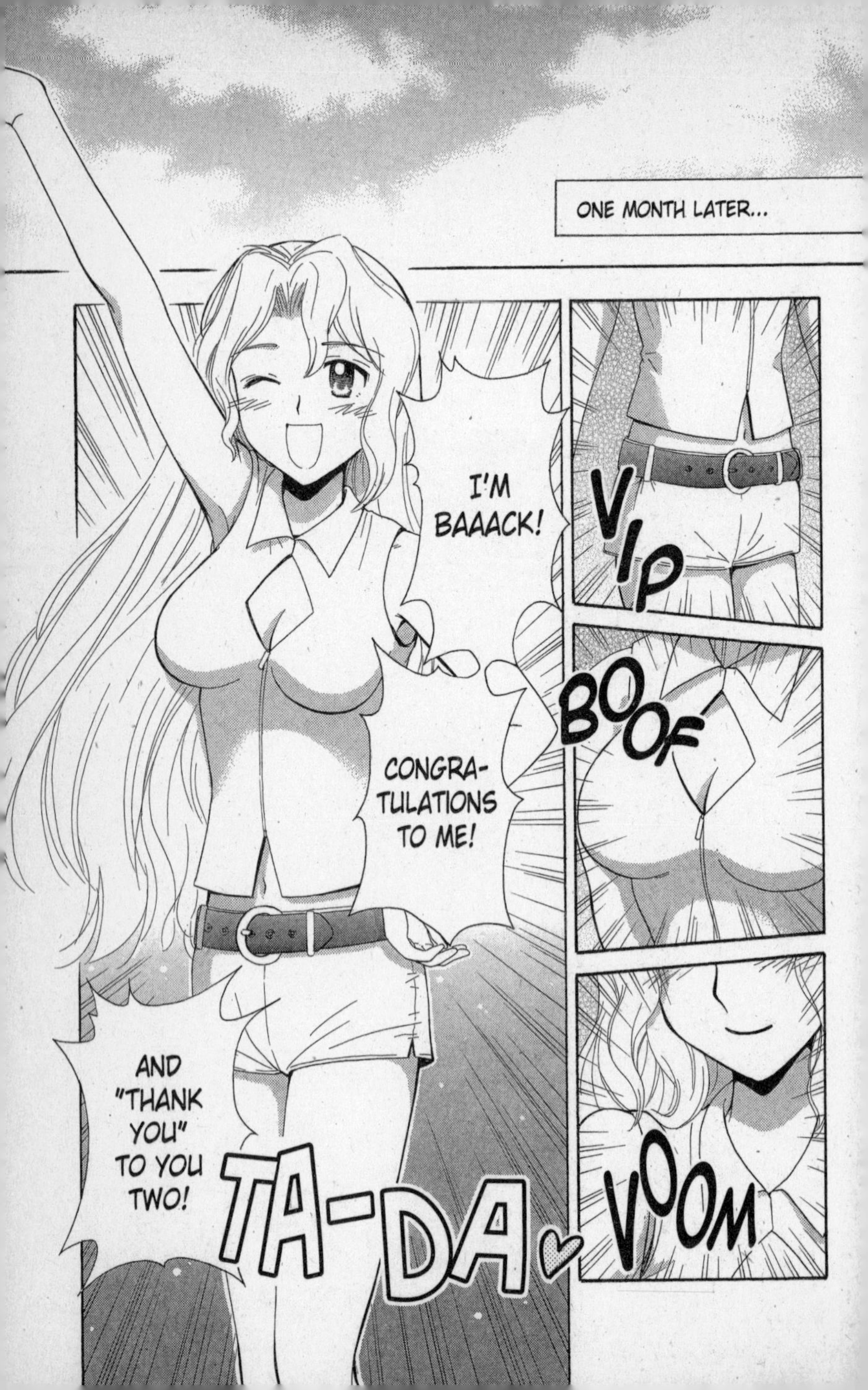
ONE MONTH LATER...
VIP
BOOF
VOOM
I'M BAAACK!
CONGRATULATIONS TO ME!
AND "THANK YOU" TO YOU TWO!
TA-DA

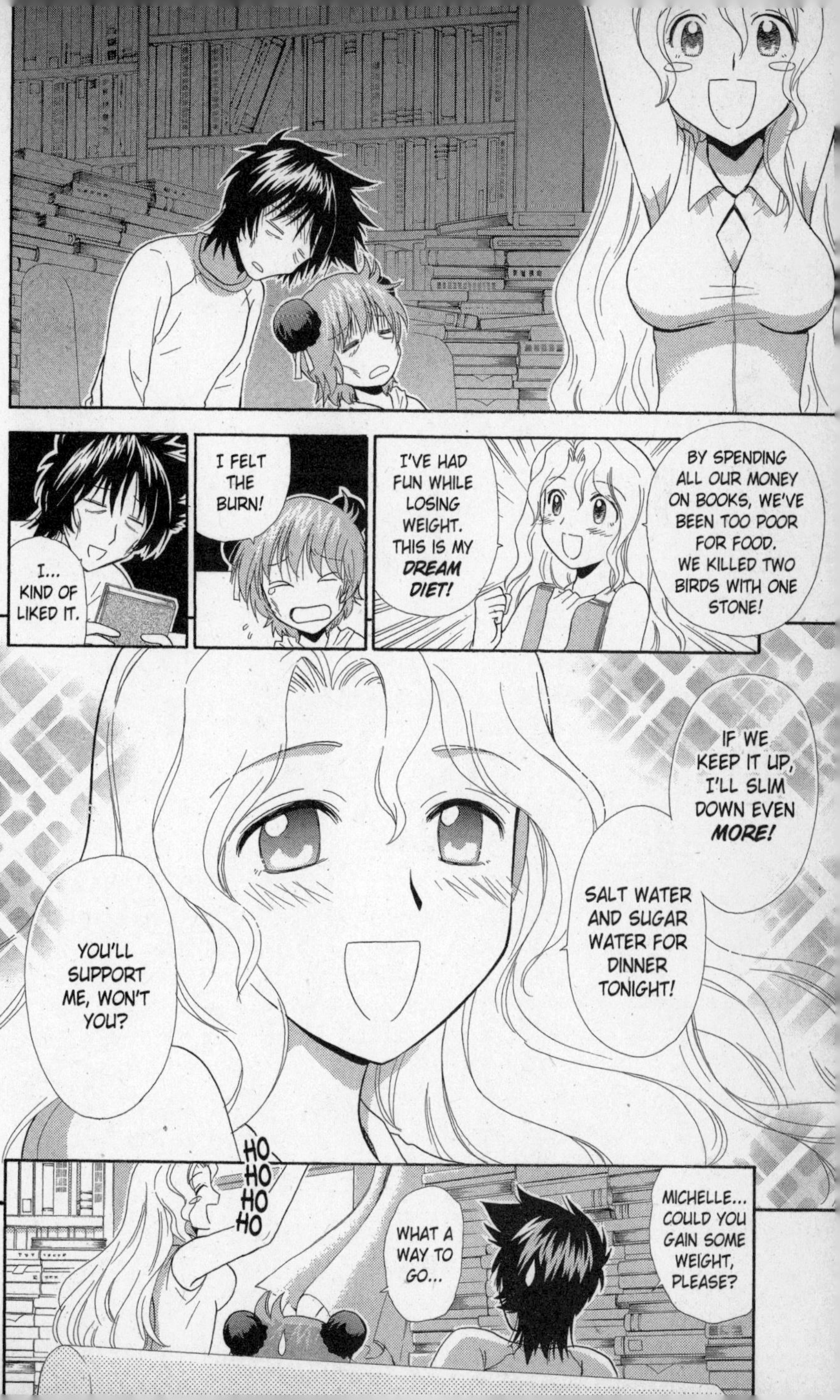
BY SPENDING ALL OUR MONEY ON BOOKS, WE'VE BEEN TOO POOR FOR FOOD. WE KILLED TWO BIRDS WITH ONE STONE!
I'VE HAD FUN WHILE LOSING WEIGHT. THIS IS MY DREAM DIET!
I FELT THE BURN!
I... KIND OF LIKED IT.
IF WE KEEP IT UP, I'LL SLIM DOWN EVEN MORE!
SALT WATER AND SUGAR WATER FOR DINNER TONIGHT!
YOU'LL SUPPORT ME, WON'T YOU?
HO HO HO HO
MICHELLE... COULD YOU GAIN SOME WEIGHT, PLEASE?
WHAT A WAY TO GO...

CHAPTER 19

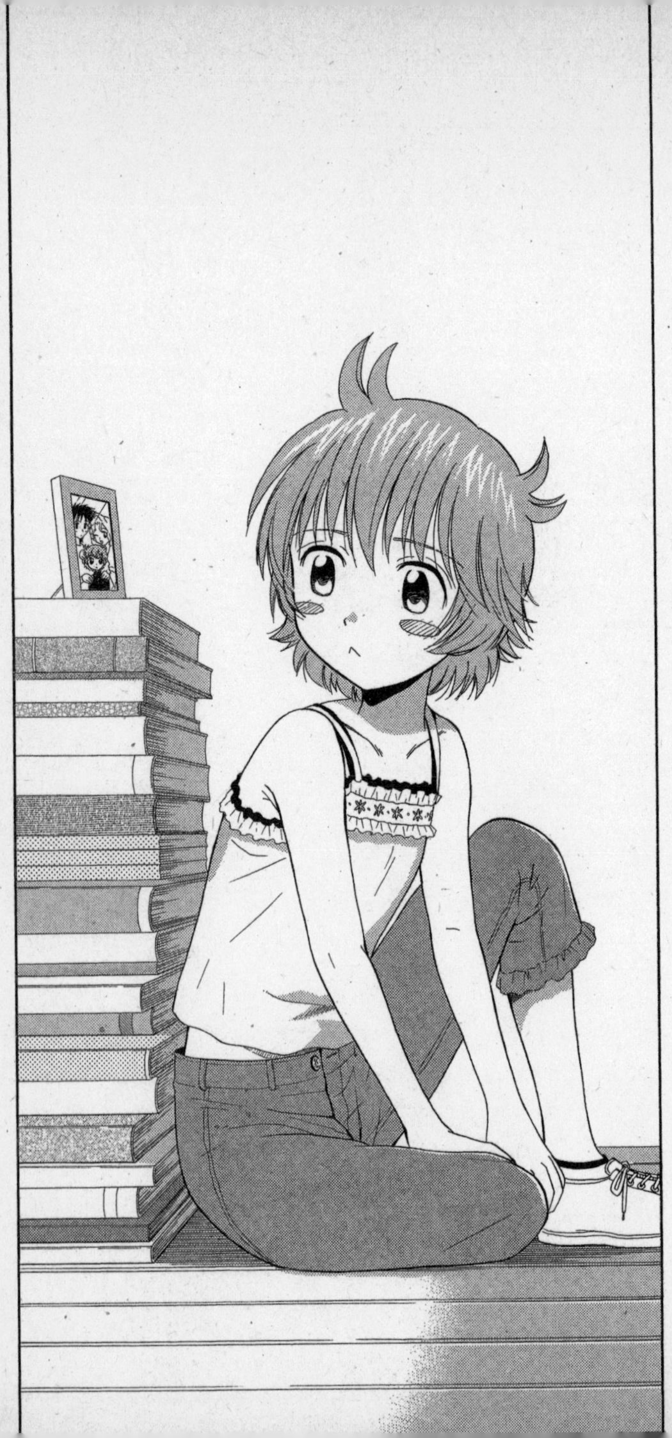

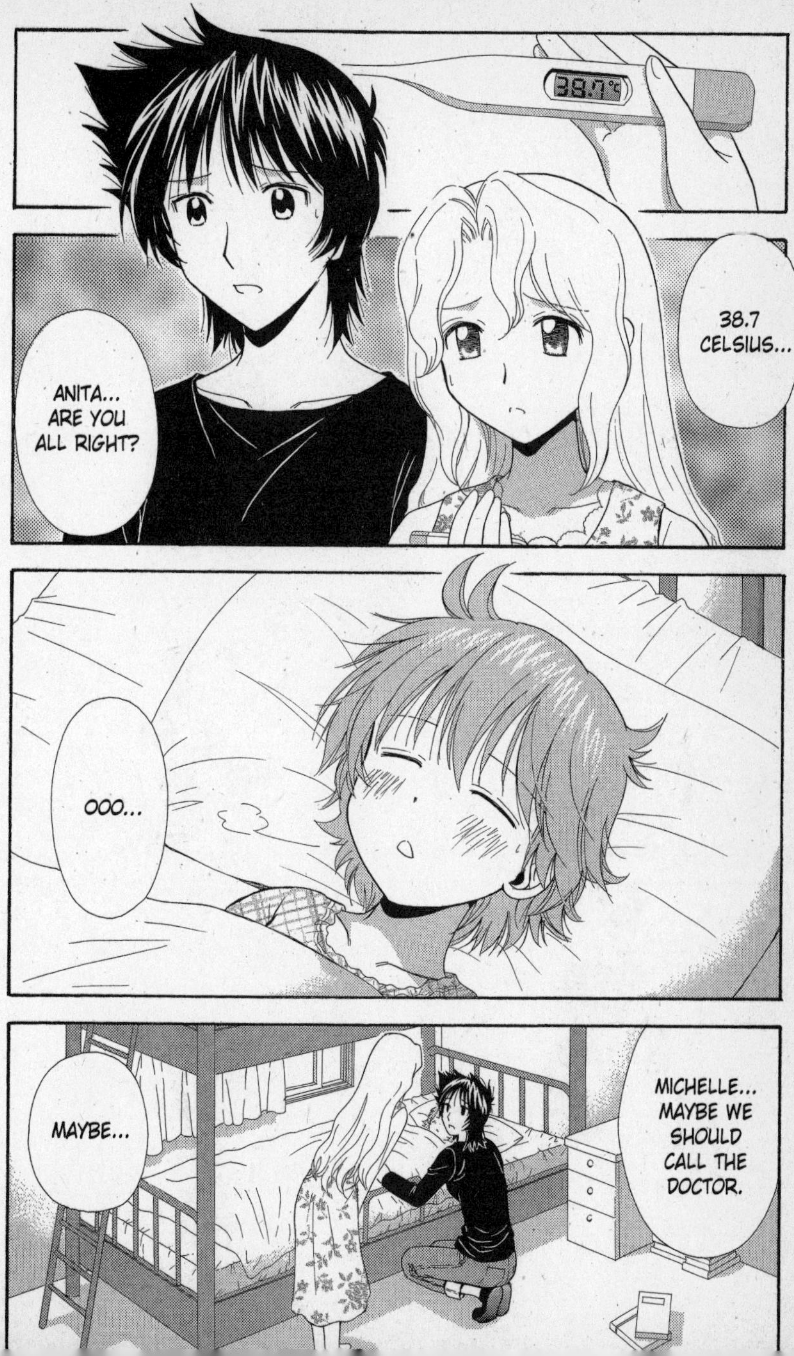
38.7°C
38.7 CELSIUS...
ANITA... ARE YOU ALL RIGHT?
OOO...
MICHELLE... MAYBE WE SHOULD CALL THE DOCTOR.
MAYBE...

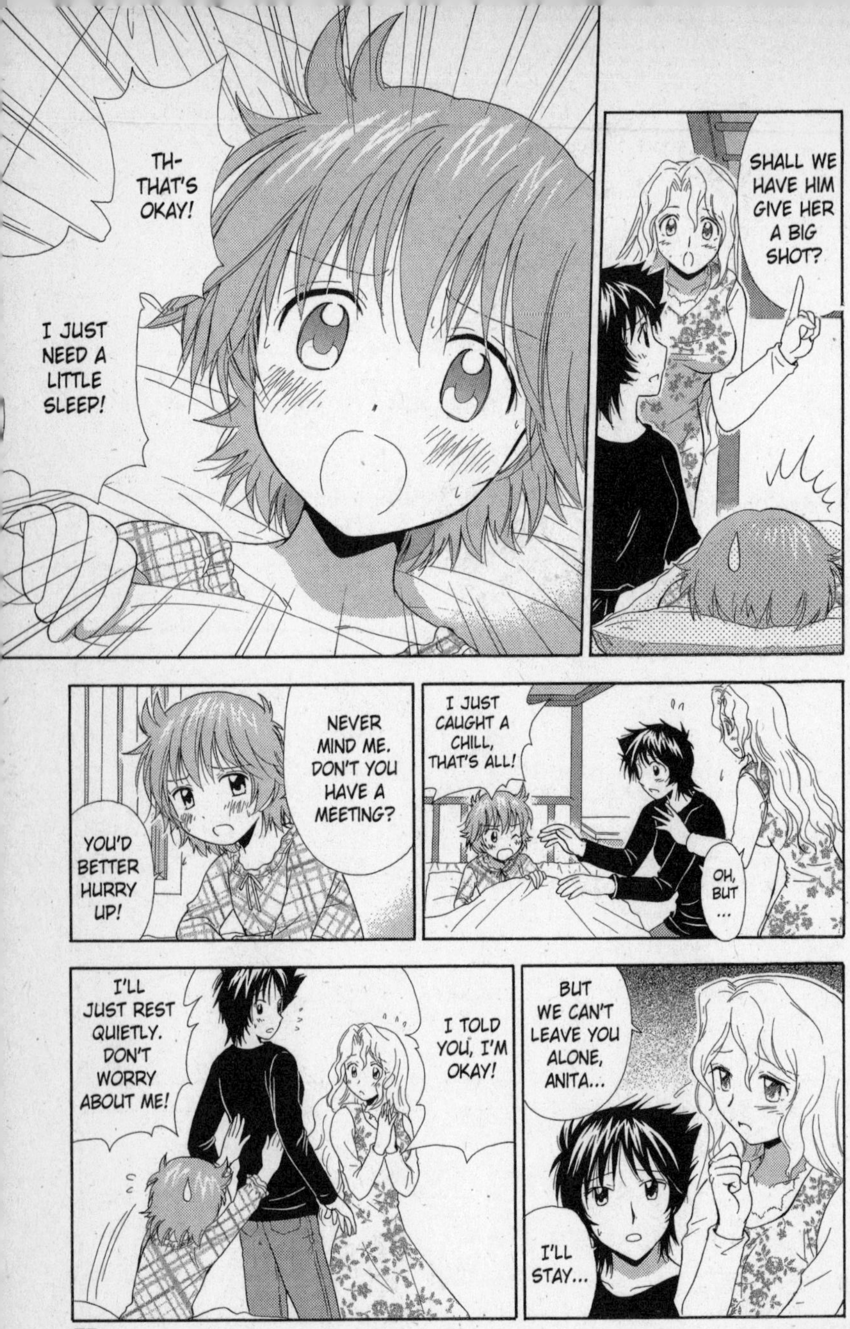
SHALL WE HAVE HIM GIVE HER A BIG SHOT?
TH- THAT'S OKAY!
I JUST NEED A LITTLE SLEEP!
I JUST CAUGHT A CHILL, THAT'S ALL!
OH, BUT...
NEVER MIND ME. DON'T YOU HAVE A MEETING?
YOU'D BETTER HURRY UP!
BUT WE CAN'T LEAVE YOU ALONE, ANITA...
I'LL STAY...
I TOLD YOU, I'M OKAY!
I'LL JUST REST QUIETLY. DON'T WORRY ABOUT ME!

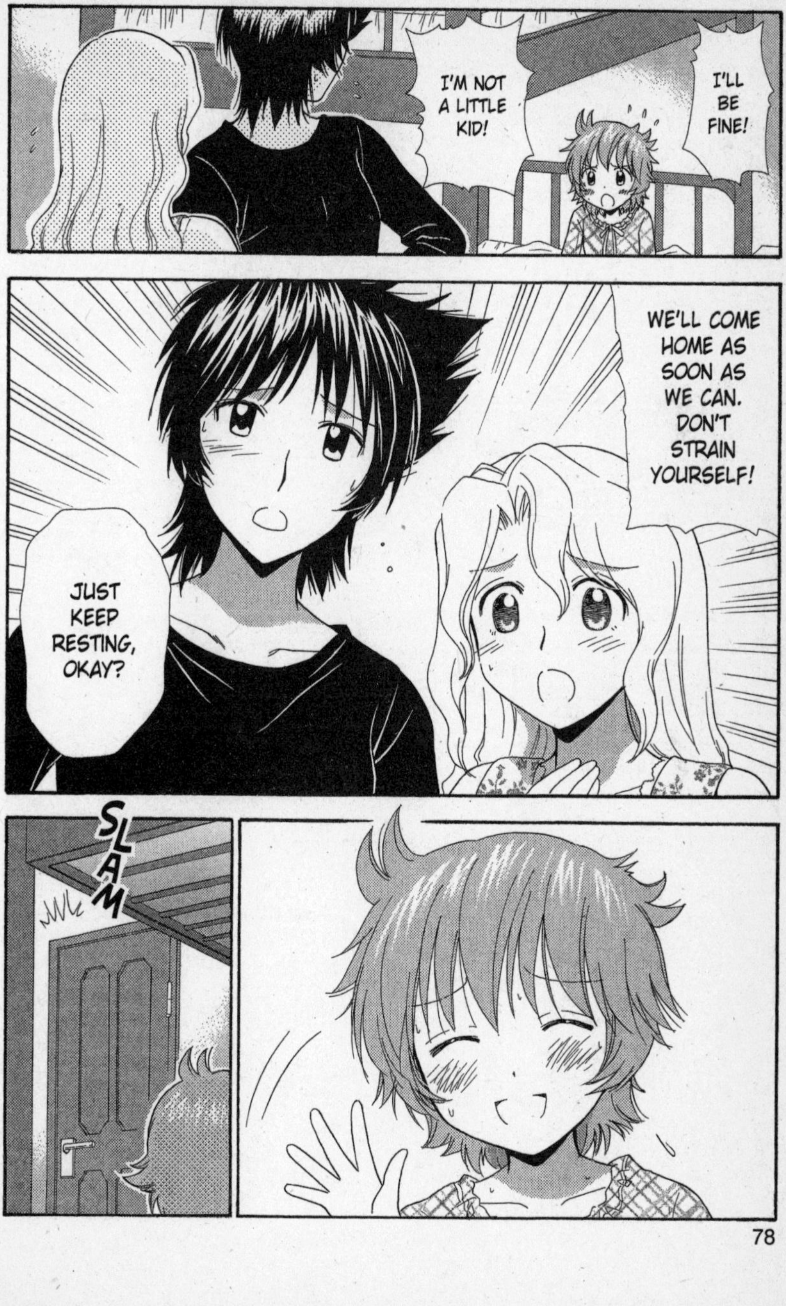
I'LL BE FINE!
I'M NOT A LITTLE KID!
WE'LL COME HOME AS SOON AS WE CAN. DON'T STRAIN YOURSELF!
JUST KEEP RESTING, OKAY?
SLAM

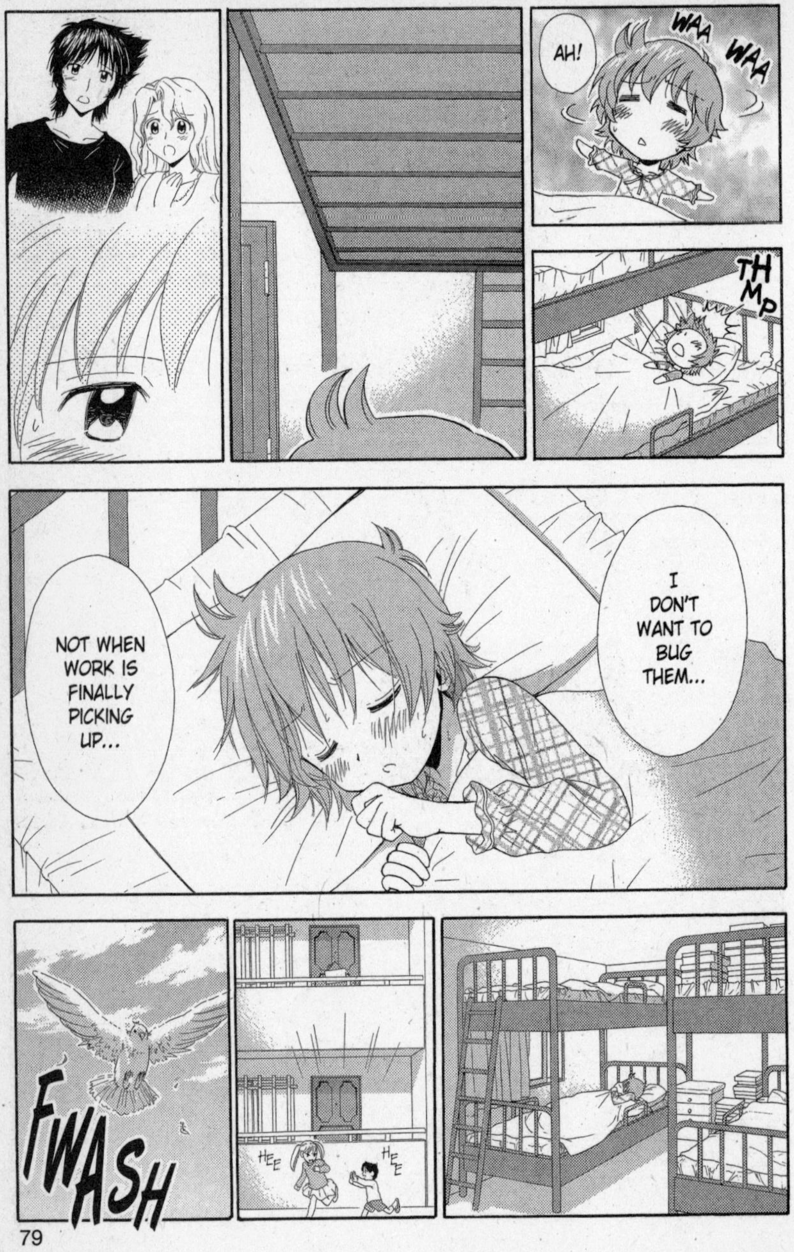
AH!
WAA WAA
THMP
I DON'T WANT TO BUG THEM...
NOT WHEN WORK IS FINALLY PICKING UP...
HEE HEE
FWASH

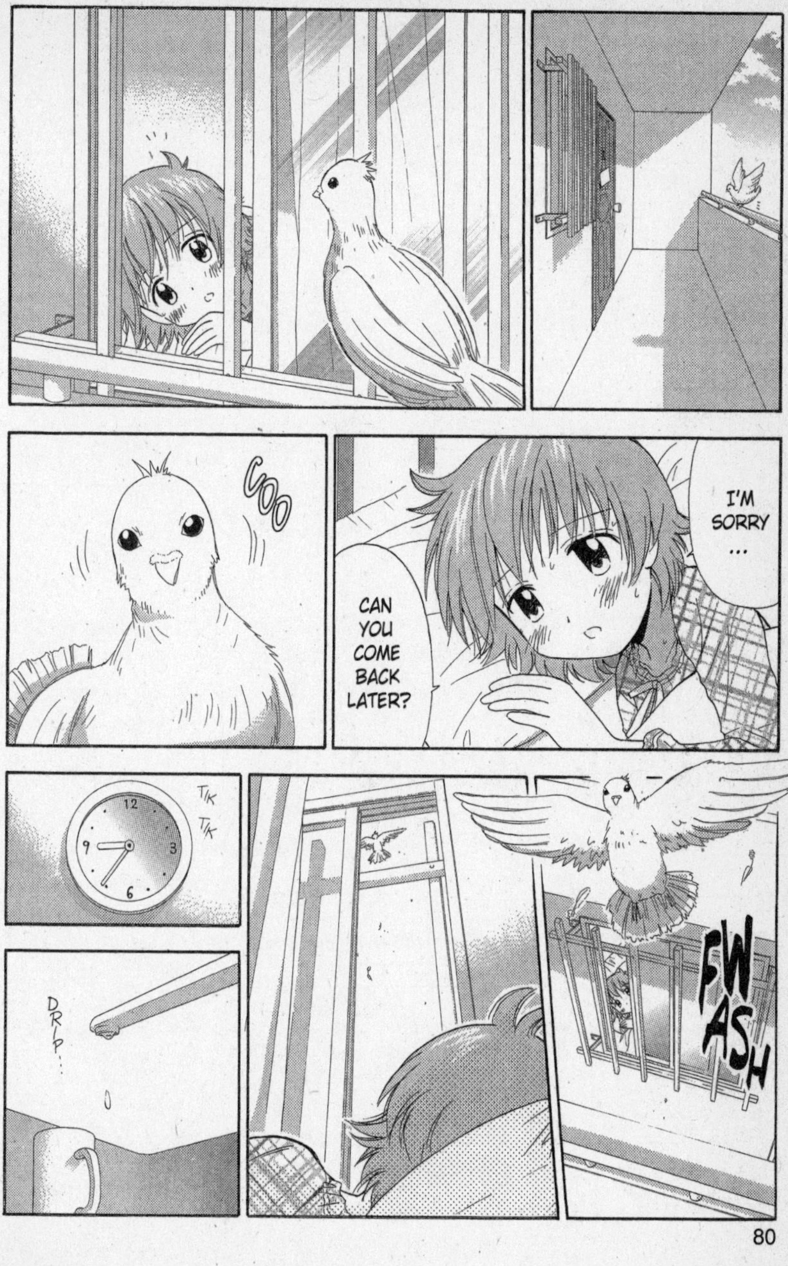
I'M SORRY ...
CAN YOU COME BACK LATER?
COO
FWASH
TIK TIK
DRIP...

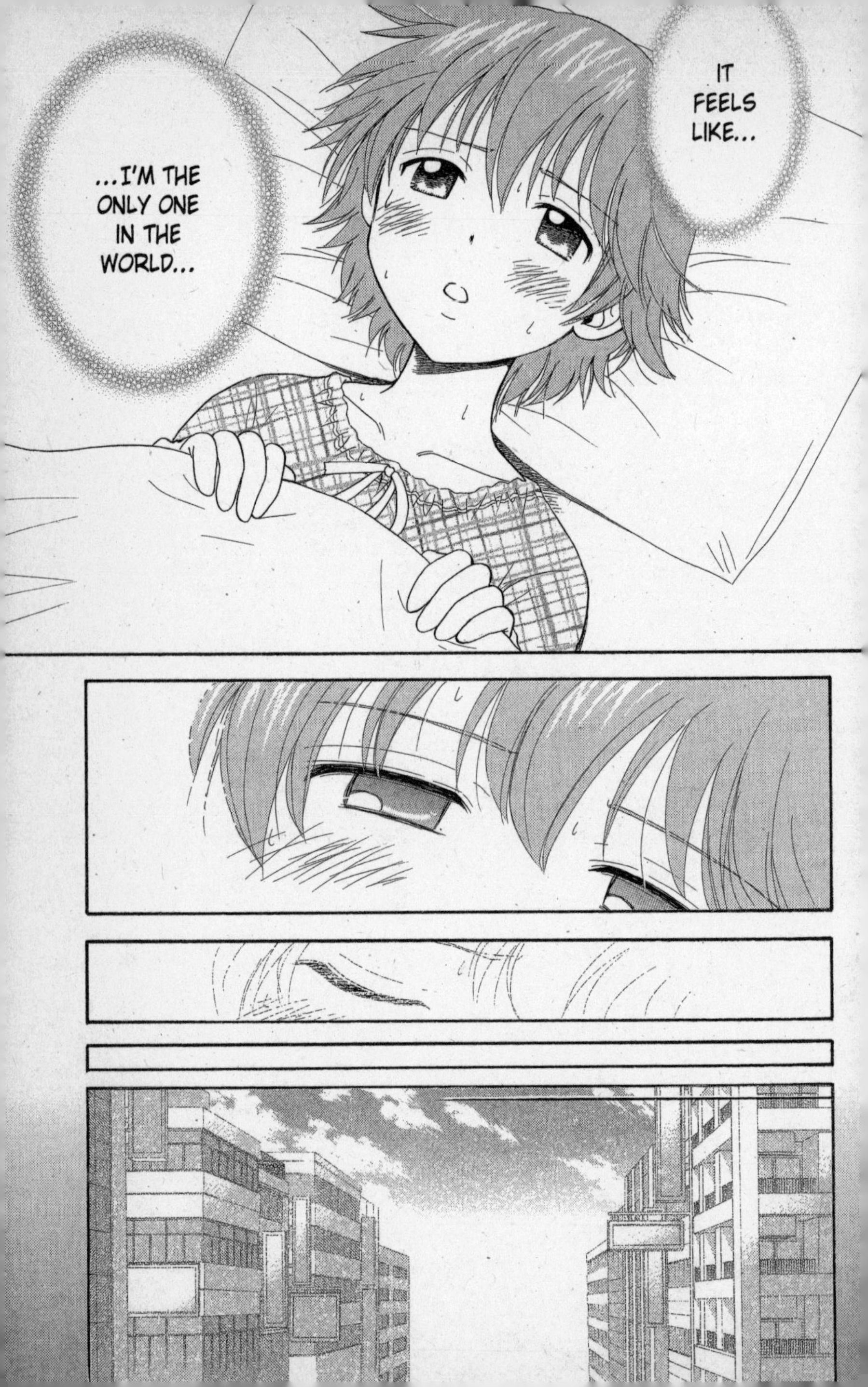
IT FEELS LIKE...
...I'M THE ONLY ONE IN THE WORLD...

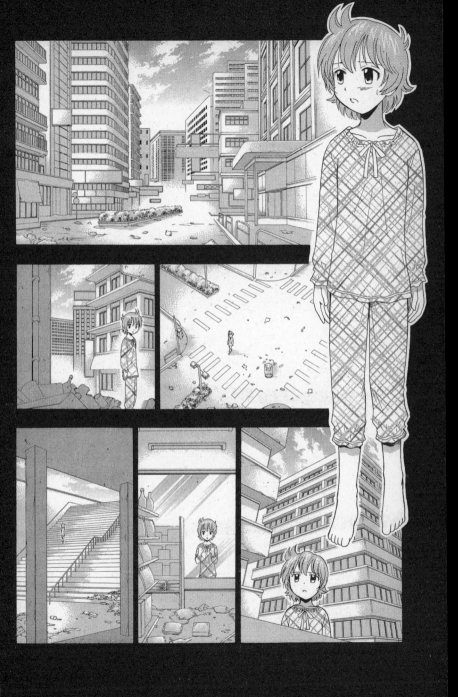

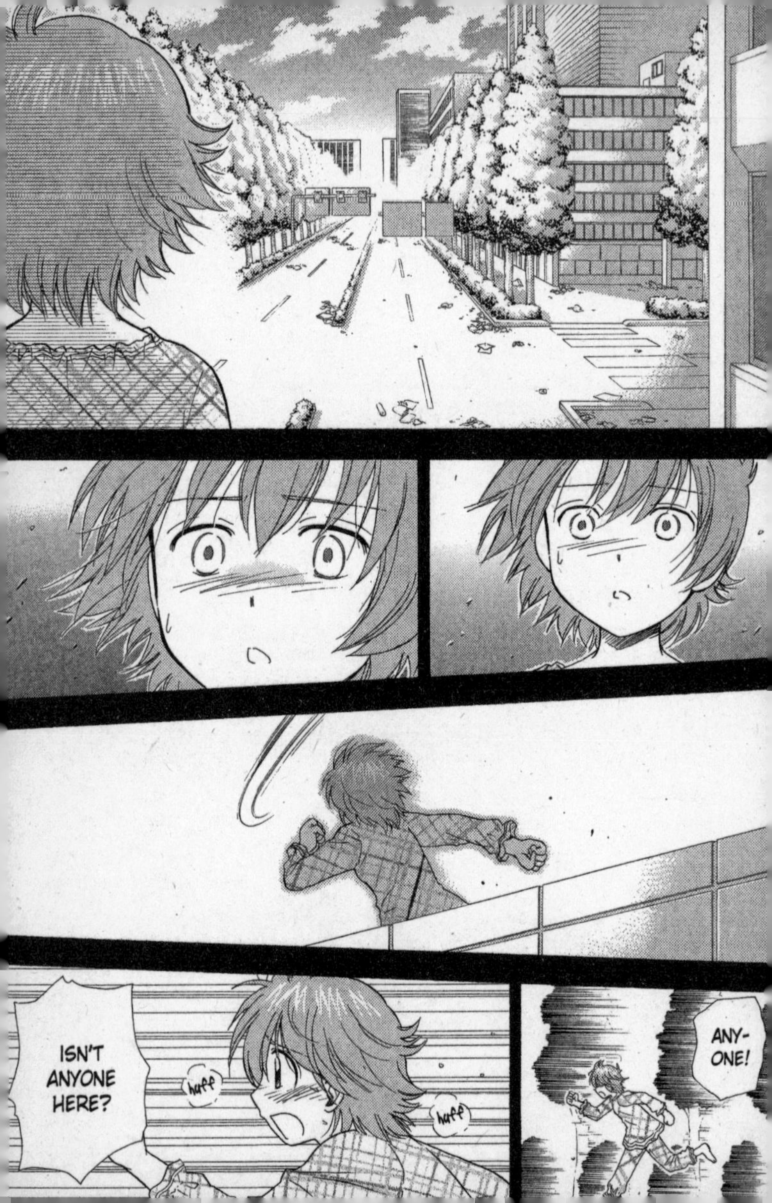
ANY-ONE!
huff
huff
ISN'T ANYONE HERE?

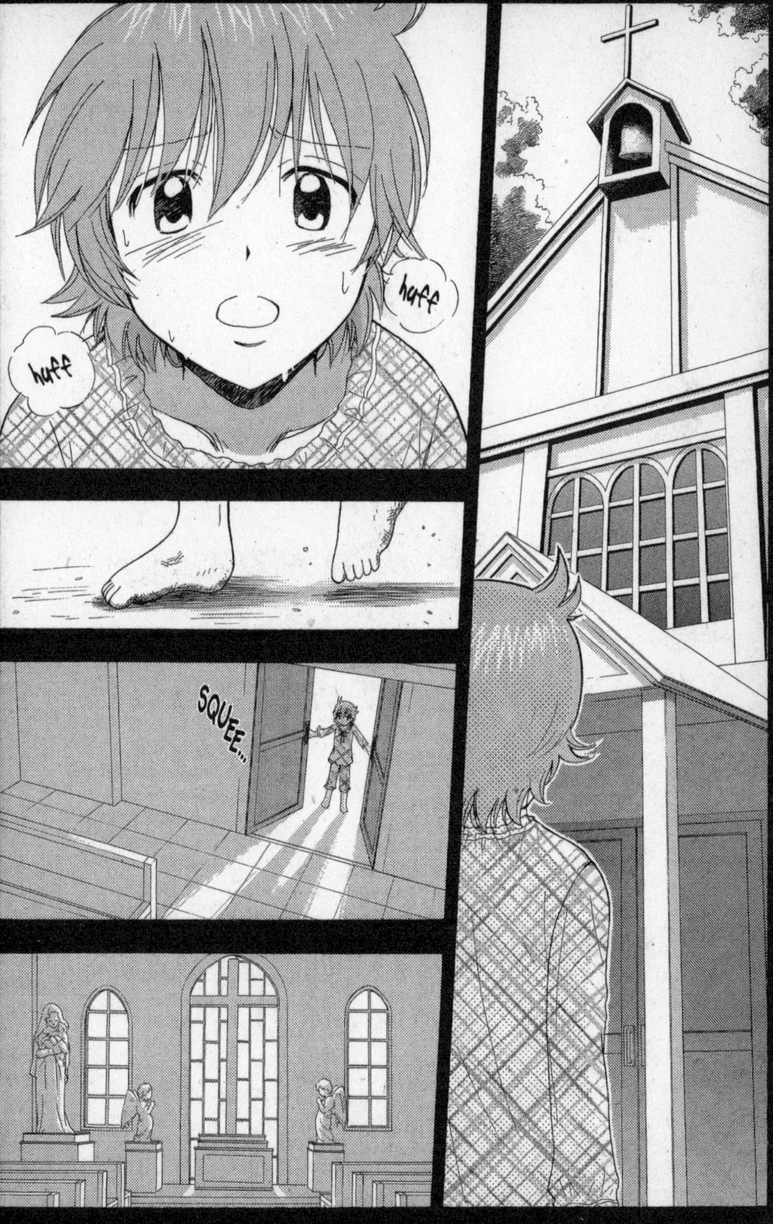
huff
huff
SQUEE...

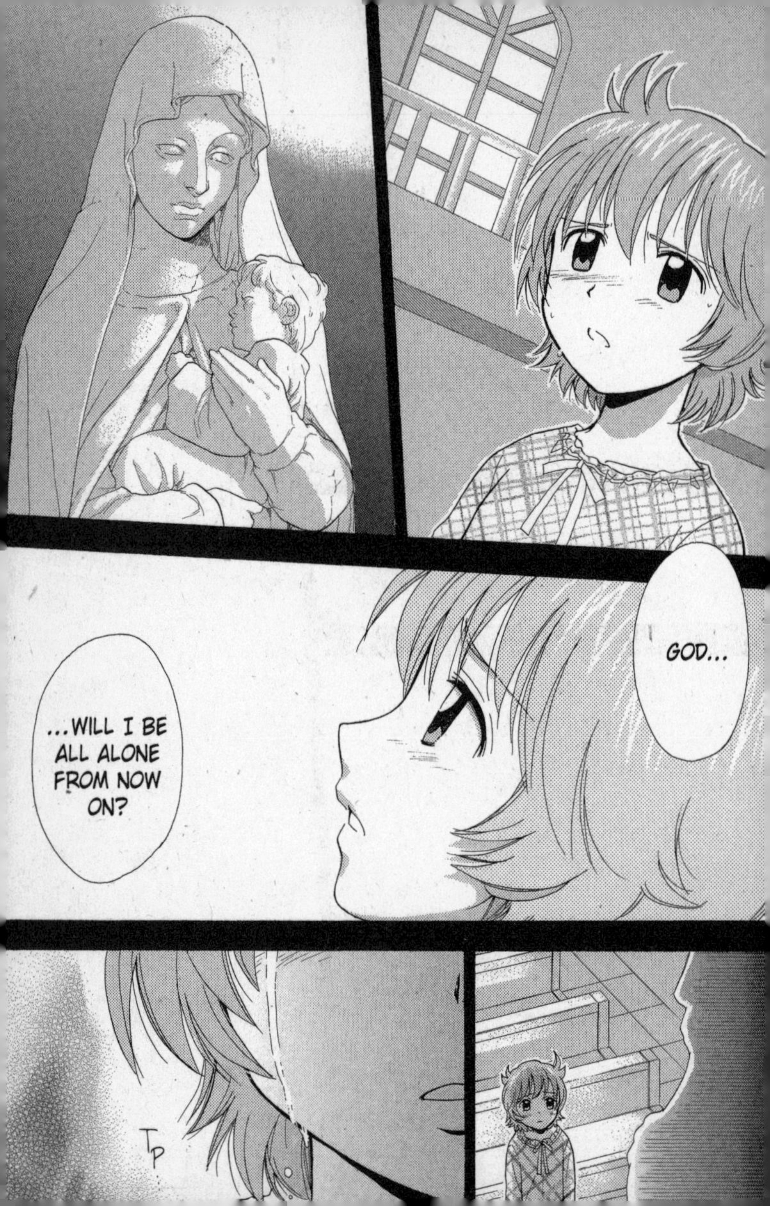
GOD...
...WILL I BE ALL ALONE FROM NOW ON?
TP

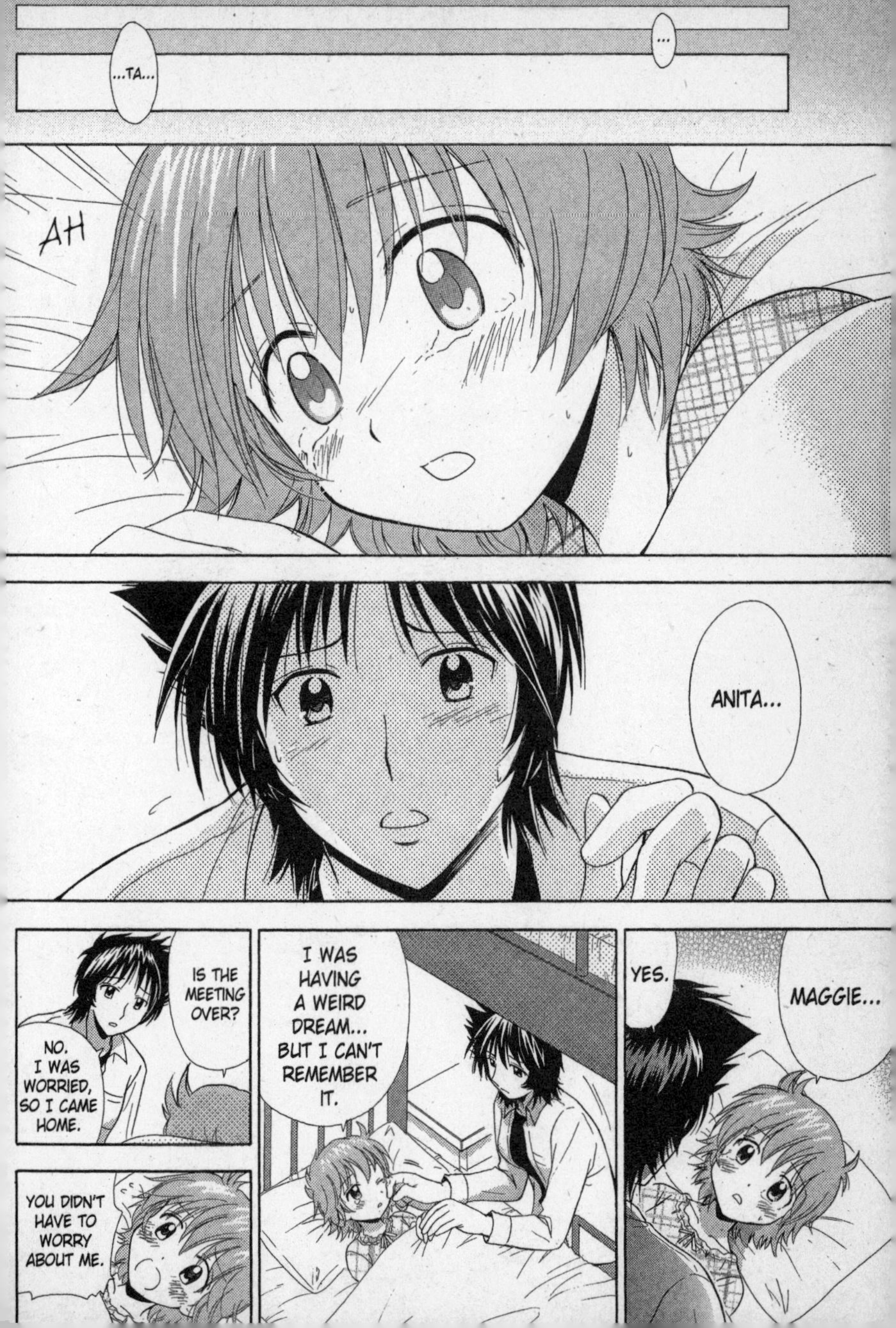
...
...TA...
AH
ANITA...
MAGGIE...
YES.
I WAS HAVING A WEIRD DREAM... BUT I CAN'T REMEMBER IT.
IS THE MEETING OVER?
NO. I WAS WORRIED, SO I CAME HOME.
YOU DIDN'T HAVE TO WORRY ABOUT ME.

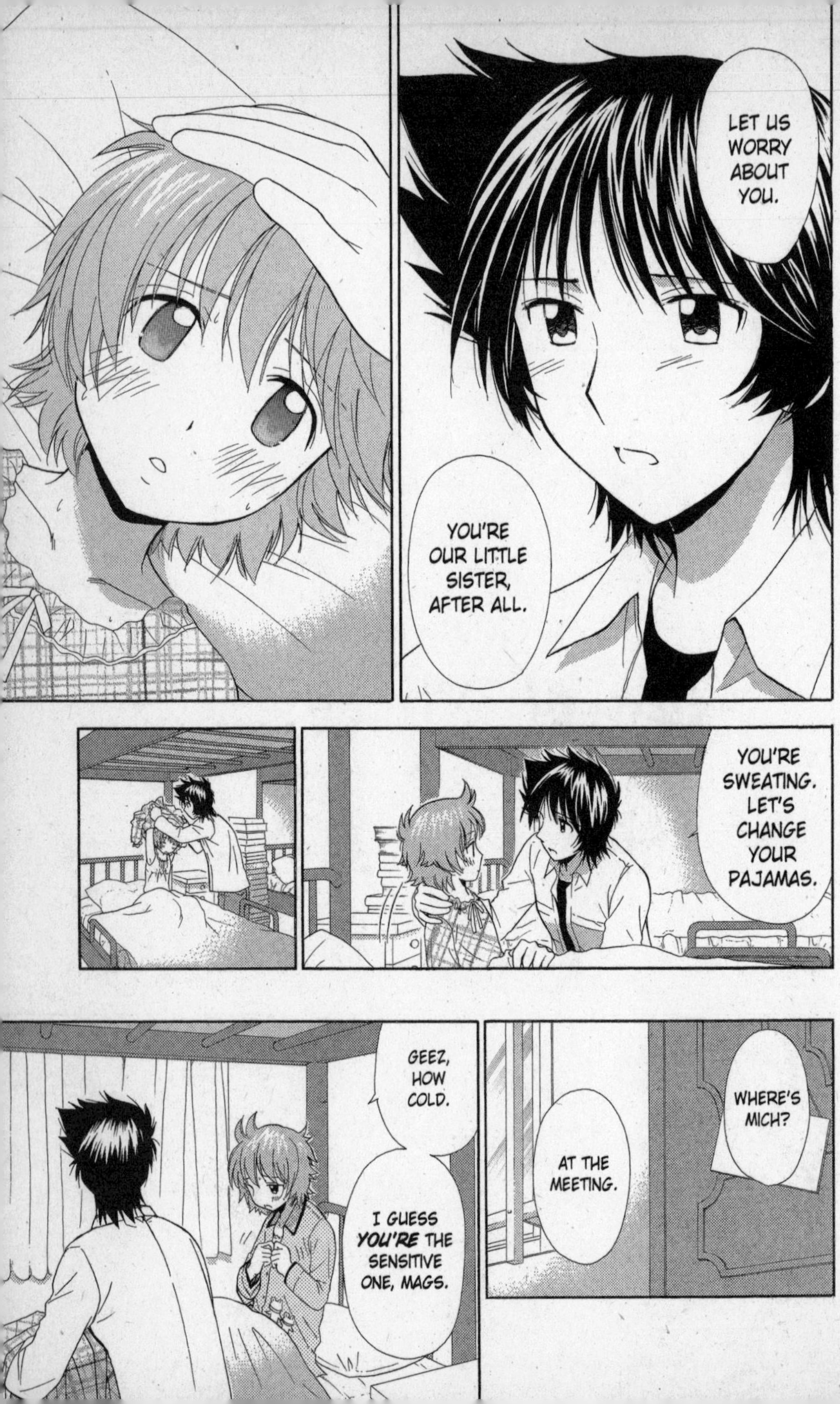
LET US WORRY ABOUT YOU.
YOU'RE OUR LITTLE SISTER, AFTER ALL.
YOU'RE SWEATING. LET'S CHANGE YOUR PAJAMAS.
WHERE'S MICH?
AT THE MEETING.
GEEZ, HOW COLD.
I GUESS *YOU'RE* THE SENSITIVE ONE, MAGS.

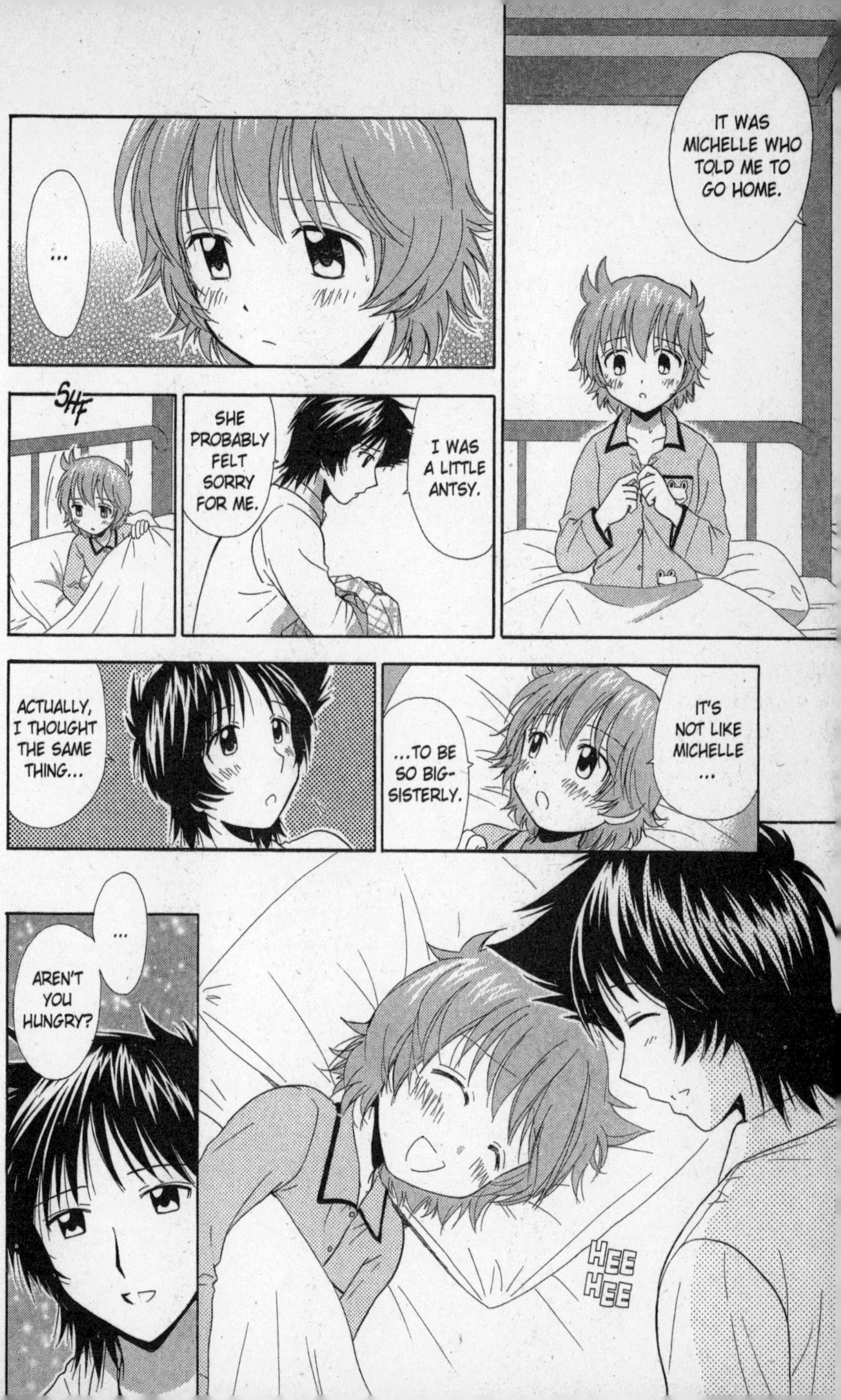
IT WAS MICHELLE WHO TOLD ME TO GO HOME.
...
I WAS A LITTLE ANTSY.
SHE PROBABLY FELT SORRY FOR ME.
SHF
IT'S NOT LIKE MICHELLE ...
...TO BE SO BIG-SISTERLY.
ACTUALLY, I THOUGHT THE SAME THING...
HEE HEE
...
AREN'T YOU HUNGRY?

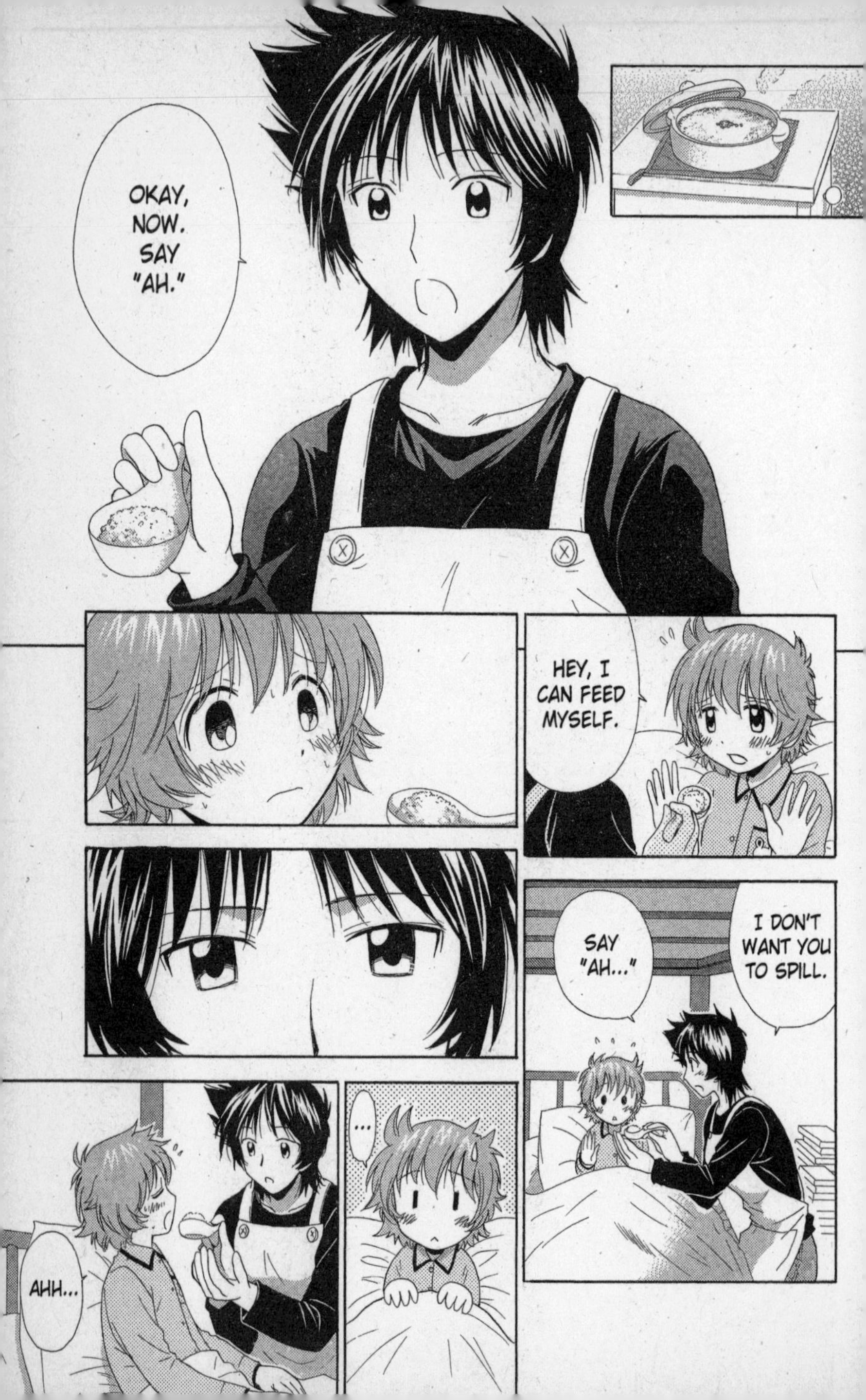
OKAY, NOW. SAY "AH."
HEY, I CAN FEED MYSELF.
I DON'T WANT YOU TO SPILL.
SAY "AH..."
...
AHH...

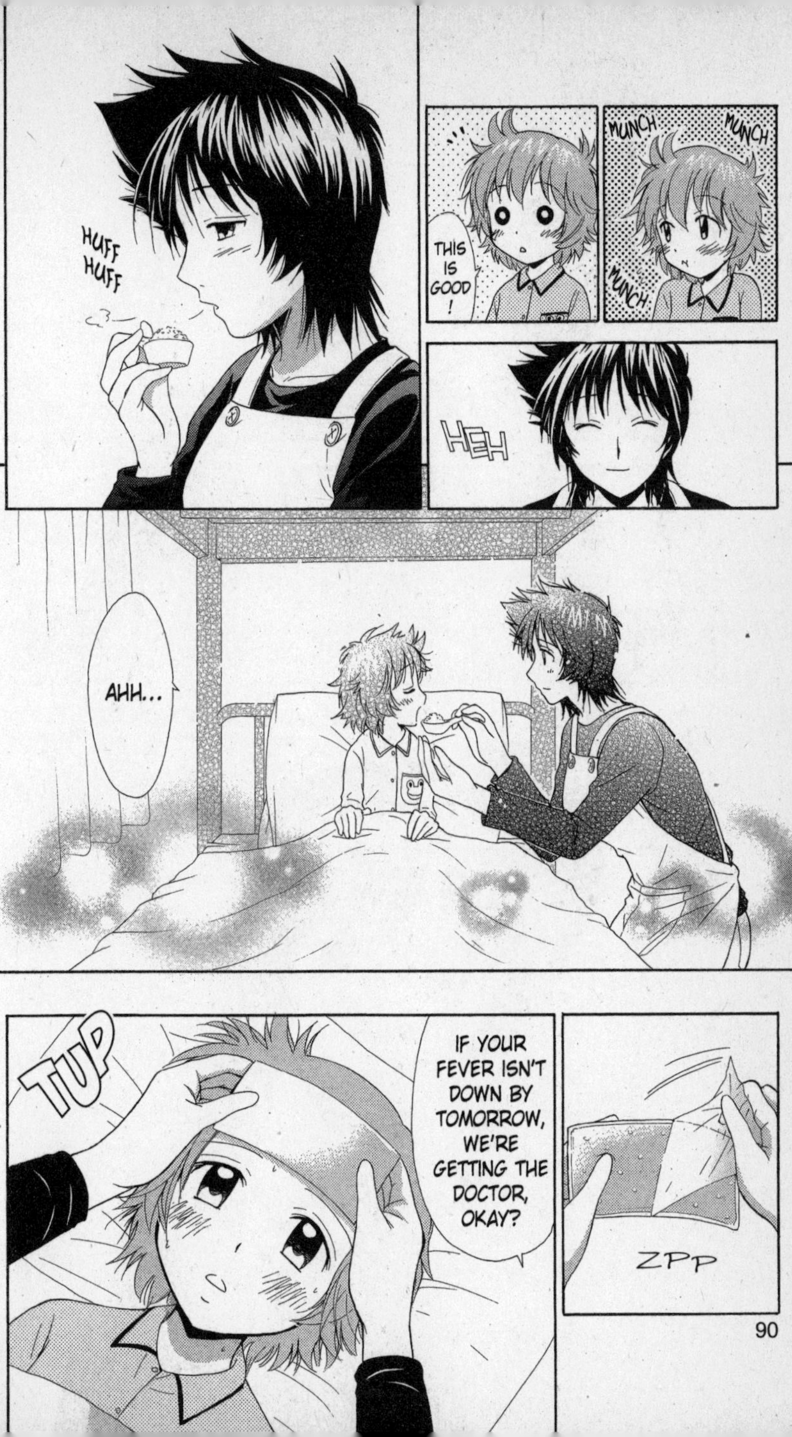
MUNCH MUNCH
MUNCH
THIS IS GOOD!
HEH
HUFF HUFF
AHH...
ZPP
IF YOUR FEVER ISN'T DOWN BY TOMORROW, WE'RE GETTING THE DOCTOR, OKAY?
TUP

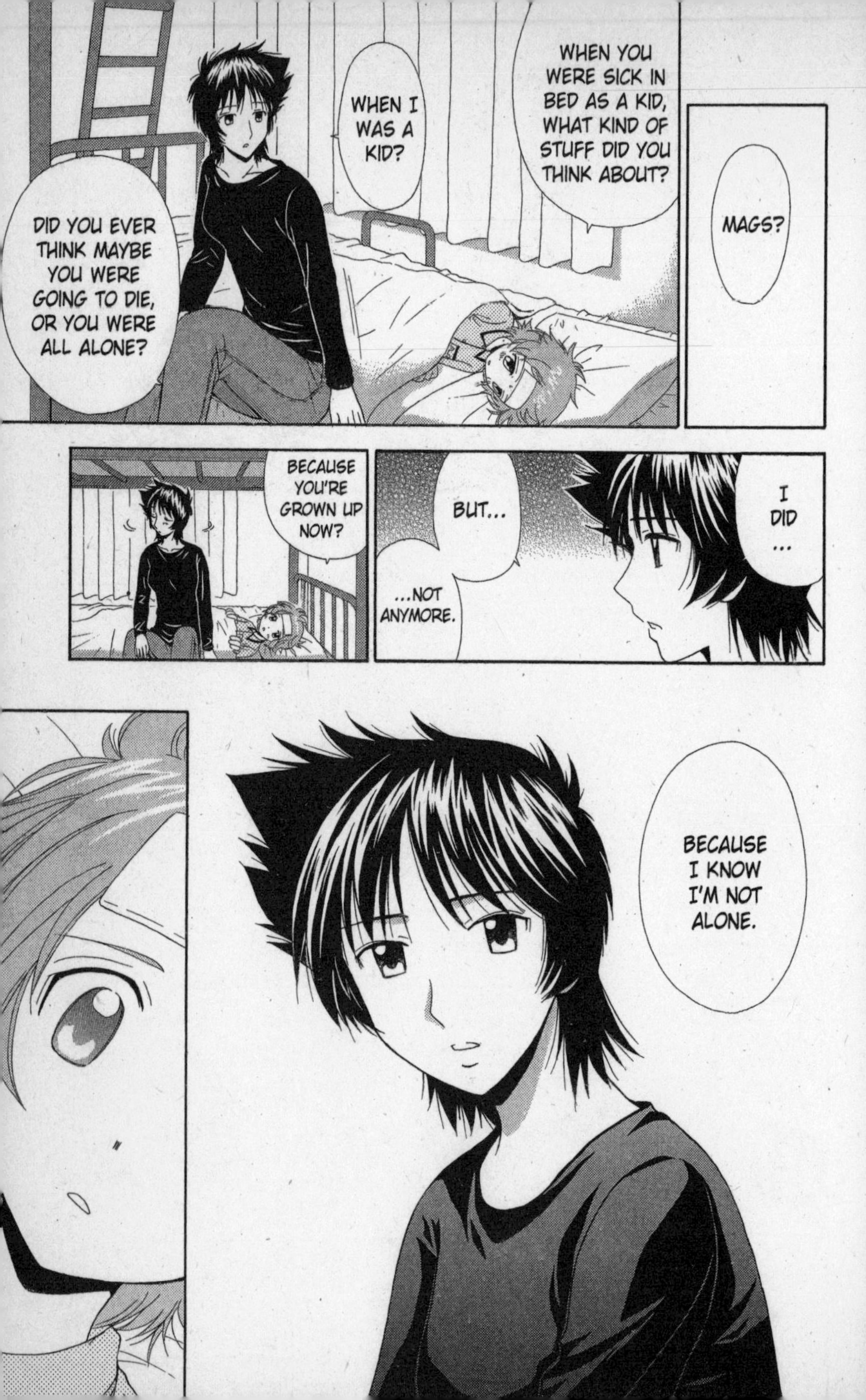
MAGS?
WHEN YOU WERE SICK IN BED AS A KID, WHAT KIND OF STUFF DID YOU THINK ABOUT?
WHEN I WAS A KID?
DID YOU EVER THINK MAYBE YOU WERE GOING TO DIE, OR YOU WERE ALL ALONE?
I DID ...
BUT...
...NOT ANYMORE.
BECAUSE YOU'RE GROWN UP NOW?
BECAUSE I KNOW I'M NOT ALONE.

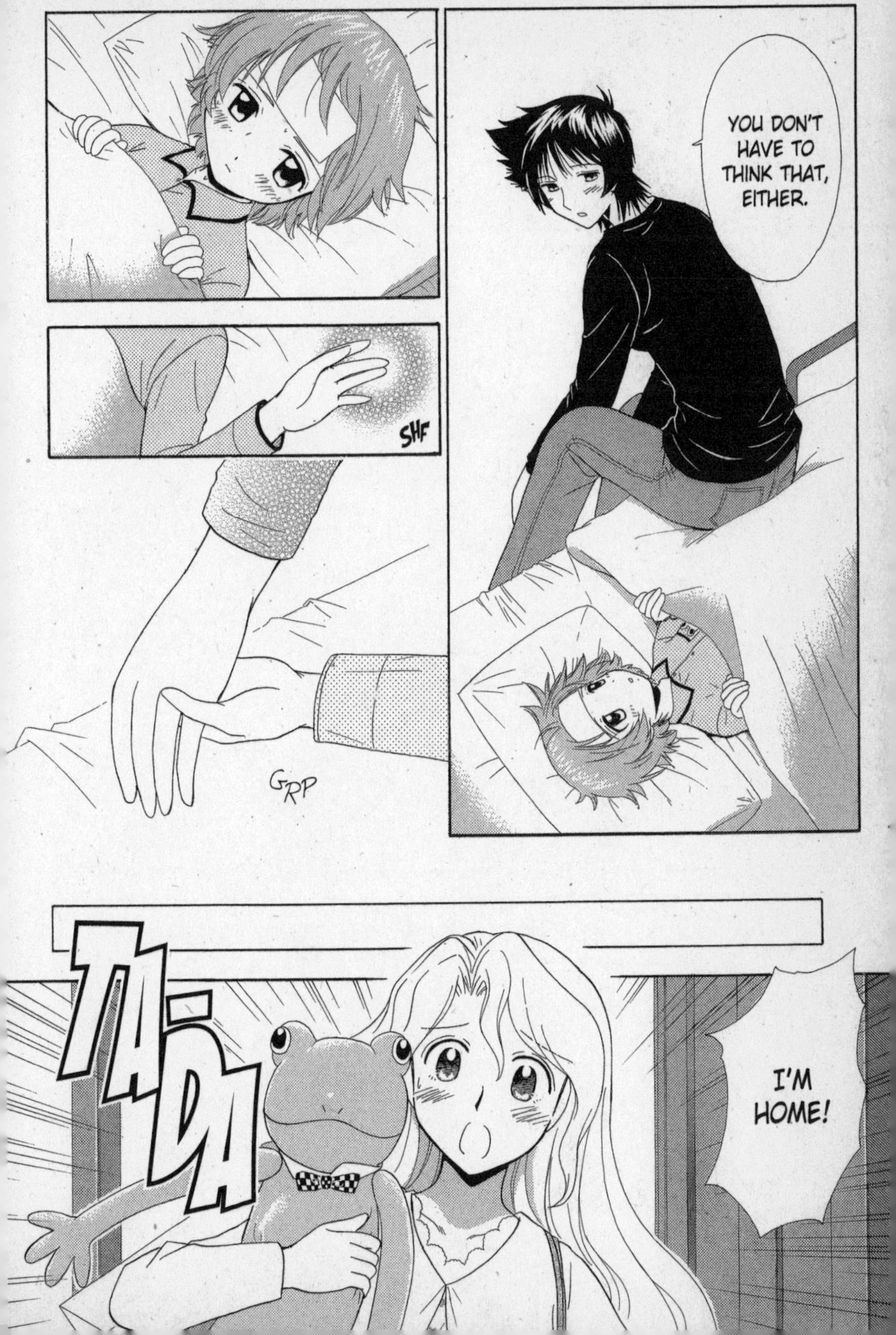
YOU DON'T HAVE TO THINK THAT, EITHER.
SHF
GRP
I'M HOME!
TA-DA

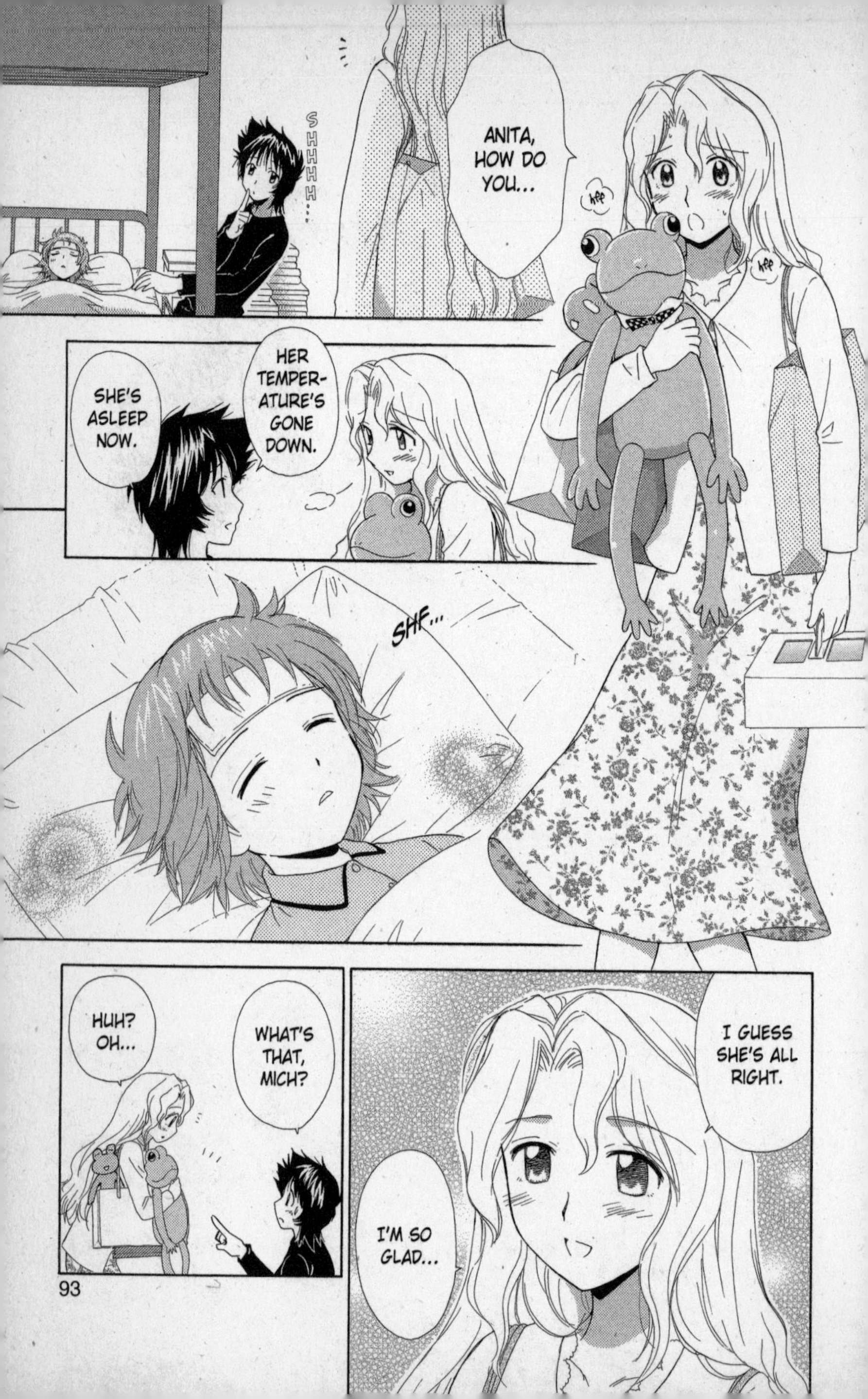
hff
hff
ANITA, HOW DO YOU...
SHHHHH...
HER TEMPERATURE'S GONE DOWN.
SHE'S ASLEEP NOW.
SHF...
I GUESS SHE'S ALL RIGHT.
I'M SO GLAD...
WHAT'S THAT, MICH?
HUH? OH...

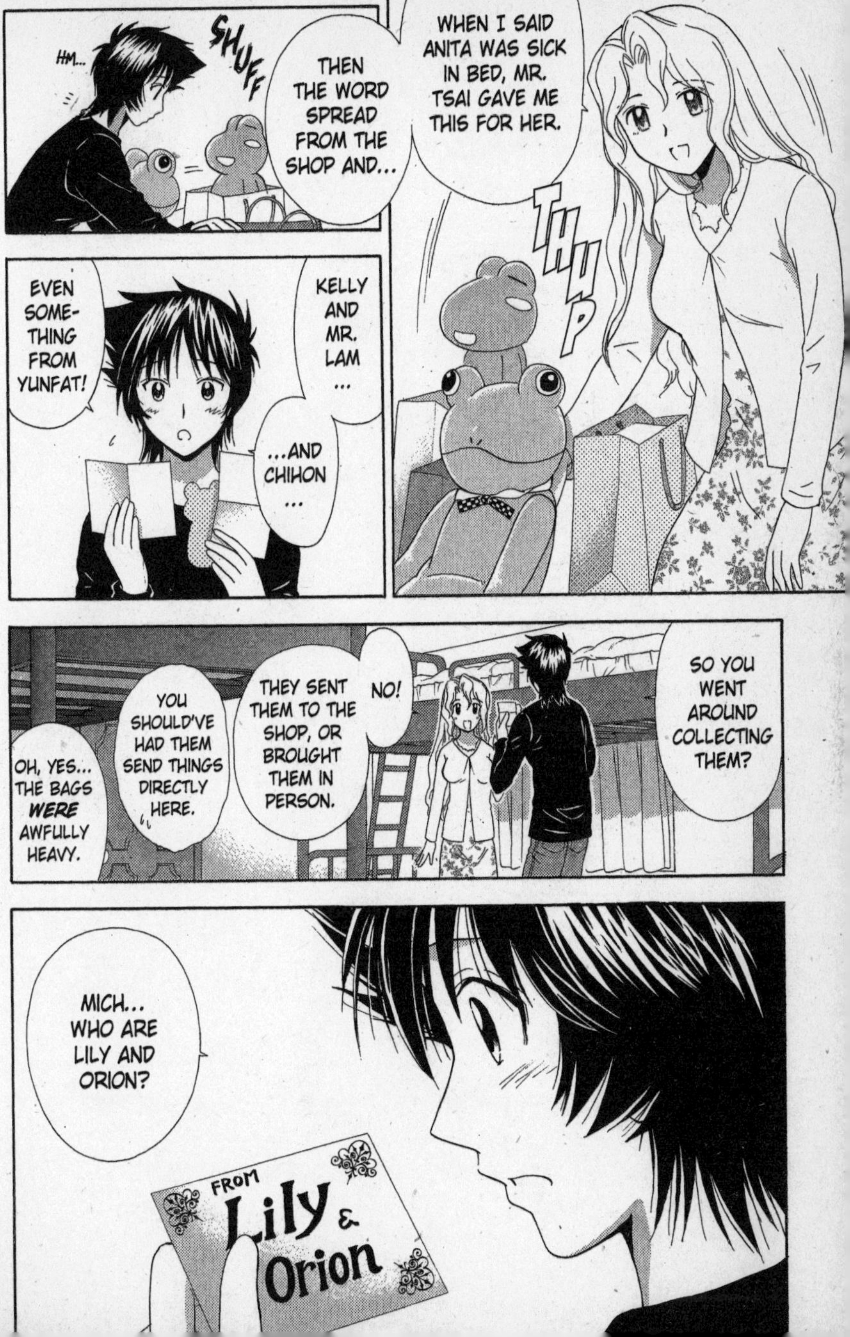
WHEN I SAID ANITA WAS SICK IN BED, MR. TSAI GAVE ME THIS FOR HER.
THUP
THEN THE WORD SPREAD FROM THE SHOP AND...
SHUFF
HM...
KELLY AND MR. LAM ...
...AND CHIHON ...
EVEN SOMETHING FROM YUNFAT!
SO YOU WENT AROUND COLLECTING THEM?
NO!
THEY SENT THEM TO THE SHOP, OR BROUGHT THEM IN PERSON.
YOU SHOULD'VE HAD THEM SEND THINGS DIRECTLY HERE.
OH, YES... THE BAGS WERE AWFULLY HEAVY.
MICH... WHO ARE LILY AND ORION?
FROM Lily & Orion

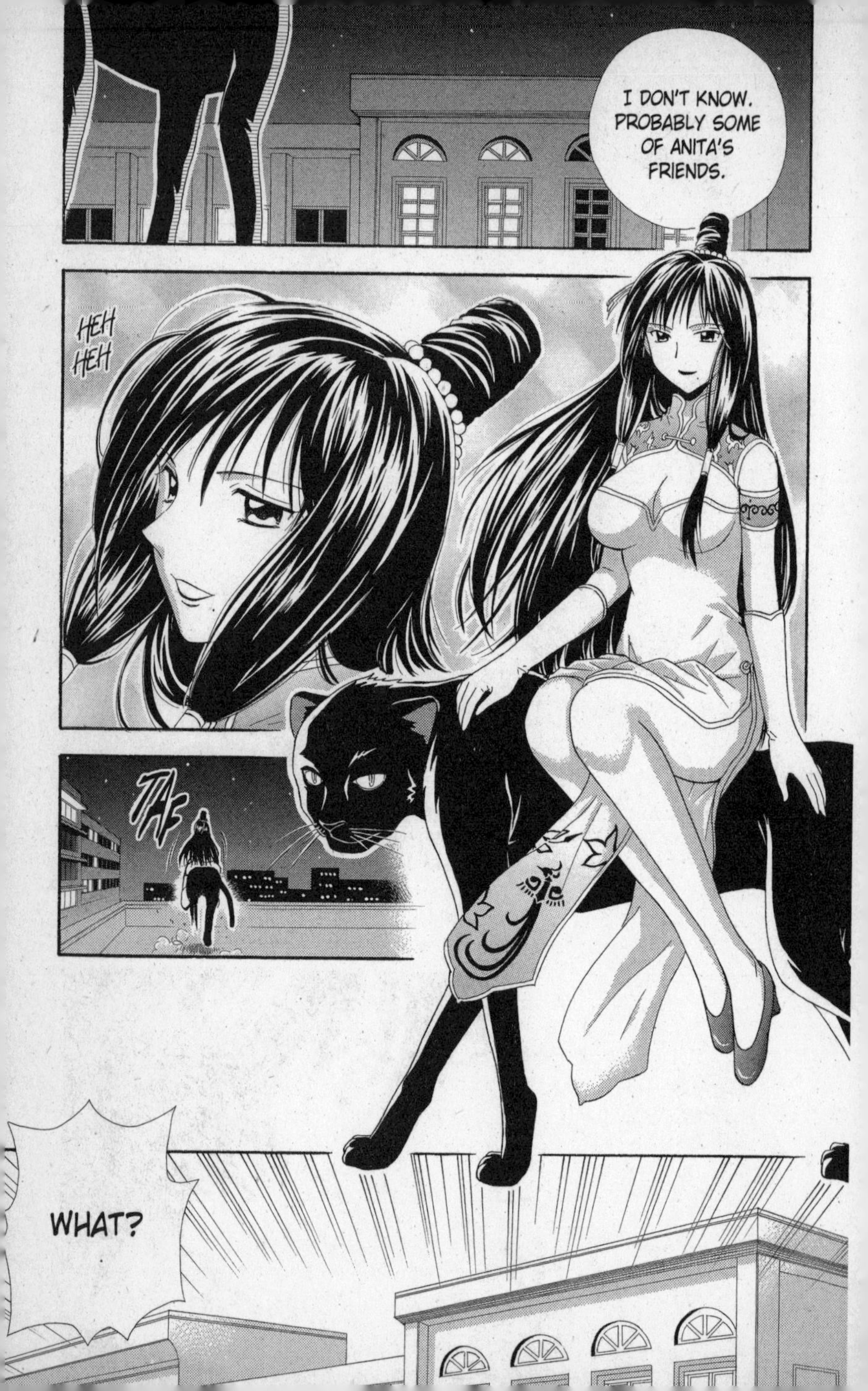
I DON'T KNOW. PROBABLY SOME OF ANITA'S FRIENDS.
HEH HEH
TAP
WHAT?

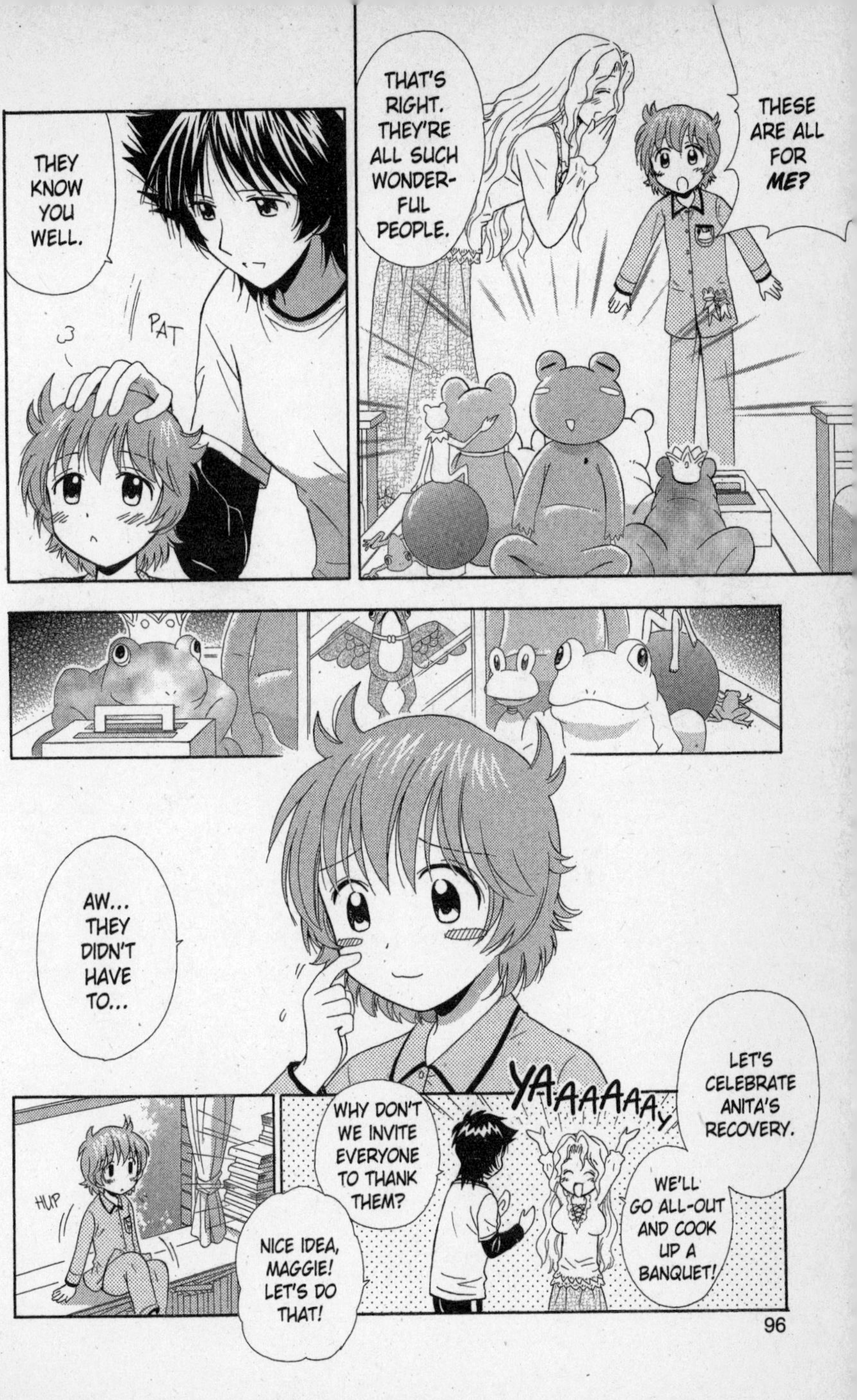
THESE ARE ALL FOR *ME?*
THAT'S RIGHT. THEY'RE ALL SUCH WONDERFUL PEOPLE.
THEY KNOW YOU WELL.
PAT
AW... THEY DIDN'T HAVE TO...
LET'S CELEBRATE ANITA'S RECOVERY.
YAAAAAAY
WHY DON'T WE INVITE EVERYONE TO THANK THEM?
WE'LL GO ALL-OUT AND COOK UP A BANQUET!
NICE IDEA, MAGGIE! LET'S DO THAT!
HUP

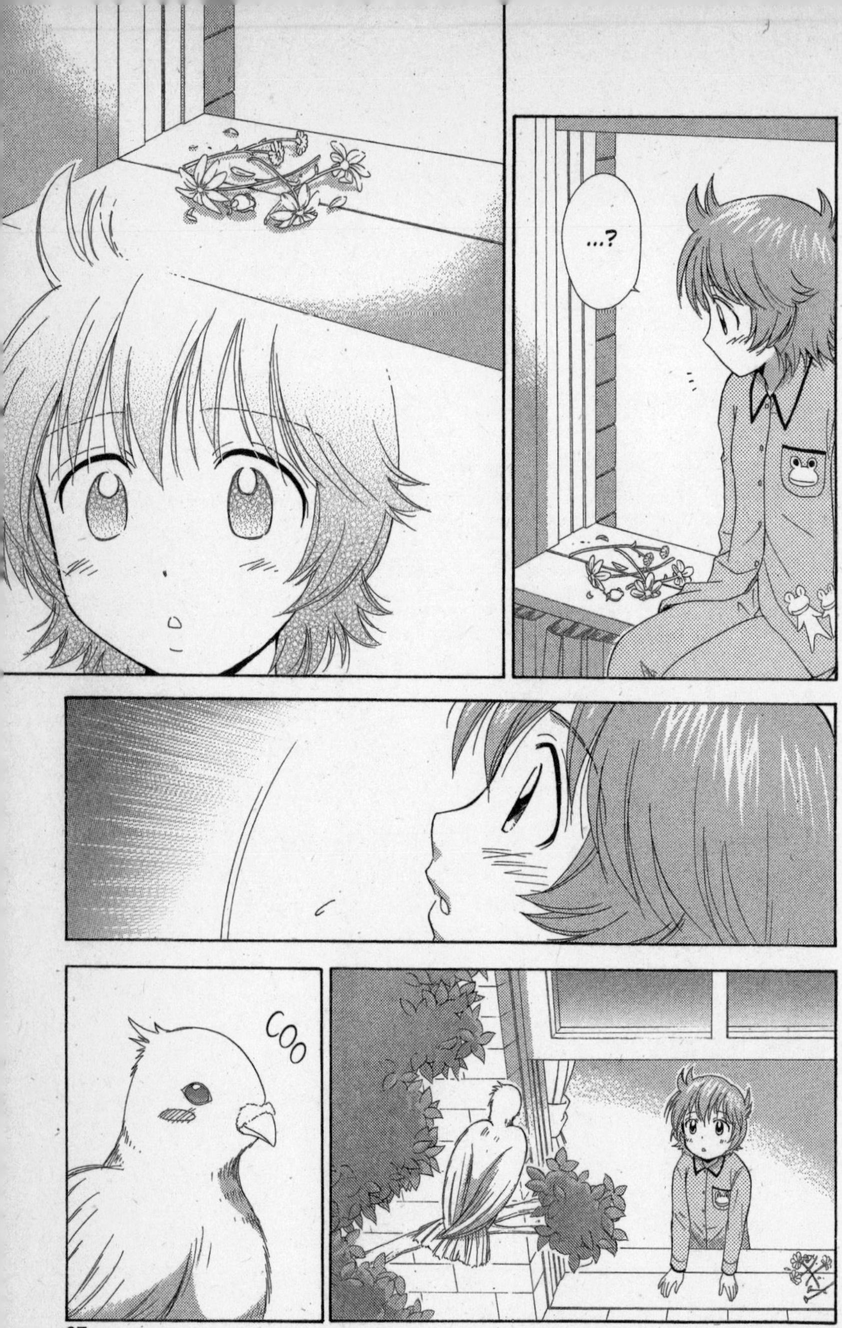
...?
COO

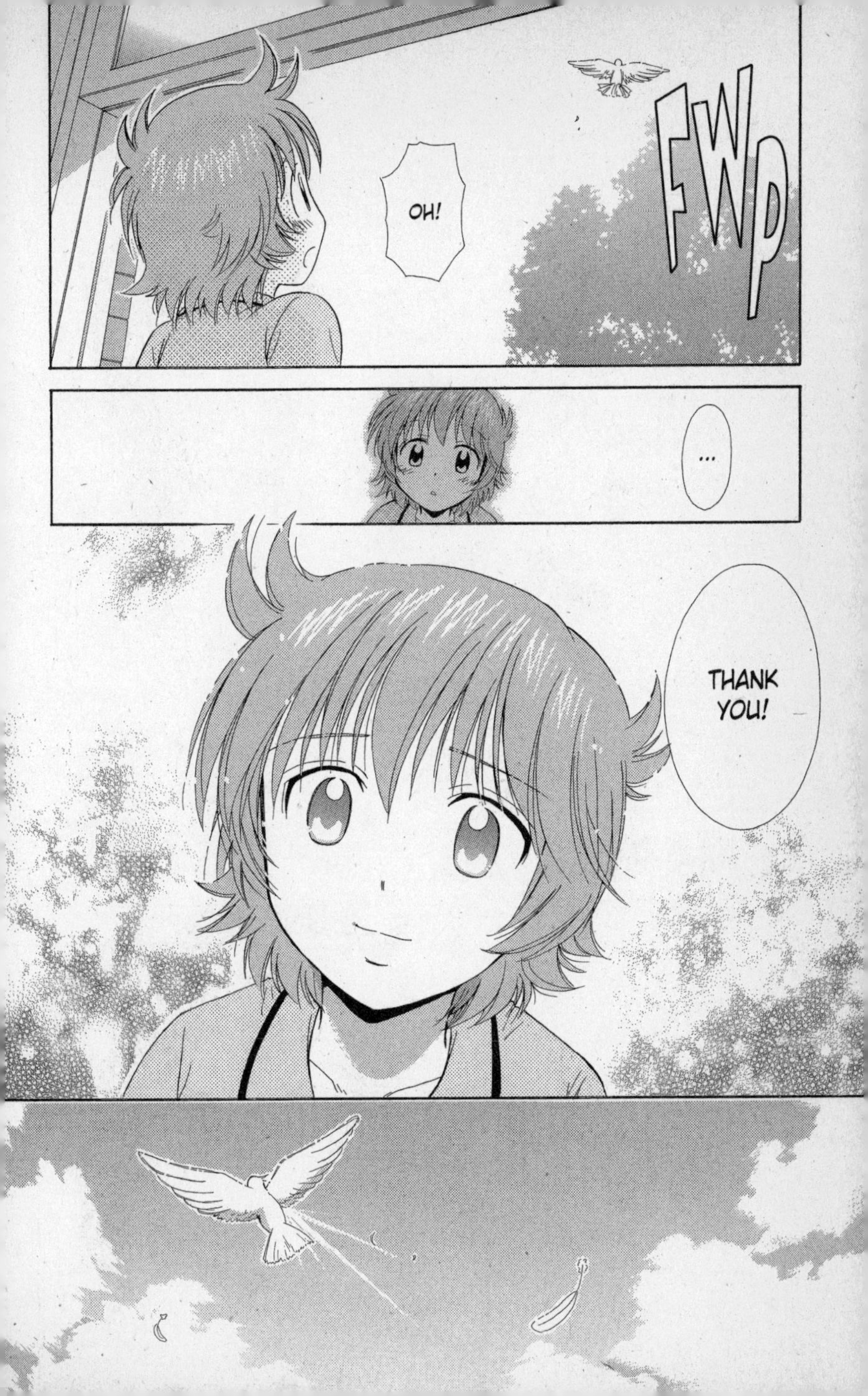
FWP
OH!
...
THANK YOU!

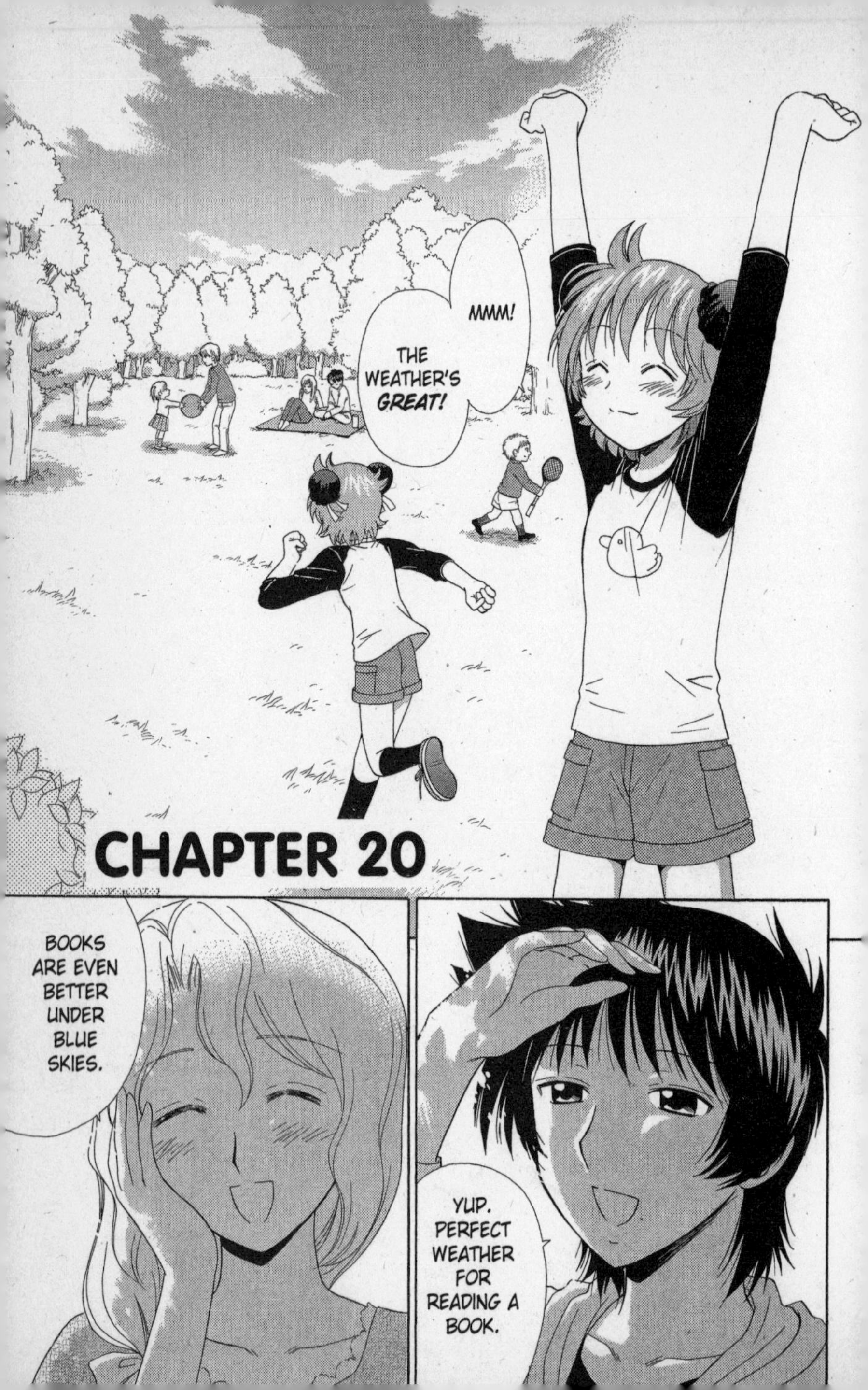
MMM!
THE WEATHER'S GREAT!
CHAPTER 20
YUP. PERFECT WEATHER FOR READING A BOOK.
BOOKS ARE EVEN BETTER UNDER BLUE SKIES.

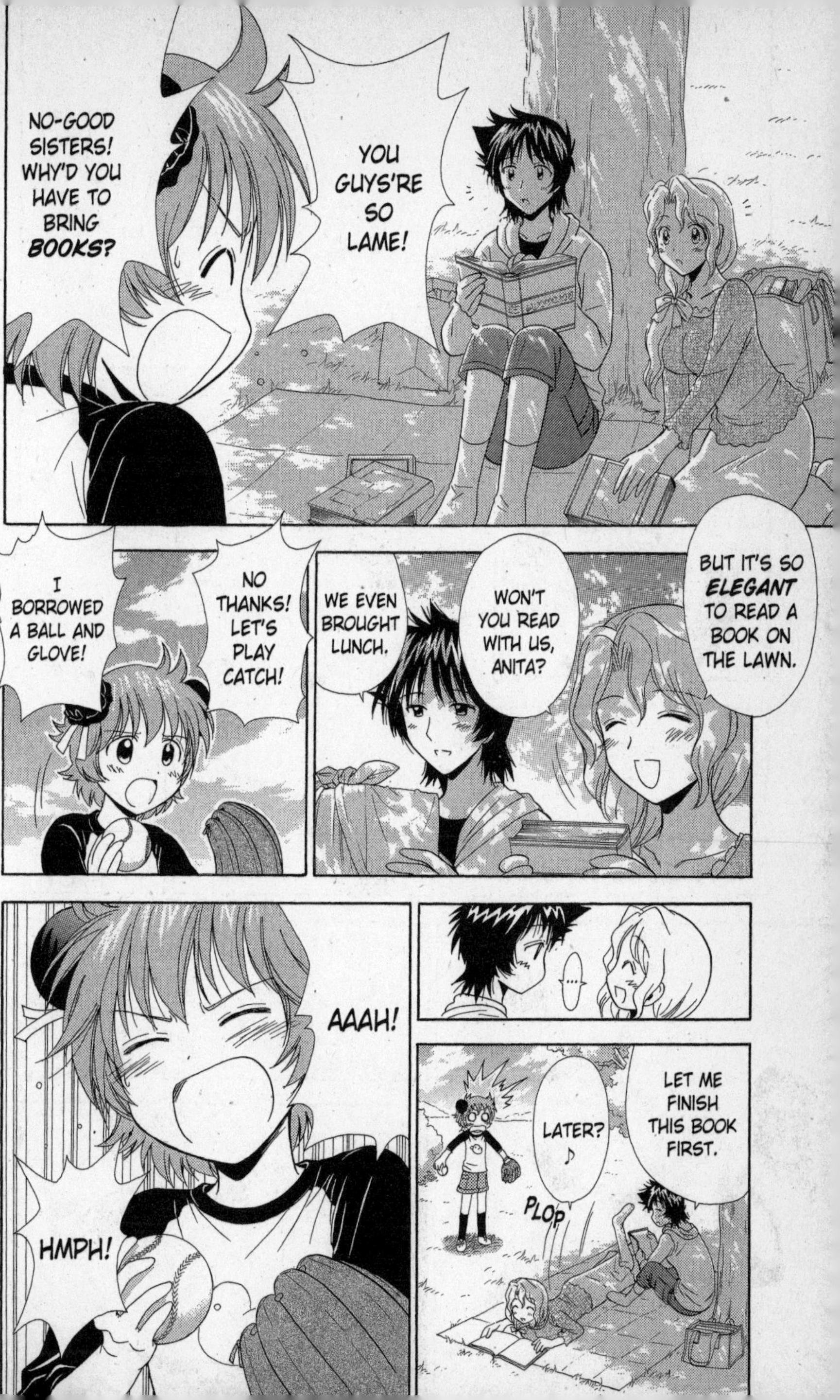
YOU GUYS'RE SO LAME!
NO-GOOD SISTERS! WHY'D YOU HAVE TO BRING BOOKS?
BUT IT'S SO ELEGANT TO READ A BOOK ON THE LAWN.
WON'T YOU READ WITH US, ANITA?
WE EVEN BROUGHT LUNCH.
NO THANKS! LET'S PLAY CATCH!
I BORROWED A BALL AND GLOVE!
...
LET ME FINISH THIS BOOK FIRST.
LATER? ♪
PLOP
AAAH!
HMPH!

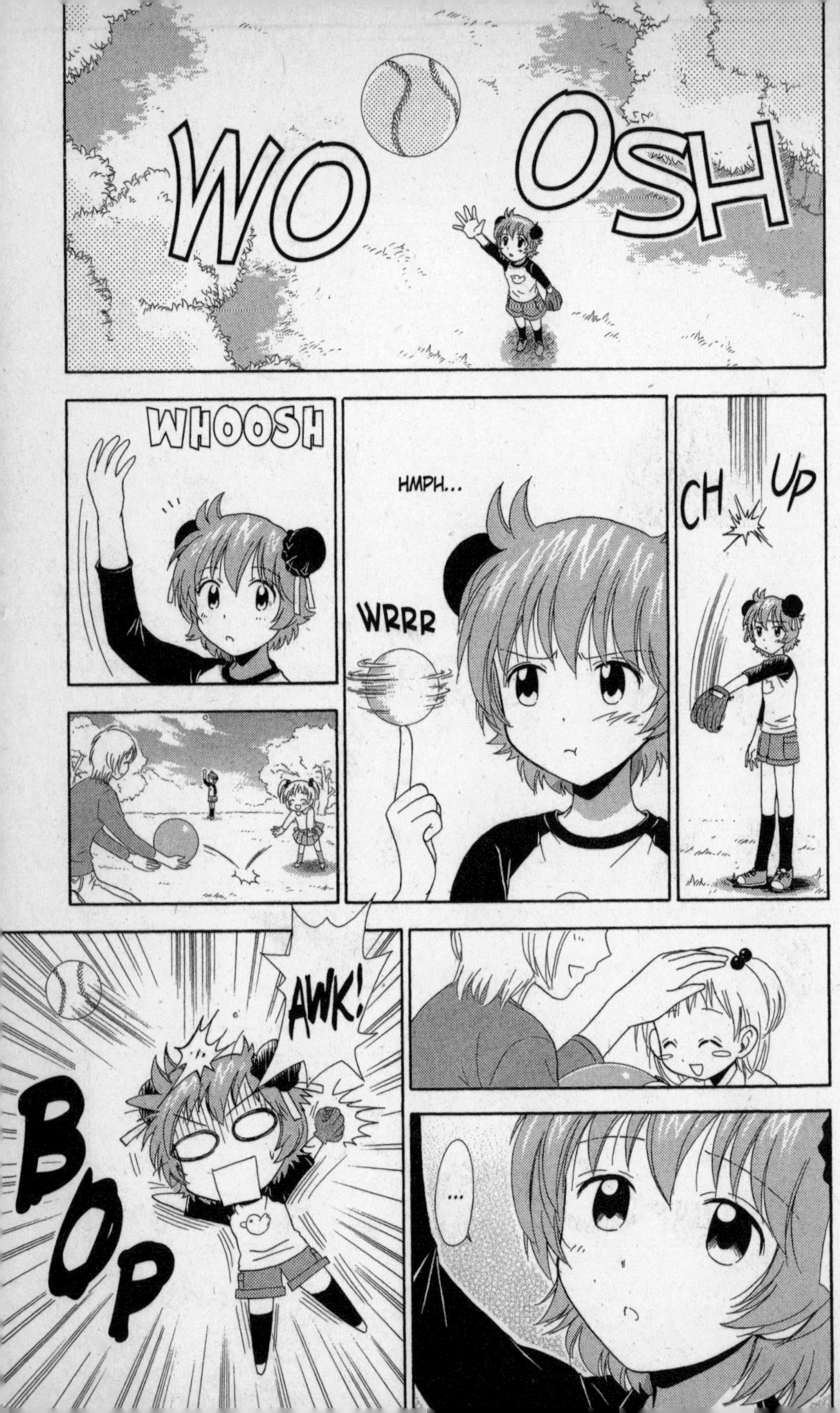
WO OSH
CH UP
HMPH...
WRRR
WHOOSH
...
AWK!
BOP

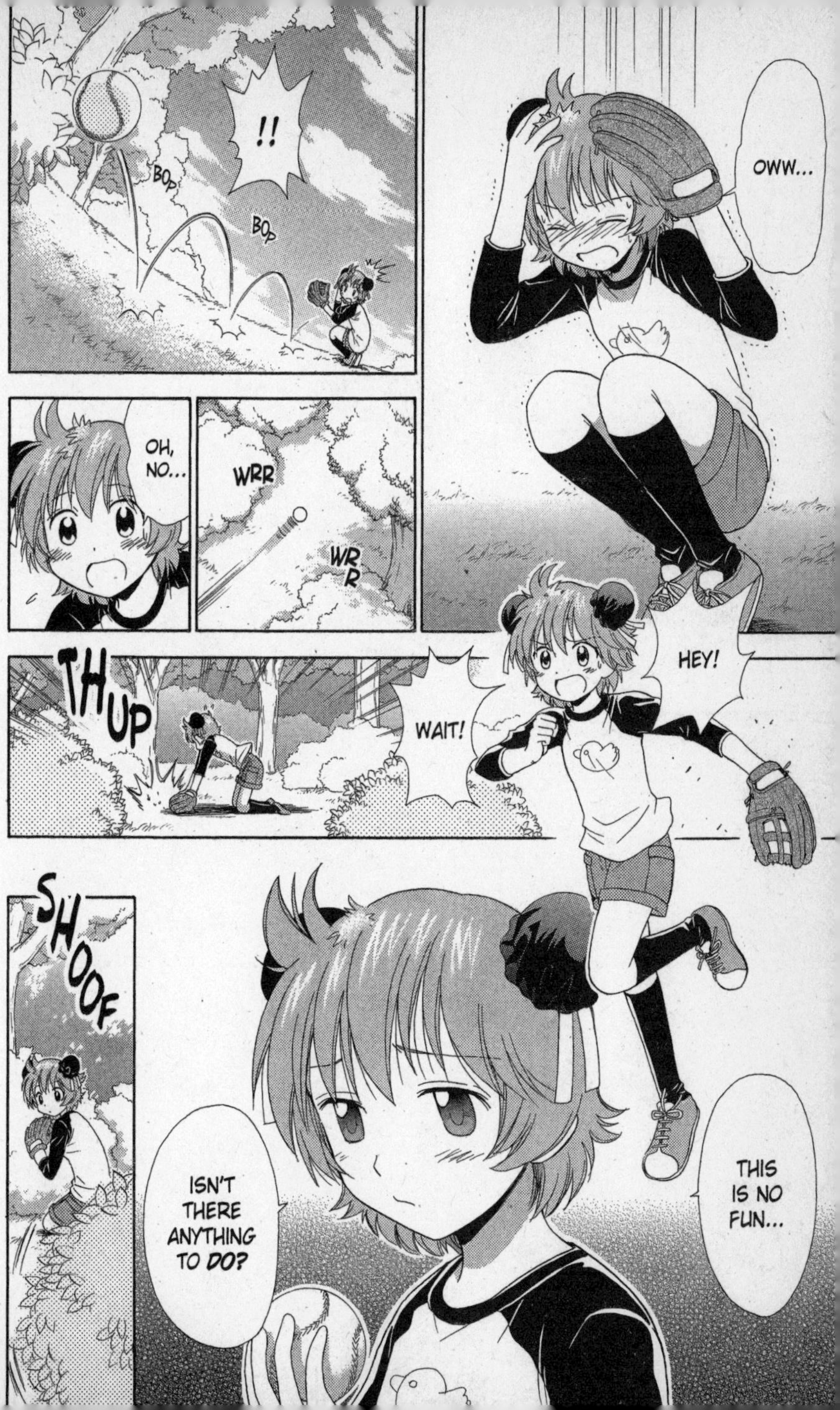
OWW...
!!
BOP
BOP
WRR
WRR
OH, NO...
HEY!
WAIT!
THUP
THIS IS NO FUN...
ISN'T THERE ANYTHING TO DO?
SHOOF

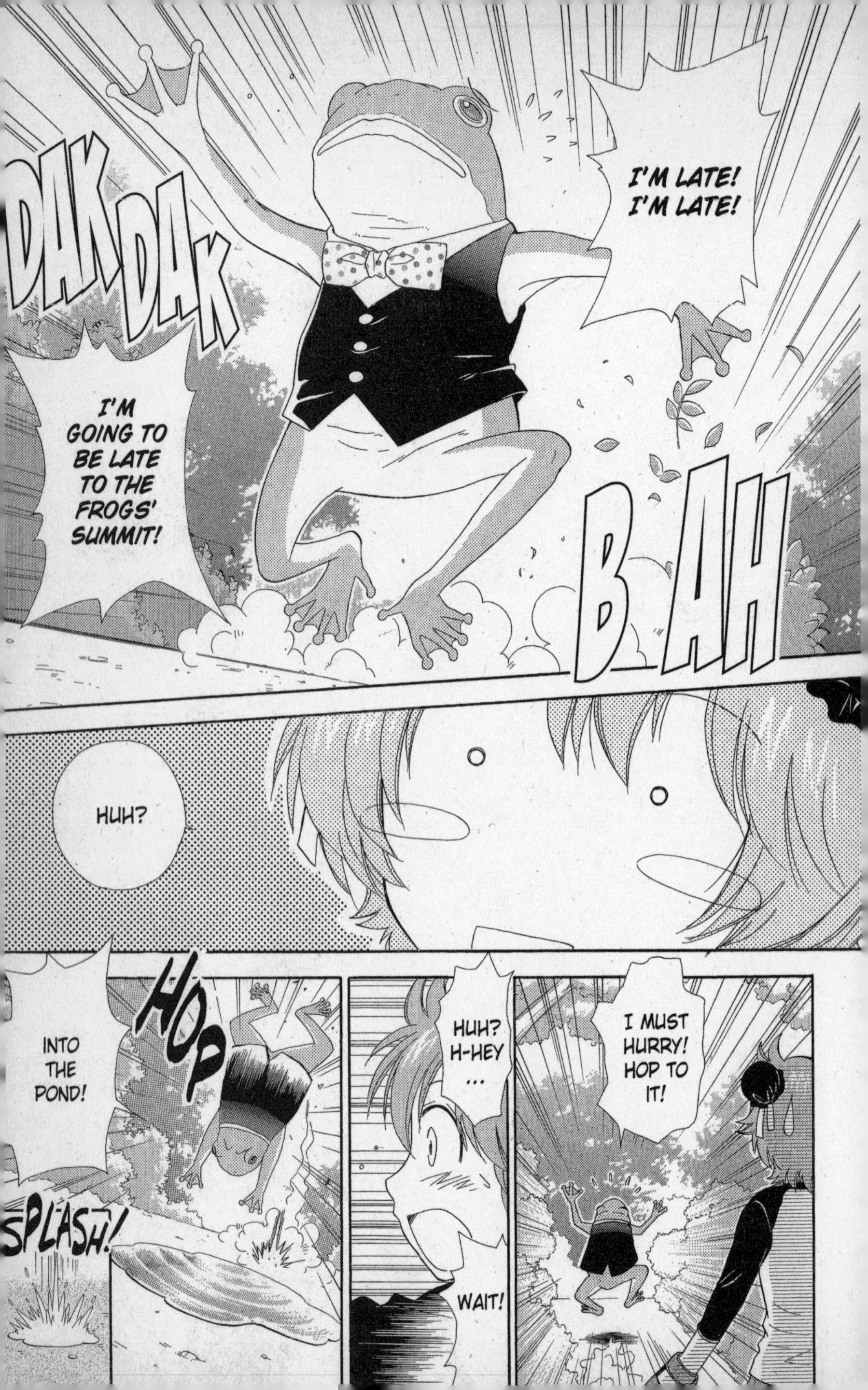
I'M LATE! I'M LATE!
DAK DAK
I'M GOING TO BE LATE TO THE FROGS' SUMMIT!
BAH
HUH?
I MUST HURRY! HOP TO IT!
HUH? H-HEY ...
WAIT!
HOP
INTO THE POND!
SPLASH!

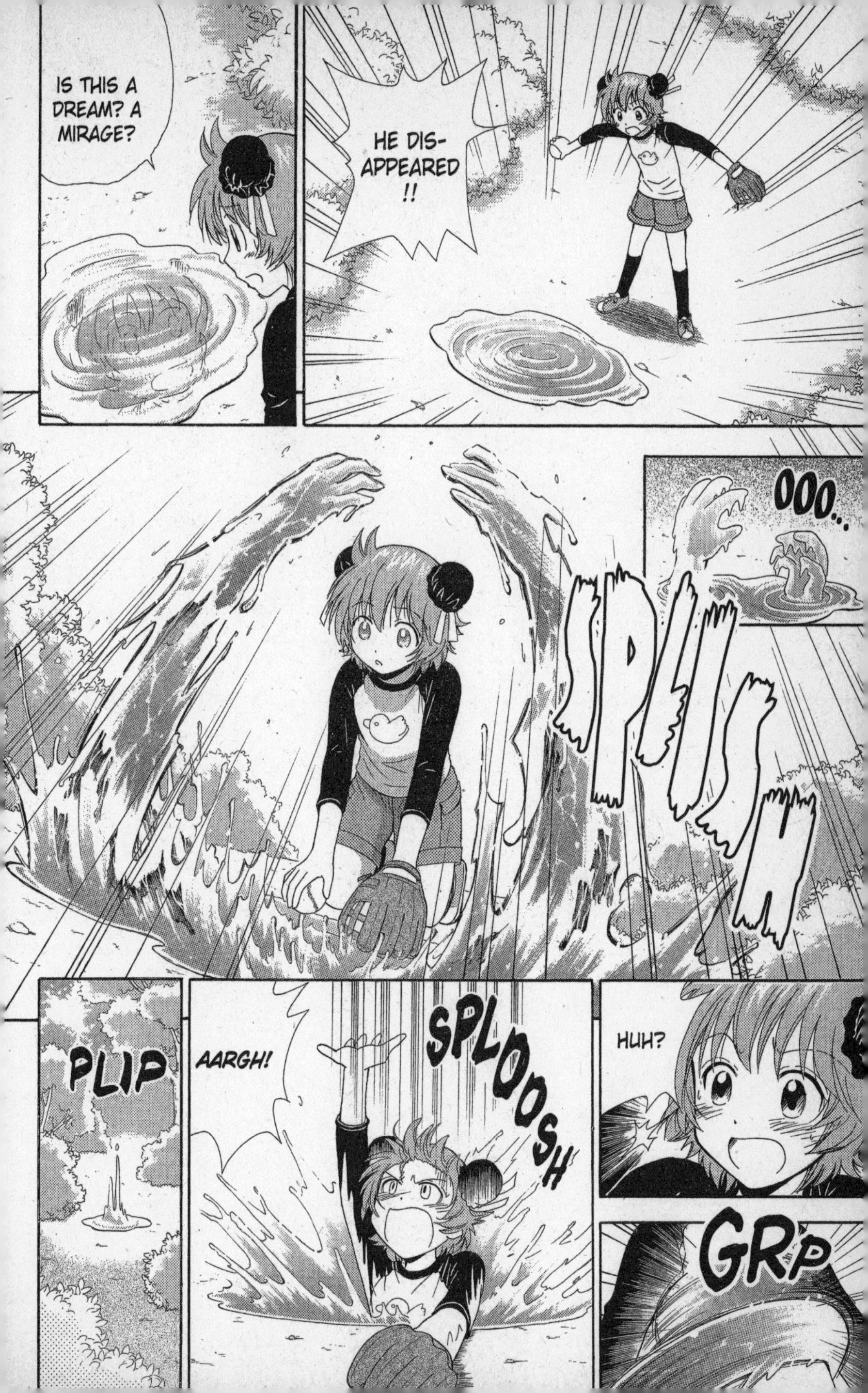
HE DIS-
APPEARED
!!
IS THIS A
DREAM? A
MIRAGE?
OOO...
SPLISH
HUH?
GRP
AARGH!
SPLOOSH
PLIP

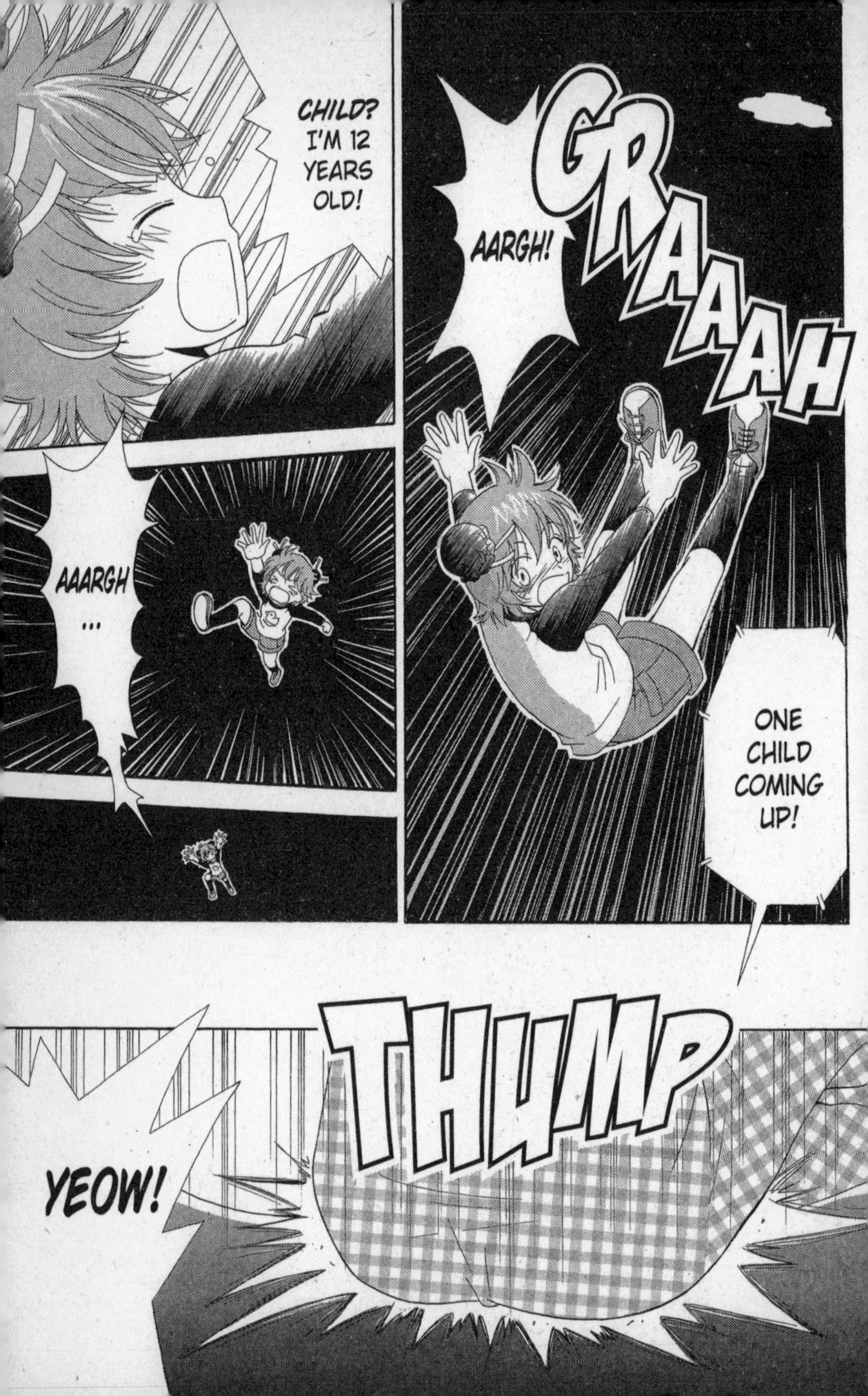
GRAAAAH
AARGH!
ONE CHILD COMING UP!
CHILD? I'M 12 YEARS OLD!
AAARGH ...
THUMP
YEOW!

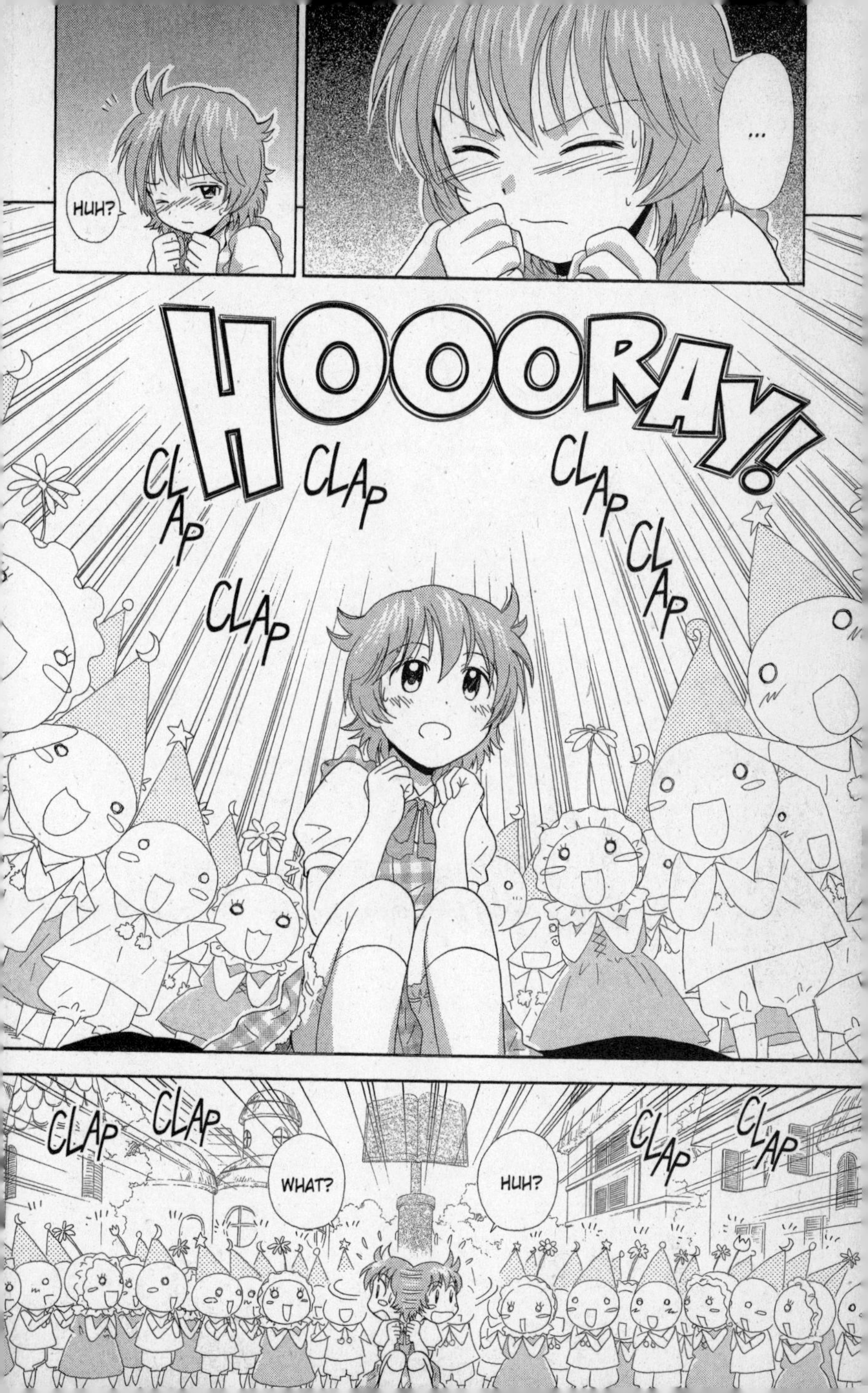
...
HUH?
HOOORAY!
CLAP
CLAP
CLAP
CLAP
CLAP
CLAP
CLAP
CLAP
HUH?
WHAT?
CLAP
CLAP

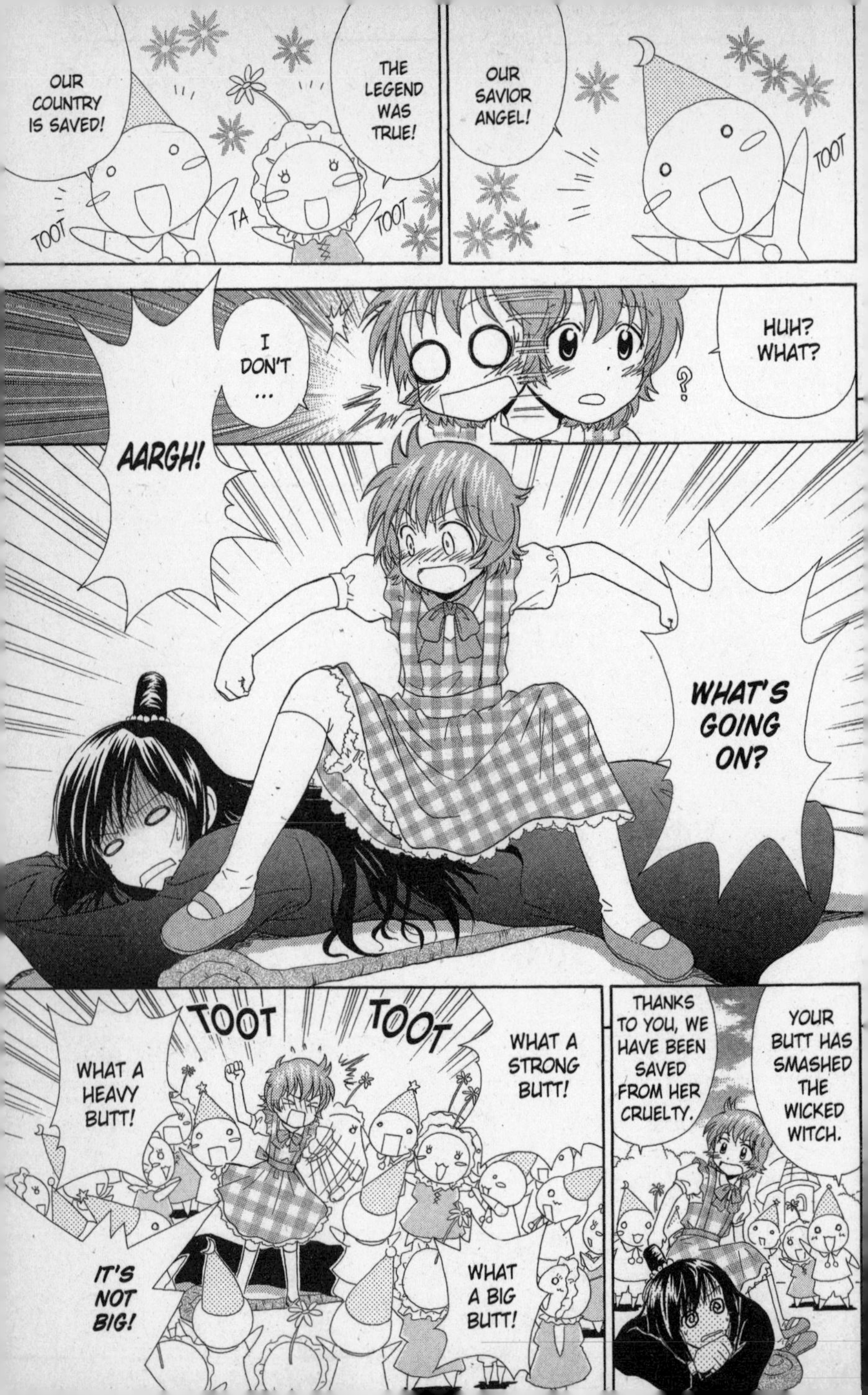
OUR SAVIOR ANGEL!
TOOT
THE LEGEND WAS TRUE!
TOOT
OUR COUNTRY IS SAVED!
TA
TOOT
HUH? WHAT?
?
I DON'T ...
WHAT'S GOING ON?
AARGH!
YOUR BUTT HAS SMASHED THE WICKED WITCH.
THANKS TO YOU, WE HAVE BEEN SAVED FROM HER CRUELTY.
TOOT
TOOT
WHAT A STRONG BUTT!
WHAT A HEAVY BUTT!
WHAT A BIG BUTT!
IT'S NOT BIG!

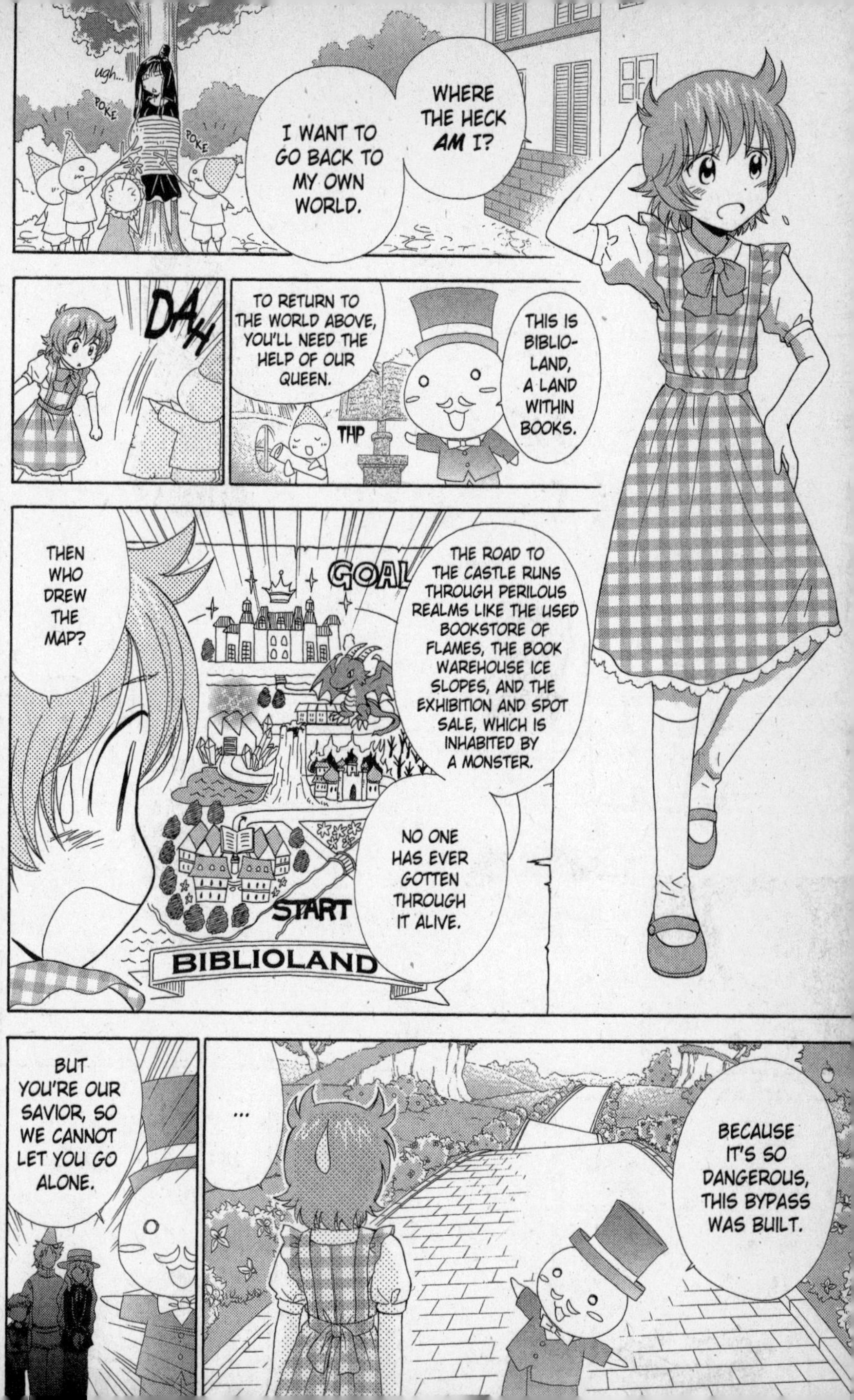
WHERE THE HECK AM I?
I WANT TO GO BACK TO MY OWN WORLD.
ugh...
POKE
POKE
THIS IS BIBLIO-LAND, A LAND WITHIN BOOKS.
TO RETURN TO THE WORLD ABOVE, YOU'LL NEED THE HELP OF OUR QUEEN.
THP
DAH
THE ROAD TO THE CASTLE RUNS THROUGH PERILOUS REALMS LIKE THE USED BOOKSTORE OF FLAMES, THE BOOK WAREHOUSE ICE SLOPES, AND THE EXHIBITION AND SPOT SALE, WHICH IS INHABITED BY A MONSTER.
NO ONE HAS EVER GOTTEN THROUGH IT ALIVE.
GOAL
START
BIBLIOLAND
THEN WHO DREW THE MAP?
BECAUSE IT'S SO DANGEROUS, THIS BYPASS WAS BUILT.
...
BUT YOU'RE OUR SAVIOR, SO WE CANNOT LET YOU GO ALONE.

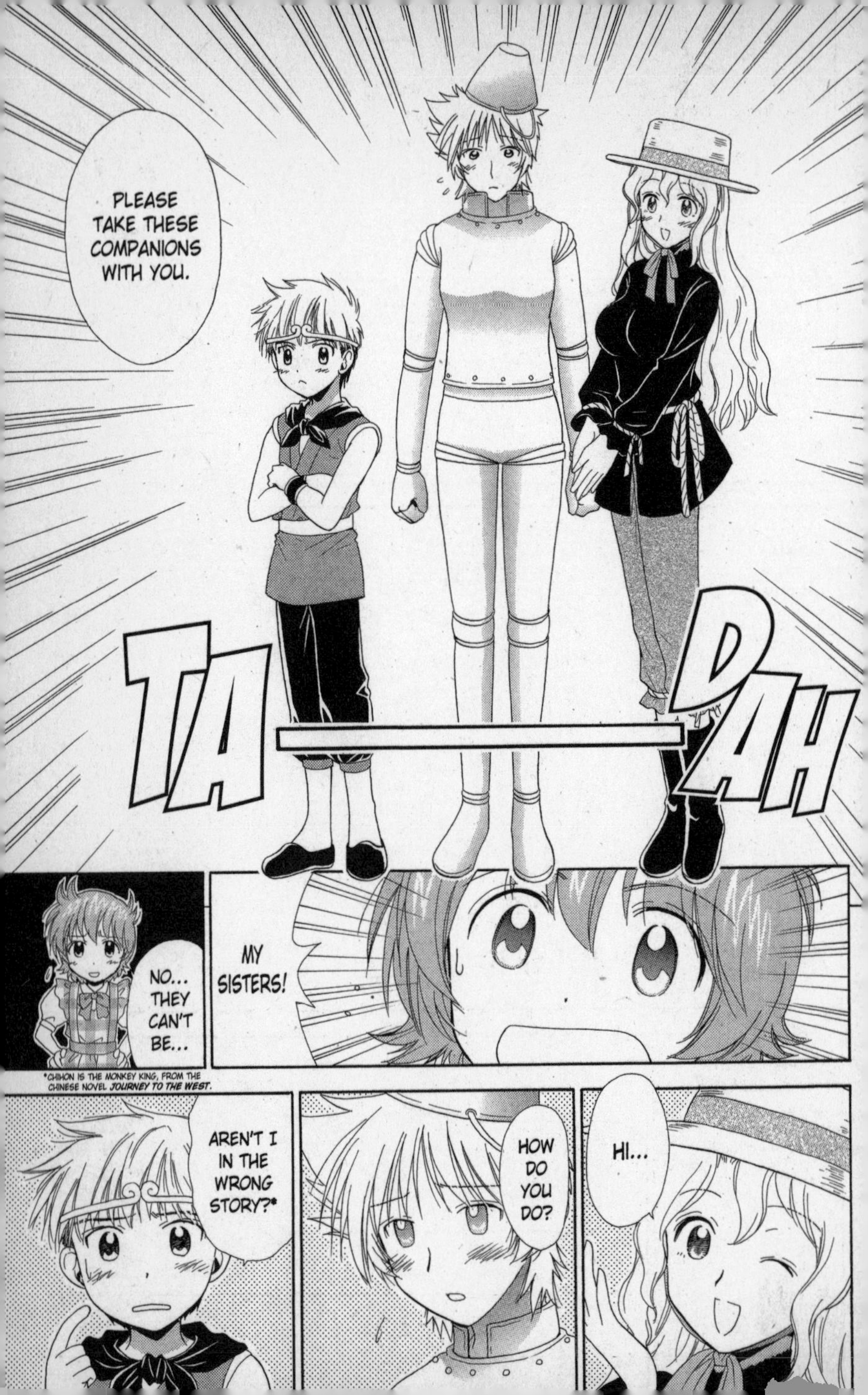
PLEASE TAKE THESE COMPANIONS WITH YOU.
TA—DAH
MY SISTERS!
NO... THEY CAN'T BE...
HI...
HOW DO YOU DO?
AREN'T I IN THE WRONG STORY?*
*CHIHON IS THE MONKEY KING, FROM THE CHINESE NOVEL *JOURNEY TO THE WEST*.

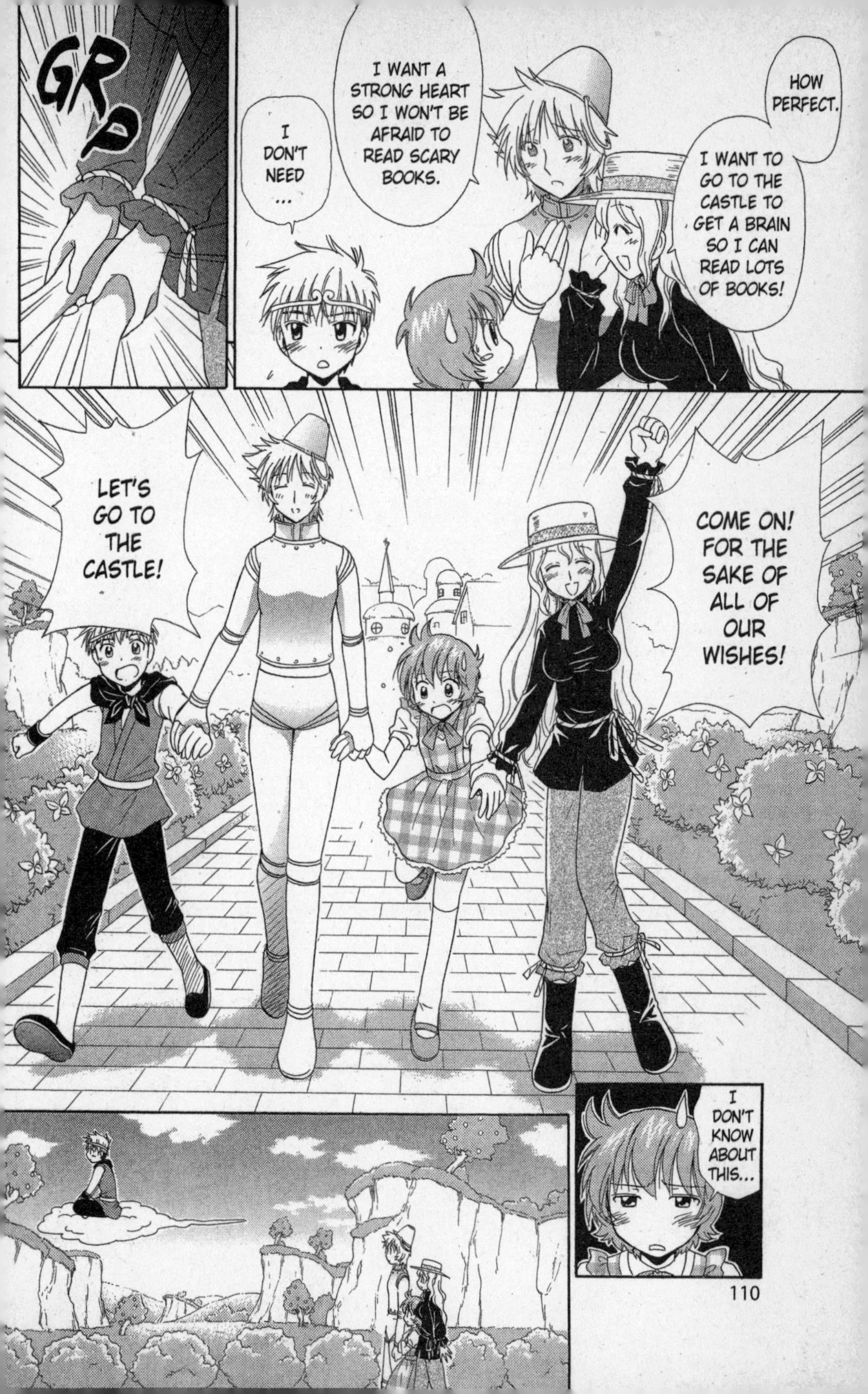
HOW PERFECT.
I WANT TO GO TO THE CASTLE TO GET A BRAIN SO I CAN READ LOTS OF BOOKS!
I WANT A STRONG HEART SO I WON'T BE AFRAID TO READ SCARY BOOKS.
I DON'T NEED ...
GRP
COME ON! FOR THE SAKE OF ALL OF OUR WISHES!
LET'S GO TO THE CASTLE!
I DON'T KNOW ABOUT THIS...

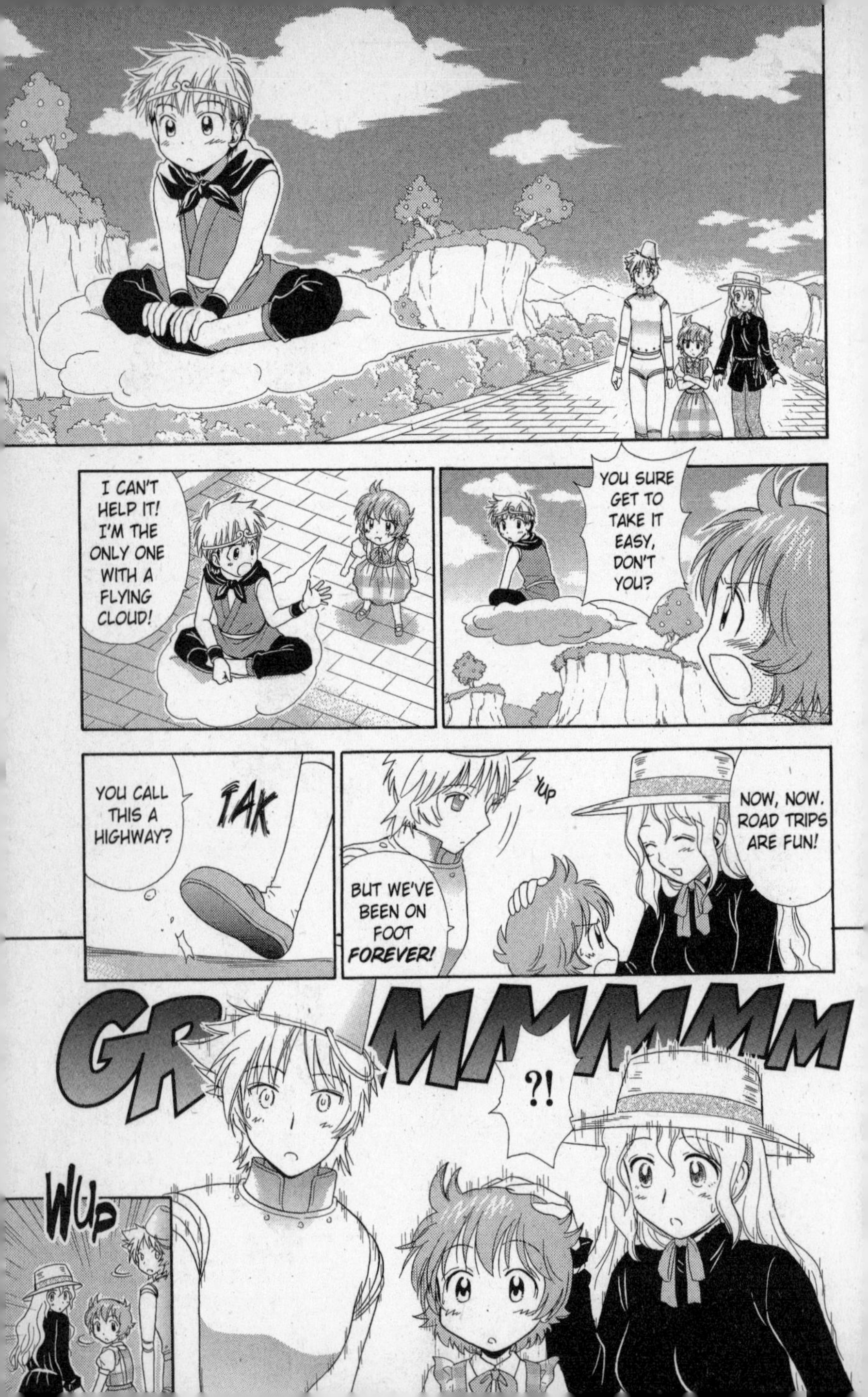

YOU SURE GET TO TAKE IT EASY, DON'T YOU?
I CAN'T HELP IT! I'M THE ONLY ONE WITH A FLYING CLOUD!
NOW, NOW. ROAD TRIPS ARE FUN!
YUP
BUT WE'VE BEEN ON FOOT FOREVER!
YOU CALL THIS A HIGHWAY?
TAK
GRMMMMMM
?!
WUP

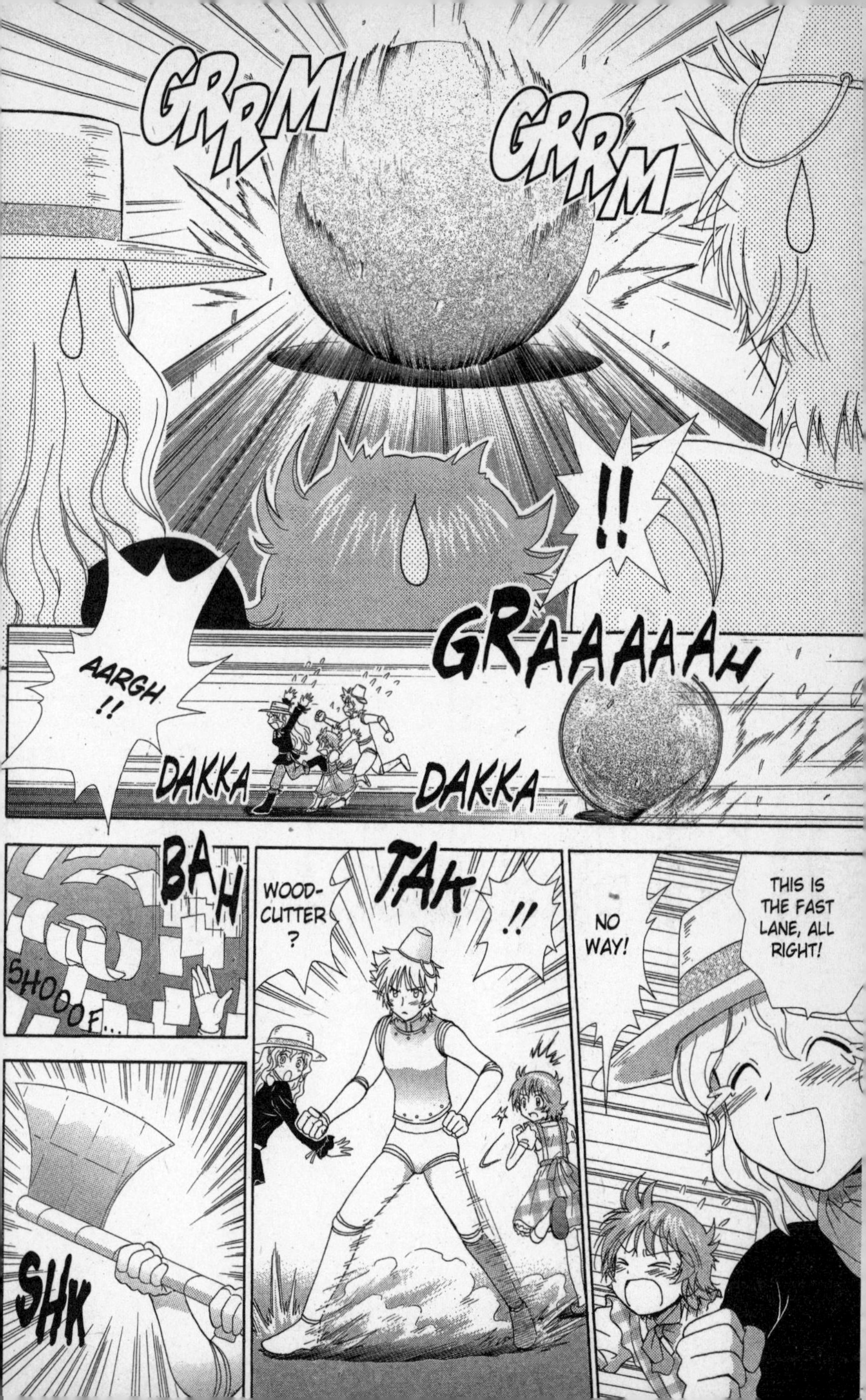
GRRM
GRRM
!!
GRAAAAAH
AARGH !!
DAKKA
DAKKA
THIS IS THE FAST LANE, ALL RIGHT!
NO WAY!
!!
TAK
WOOD-CUTTER ?
BAH
SHOOOF...
SHK

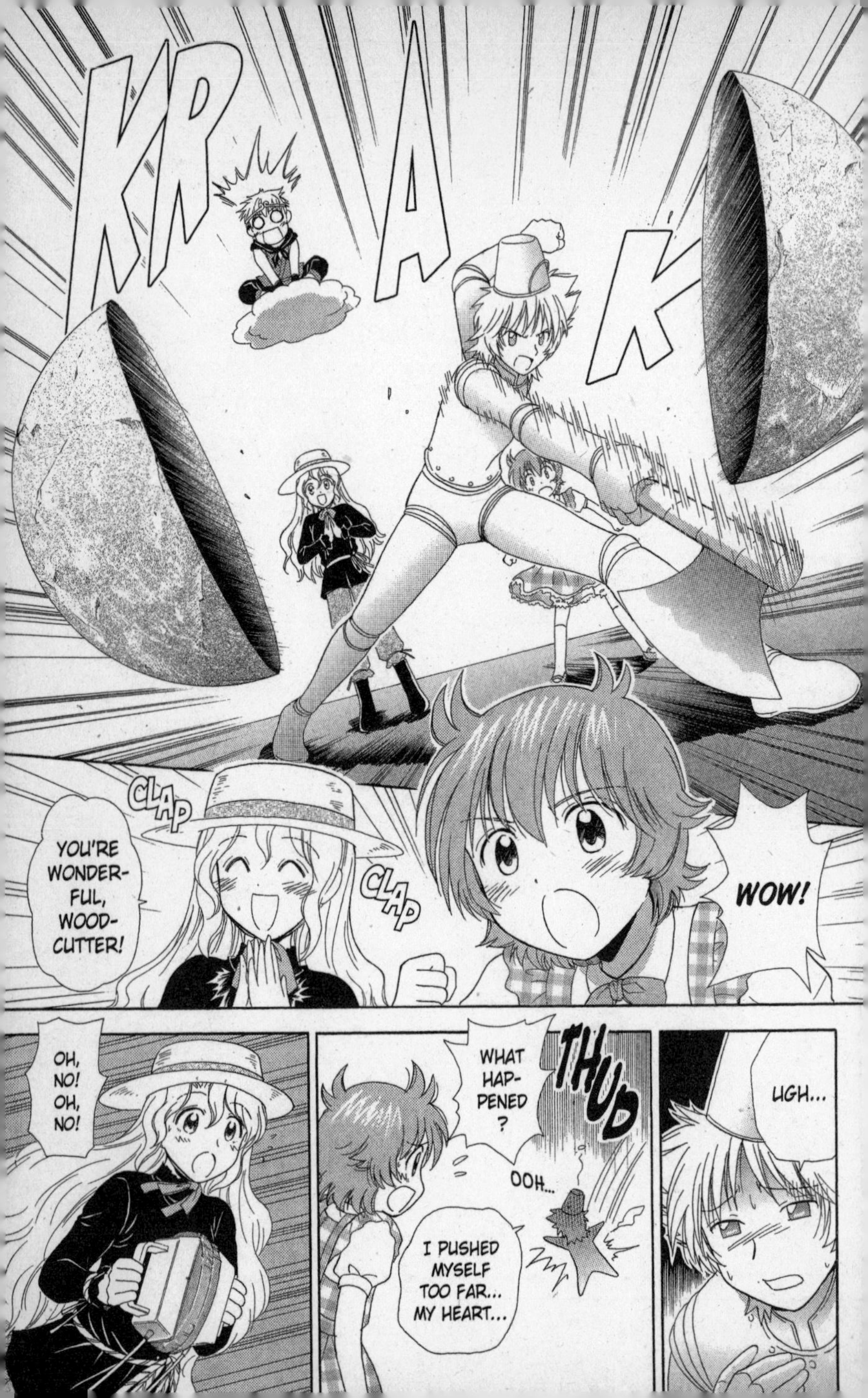
KRAK
WOW!
CLAP
CLAP
YOU'RE WONDERFUL, WOODCUTTER!
UGH...
THUD
WHAT HAPPENED?
OOH...
I PUSHED MYSELF TOO FAR... MY HEART...
OH, NO! OH, NO!

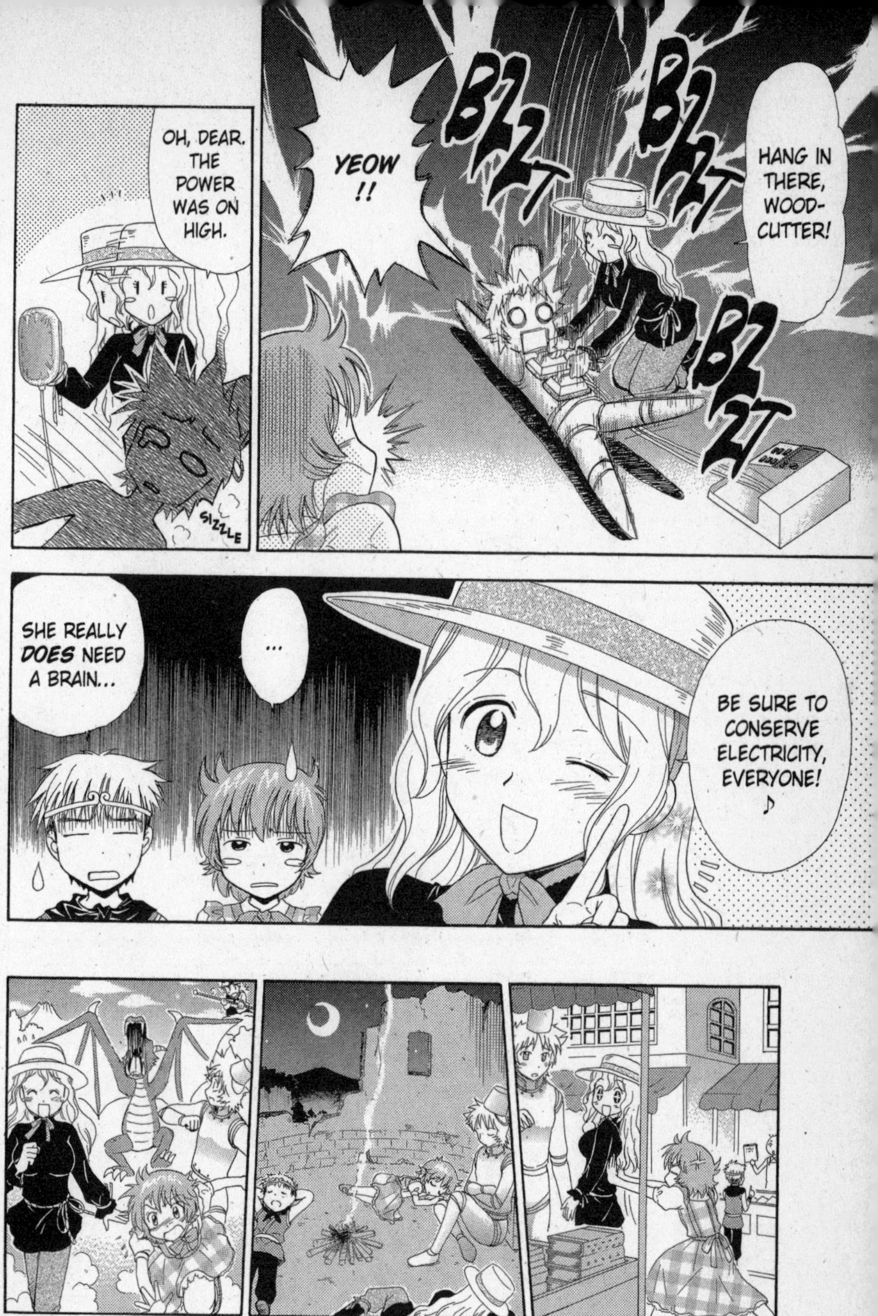
HANG IN THERE, WOOD-CUTTER!
BZZT
BZZT
BZZT
YEOW!!
OH, DEAR. THE POWER WAS ON HIGH.
SIZZLE
BE SURE TO CONSERVE ELECTRICITY, EVERYONE! ♪
...
SHE REALLY DOES NEED A BRAIN...

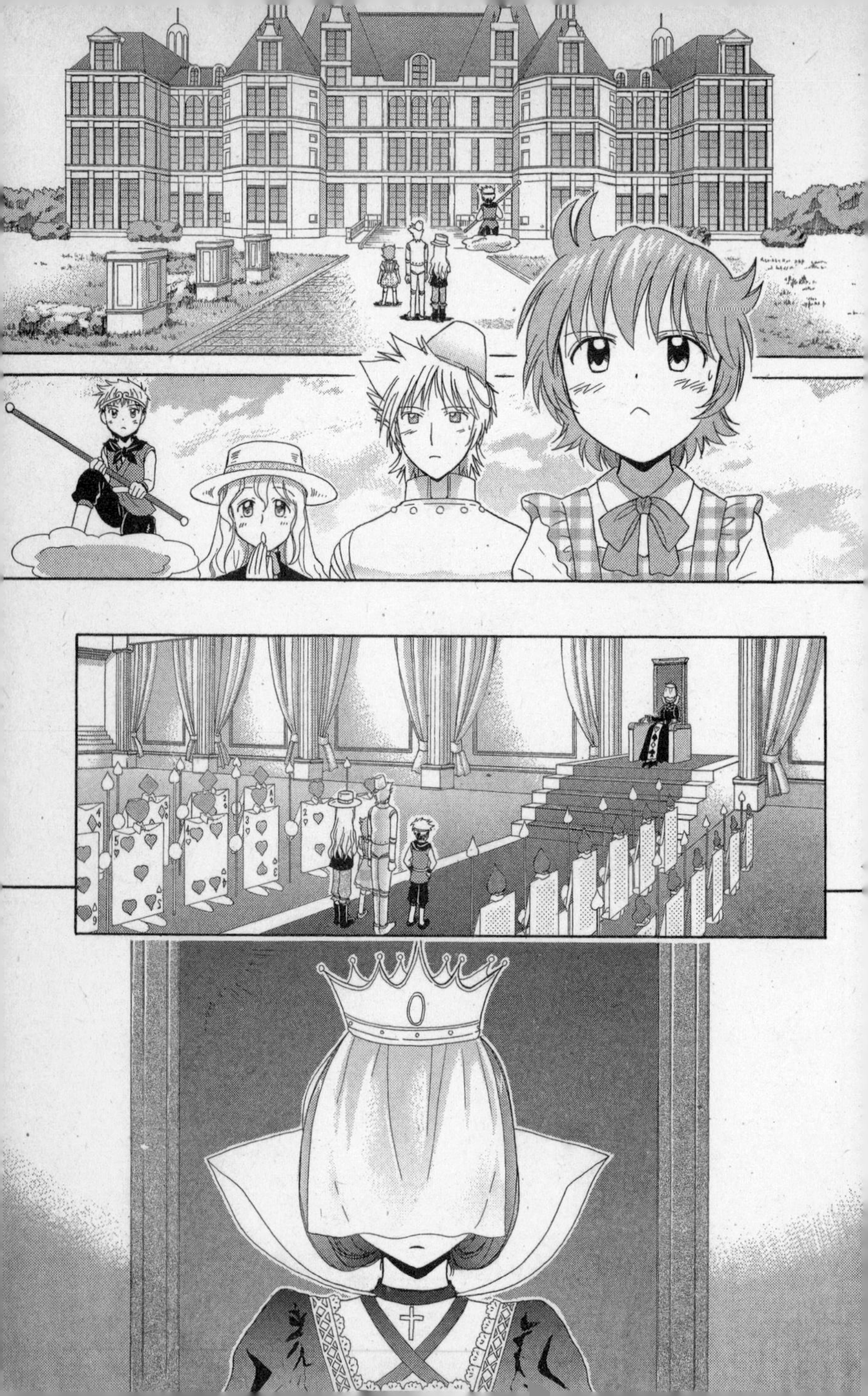

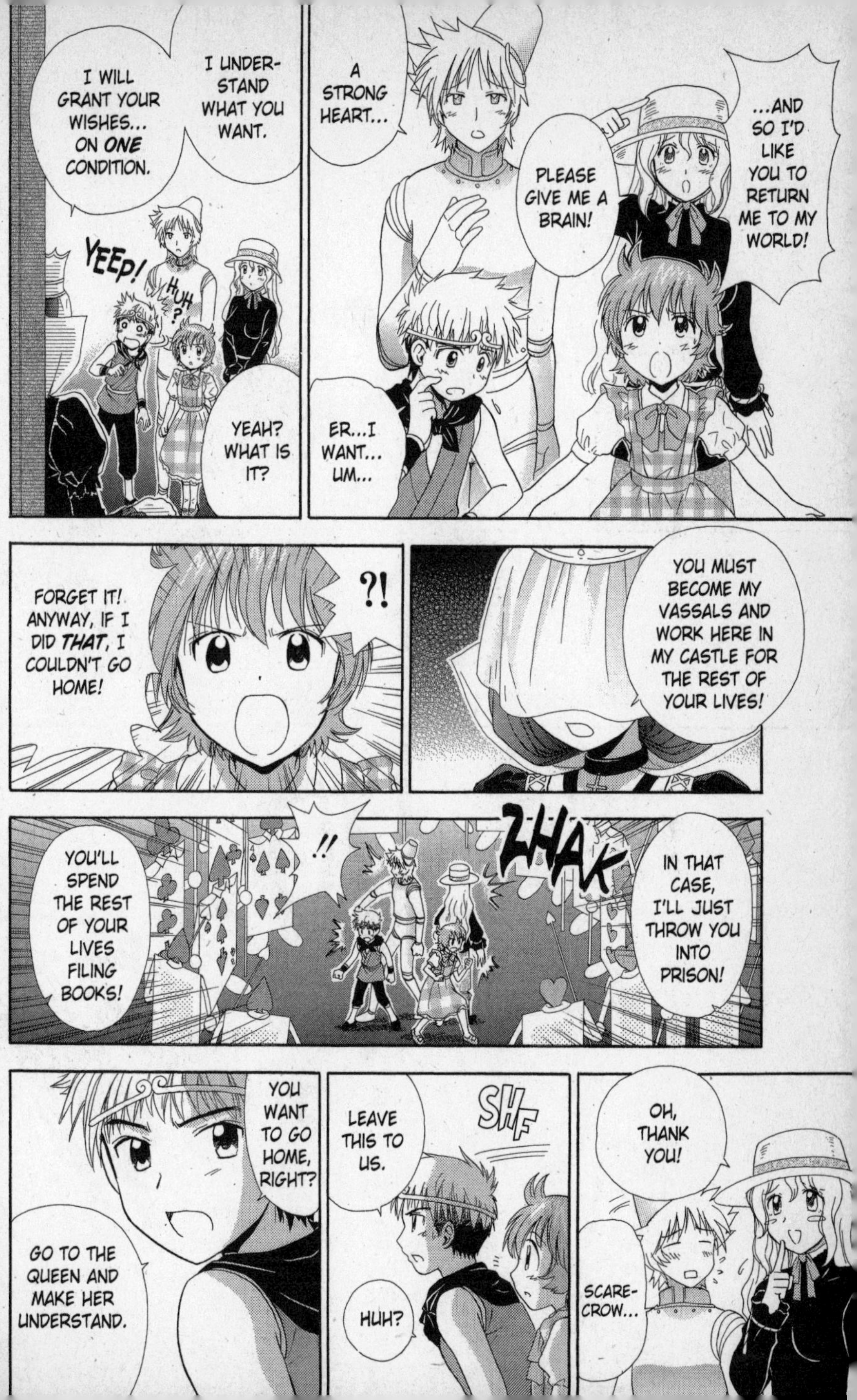
...AND SO I'D LIKE YOU TO RETURN ME TO MY WORLD!
PLEASE GIVE ME A BRAIN!
A STRONG HEART...
ER...I WANT... UM...
I UNDER-STAND WHAT YOU WANT.
I WILL GRANT YOUR WISHES... ON ONE CONDITION.
YEEP!
HUH?
YEAH? WHAT IS IT?
YOU MUST BECOME MY VASSALS AND WORK HERE IN MY CASTLE FOR THE REST OF YOUR LIVES!
?!
FORGET IT! ANYWAY, IF I DID THAT, I COULDN'T GO HOME!
IN THAT CASE, I'LL JUST THROW YOU INTO PRISON!
ZHAK
!!
YOU'LL SPEND THE REST OF YOUR LIVES FILING BOOKS!
OH, THANK YOU!
SCARE-CROW...
SHF
LEAVE THIS TO US.
HUH?
YOU WANT TO GO HOME, RIGHT?
GO TO THE QUEEN AND MAKE HER UNDERSTAND.

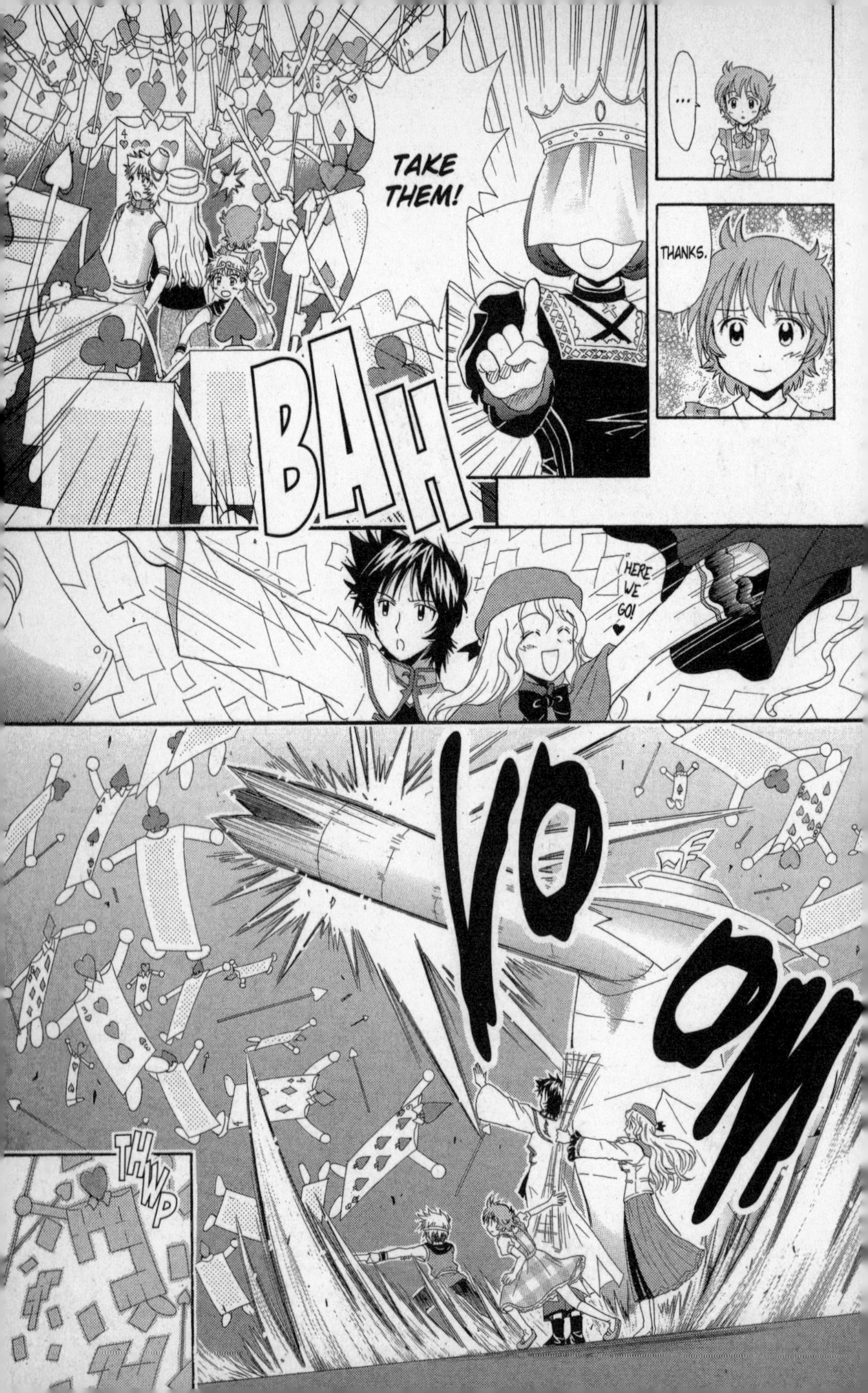
...
THANKS.
TAKE THEM!
BAH
HERE WE GO! ♥
VOOM
THWP

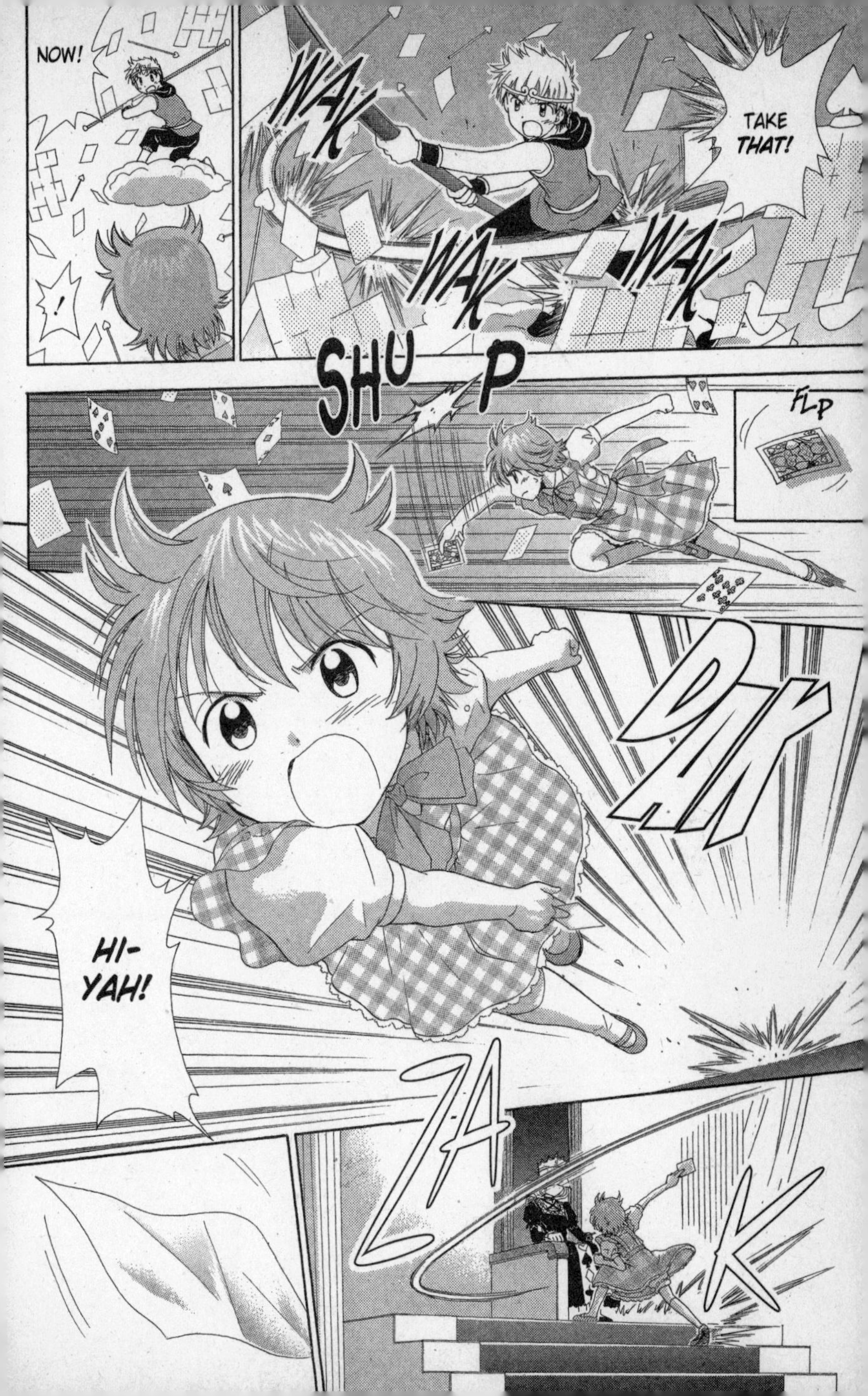
TAKE THAT!
WAK
WAK
WAK
NOW!
!
FLP
SHUP
DAK
HI-YAH!
ZAK

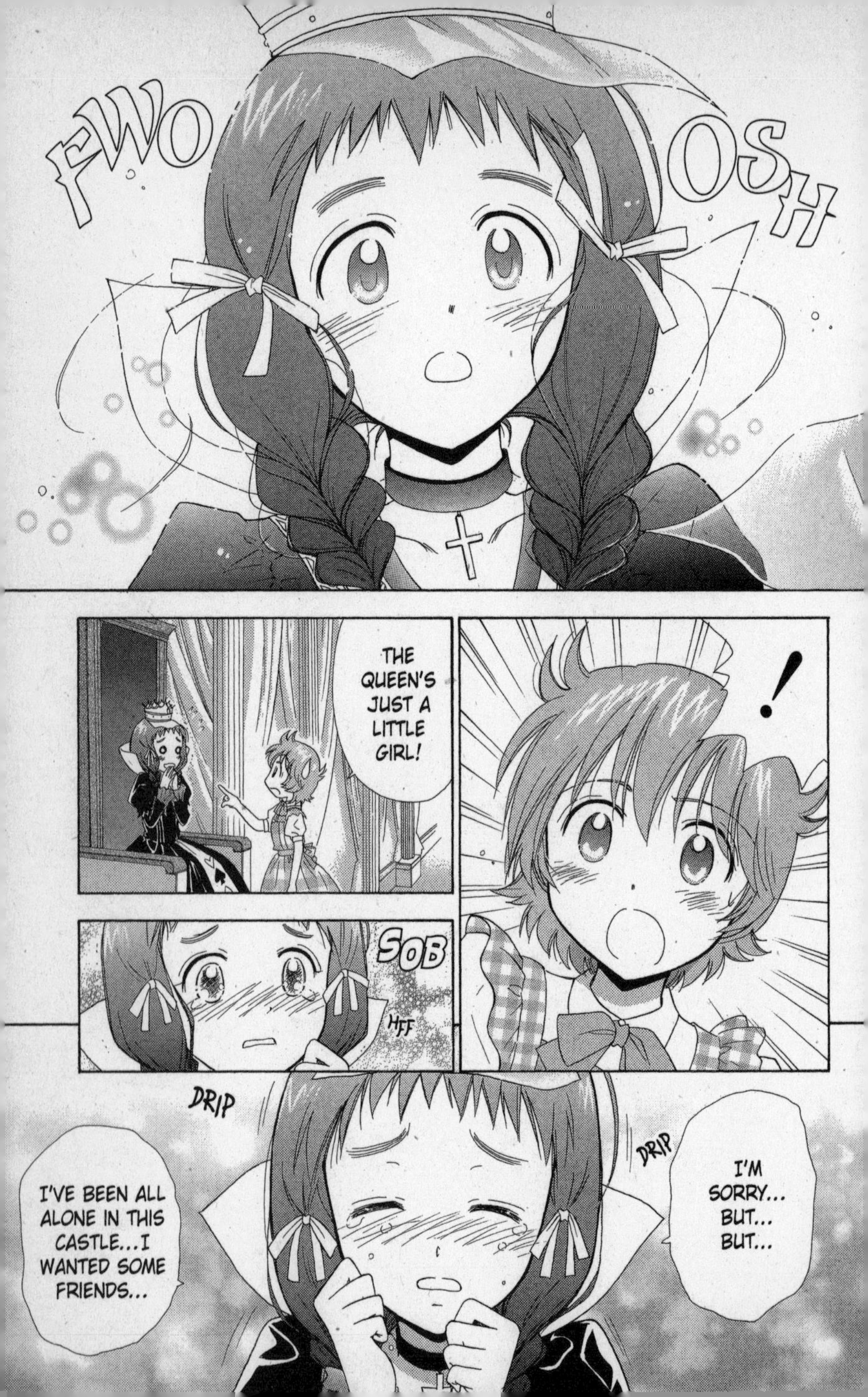
FWOOSH
!
THE QUEEN'S JUST A LITTLE GIRL!
SOB
HFF
I'M SORRY... BUT... BUT...
DRIP
DRIP
I'VE BEEN ALL ALONE IN THIS CASTLE...I WANTED SOME FRIENDS...

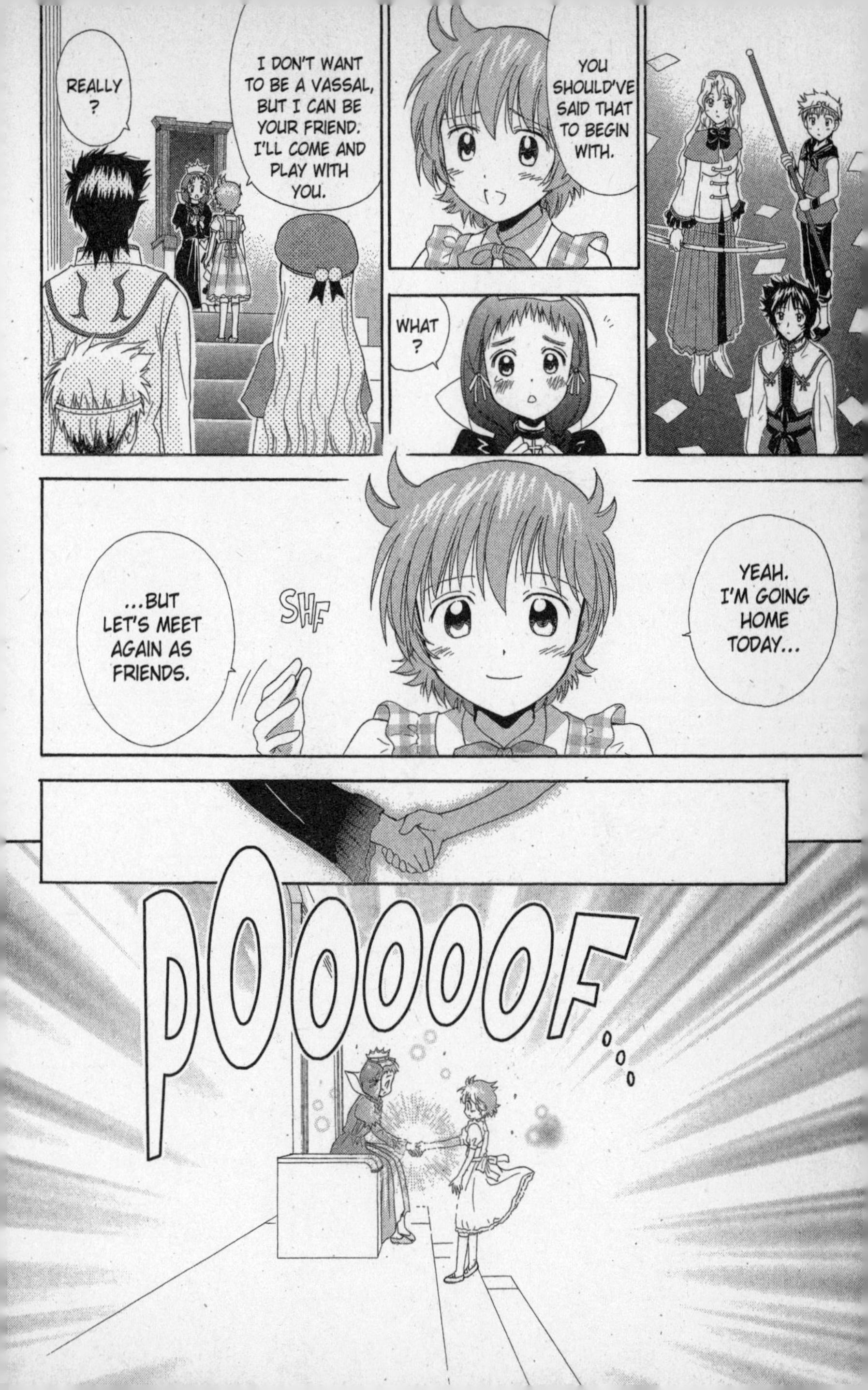
YOU SHOULD'VE SAID THAT TO BEGIN WITH.
WHAT?
I DON'T WANT TO BE A VASSAL, BUT I CAN BE YOUR FRIEND. I'LL COME AND PLAY WITH YOU.
REALLY?
YEAH. I'M GOING HOME TODAY...
SHF
...BUT LET'S MEET AGAIN AS FRIENDS.
POOOOOF

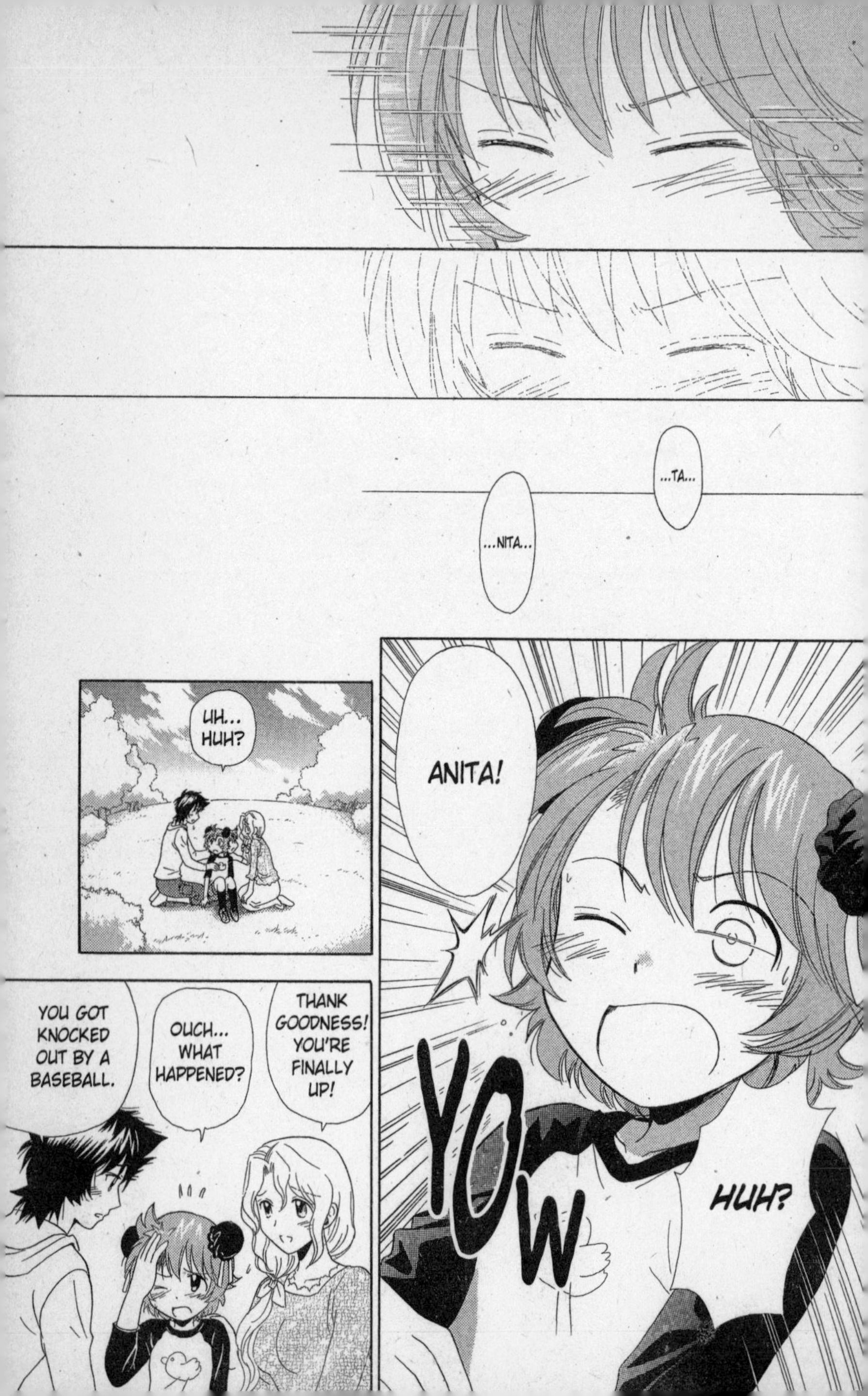
...TA...
...NITA...
ANITA!
YOW
HUH?
UH... HUH?
THANK GOODNESS! YOU'RE FINALLY UP!
OUCH... WHAT HAPPENED?
YOU GOT KNOCKED OUT BY A BASEBALL.

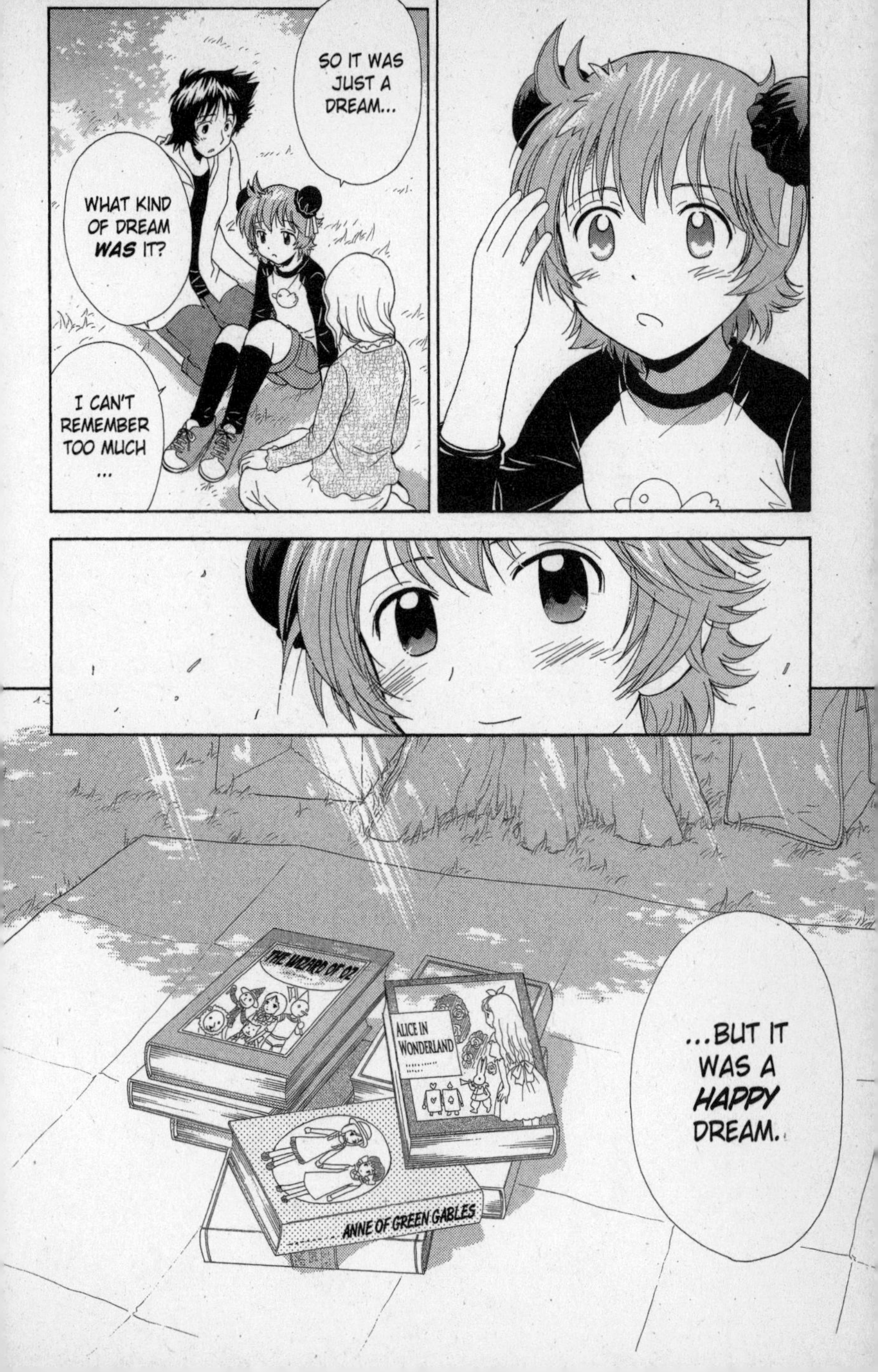
SO IT WAS JUST A DREAM...
WHAT KIND OF DREAM *WAS* IT?
I CAN'T REMEMBER TOO MUCH ...
...BUT IT WAS A *HAPPY* DREAM.
THE WIZARD OF OZ
ALICE IN WONDERLAND
ANNE OF GREEN GABLES

CHAPTER 21

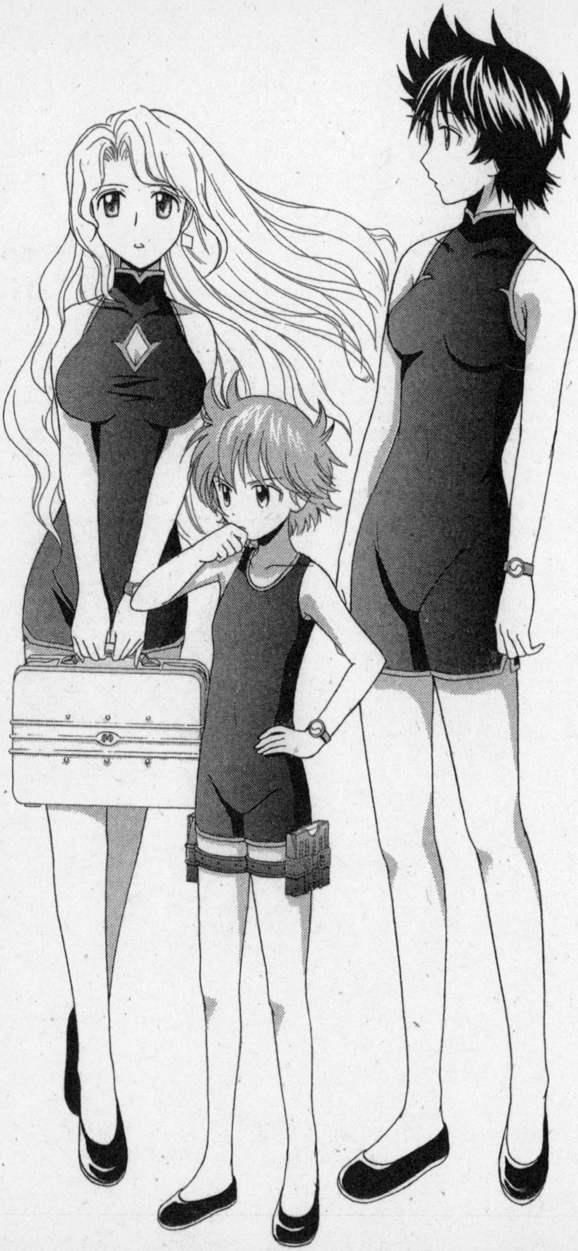

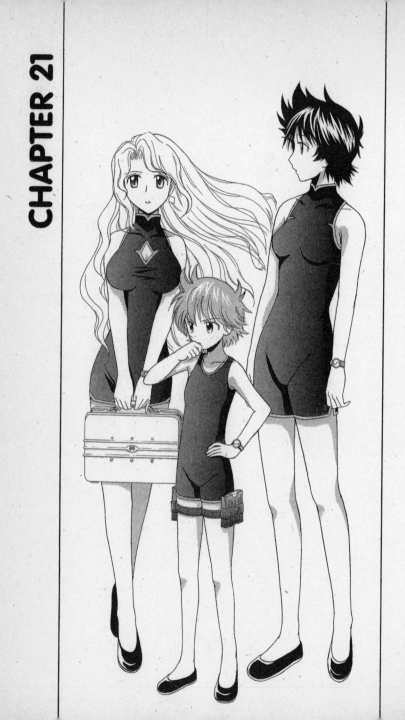

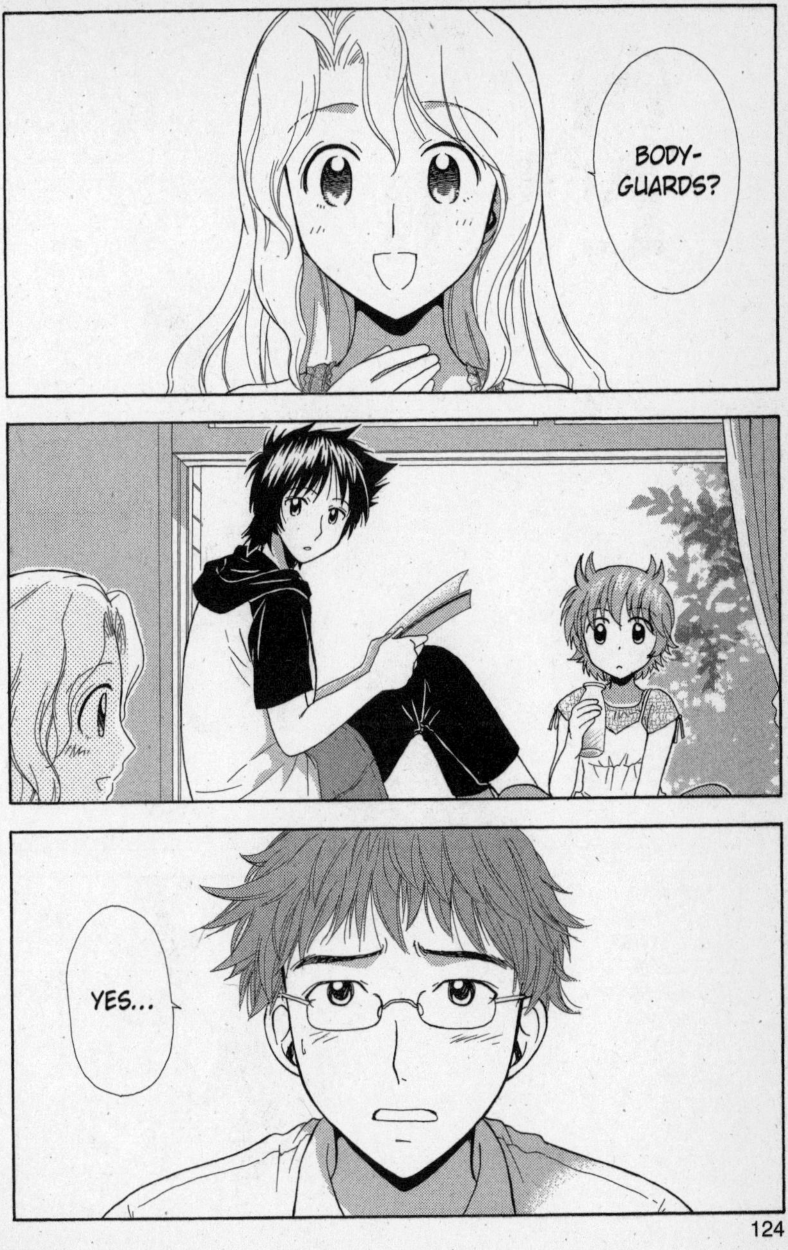
BODY-
GUARDS?
YES...

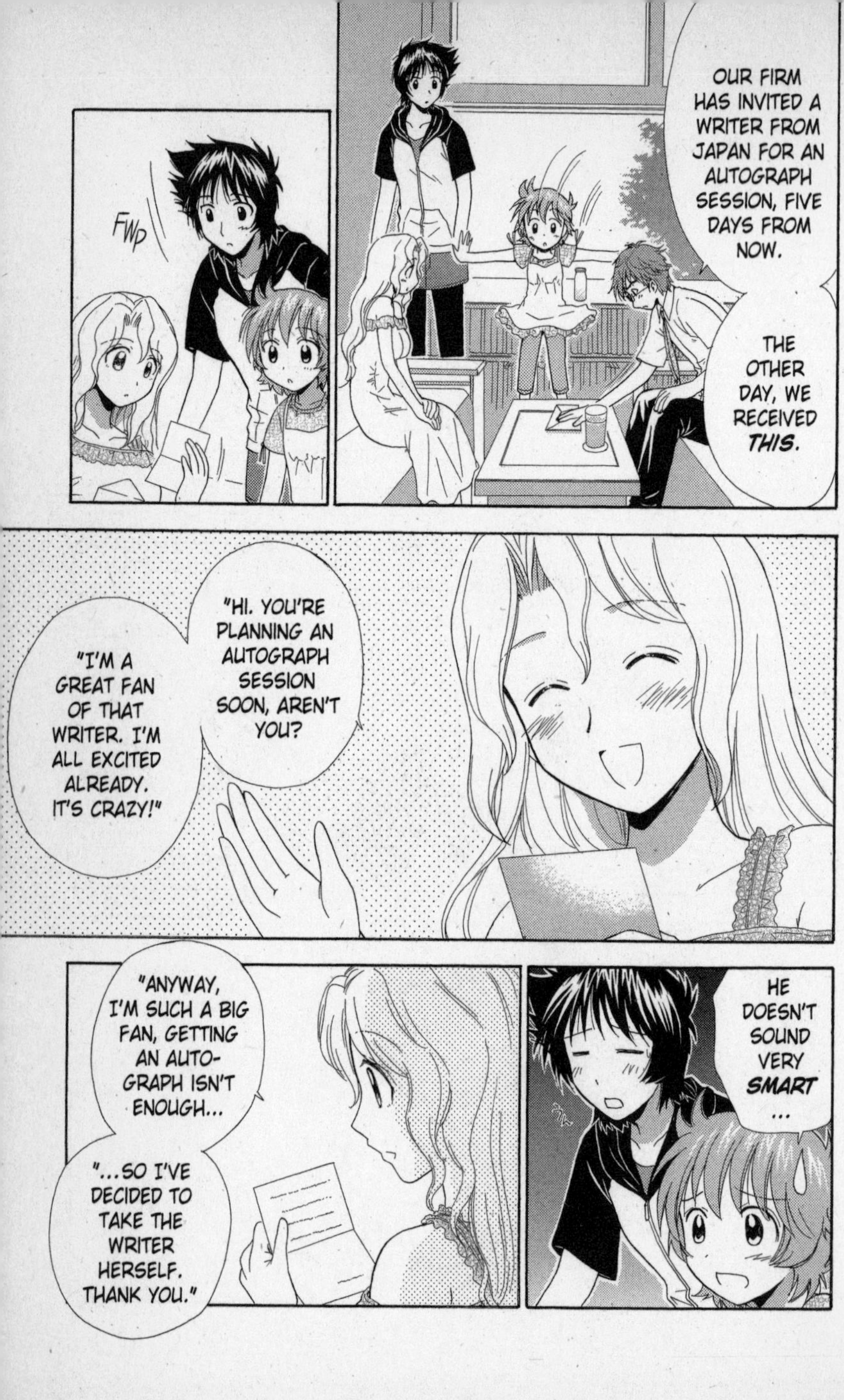
OUR FIRM HAS INVITED A WRITER FROM JAPAN FOR AN AUTOGRAPH SESSION, FIVE DAYS FROM NOW.
THE OTHER DAY, WE RECEIVED THIS.
FWP
"HI. YOU'RE PLANNING AN AUTOGRAPH SESSION SOON, AREN'T YOU?
"I'M A GREAT FAN OF THAT WRITER. I'M ALL EXCITED ALREADY. IT'S CRAZY!"
HE DOESN'T SOUND VERY SMART...
"ANYWAY, I'M SUCH A BIG FAN, GETTING AN AUTO-GRAPH ISN'T ENOUGH...
"...SO I'VE DECIDED TO TAKE THE WRITER HERSELF. THANK YOU."

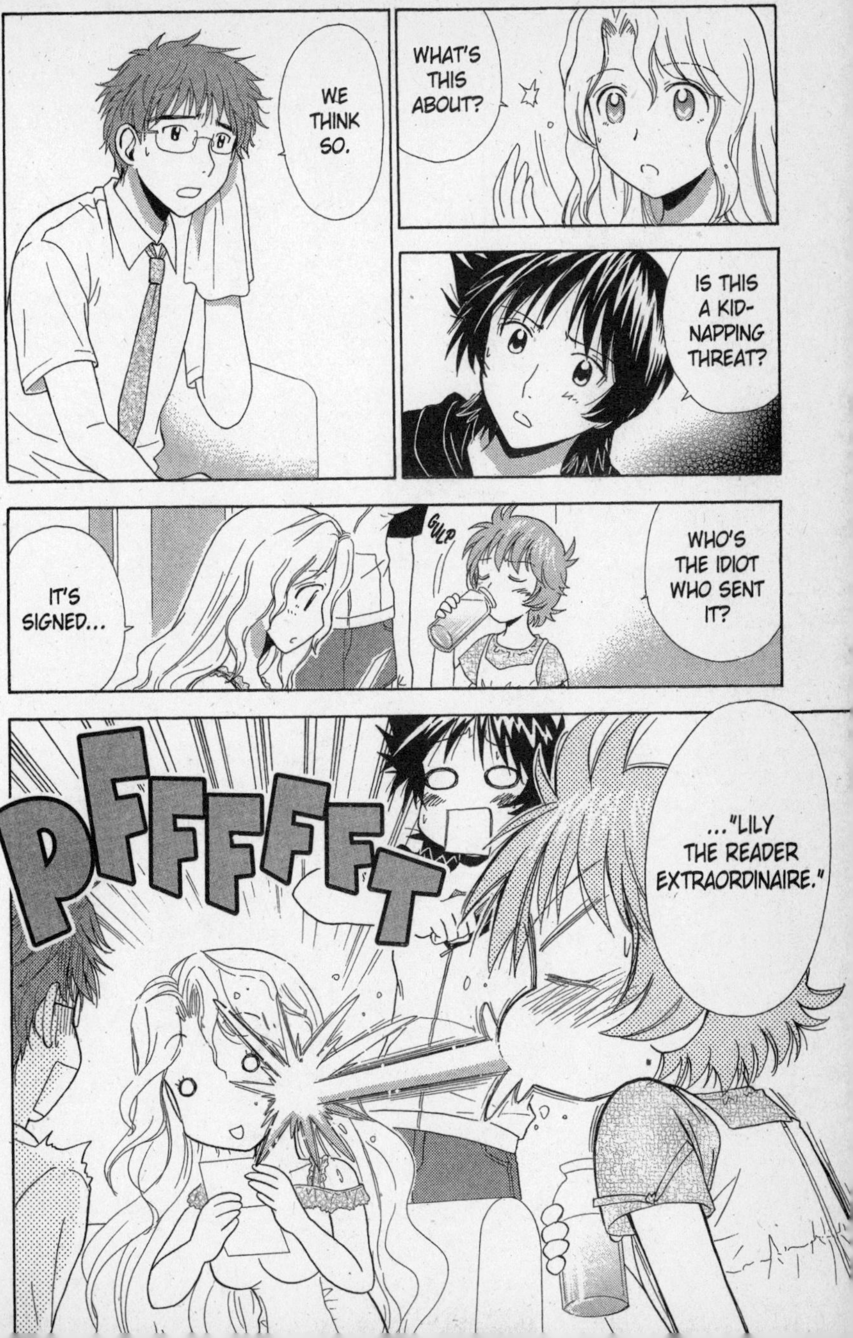
WHAT'S THIS ABOUT?
IS THIS A KID-NAPPING THREAT?
WE THINK SO.
WHO'S THE IDIOT WHO SENT IT?
GULP
IT'S SIGNED...
..."LILY THE READER EXTRAORDINAIRE."
PFFFFFT

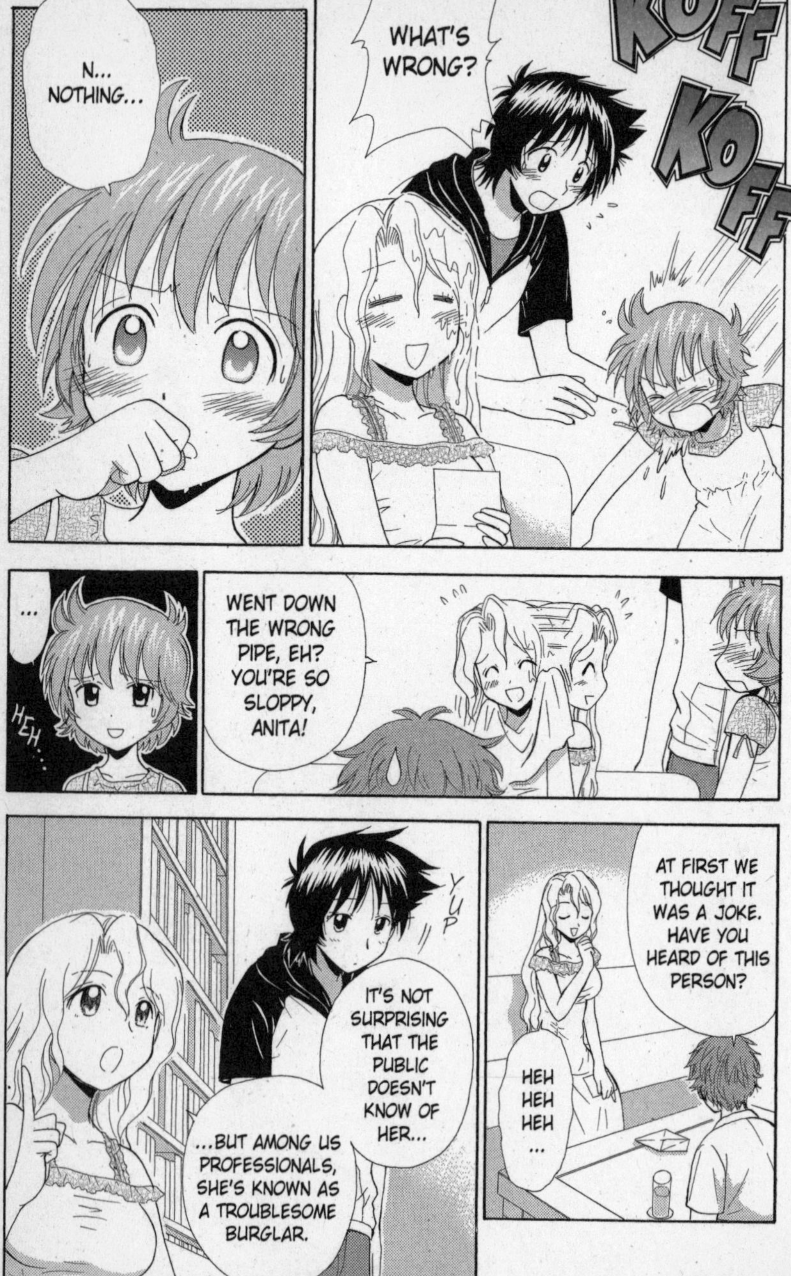
KOFF KOFF
WHAT'S WRONG?
N... NOTHING...
WENT DOWN THE WRONG PIPE, EH? YOU'RE SO SLOPPY, ANITA!
...
HEH...
AT FIRST WE THOUGHT IT WAS A JOKE. HAVE YOU HEARD OF THIS PERSON?
HEH HEH HEH ...
YUP
IT'S NOT SURPRISING THAT THE PUBLIC DOESN'T KNOW OF HER...
...BUT AMONG US PROFESSIONALS, SHE'S KNOWN AS A TROUBLESOME BURGLAR.

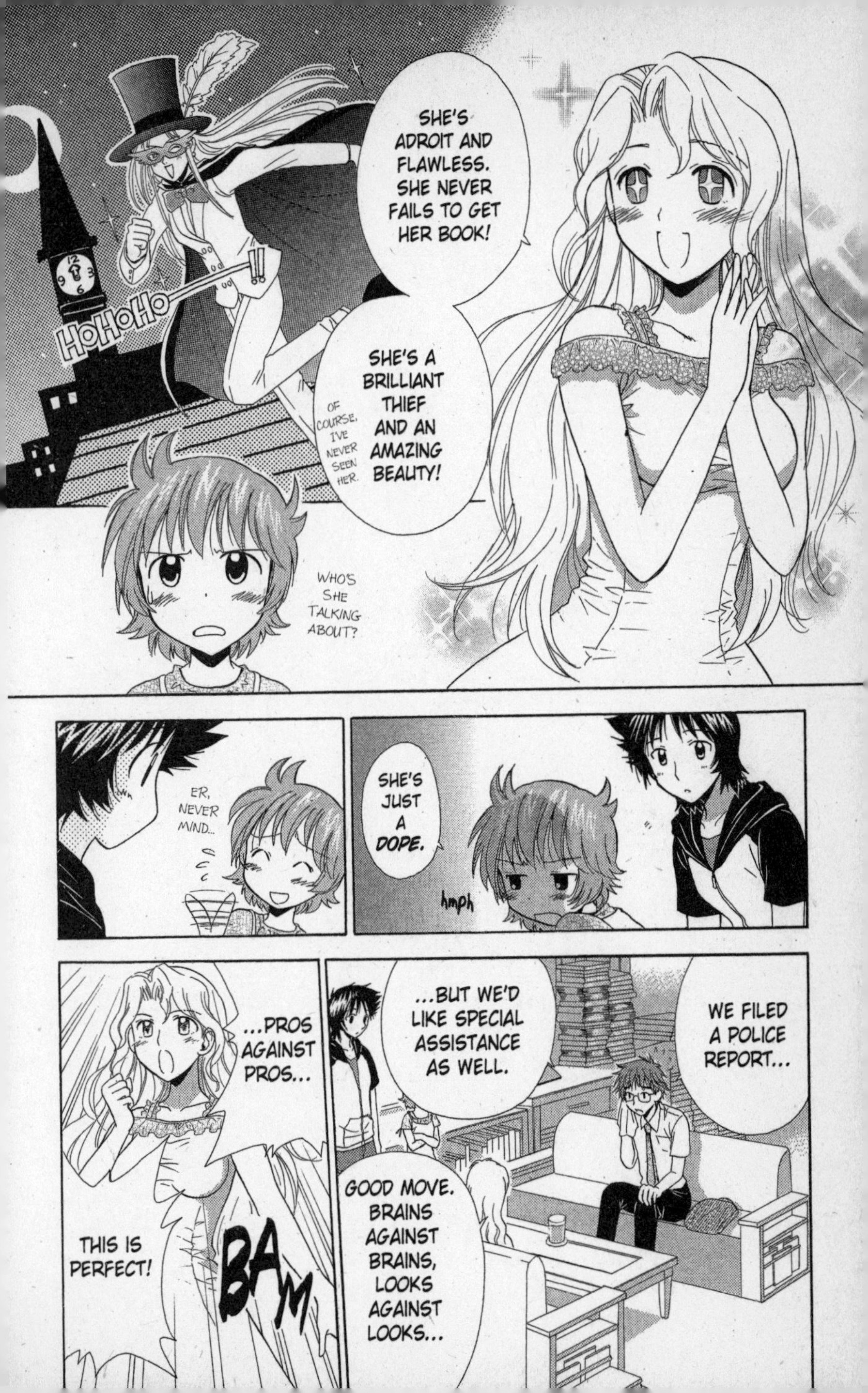
SHE'S ADROIT AND FLAWLESS. SHE NEVER FAILS TO GET HER BOOK!
SHE'S A BRILLIANT THIEF AND AN AMAZING BEAUTY!
OF COURSE, I'VE NEVER SEEN HER.
HOHOHO
WHO'S SHE TALKING ABOUT?
SHE'S JUST A DOPE.
hmph
ER, NEVER MIND...
WE FILED A POLICE REPORT...
...BUT WE'D LIKE SPECIAL ASSISTANCE AS WELL.
GOOD MOVE. BRAINS AGAINST BRAINS, LOOKS AGAINST LOOKS...
...PROS AGAINST PROS...
THIS IS PERFECT!
BAM

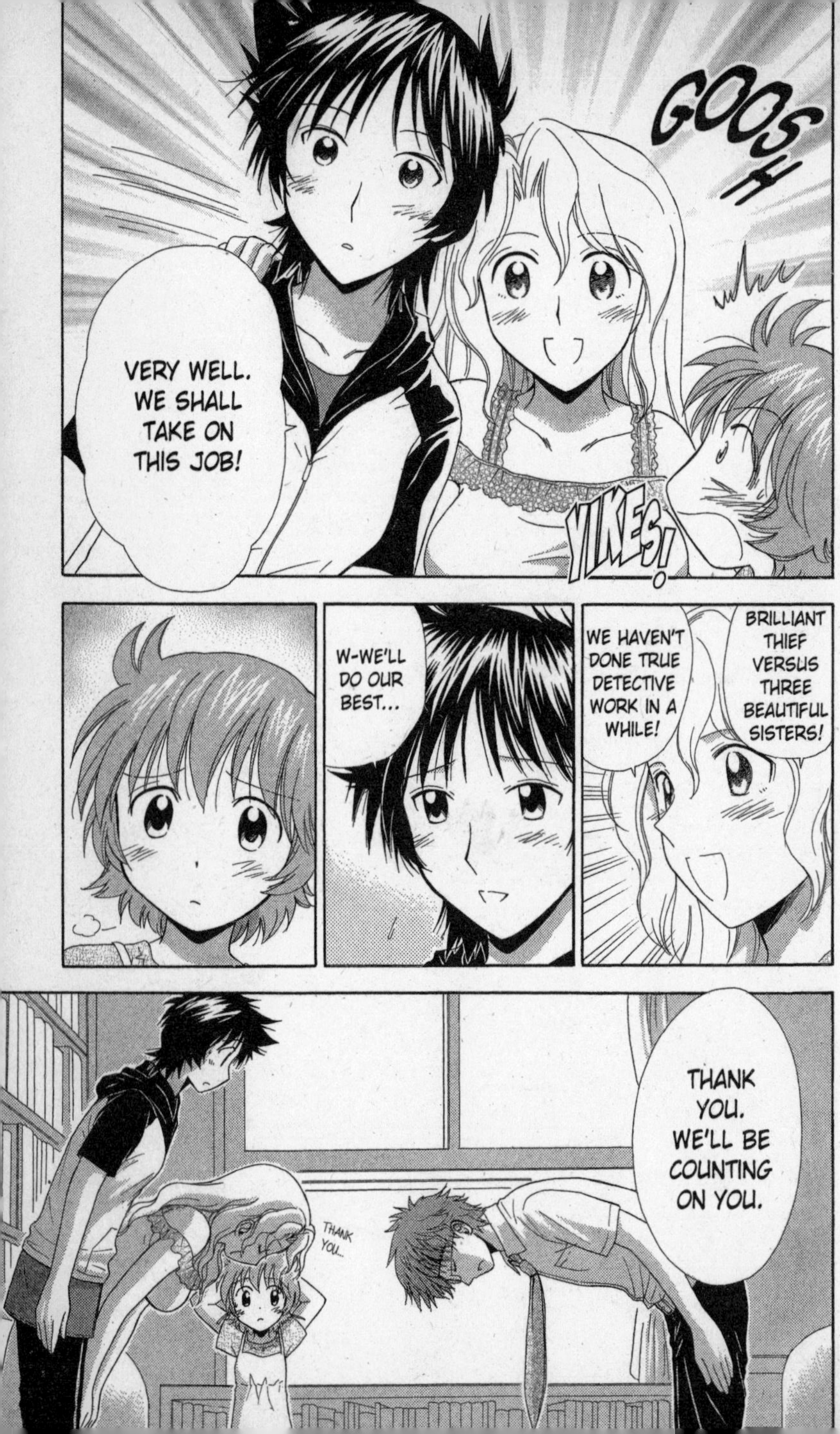
GOOSH
VERY WELL. WE SHALL TAKE ON THIS JOB!
YIKES!
BRILLIANT THIEF VERSUS THREE BEAUTIFUL SISTERS!
WE HAVEN'T DONE TRUE DETECTIVE WORK IN A WHILE!
W-WE'LL DO OUR BEST...
THANK YOU. WE'LL BE COUNTING ON YOU.
THANK YOU...

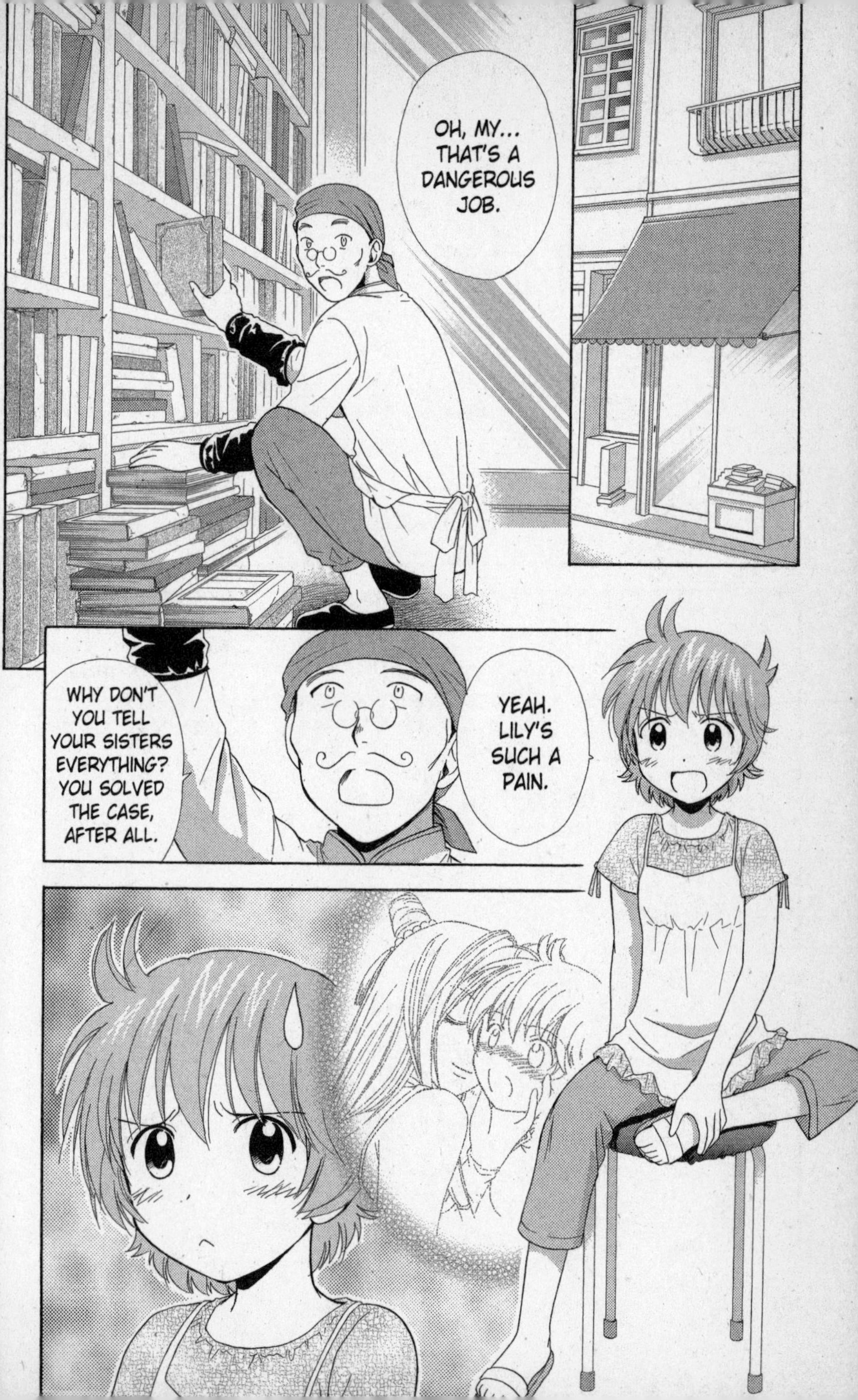
OH, MY... THAT'S A DANGEROUS JOB.
YEAH. LILY'S SUCH A PAIN.
WHY DON'T YOU TELL YOUR SISTERS EVERYTHING? YOU SOLVED THE CASE, AFTER ALL.

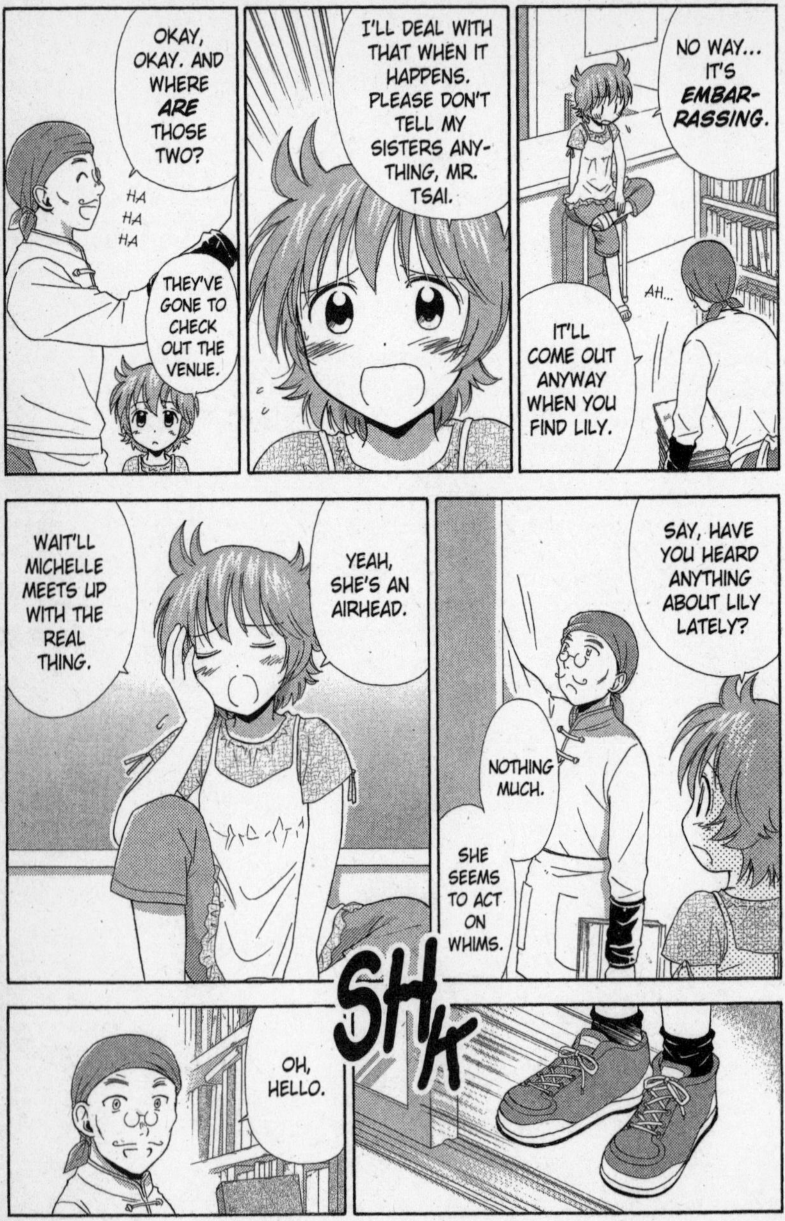
NO WAY... IT'S EMBARRASSING.
AH...
IT'LL COME OUT ANYWAY WHEN YOU FIND LILY.
I'LL DEAL WITH THAT WHEN IT HAPPENS. PLEASE DON'T TELL MY SISTERS ANYTHING, MR. TSAI.
OKAY, OKAY. AND WHERE ARE THOSE TWO?
HA HA HA
THEY'VE GONE TO CHECK OUT THE VENUE.
SAY, HAVE YOU HEARD ANYTHING ABOUT LILY LATELY?
NOTHING MUCH.
SHE SEEMS TO ACT ON WHIMS.
YEAH, SHE'S AN AIRHEAD.
WAIT'LL MICHELLE MEETS UP WITH THE REAL THING.
SHK
OH, HELLO.

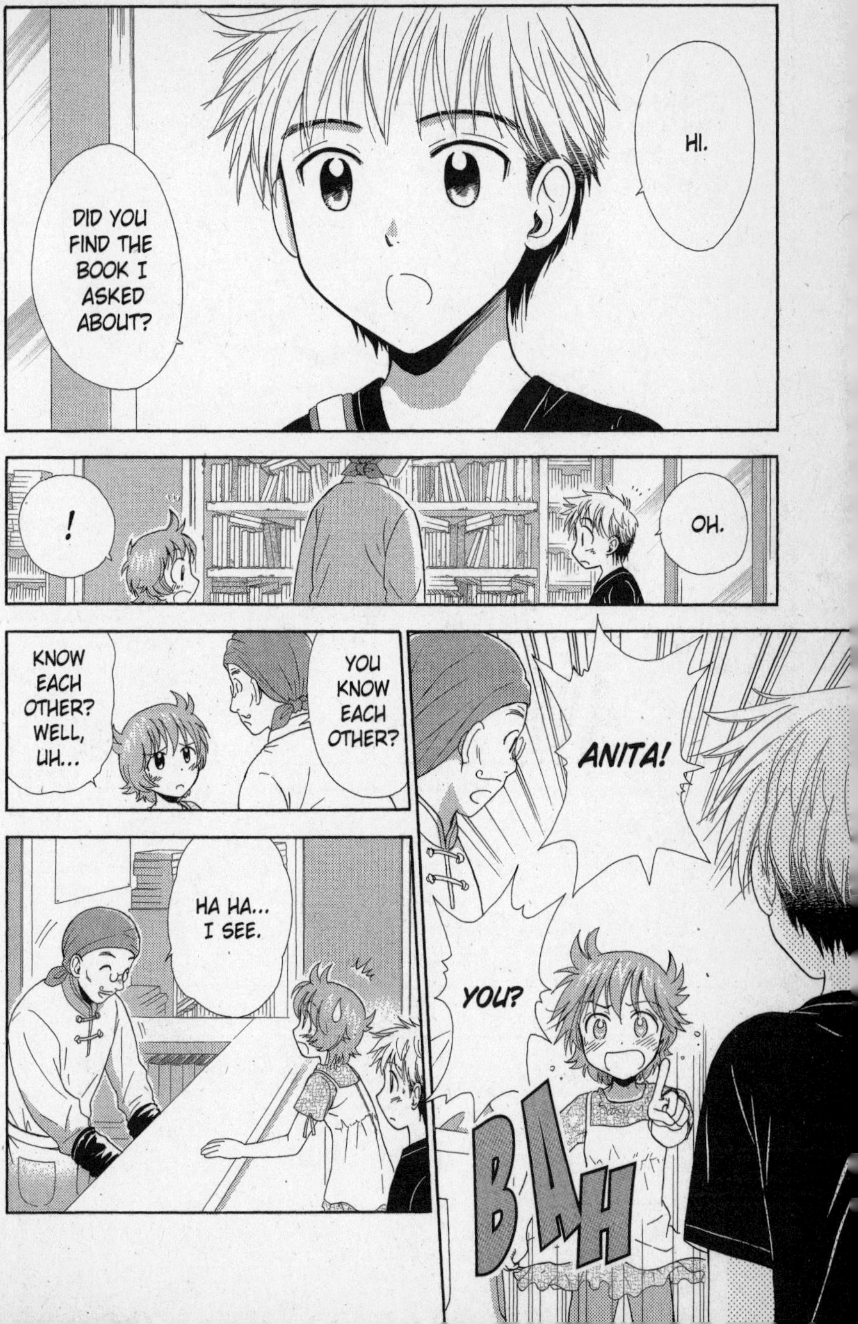
HI.
DID YOU FIND THE BOOK I ASKED ABOUT?
OH.
!
ANITA!
YOU?
BAH
YOU KNOW EACH OTHER?
KNOW EACH OTHER? WELL, UH...
HA HA... I SEE.

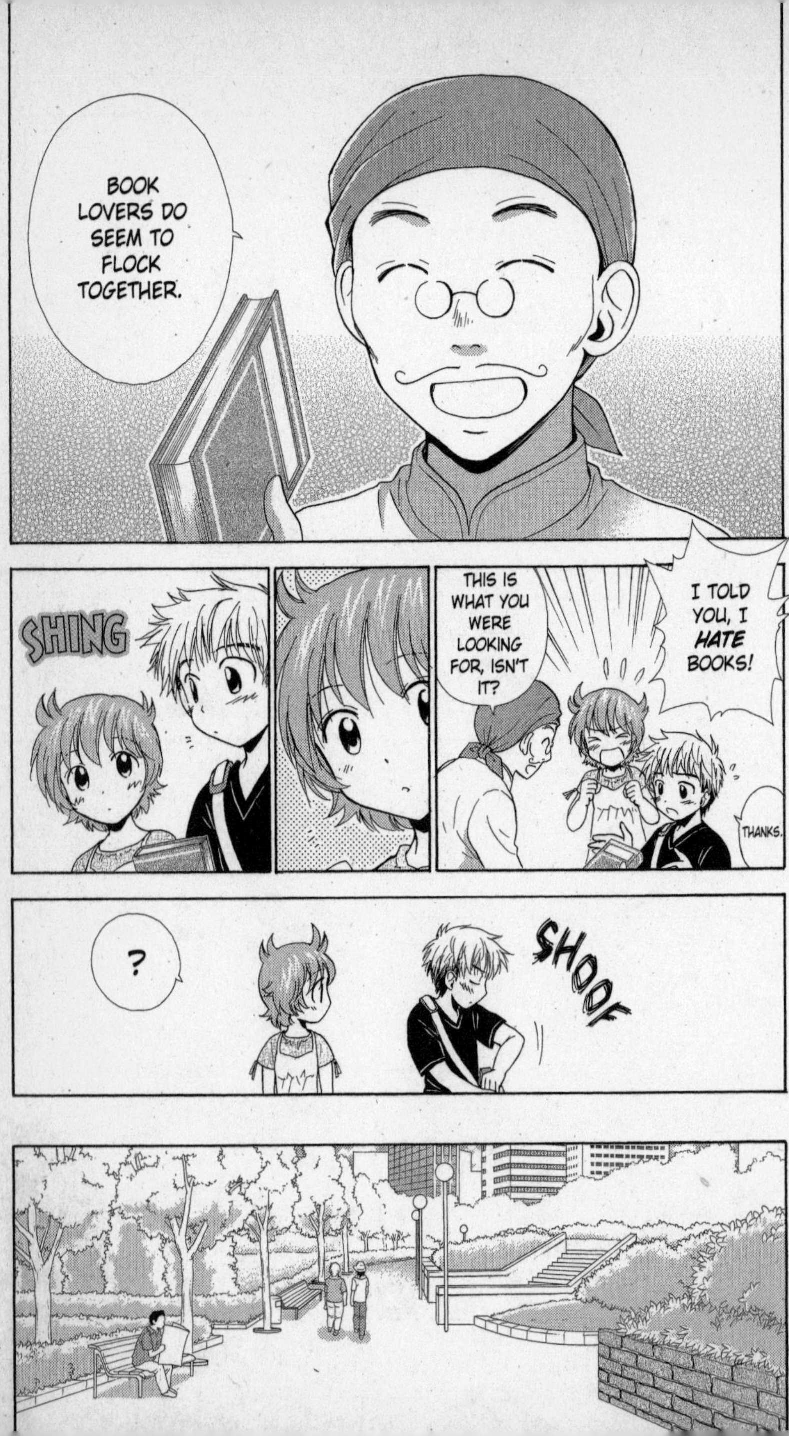
BOOK LOVERS DO SEEM TO FLOCK TOGETHER.
I TOLD YOU, I HATE BOOKS!
THIS IS WHAT YOU WERE LOOKING FOR, ISN'T IT?
THANKS.
SHING
SHOOF
?

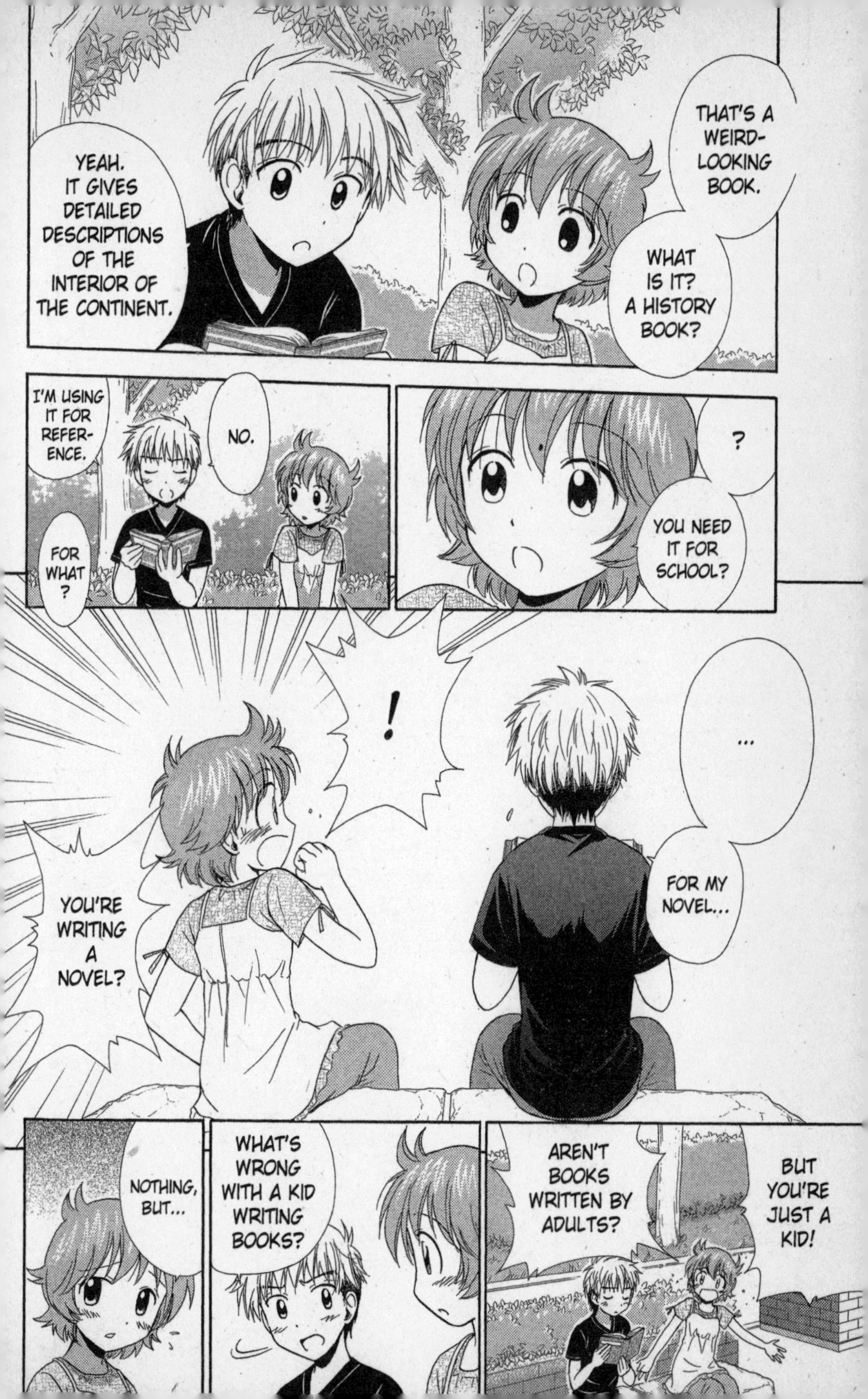
THAT'S A WEIRD-LOOKING BOOK.
WHAT IS IT? A HISTORY BOOK?
YEAH. IT GIVES DETAILED DESCRIPTIONS OF THE INTERIOR OF THE CONTINENT.
?
YOU NEED IT FOR SCHOOL?
NO.
I'M USING IT FOR REFERENCE.
FOR WHAT?
...
FOR MY NOVEL...
!
YOU'RE WRITING A NOVEL?
BUT YOU'RE JUST A KID!
AREN'T BOOKS WRITTEN BY ADULTS?
WHAT'S WRONG WITH A KID WRITING BOOKS?
NOTHING, BUT...

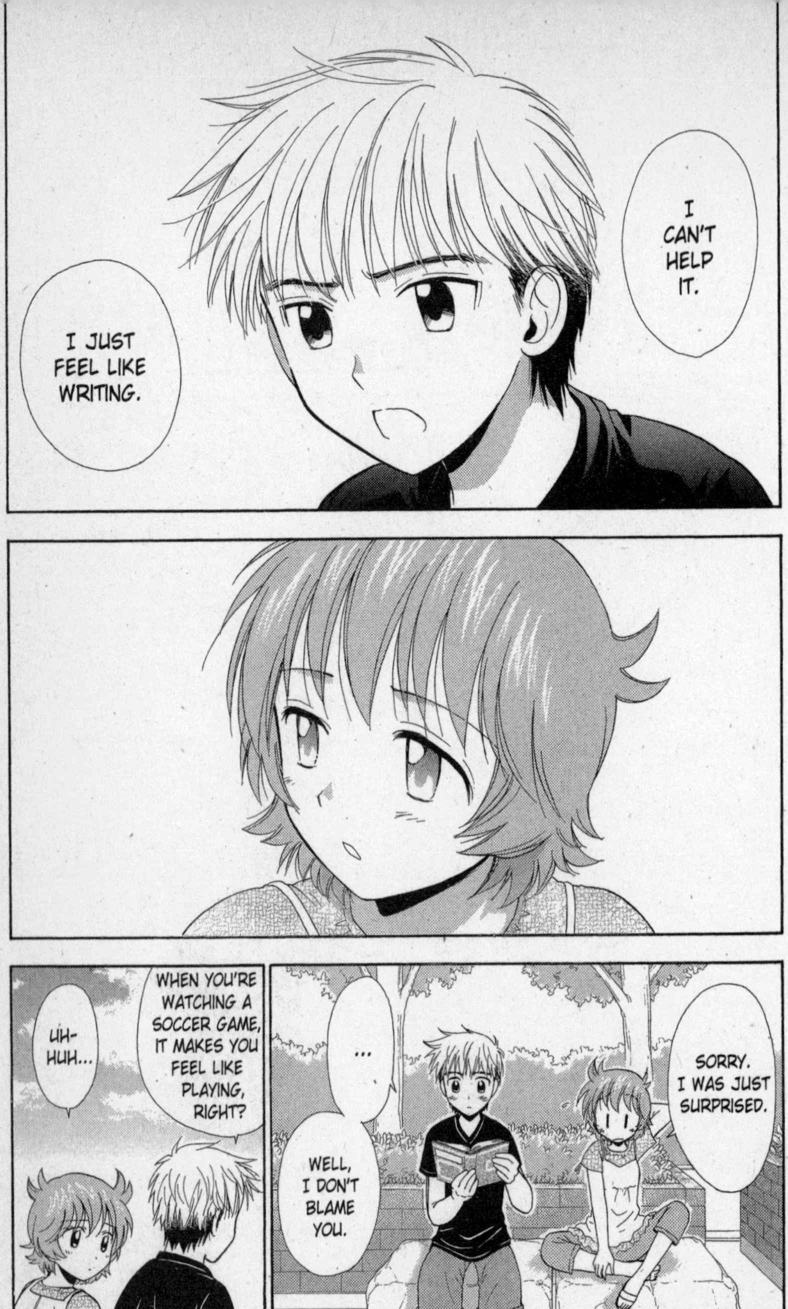
I CAN'T HELP IT.
I JUST FEEL LIKE WRITING.
SORRY. I WAS JUST SURPRISED.
...
WELL, I DON'T BLAME YOU.
WHEN YOU'RE WATCHING A SOCCER GAME, IT MAKES YOU FEEL LIKE PLAYING, RIGHT?
UH-HUH...

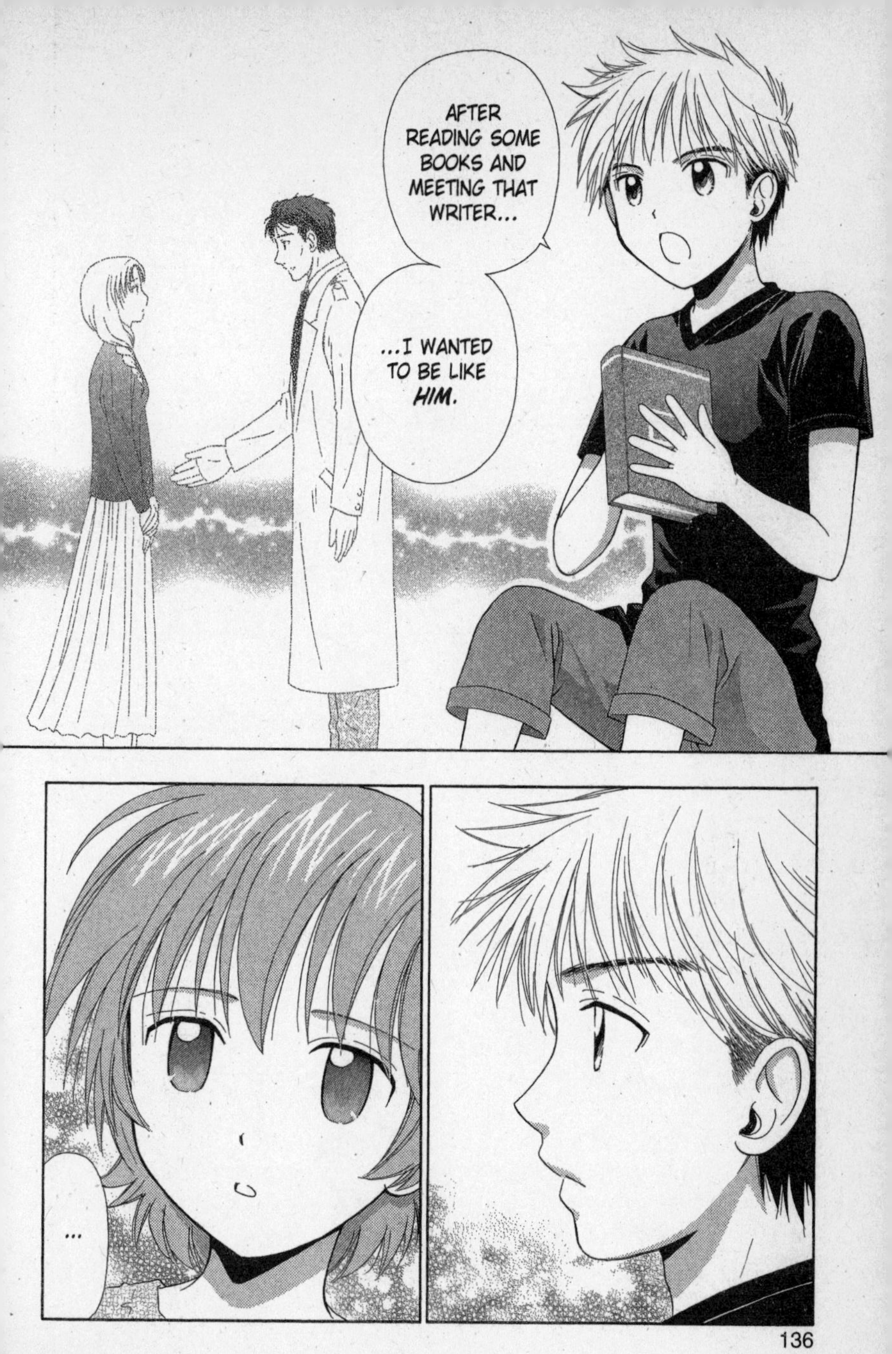

AFTER READING SOME BOOKS AND MEETING THAT WRITER...
...I WANTED TO BE LIKE *HIM*.
...

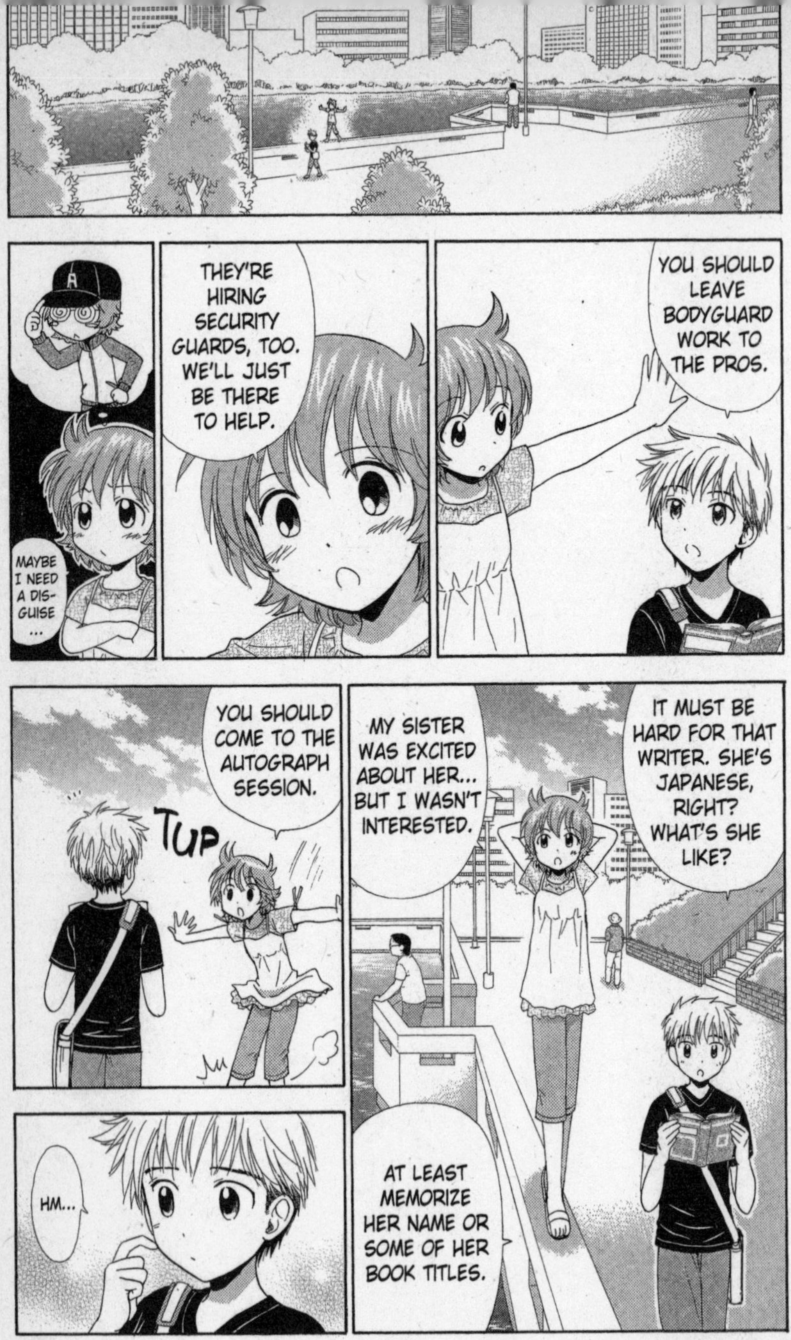
YOU SHOULD LEAVE BODYGUARD WORK TO THE PROS.
THEY'RE HIRING SECURITY GUARDS, TOO. WE'LL JUST BE THERE TO HELP.
MAYBE I NEED A DISGUISE ...
IT MUST BE HARD FOR THAT WRITER. SHE'S JAPANESE, RIGHT? WHAT'S SHE LIKE?
MY SISTER WAS EXCITED ABOUT HER... BUT I WASN'T INTERESTED.
AT LEAST MEMORIZE HER NAME OR SOME OF HER BOOK TITLES.
YOU SHOULD COME TO THE AUTOGRAPH SESSION.
TUP
...
HM...

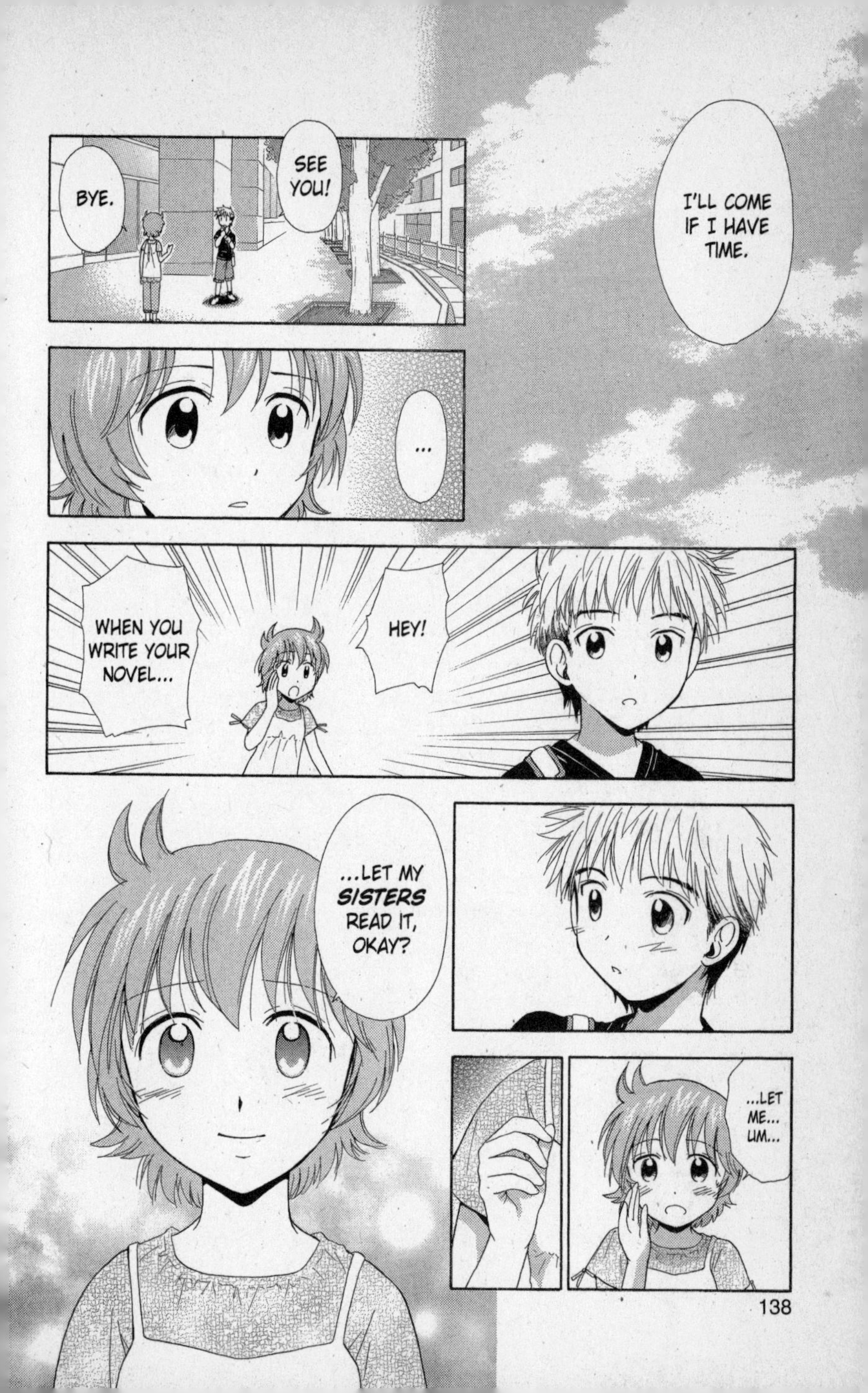
I'LL COME IF I HAVE TIME.
SEE YOU!
BYE.
...
HEY!
WHEN YOU WRITE YOUR NOVEL...
...LET ME... UM...
...LET MY SISTERS READ IT, OKAY?

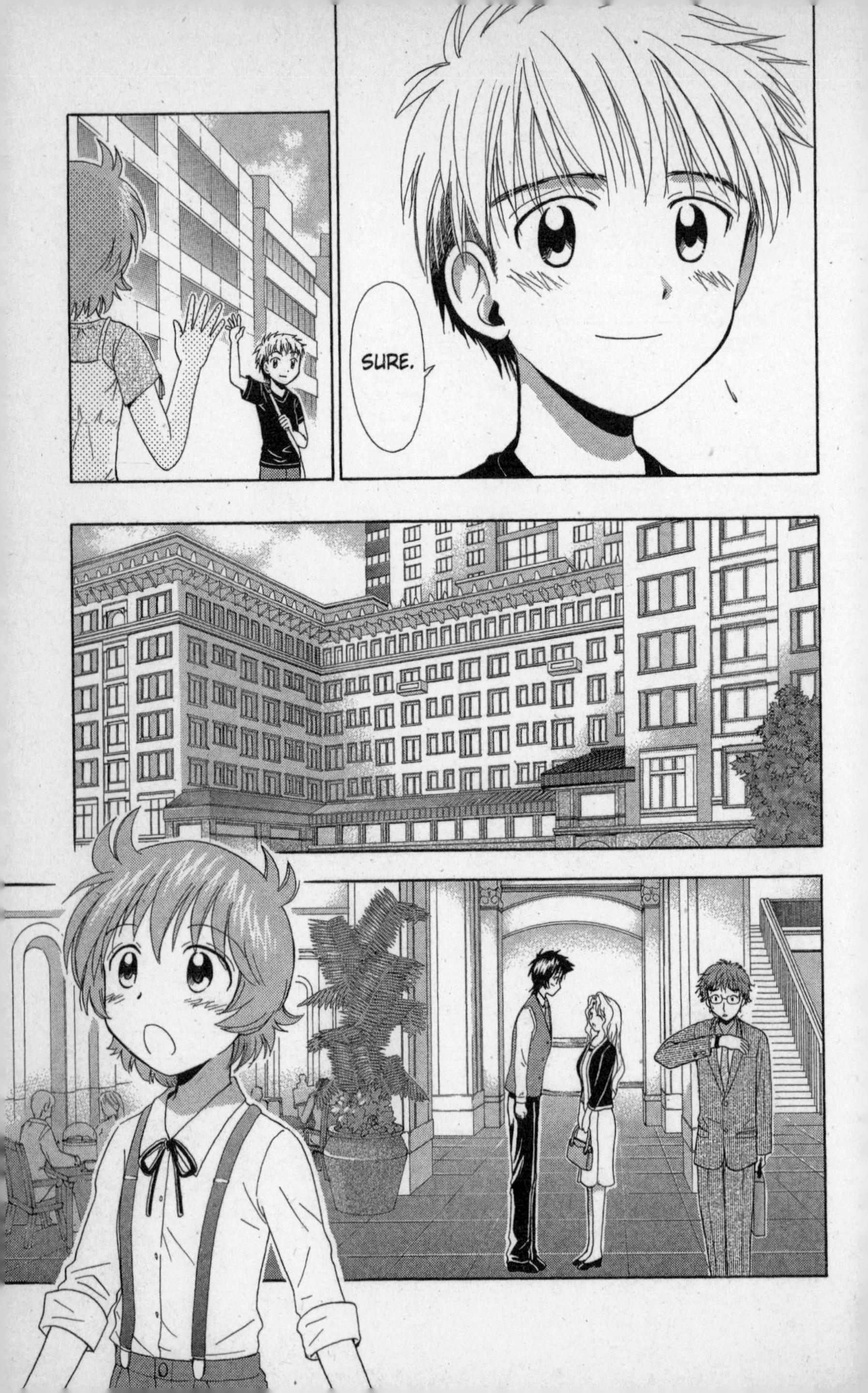
SURE.

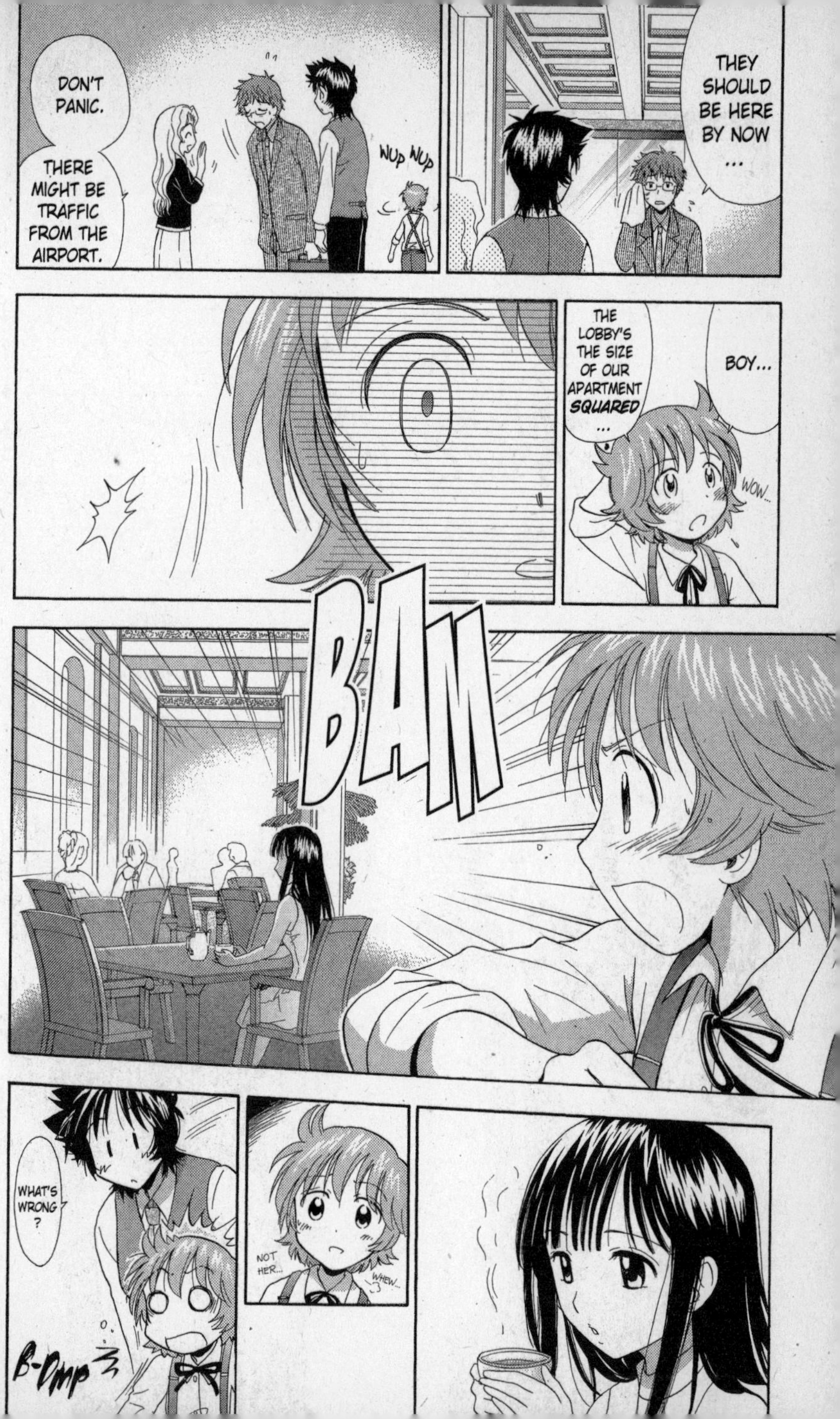
THEY SHOULD BE HERE BY NOW ...
DON'T PANIC.
THERE MIGHT BE TRAFFIC FROM THE AIRPORT.
WUP WUP
BOY...
THE LOBBY'S THE SIZE OF OUR APARTMENT SQUARED ...
WOW...
BAM
NOT HER...
WHEW...
WHAT'S WRONG ?
B-DMP

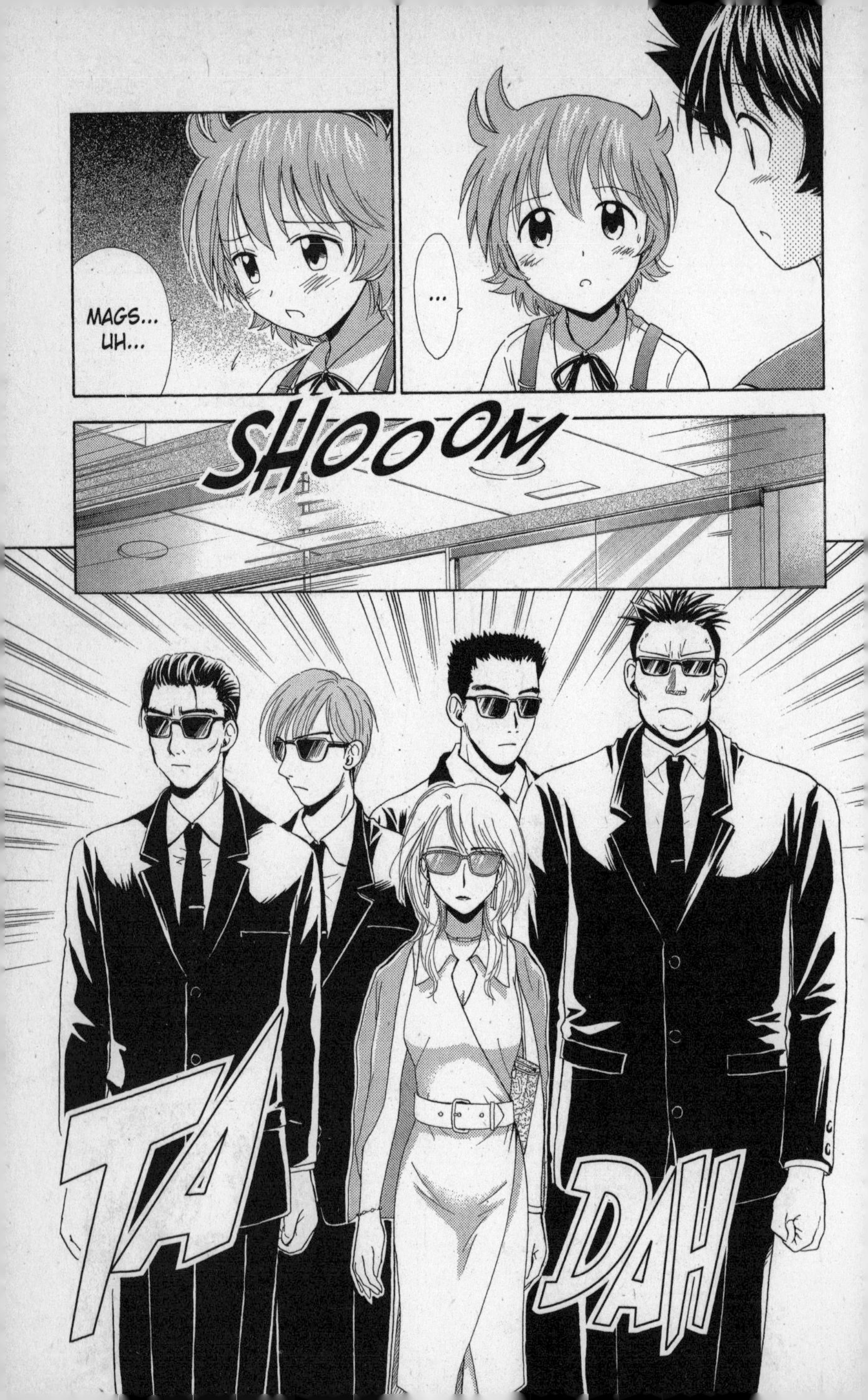
...
MAGS... UH...
SHOOOM
TA
DAH

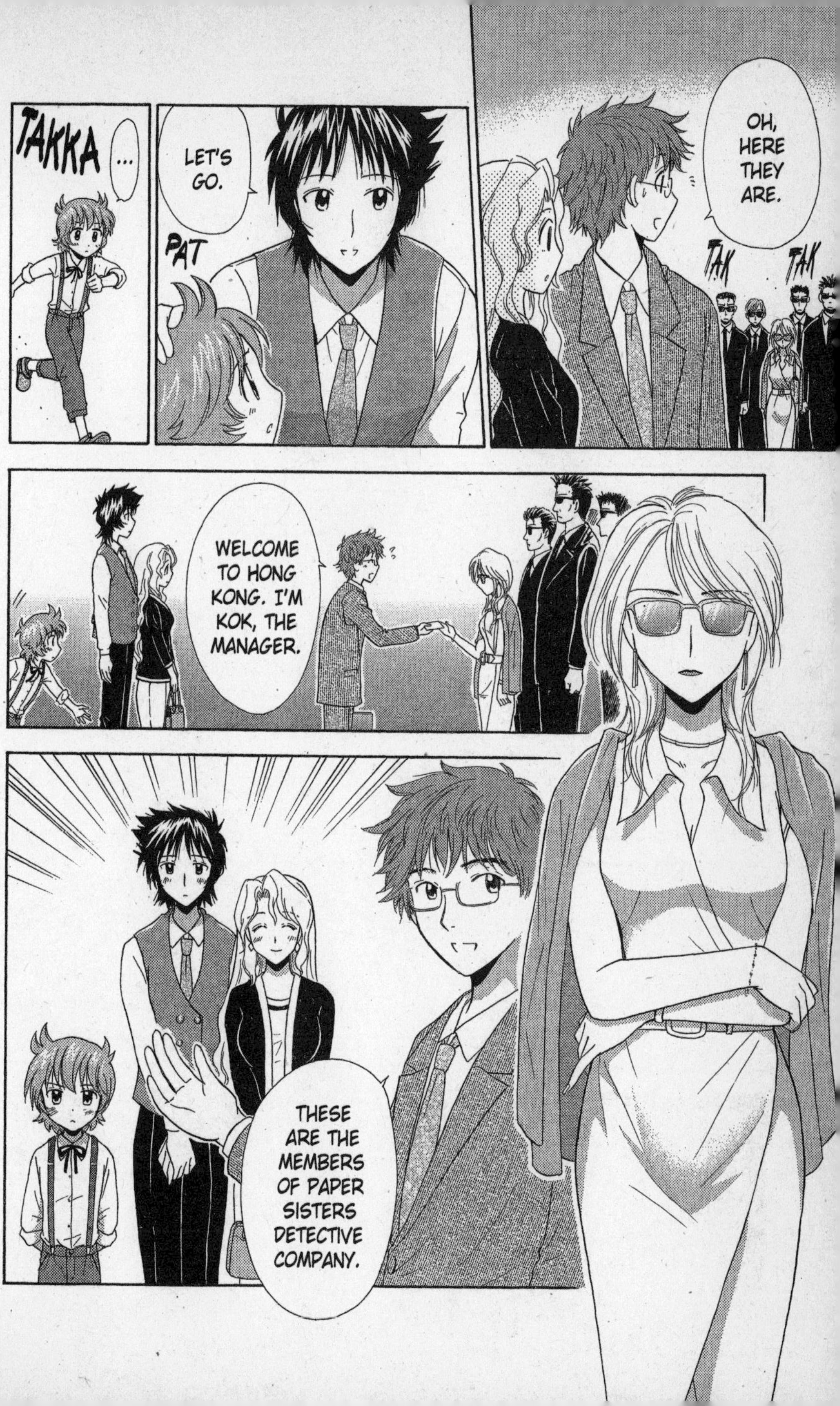
OH, HERE THEY ARE.
TAK
TAK
LET'S GO.
PAT
TAKKA
...
WELCOME TO HONG KONG. I'M KOK, THE MANAGER.
THESE ARE THE MEMBERS OF PAPER SISTERS DETECTIVE COMPANY.

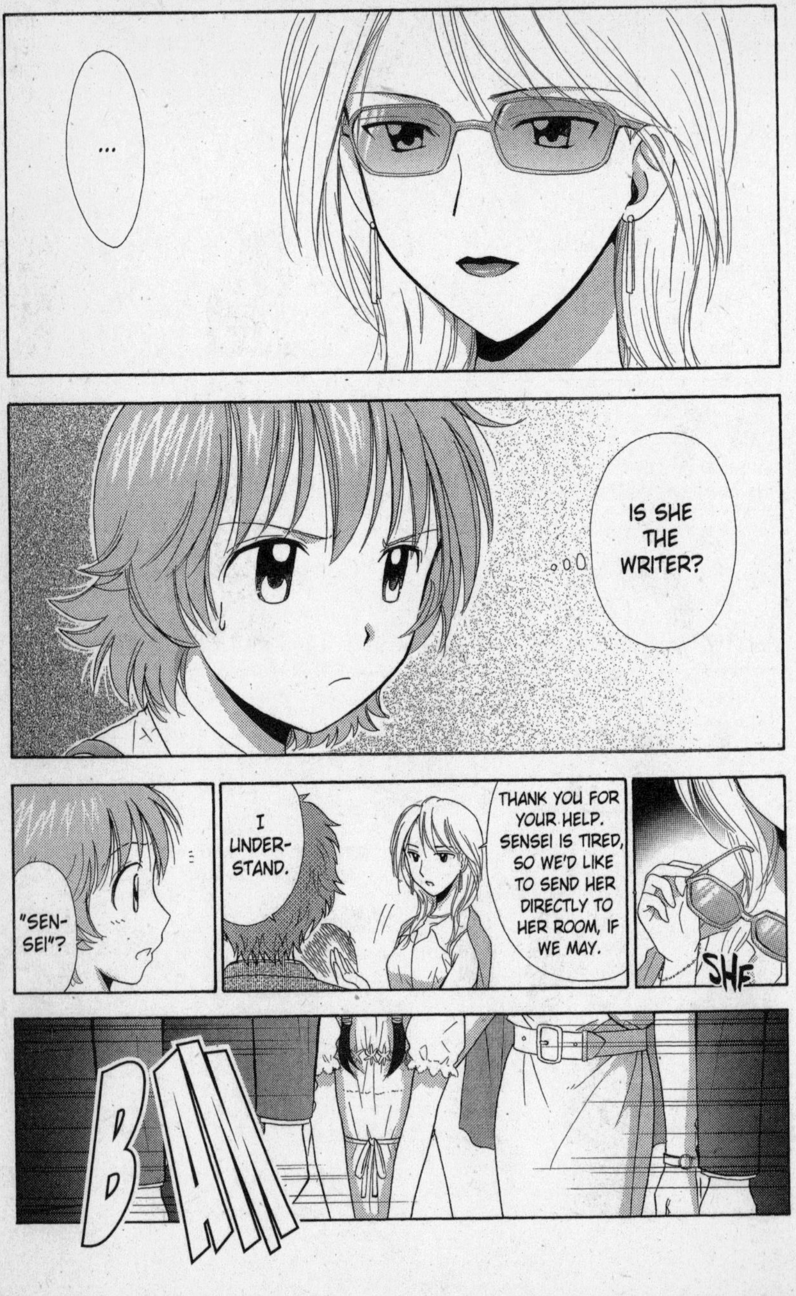
...
IS SHE THE WRITER?
SHF
THANK YOU FOR YOUR HELP. SENSEI IS TIRED, SO WE'D LIKE TO SEND HER DIRECTLY TO HER ROOM, IF WE MAY.
I UNDERSTAND.
"SEN-SEI"?
BAM

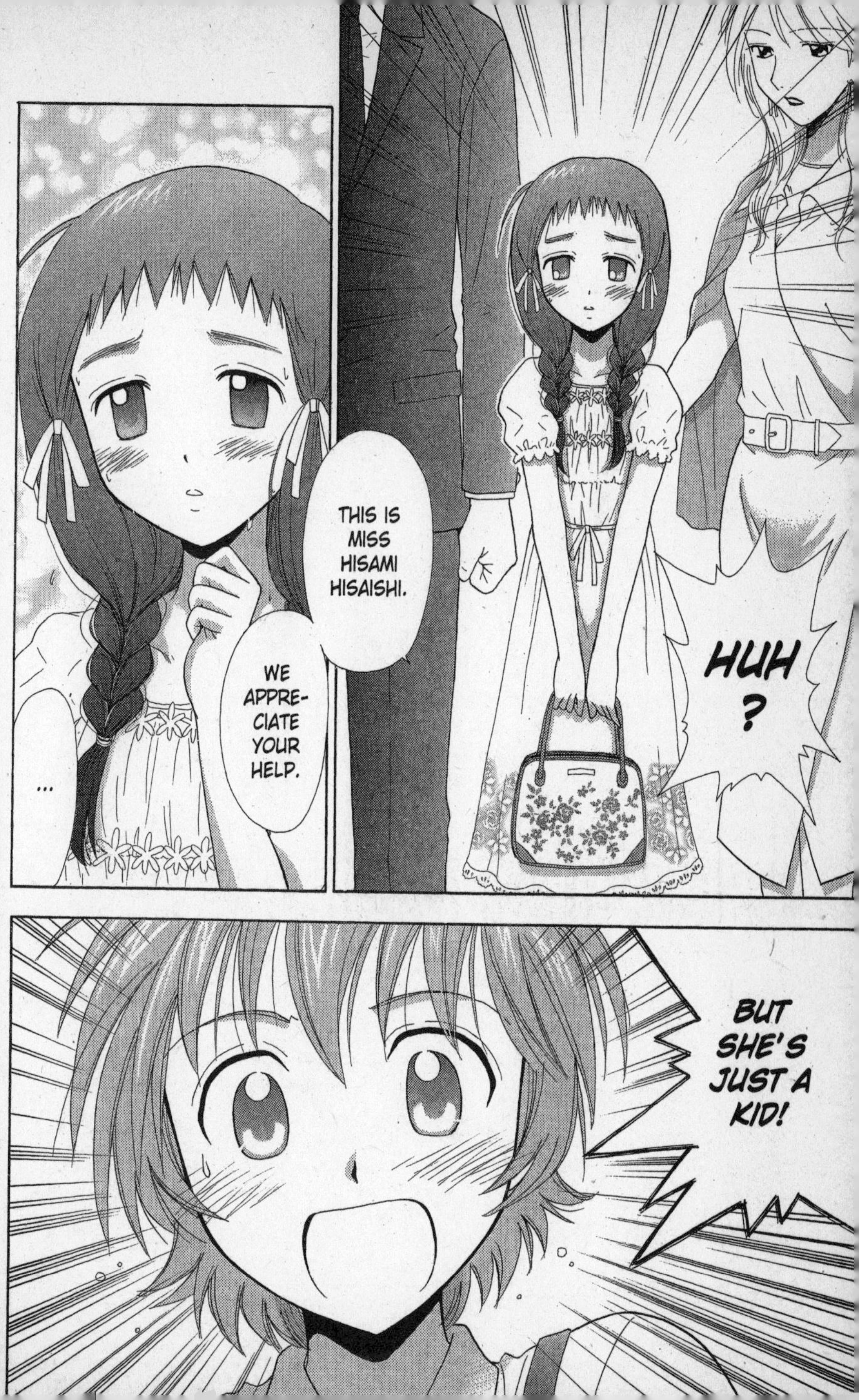
HUH ?
THIS IS MISS HISAMI HISAISHI.
WE APPRE-CIATE YOUR HELP.
...
BUT SHE'S JUST A KID!

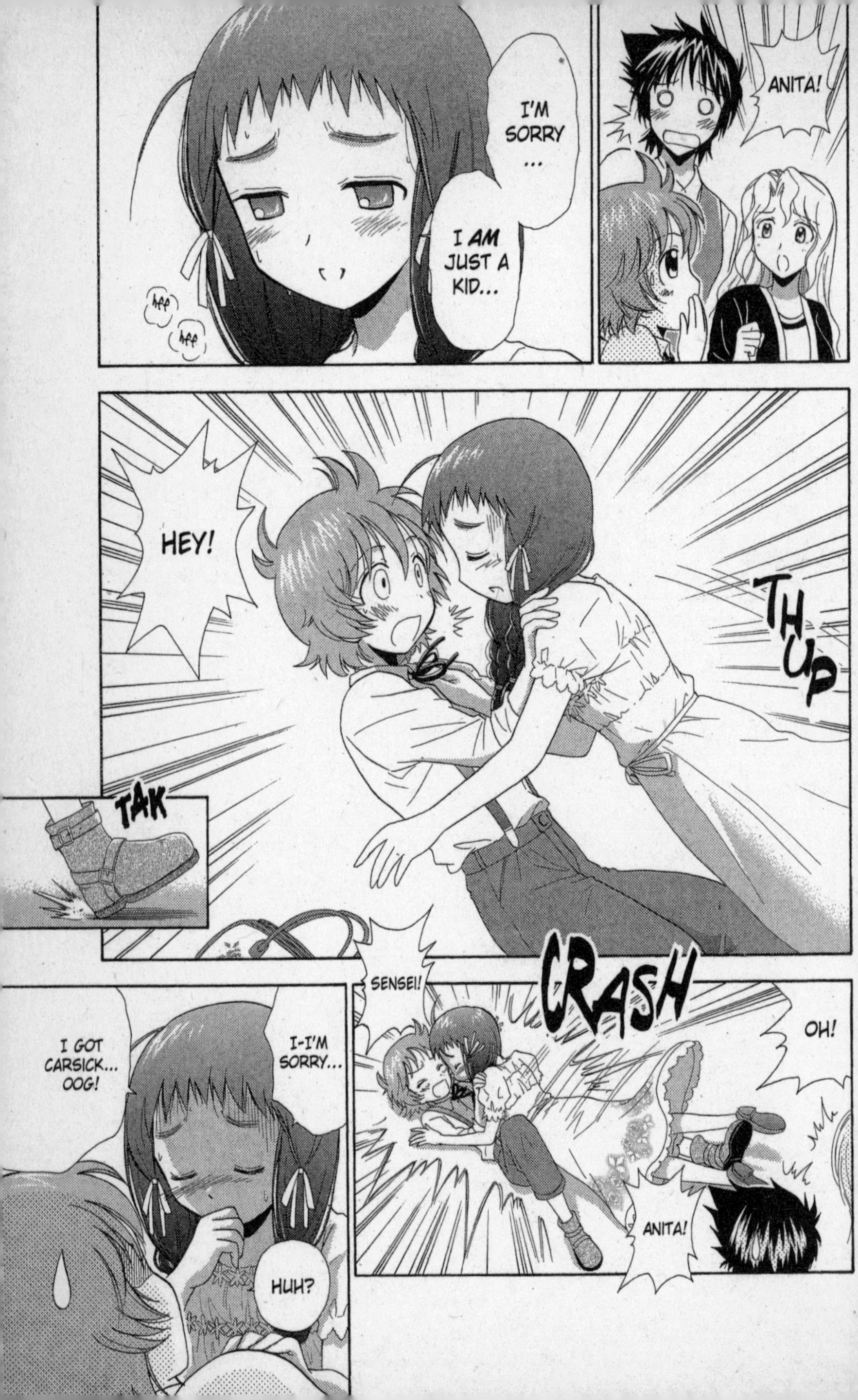
ANITA!
I'M SORRY ...
I AM JUST A KID...
hff
hff
HEY!
THUP
TAK
SENSEI!
CRASH
OH!
ANITA!
I-I'M SORRY...
I GOT CARSICK... OOG!
HUH?

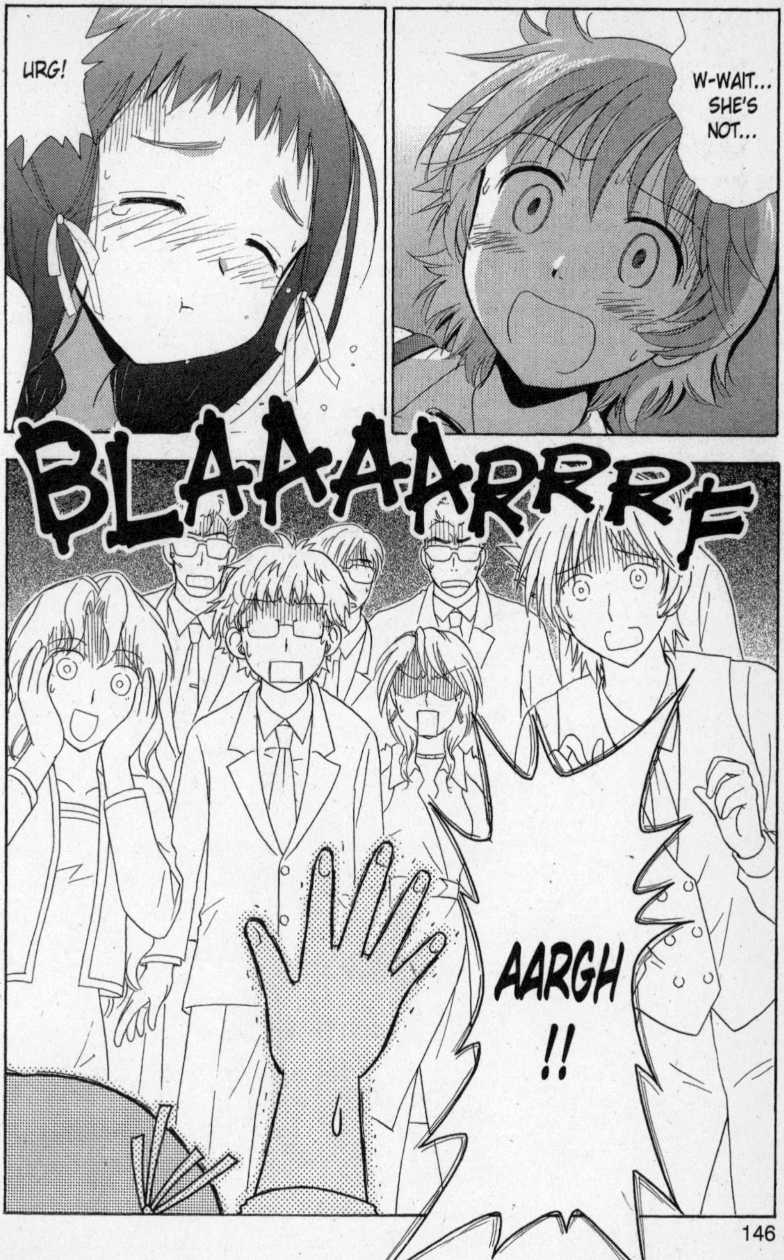
W-WAIT... SHE'S NOT...
URG!
BLAAAARRRF
AARGH !!

CHAPTER 22

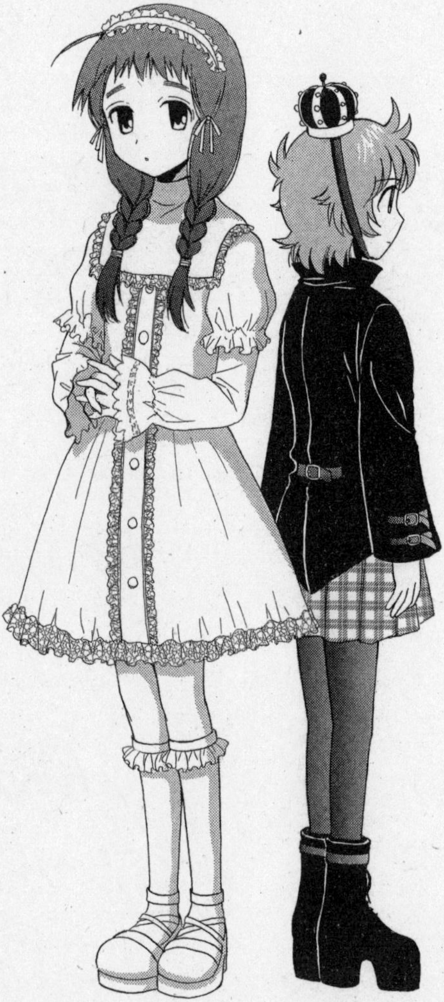

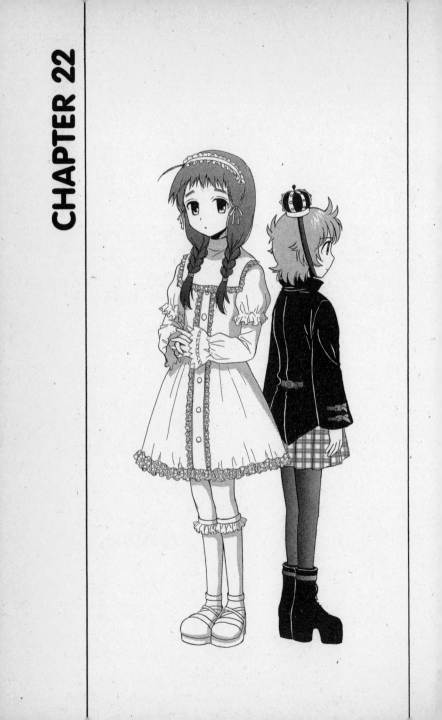

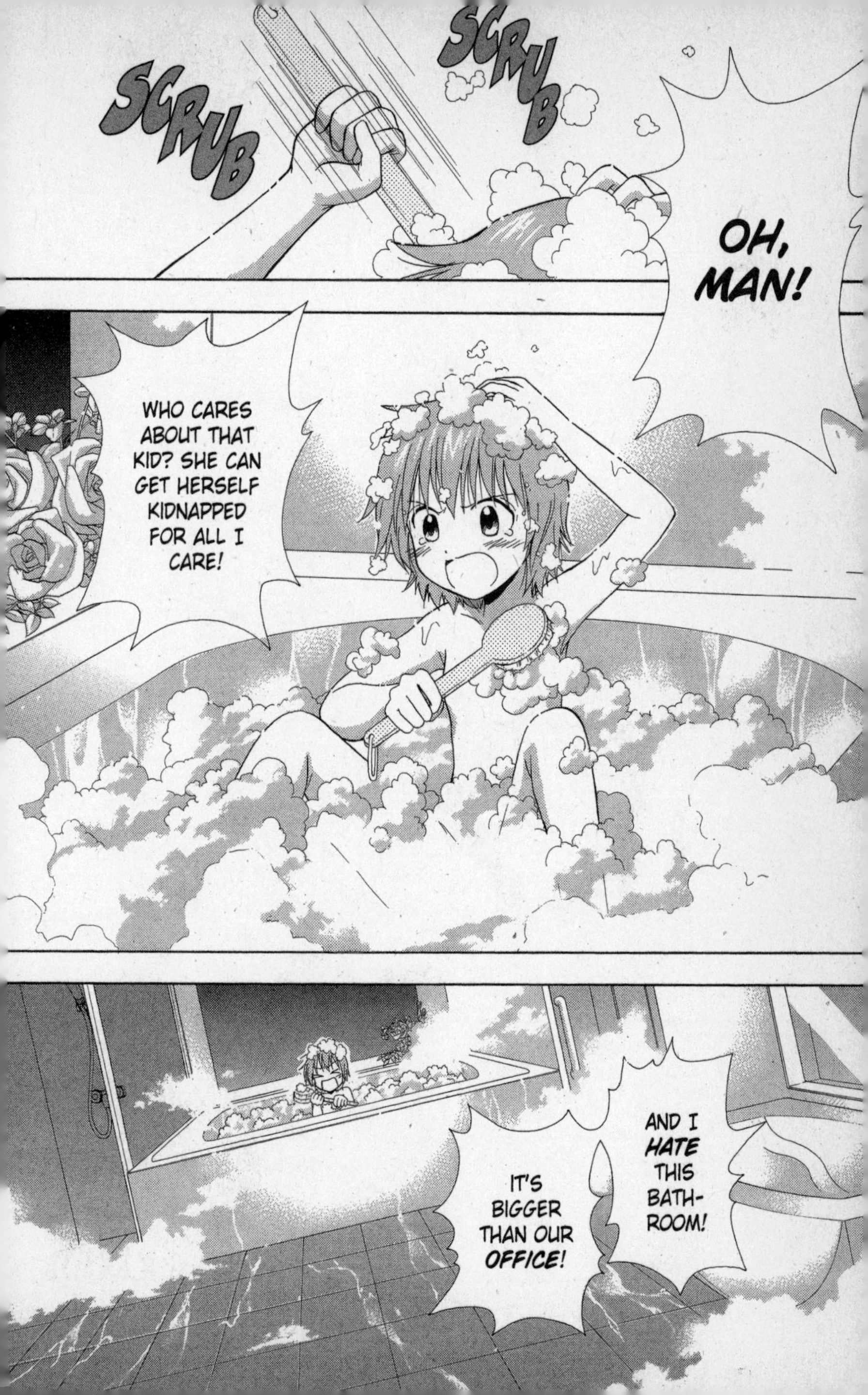
SCRUB
SCRUB
OH, MAN!
WHO CARES ABOUT THAT KID? SHE CAN GET HERSELF KIDNAPPED FOR ALL I CARE!
AND I *HATE* THIS BATH-ROOM!
IT'S BIGGER THAN OUR *OFFICE*!

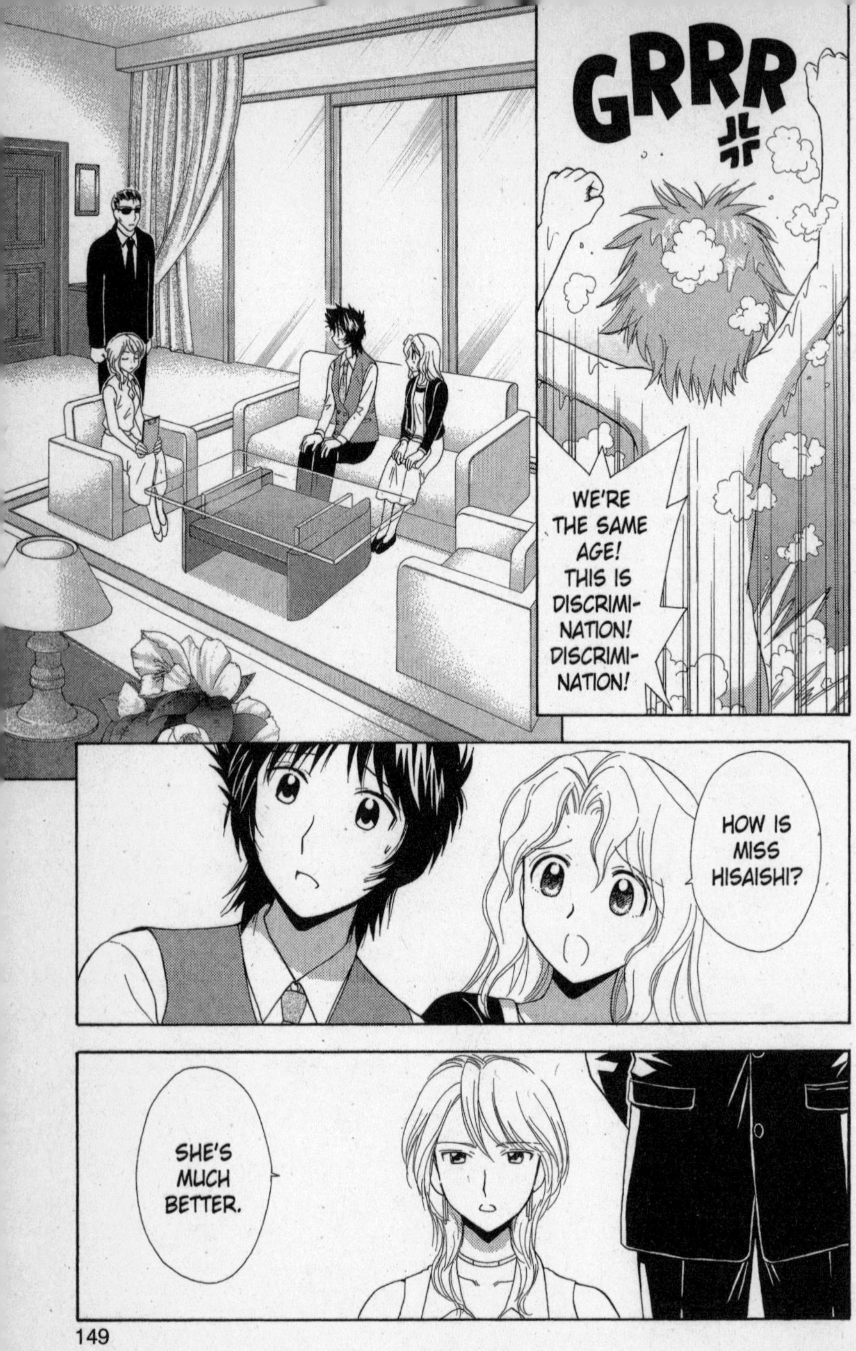
GRRR
WE'RE THE SAME AGE! THIS IS DISCRIMINATION! DISCRIMINATION!
HOW IS MISS HISAISHI?
SHE'S MUCH BETTER.

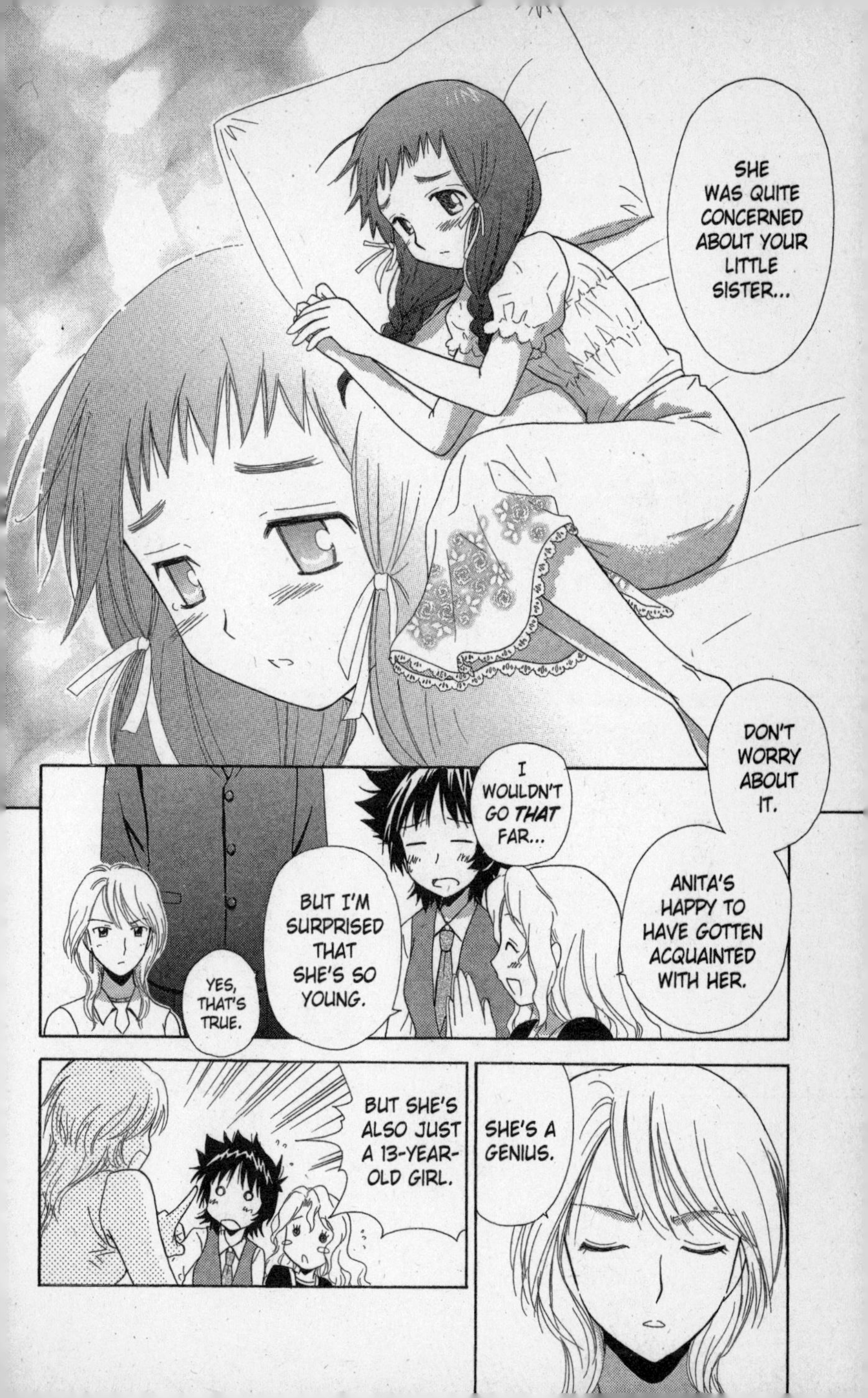
SHE WAS QUITE CONCERNED ABOUT YOUR LITTLE SISTER...
DON'T WORRY ABOUT IT.
ANITA'S HAPPY TO HAVE GOTTEN ACQUAINTED WITH HER.
I WOULDN'T GO *THAT* FAR...
BUT I'M SURPRISED THAT SHE'S SO YOUNG.
YES, THAT'S TRUE.
SHE'S A GENIUS.
BUT SHE'S ALSO JUST A 13-YEAR-OLD GIRL.

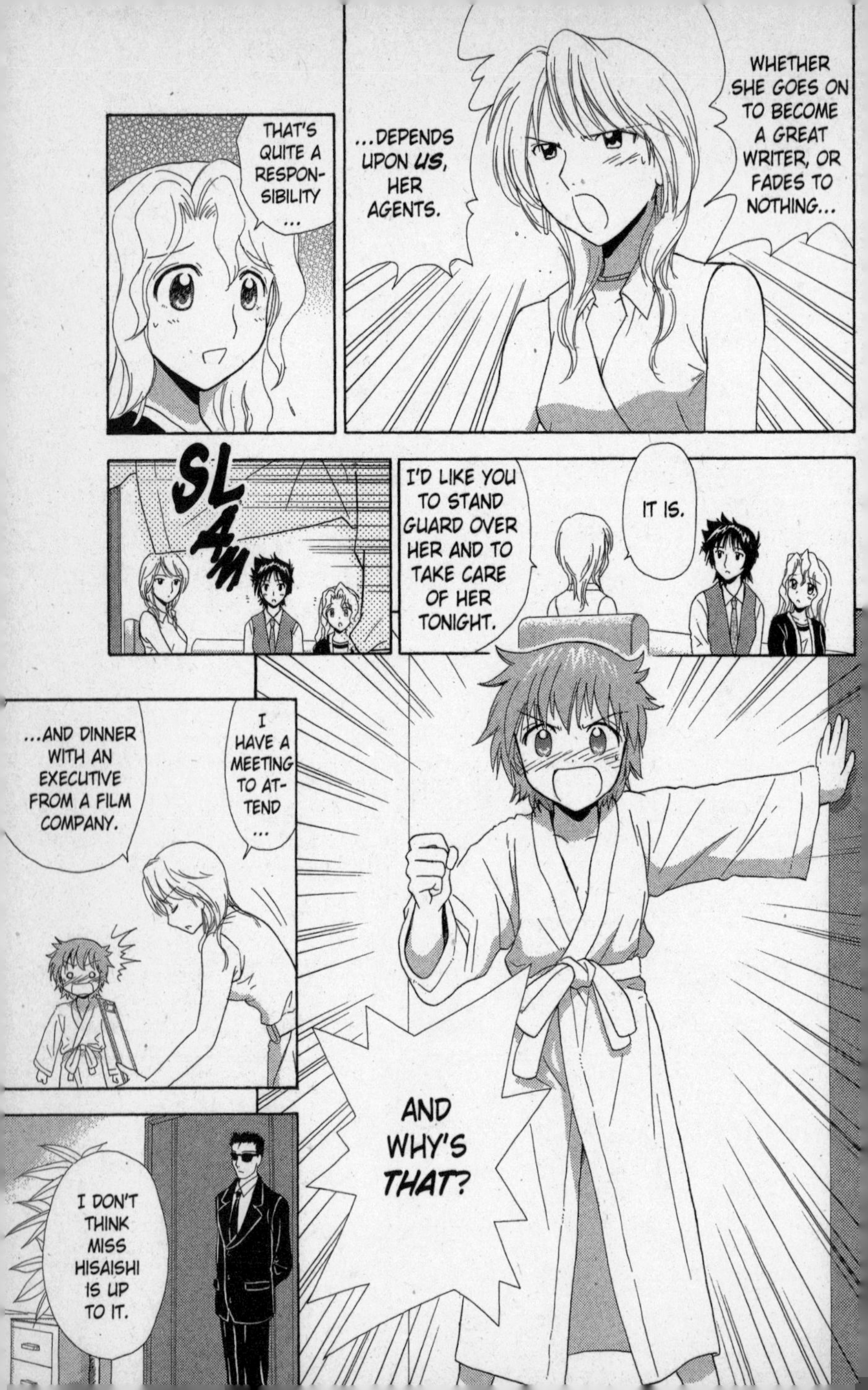
WHETHER SHE GOES ON TO BECOME A GREAT WRITER, OR FADES TO NOTHING...
...DEPENDS UPON *US*, HER AGENTS.
THAT'S QUITE A RESPONSIBILITY ...
IT IS.
I'D LIKE YOU TO STAND GUARD OVER HER AND TO TAKE CARE OF HER TONIGHT.
SLAM
AND WHY'S *THAT*?
I HAVE A MEETING TO ATTEND ...
...AND DINNER WITH AN EXECUTIVE FROM A FILM COMPANY.
I DON'T THINK MISS HISAISHI IS UP TO IT.

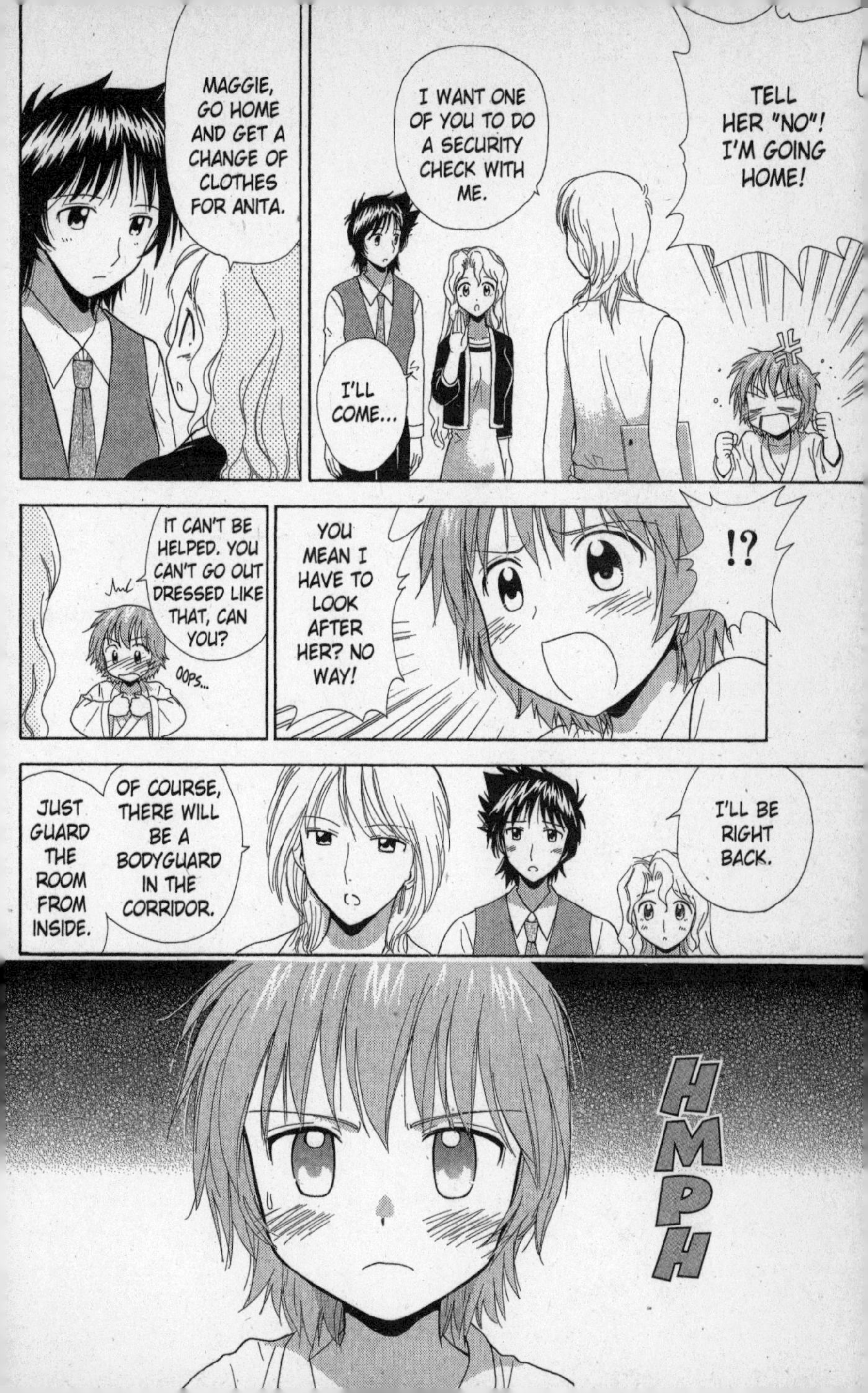

TELL HER "NO"! I'M GOING HOME!
I WANT ONE OF YOU TO DO A SECURITY CHECK WITH ME.
I'LL COME...
MAGGIE, GO HOME AND GET A CHANGE OF CLOTHES FOR ANITA.
!?
YOU MEAN I HAVE TO LOOK AFTER HER? NO WAY!
IT CAN'T BE HELPED. YOU CAN'T GO OUT DRESSED LIKE THAT, CAN YOU?
OOPS...
I'LL BE RIGHT BACK.
OF COURSE, THERE WILL BE A BODYGUARD IN THE CORRIDOR.
JUST GUARD THE ROOM FROM INSIDE.
HMPH

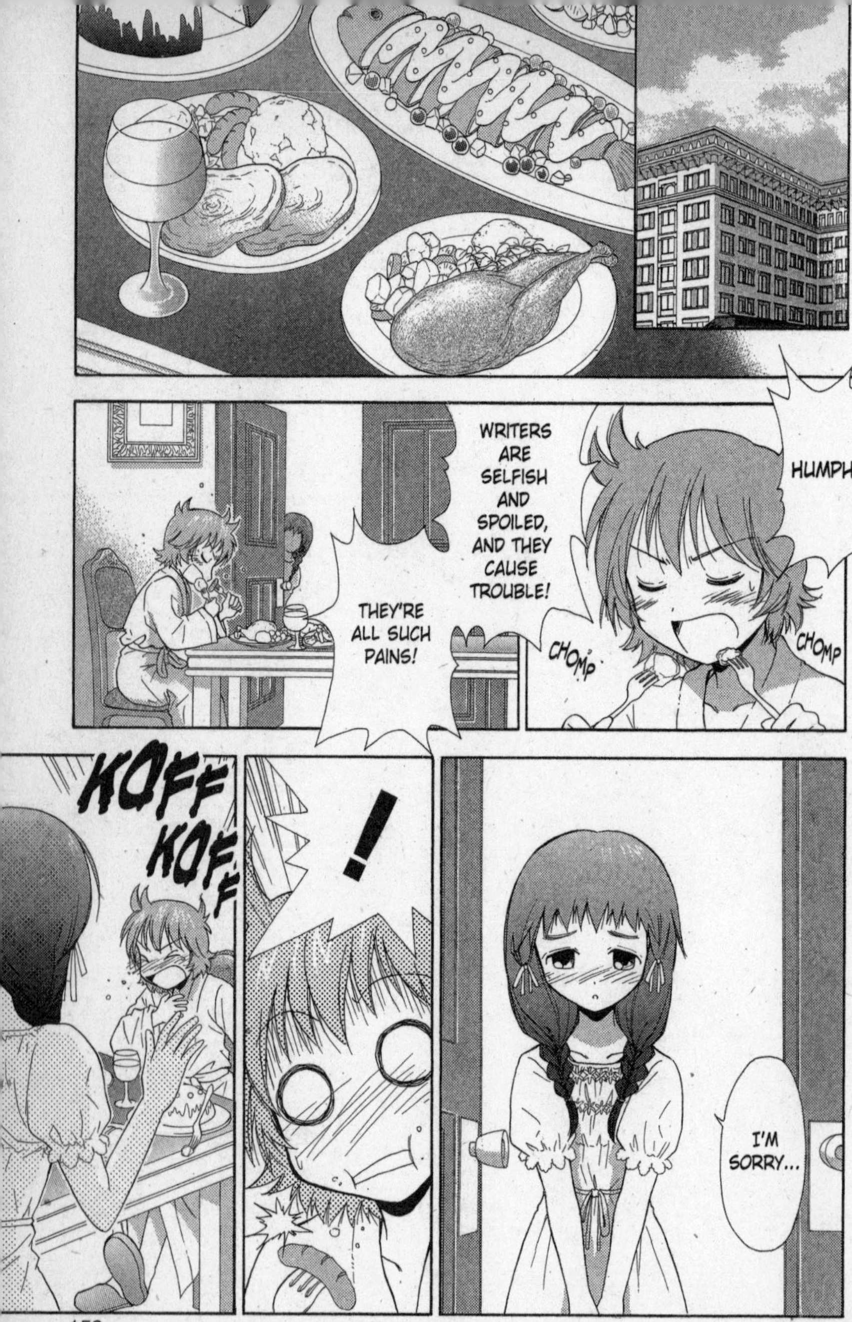
HUMPH!
WRITERS ARE SELFISH AND SPOILED, AND THEY CAUSE TROUBLE!
CHOMP
CHOMP
THEY'RE ALL SUCH PAINS!
I'M SORRY...
!
KOFF KOFF

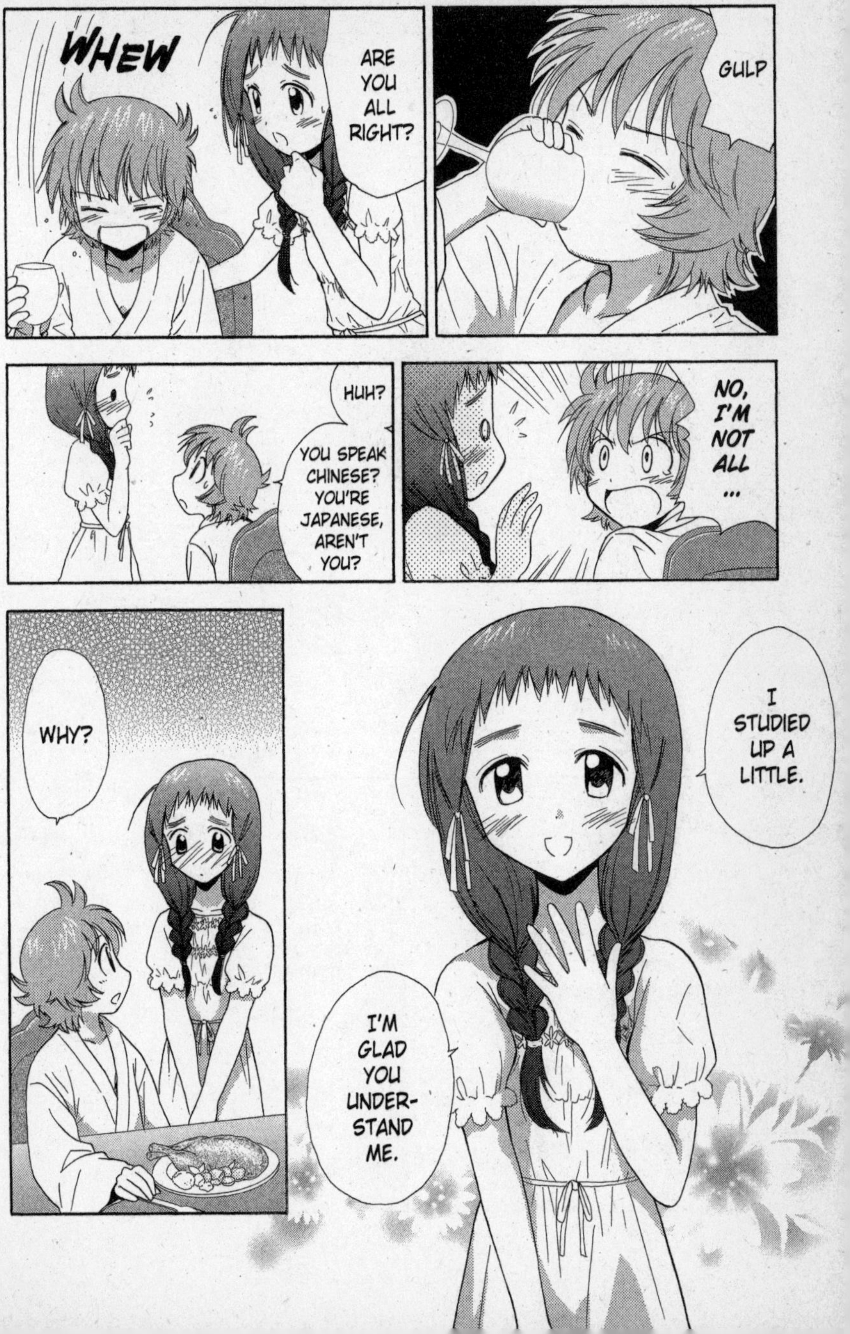
GULP
WHEW
ARE YOU ALL RIGHT?
NO, I'M NOT ALL ...
HUH?
YOU SPEAK CHINESE? YOU'RE JAPANESE, AREN'T YOU?
I STUDIED UP A LITTLE.
I'M GLAD YOU UNDERSTAND ME.
WHY?

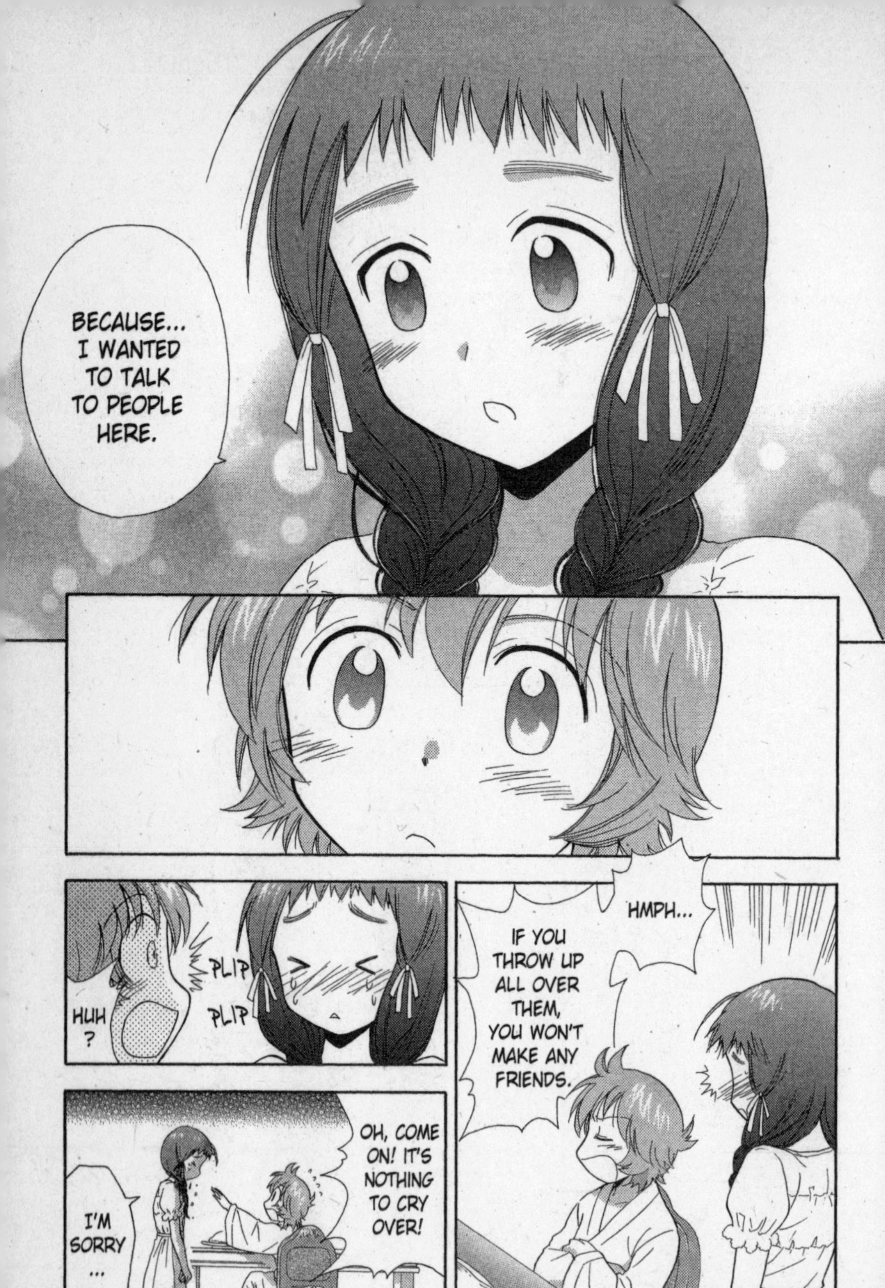
BECAUSE... I WANTED TO TALK TO PEOPLE HERE.
HMPH...
IF YOU THROW UP ALL OVER THEM, YOU WON'T MAKE ANY FRIENDS.
PLIP
PLIP
HUH?
OH, COME ON! IT'S NOTHING TO CRY OVER!
I'M SORRY...

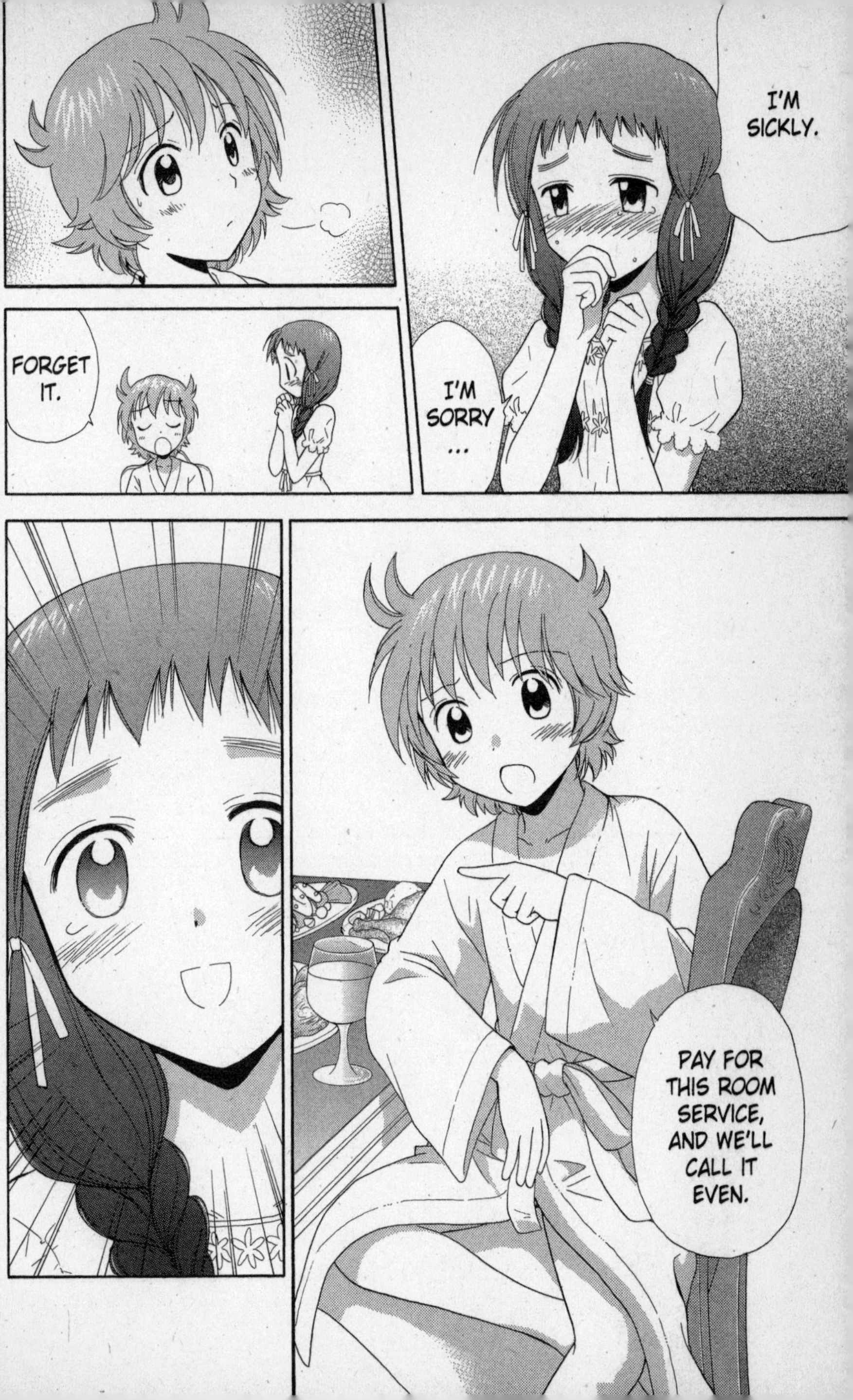
I'M SICKLY.
I'M SORRY …
FORGET IT.
PAY FOR THIS ROOM SERVICE, AND WE'LL CALL IT EVEN.

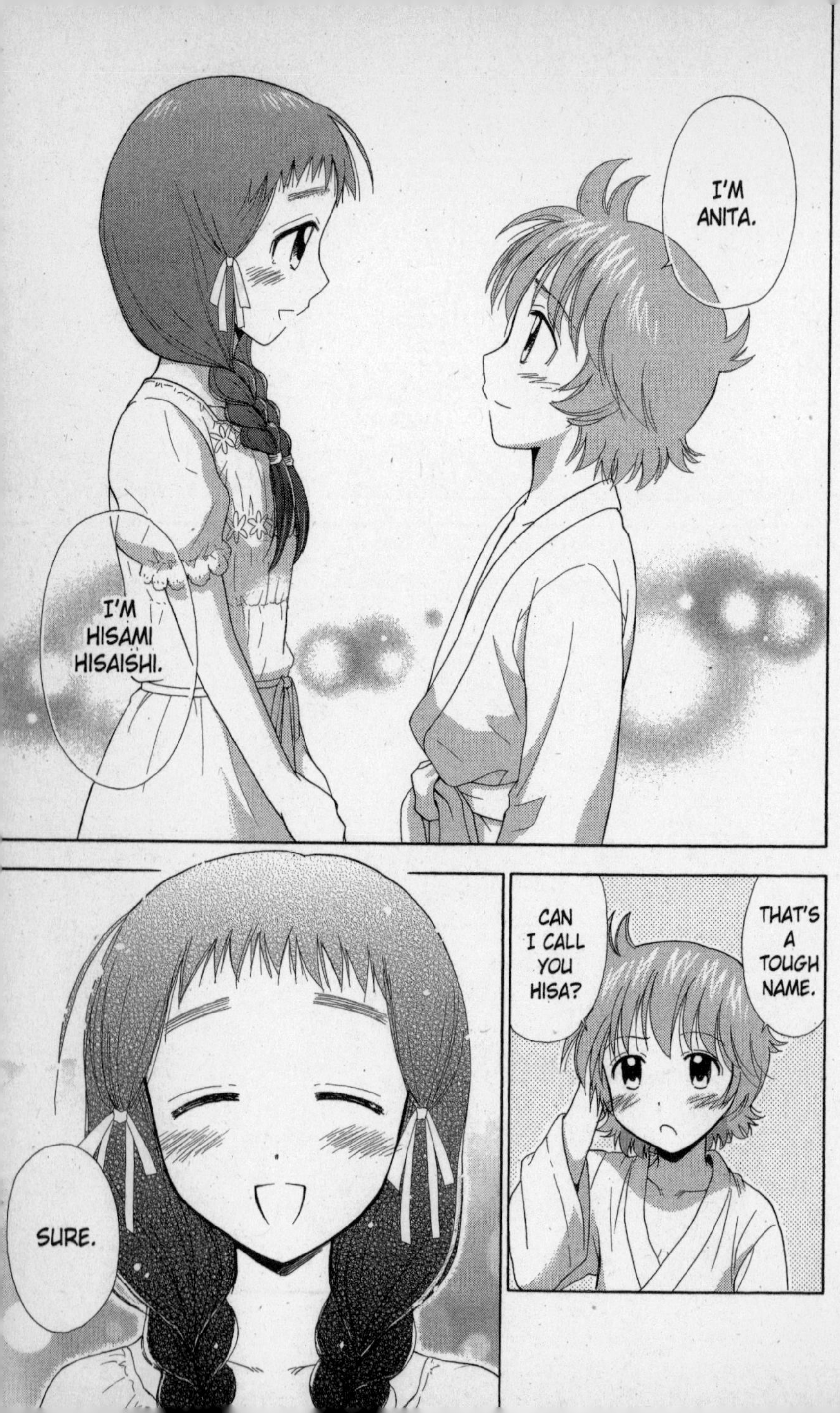

I'M ANITA.
I'M HISAMI HISAISHI.
THAT'S A TOUGH NAME.
CAN I CALL YOU HISA?
SURE.

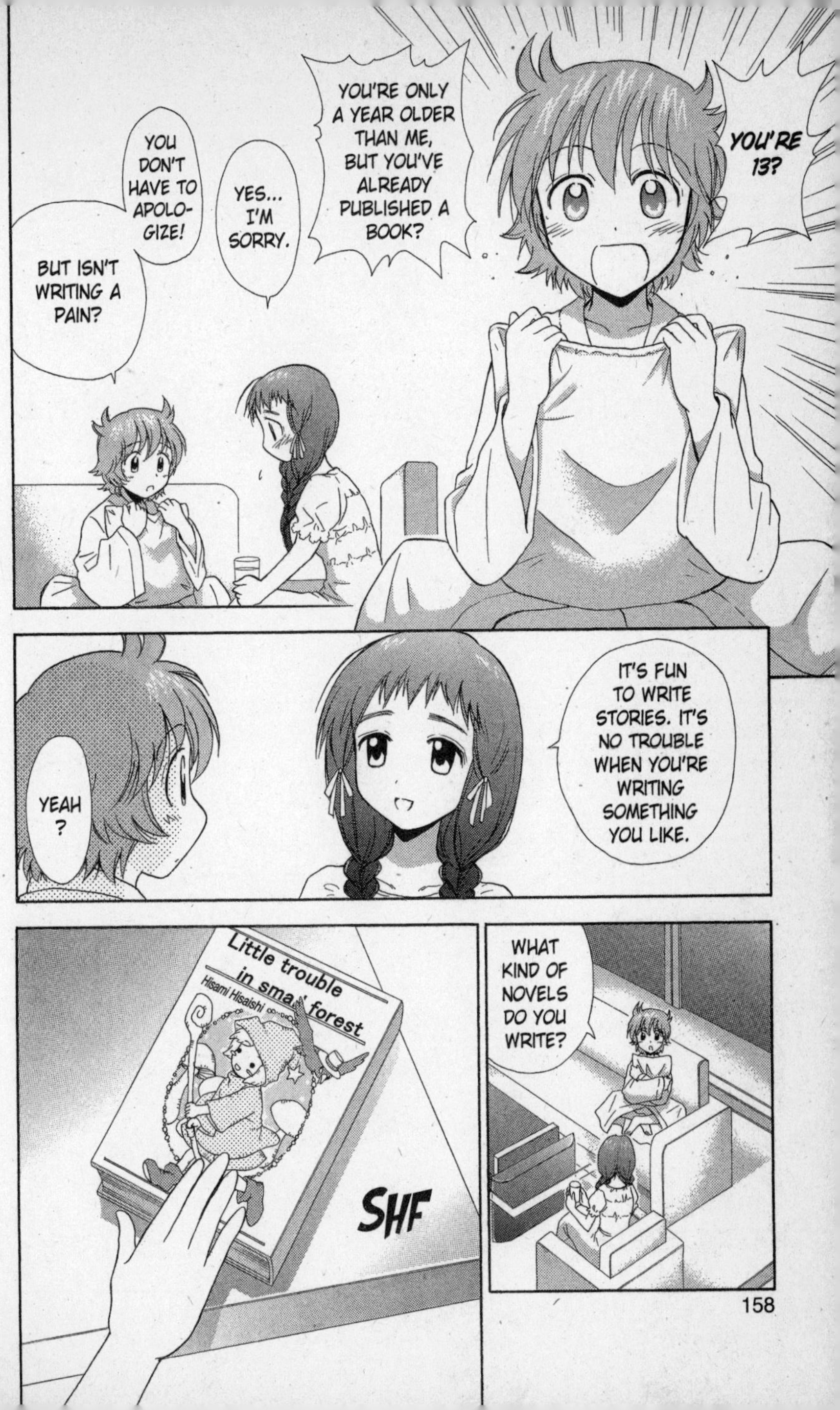
YOU'RE 13?
YOU'RE ONLY A YEAR OLDER THAN ME, BUT YOU'VE ALREADY PUBLISHED A BOOK?
YES... I'M SORRY.
YOU DON'T HAVE TO APOLOGIZE!
BUT ISN'T WRITING A PAIN?
IT'S FUN TO WRITE STORIES. IT'S NO TROUBLE WHEN YOU'RE WRITING SOMETHING YOU LIKE.
YEAH?
WHAT KIND OF NOVELS DO YOU WRITE?
Little trouble
Hisami Hisaishi
SHF

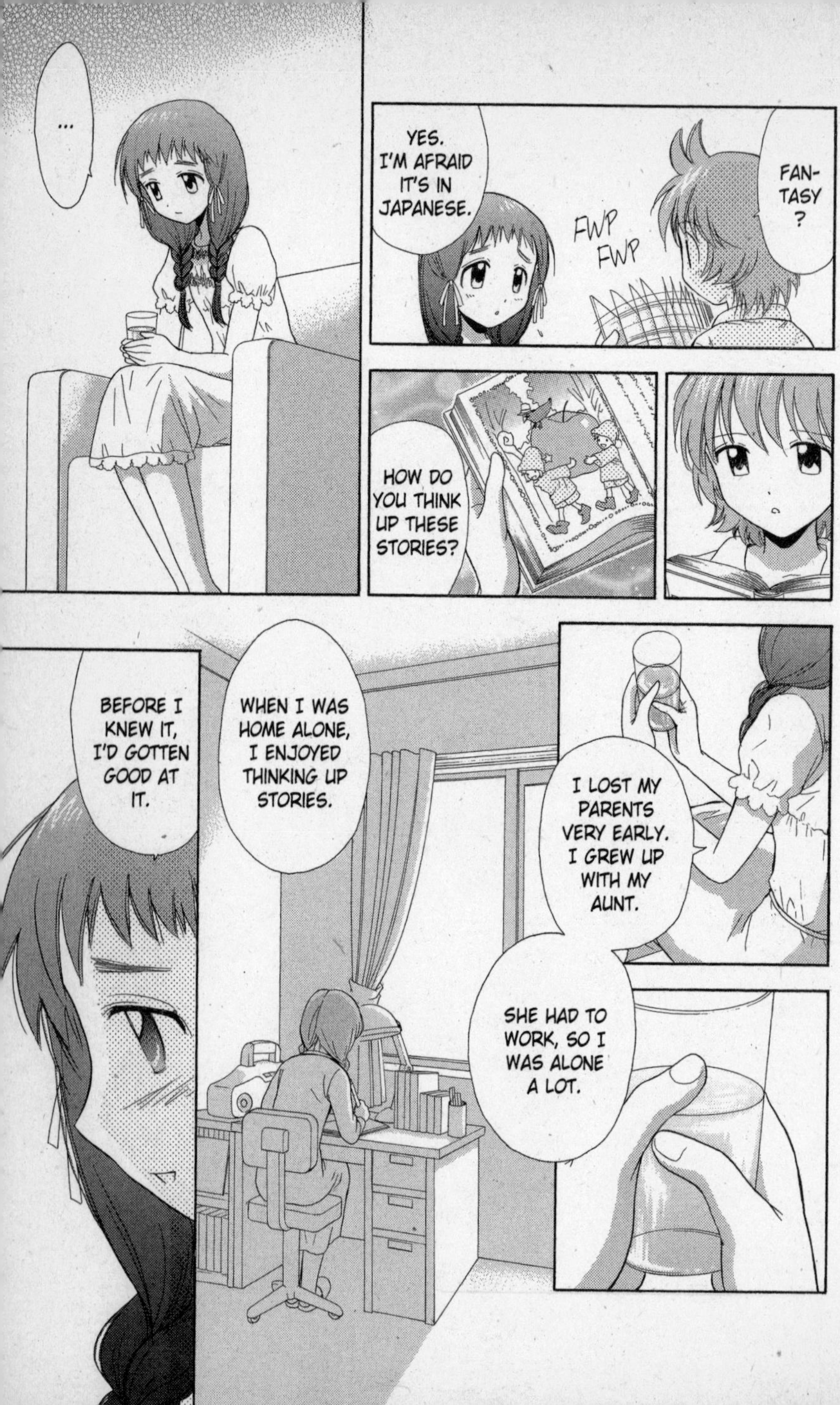
FAN-TASY?
FWP FWP
YES. I'M AFRAID IT'S IN JAPANESE.
HOW DO YOU THINK UP THESE STORIES?
...
I LOST MY PARENTS VERY EARLY. I GREW UP WITH MY AUNT.
SHE HAD TO WORK, SO I WAS ALONE A LOT.
WHEN I WAS HOME ALONE, I ENJOYED THINKING UP STORIES.
BEFORE I KNEW IT, I'D GOTTEN GOOD AT IT.

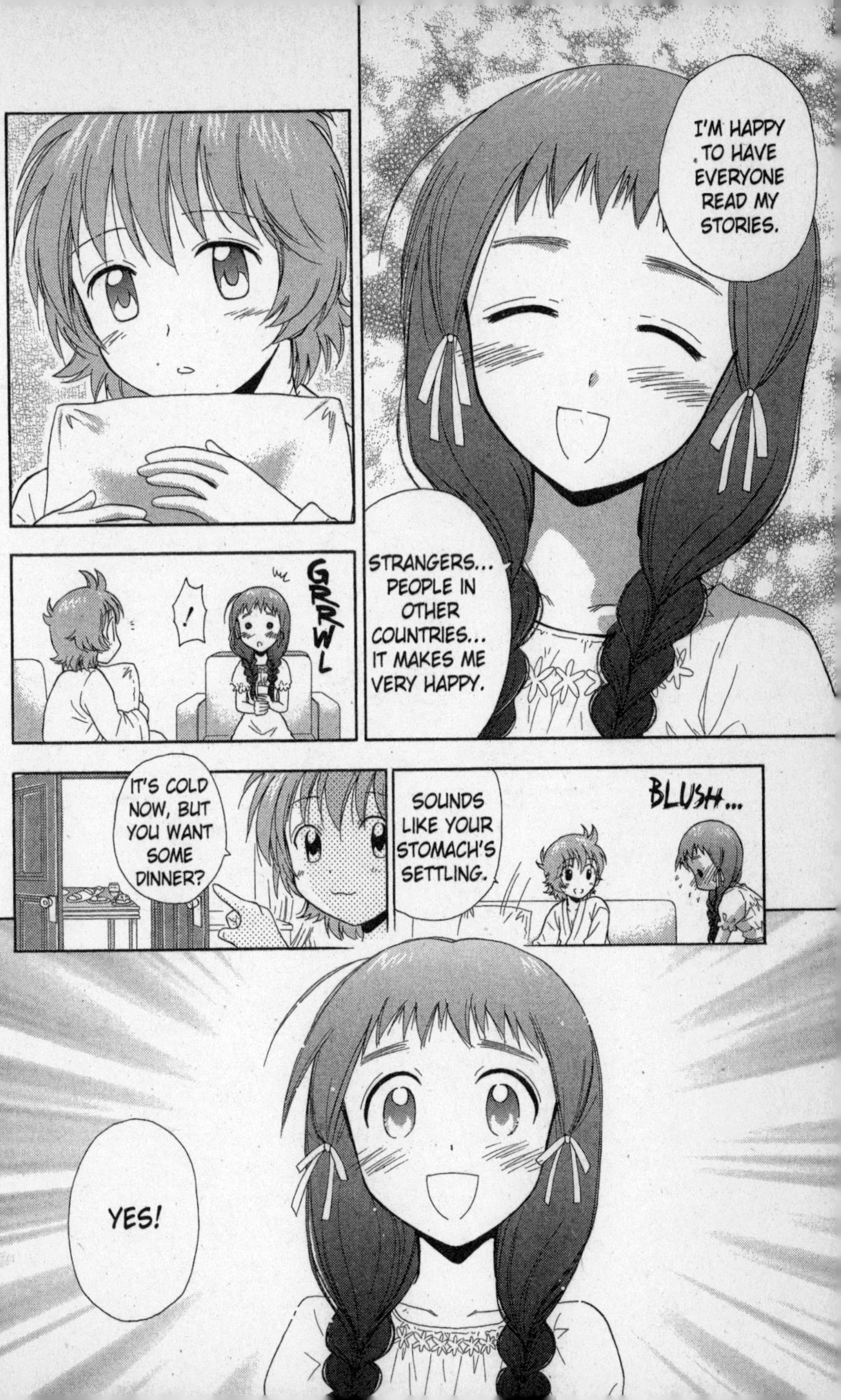
I'M HAPPY TO HAVE EVERYONE READ MY STORIES.
STRANGERS... PEOPLE IN OTHER COUNTRIES... IT MAKES ME VERY HAPPY.
GRRWL
!
SOUNDS LIKE YOUR STOMACH'S SETTLING.
BLUSH...
IT'S COLD NOW, BUT YOU WANT SOME DINNER?
YES!

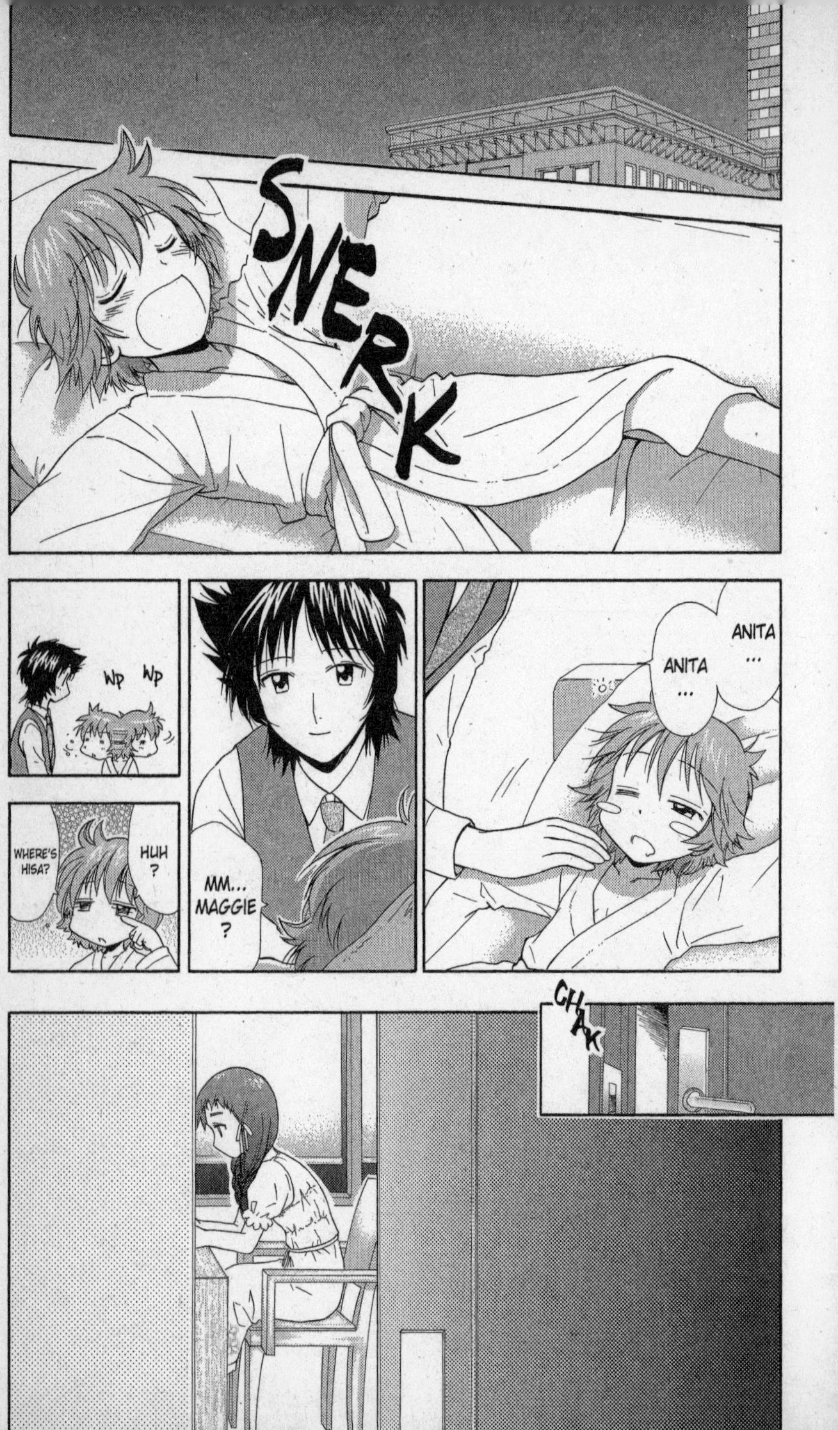
SNERK
ANITA ...
ANITA ...
MM... MAGGIE ?
WP WP
HUH ?
WHERE'S HISA?
CHAK

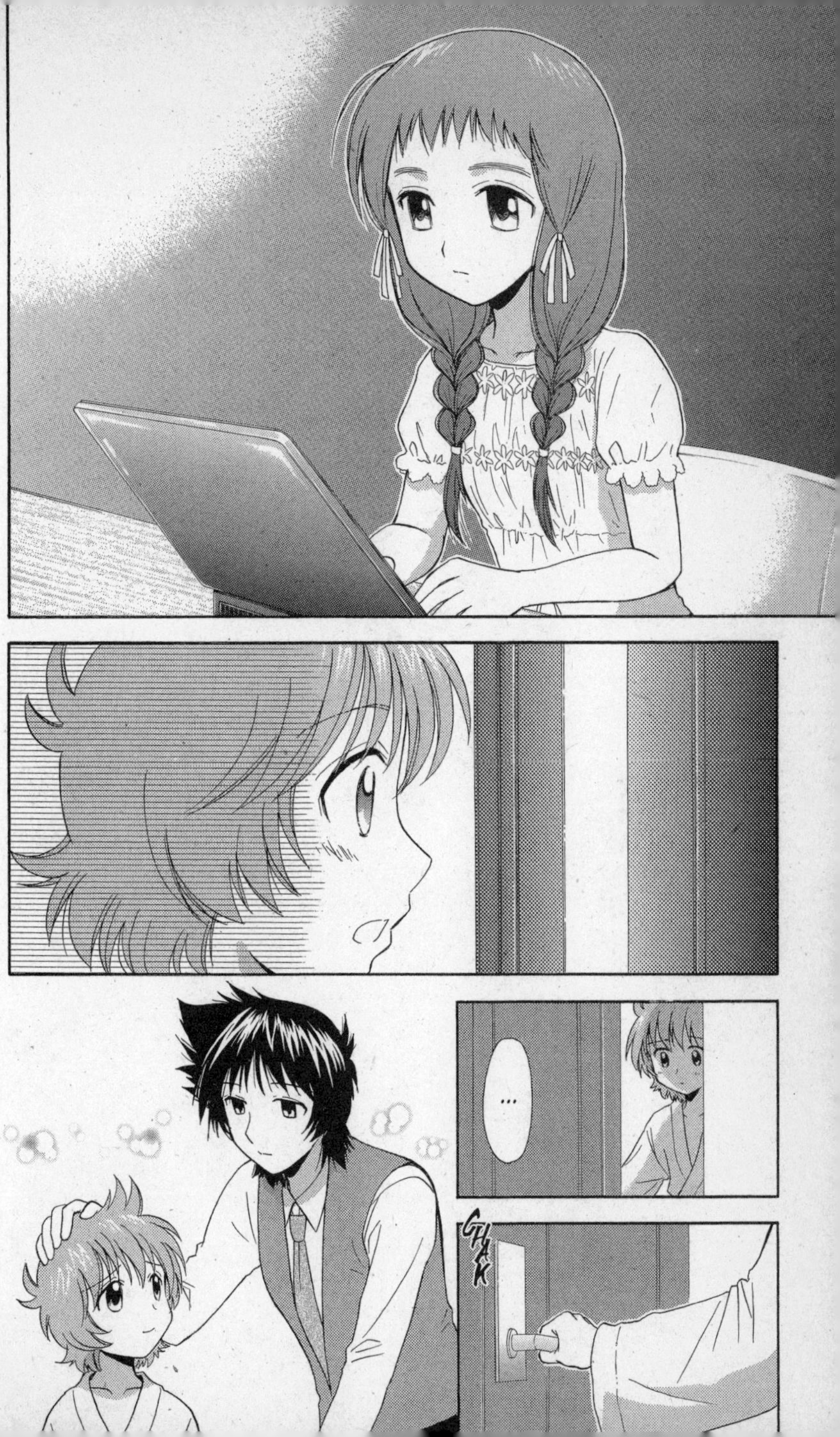
...
CHAK

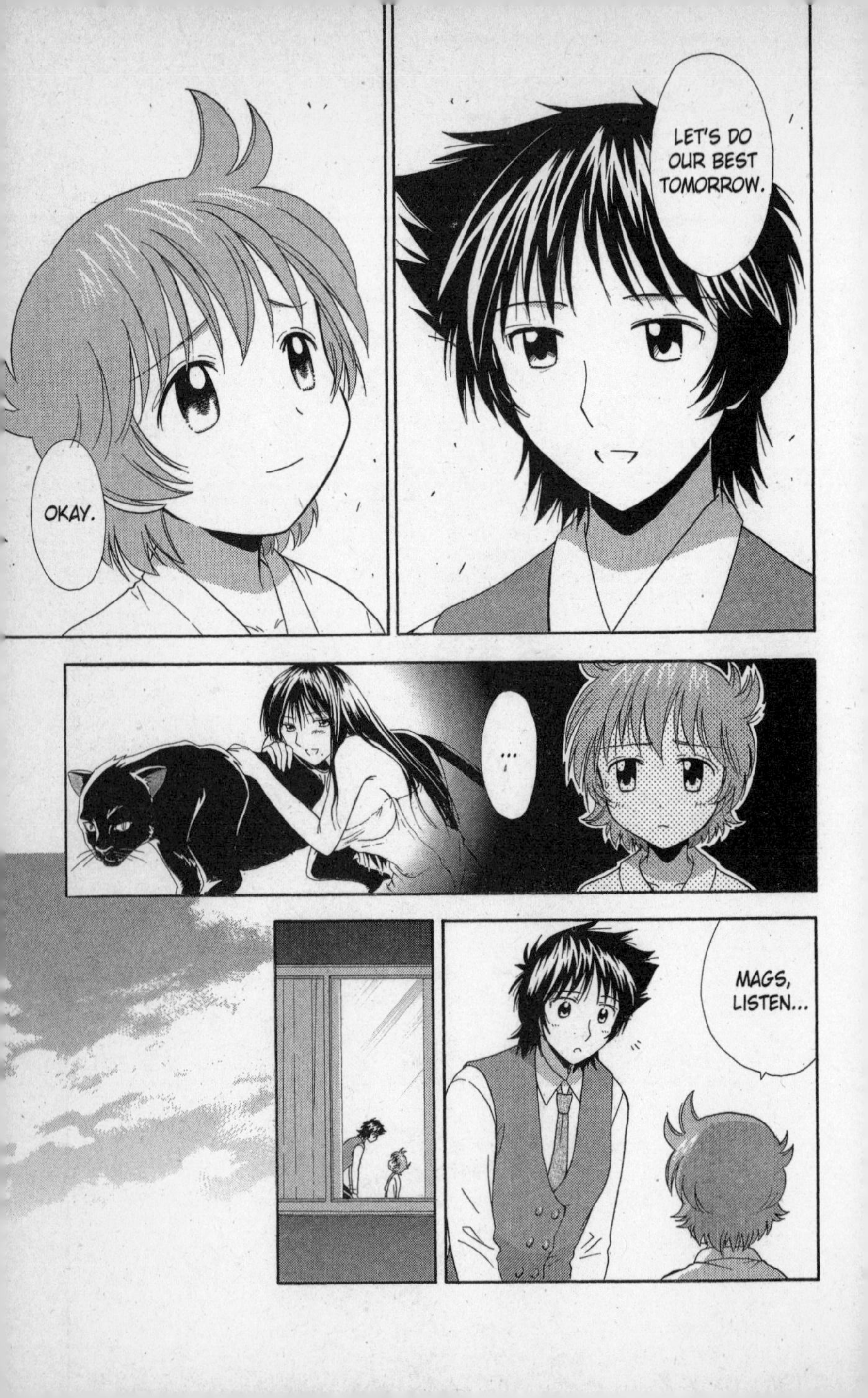
LET'S DO OUR BEST TOMORROW.
OKAY.
...
MAGS, LISTEN...

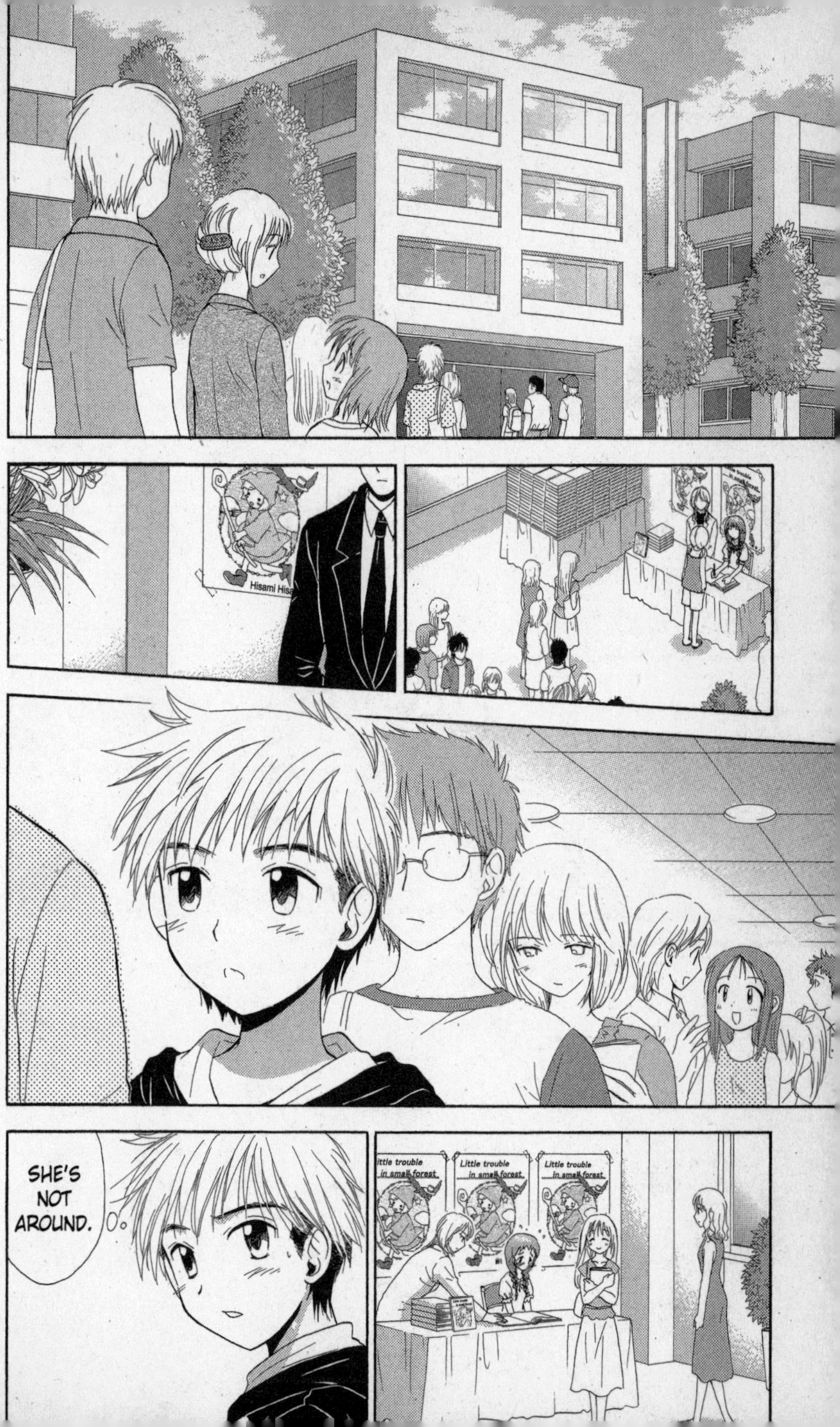
Little trouble in small forest
Little trouble in small forest
Little trouble in small forest
SHE'S NOT AROUND.

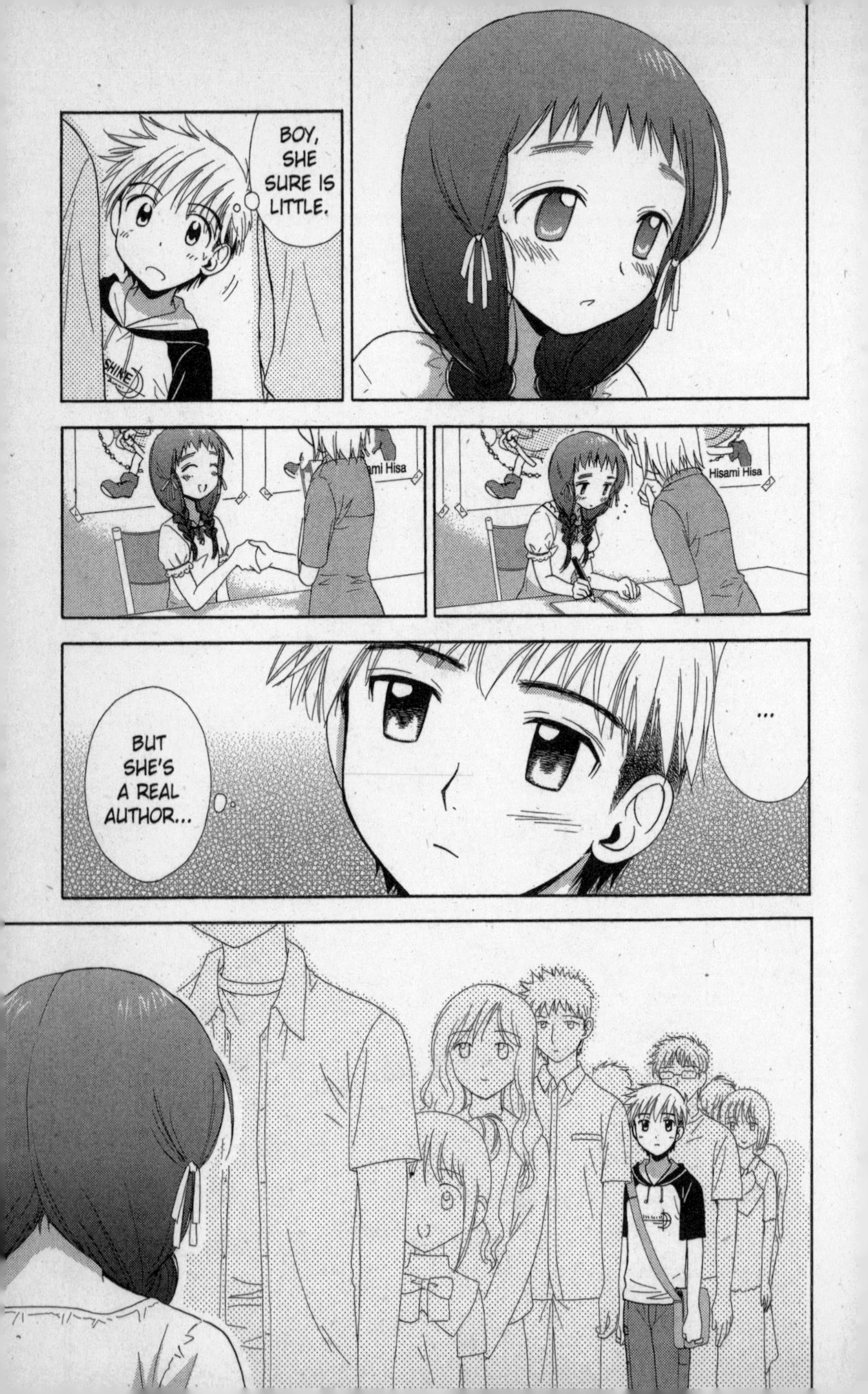
BOY, SHE SURE IS LITTLE.
SHINE
Hisami Hisa
...
BUT SHE'S A REAL AUTHOR...

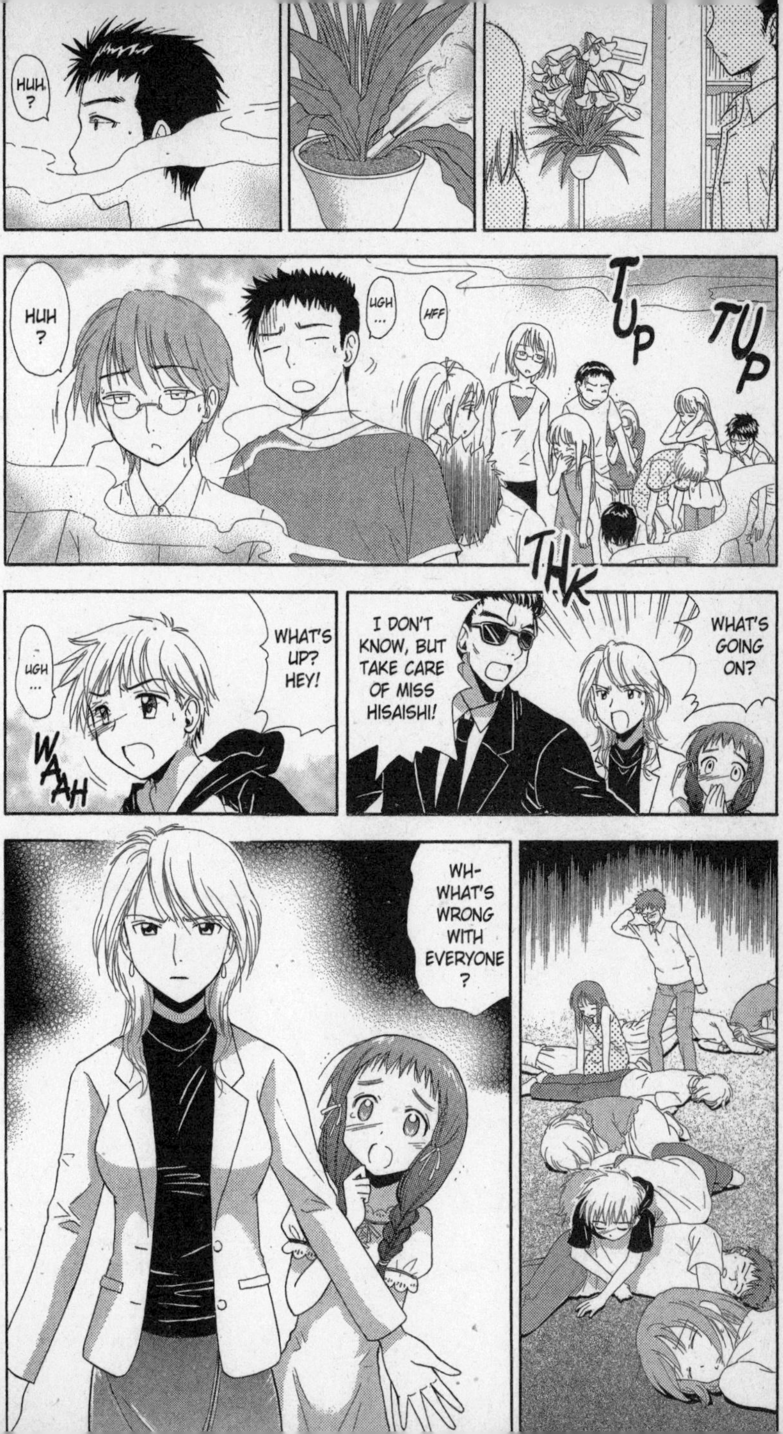
HUH ?
TUP
TUP
HFF
UGH ...
HUH ?
THK
WHAT'S GOING ON?
I DON'T KNOW, BUT TAKE CARE OF MISS HISAISHI!
WHAT'S UP? HEY!
UGH ...
WAAH
WH- WHAT'S WRONG WITH EVERYONE ?

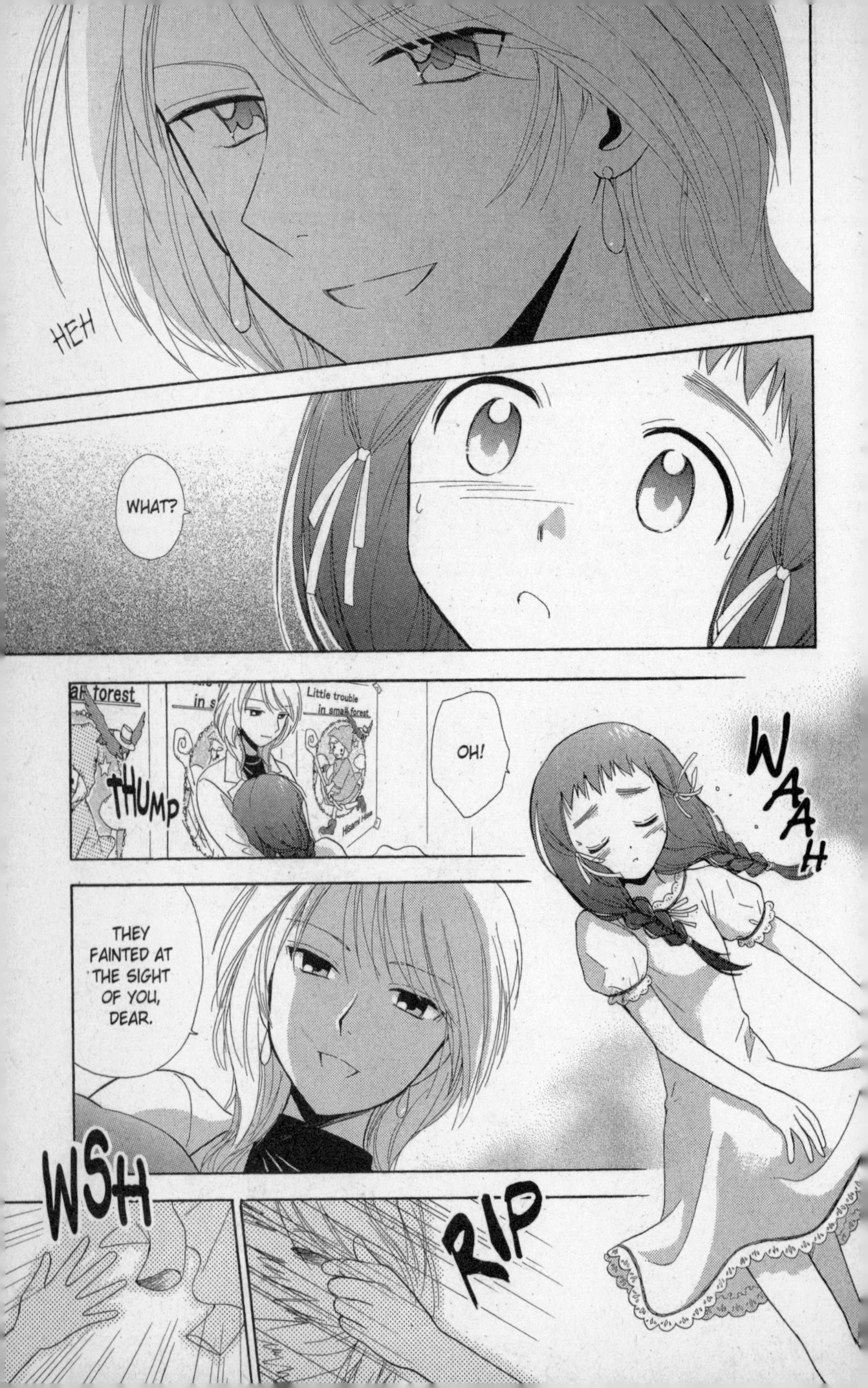
HEH
WHAT?
WAAAH
OH!
THUMP
THEY FAINTED AT THE SIGHT OF YOU, DEAR.
RIP
WSH

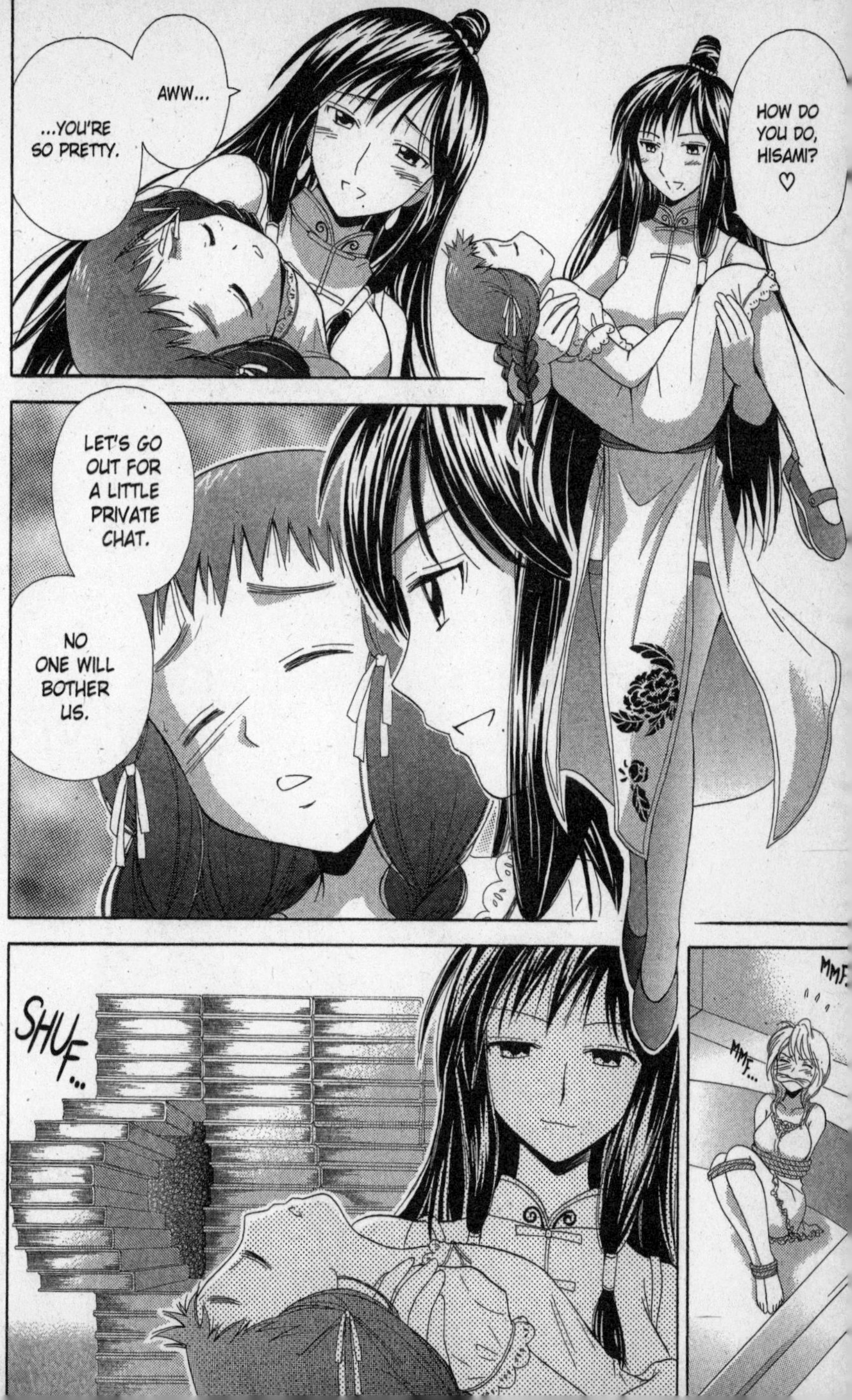
HOW DO YOU DO, HISAMI? ♡
AWW...
...YOU'RE SO PRETTY.
LET'S GO OUT FOR A LITTLE PRIVATE CHAT.
NO ONE WILL BOTHER US.
MMF.
MMF...
SHUF...

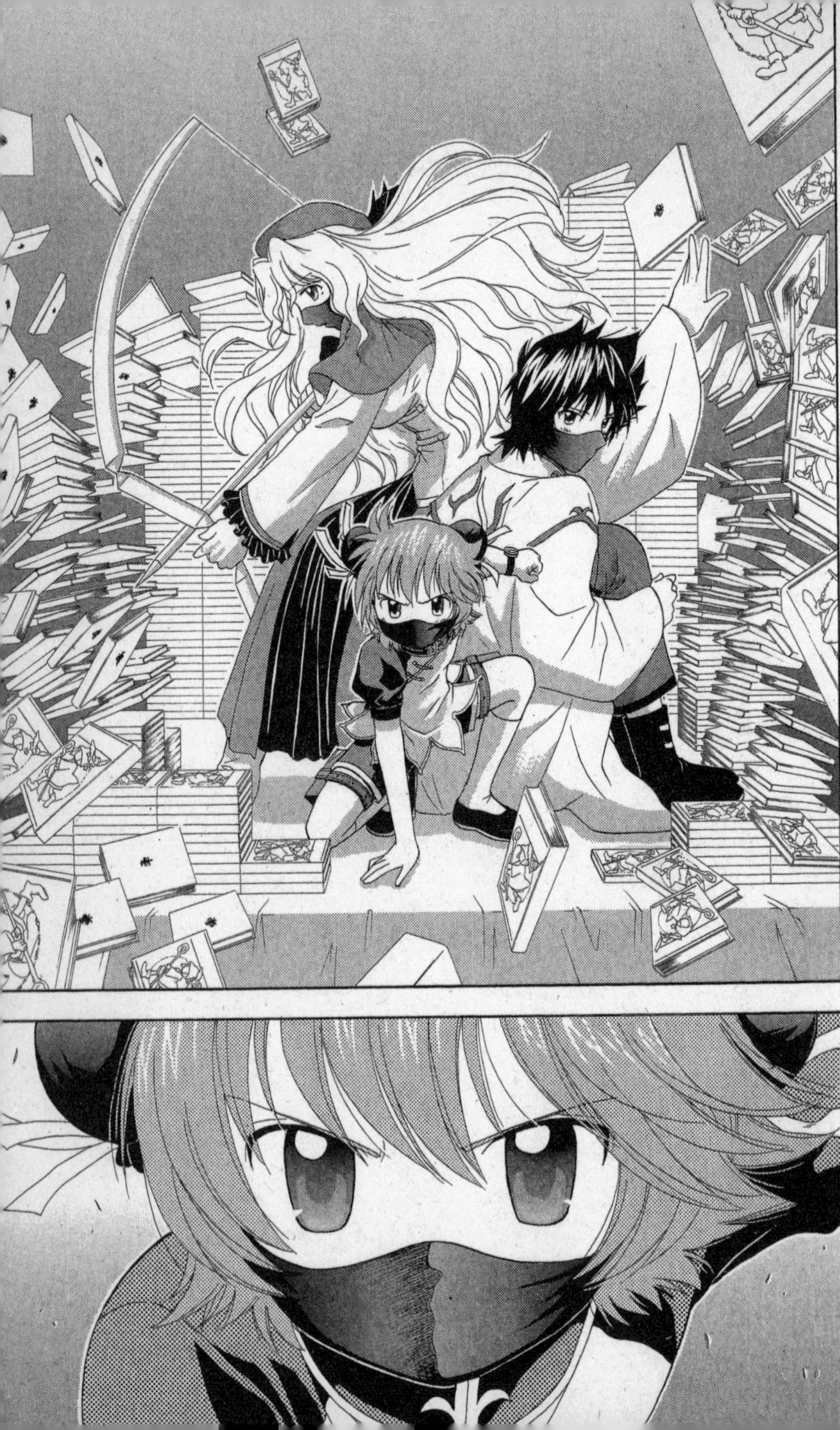

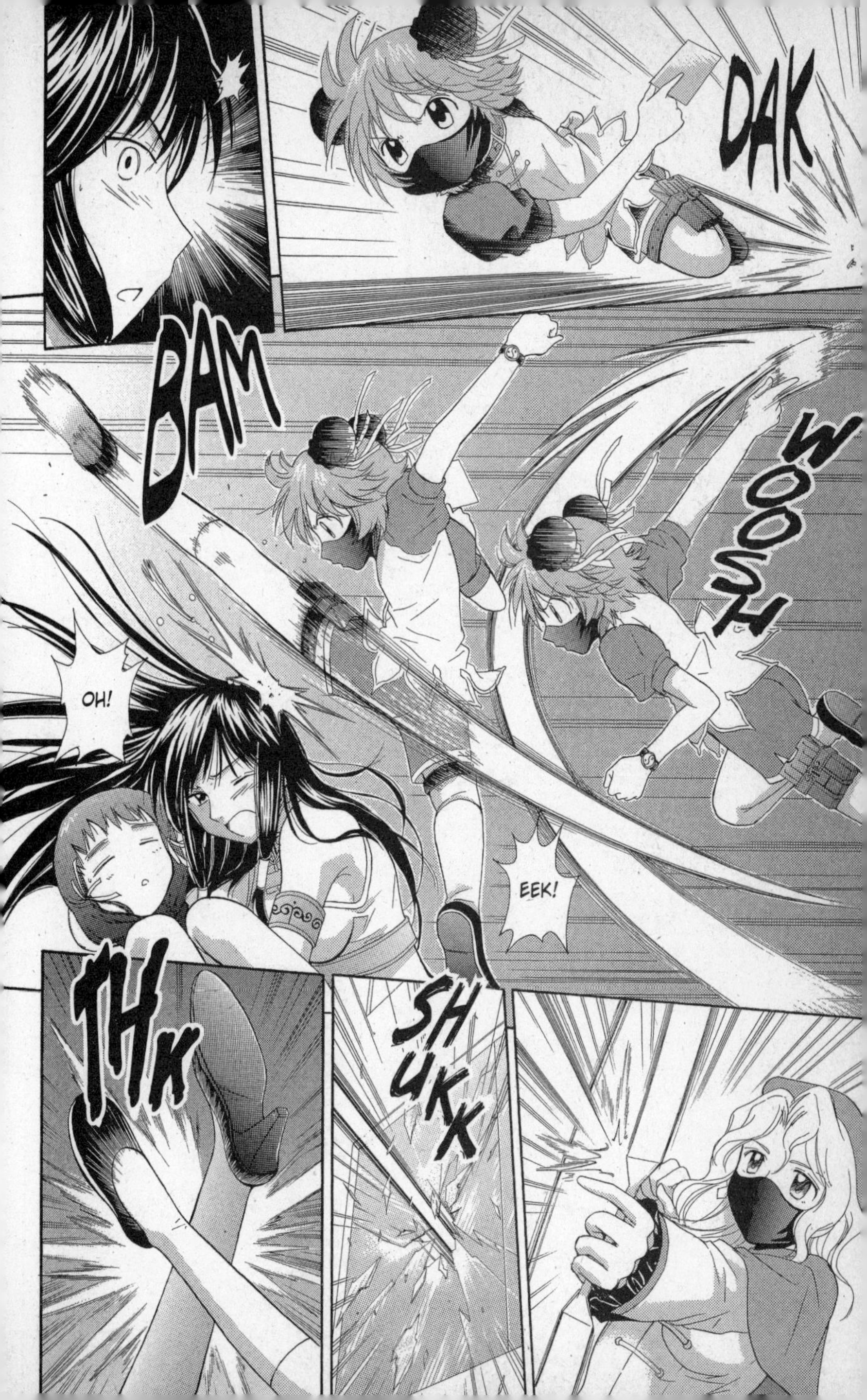
DAK
WOOSH
BAM
OH!
EEK!
SHUKK
THK

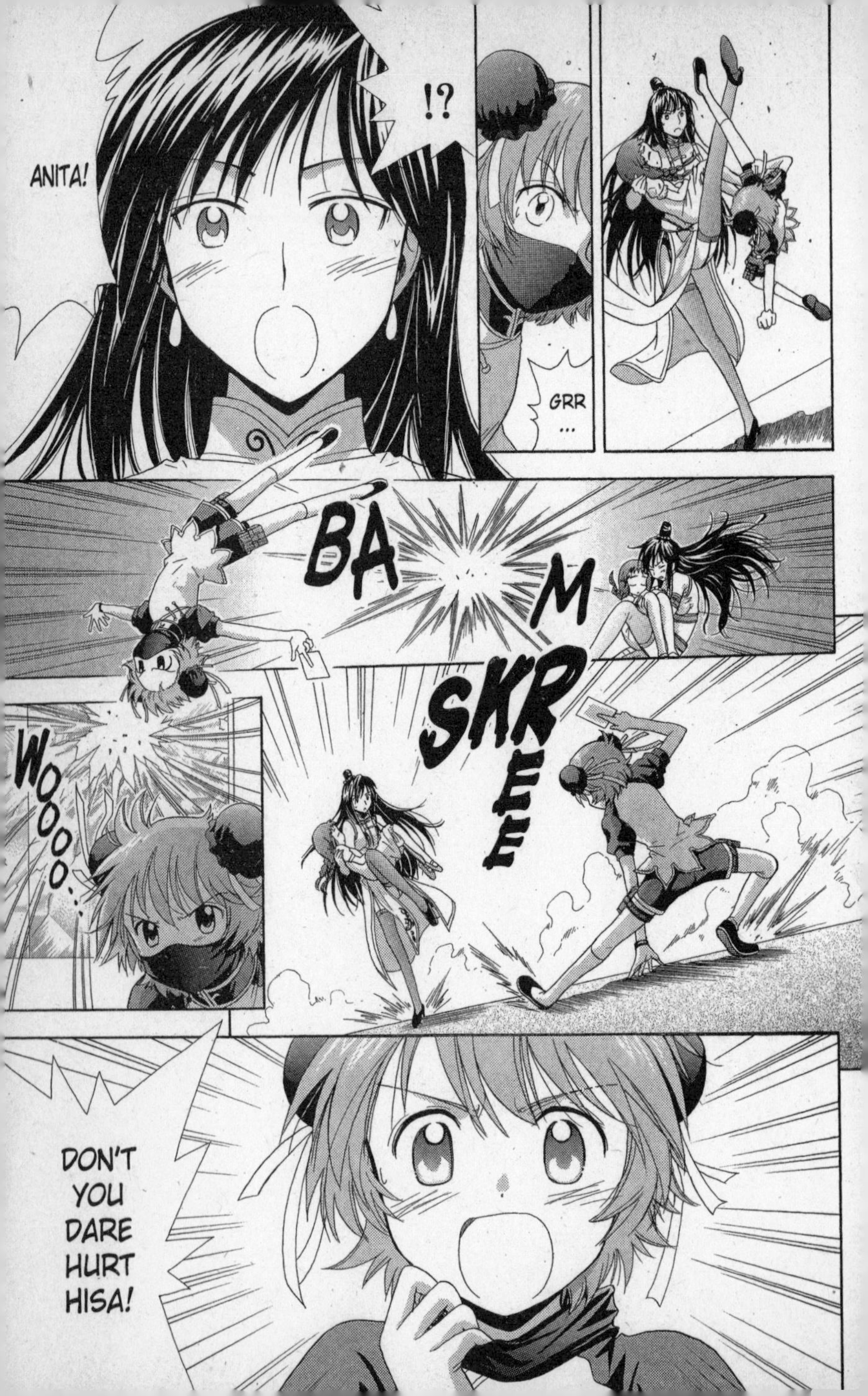
GRR ...
!?
ANITA!
BAM
SKREEE
WOOOO..
DON'T YOU DARE HURT HISA!

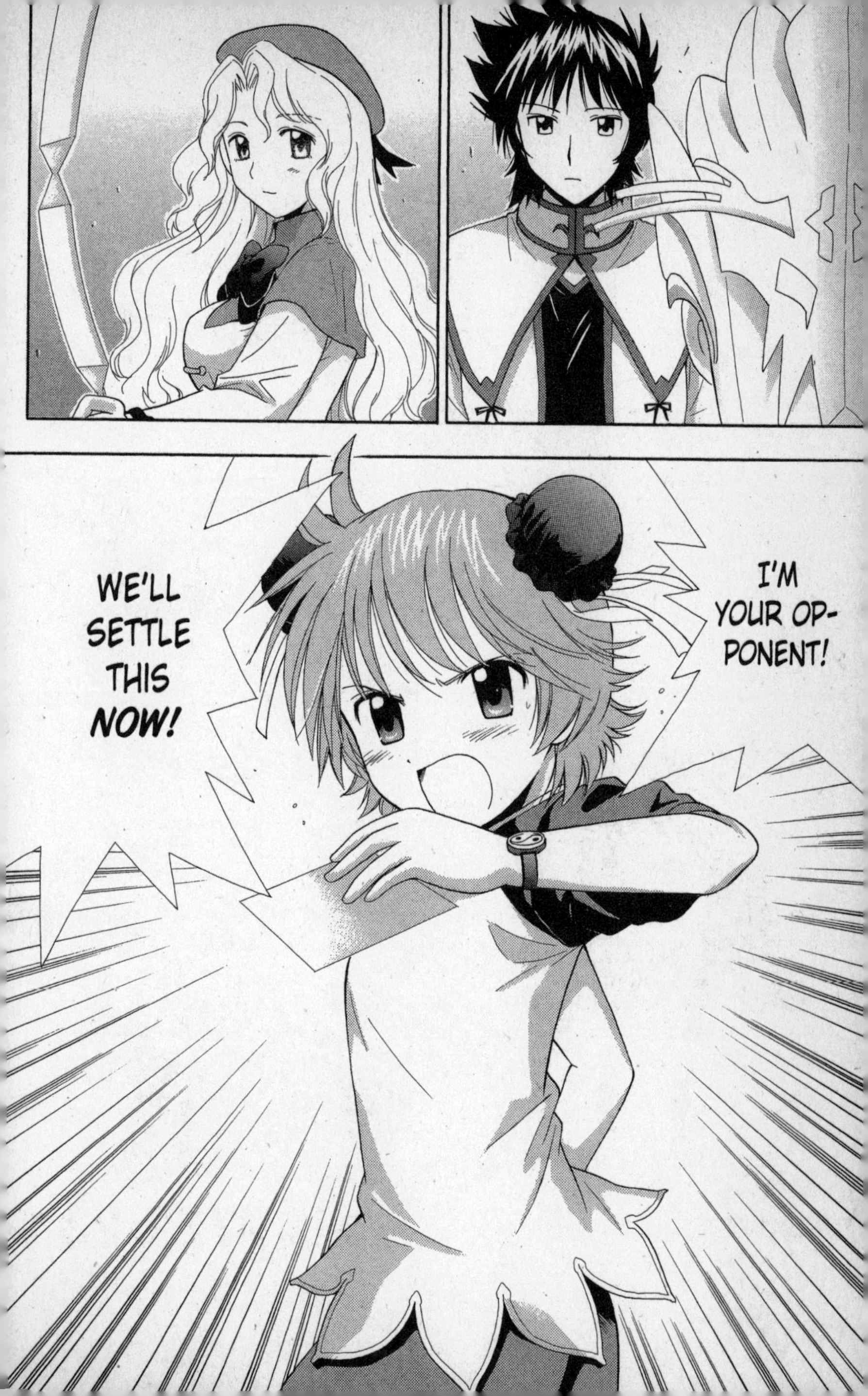
I'M YOUR OP-PONENT!
WE'LL SETTLE THIS NOW!

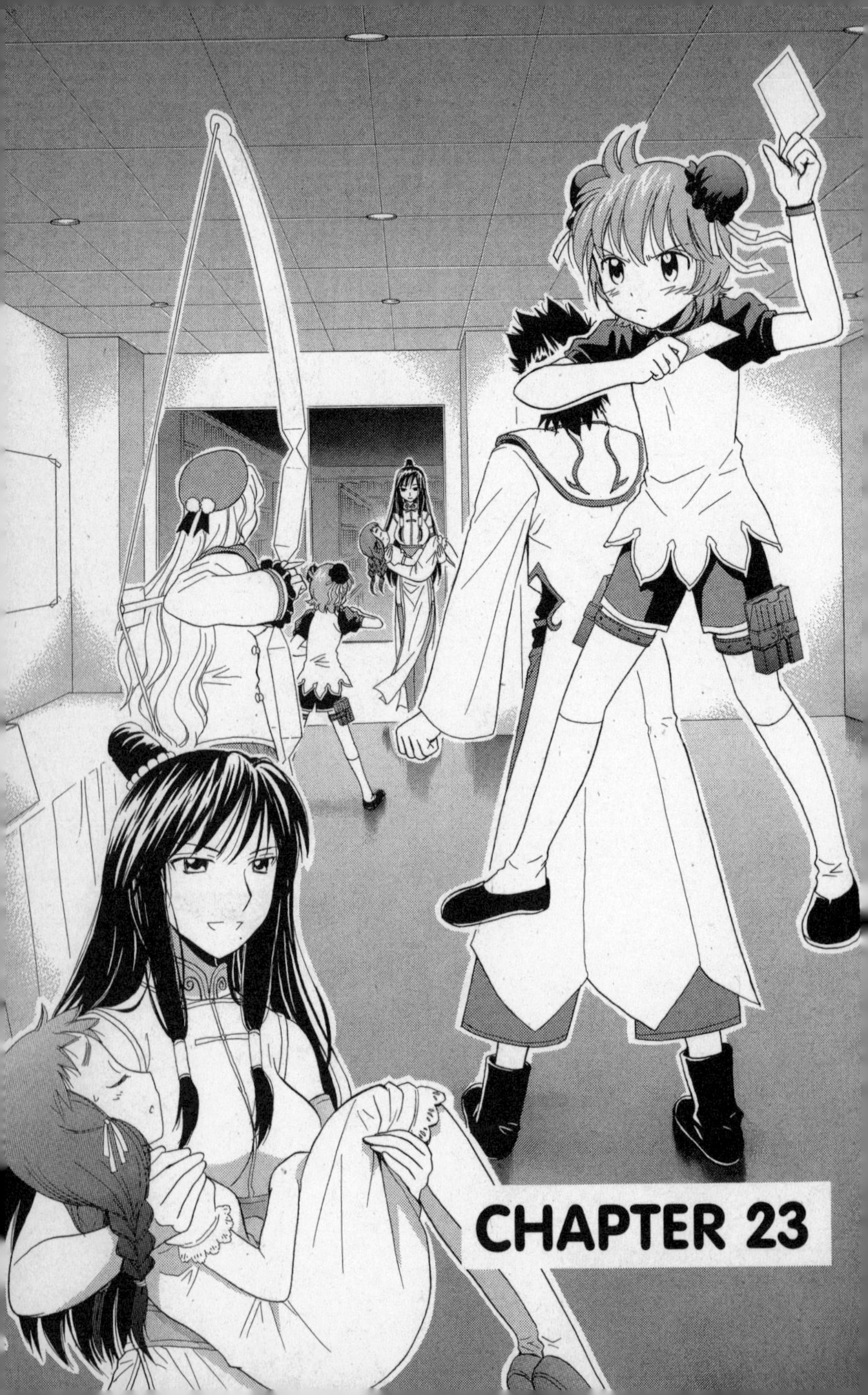
CHAPTER 23

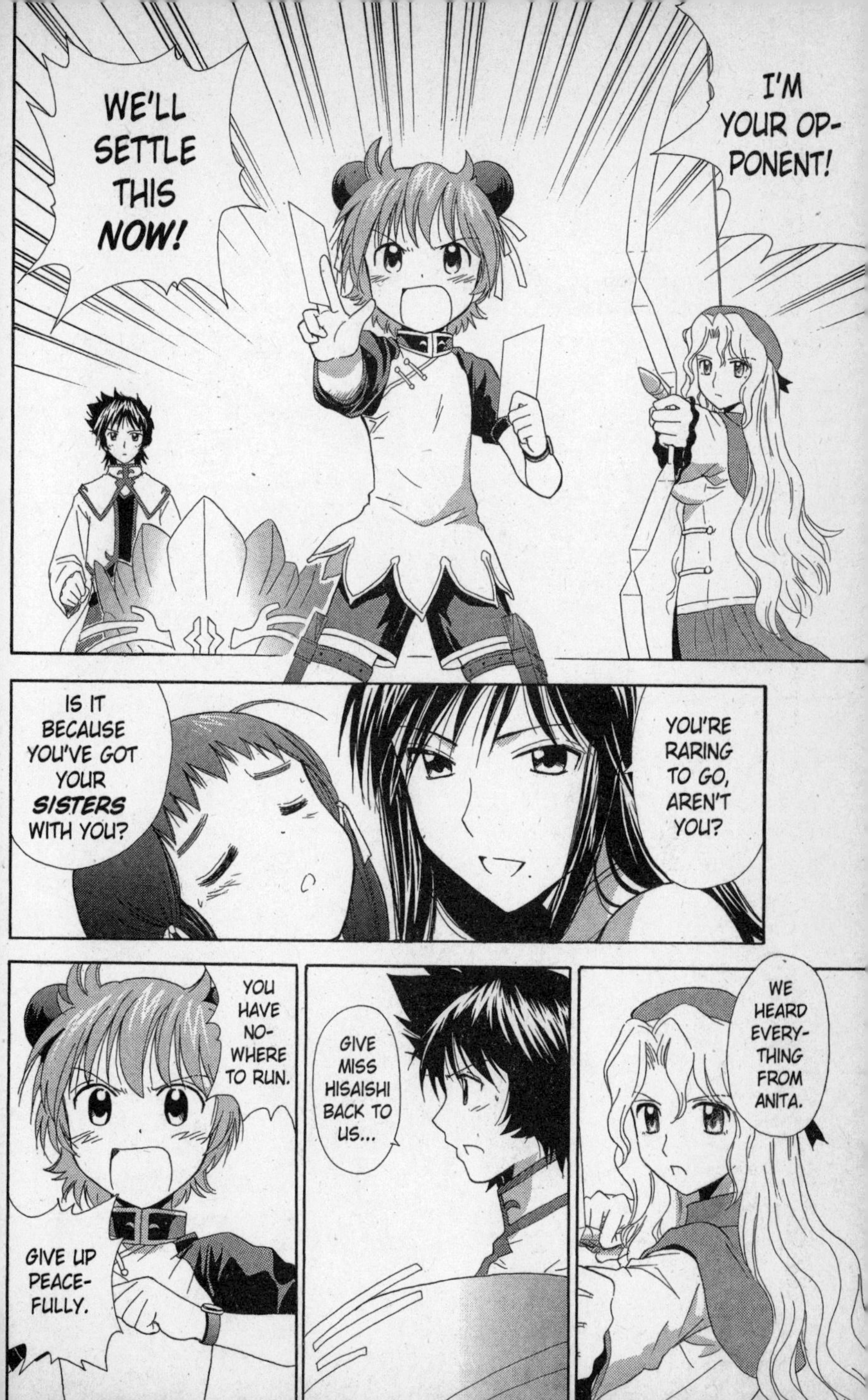
I'M YOUR OP-PONENT!
WE'LL SETTLE THIS NOW!
YOU'RE RARING TO GO, AREN'T YOU?
IS IT BECAUSE YOU'VE GOT YOUR SISTERS WITH YOU?
WE HEARD EVERY-THING FROM ANITA.
GIVE MISS HISAISHI BACK TO US...
YOU HAVE NO-WHERE TO RUN.
GIVE UP PEACE-FULLY.

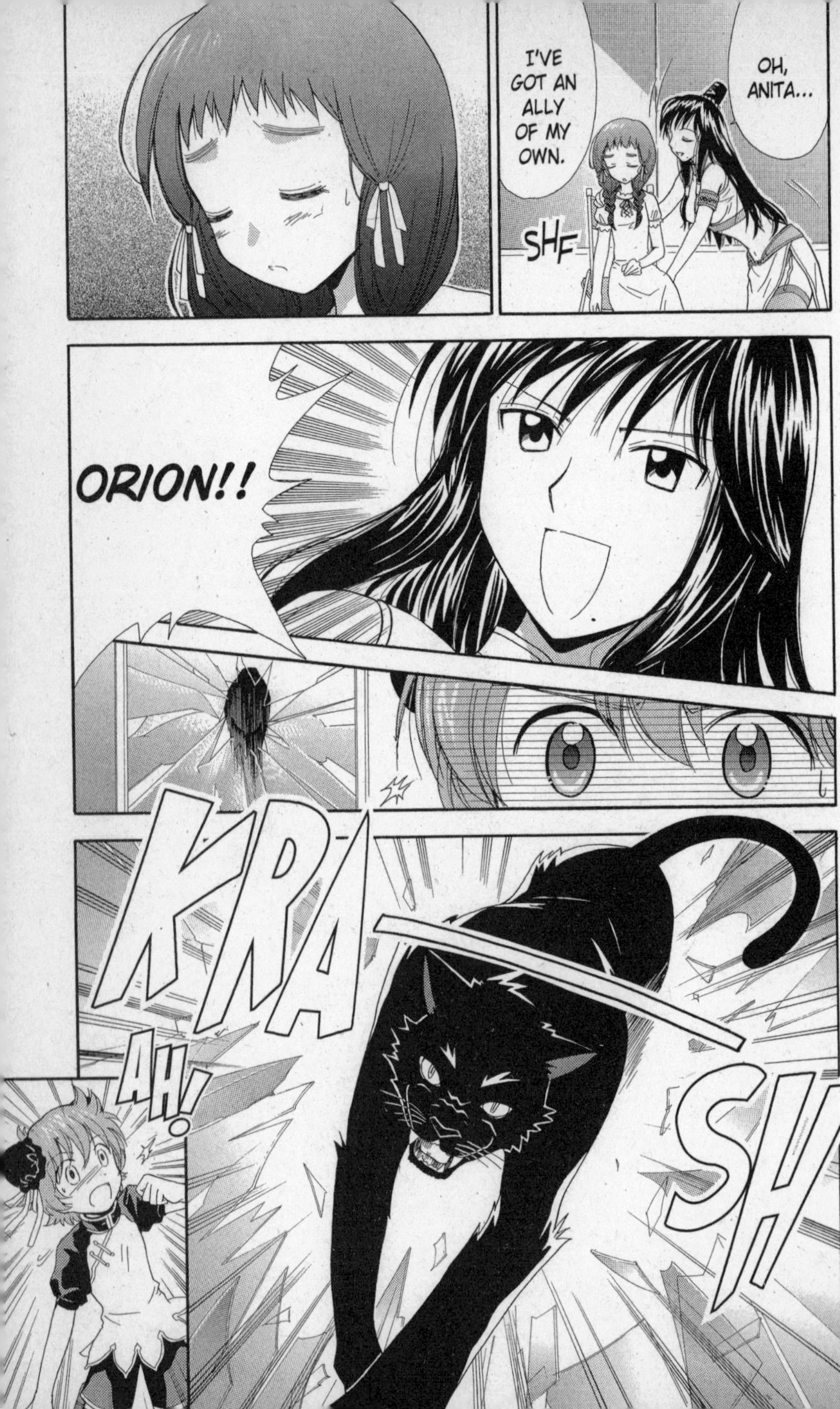
OH, ANITA...
I'VE GOT AN ALLY OF MY OWN.
SHF
ORION!!
KRASH
AH!

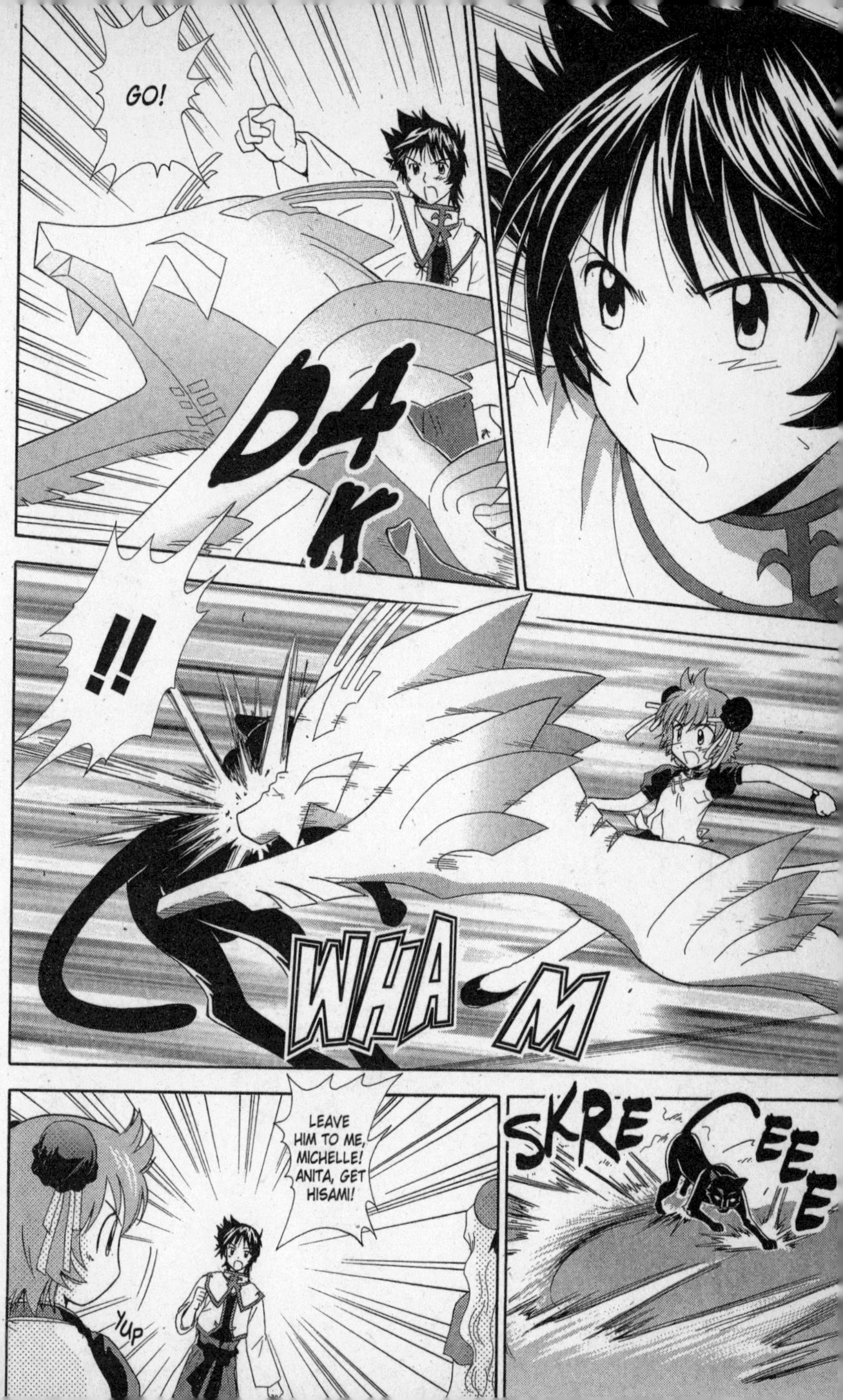
GO!
DAK
!!
WHAM
SKREEEE
LEAVE HIM TO ME, MICHELLE! ANITA, GET HISAMI!
YUP

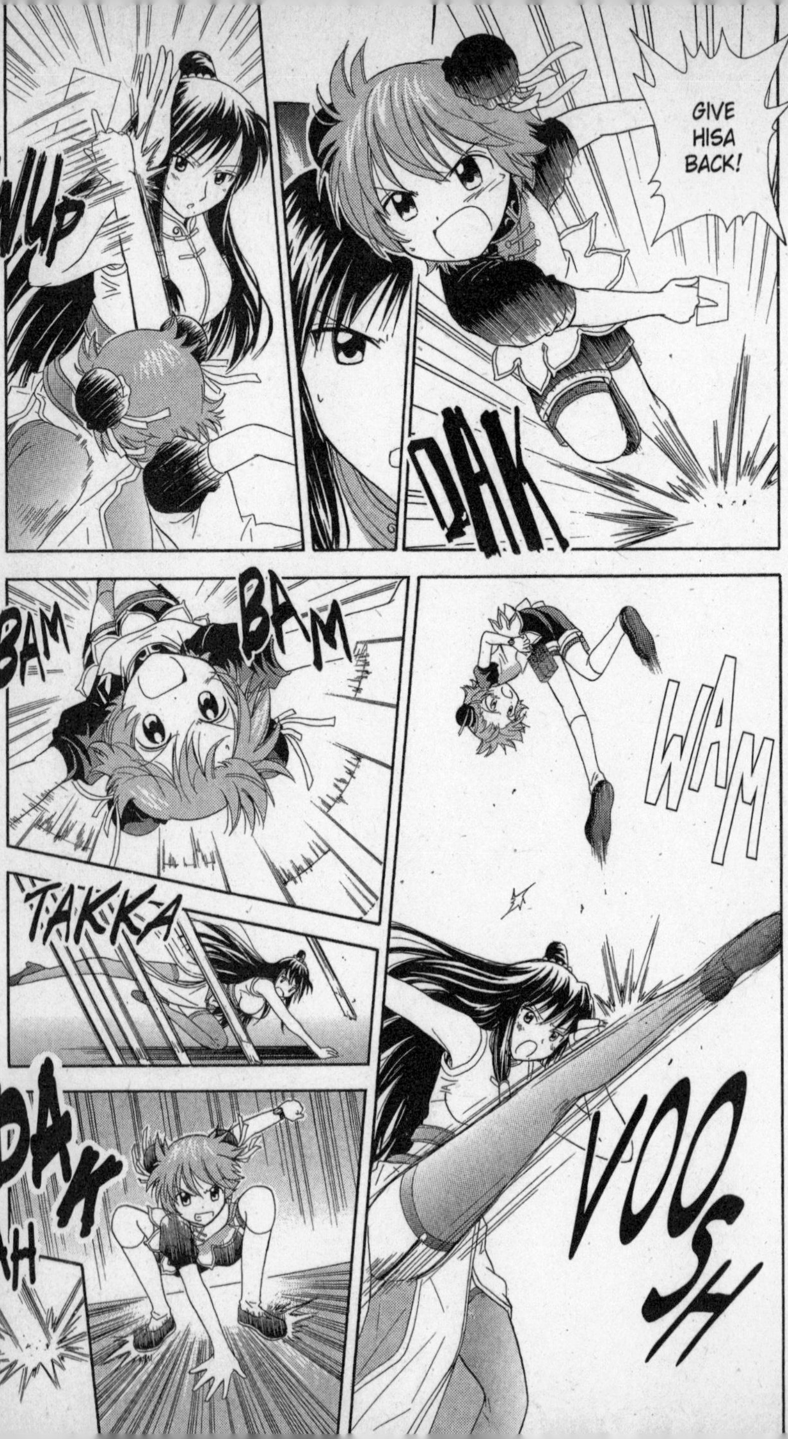
GIVE HISA BACK!
DAK
WUP
WAM
BAM BAM
TAKKA
VOOSH
DAK
BAH

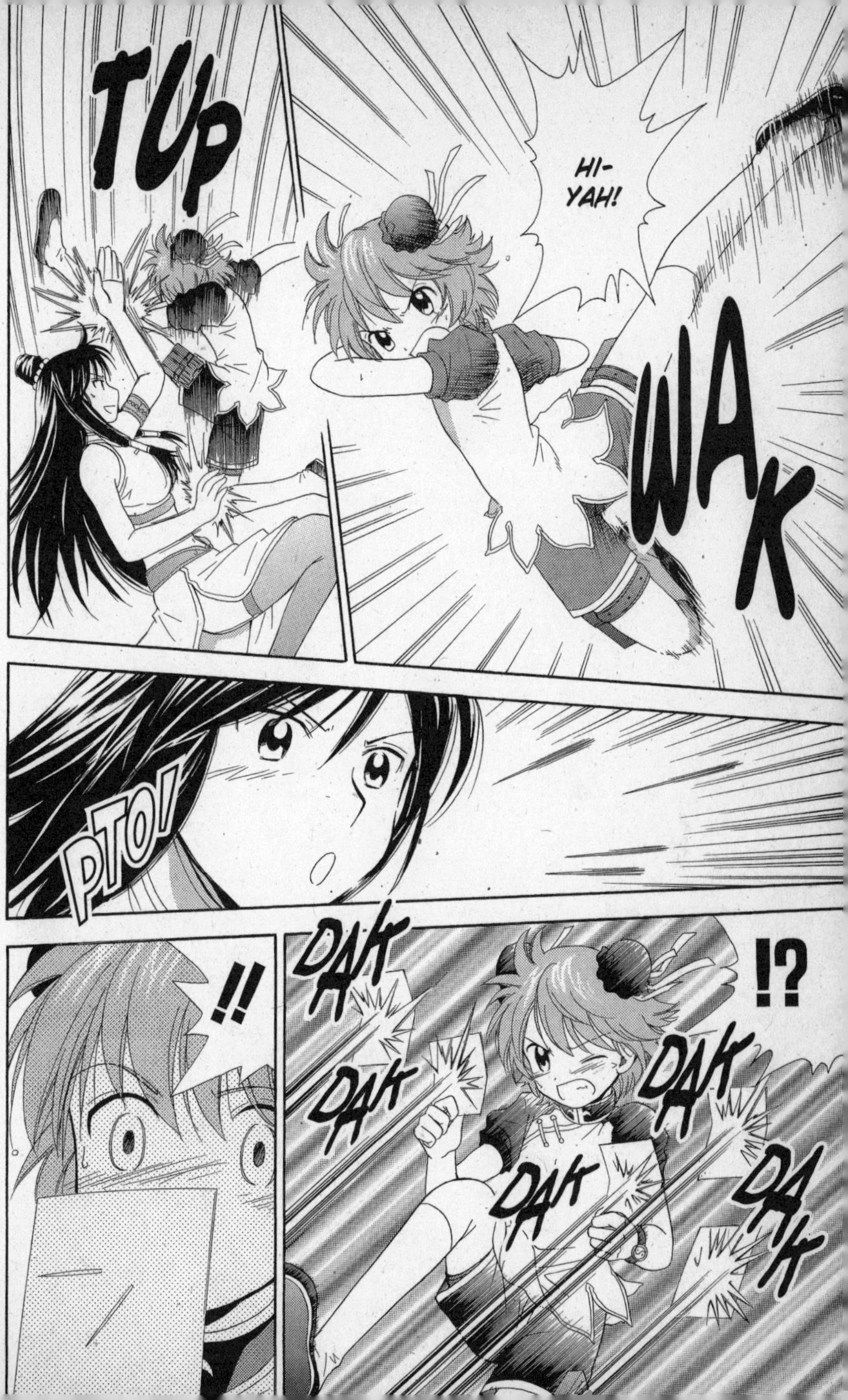
HI-
YAH!
WAK
TUP
PTOI
!?
DAK
DAK
DAK
DAK
DAK
!!

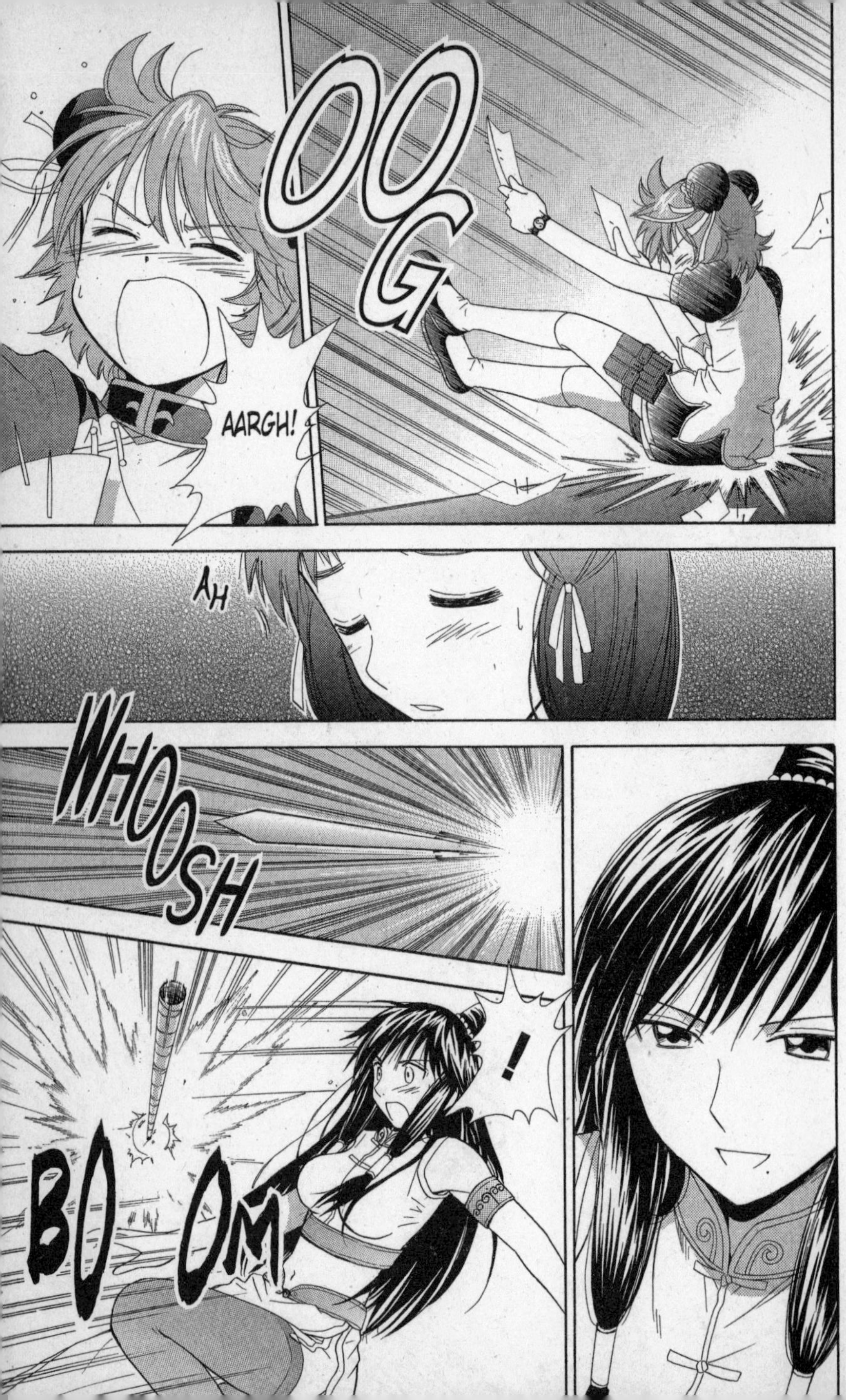
OOG
AARGH!
AH
WHOOSH
!
BOOM

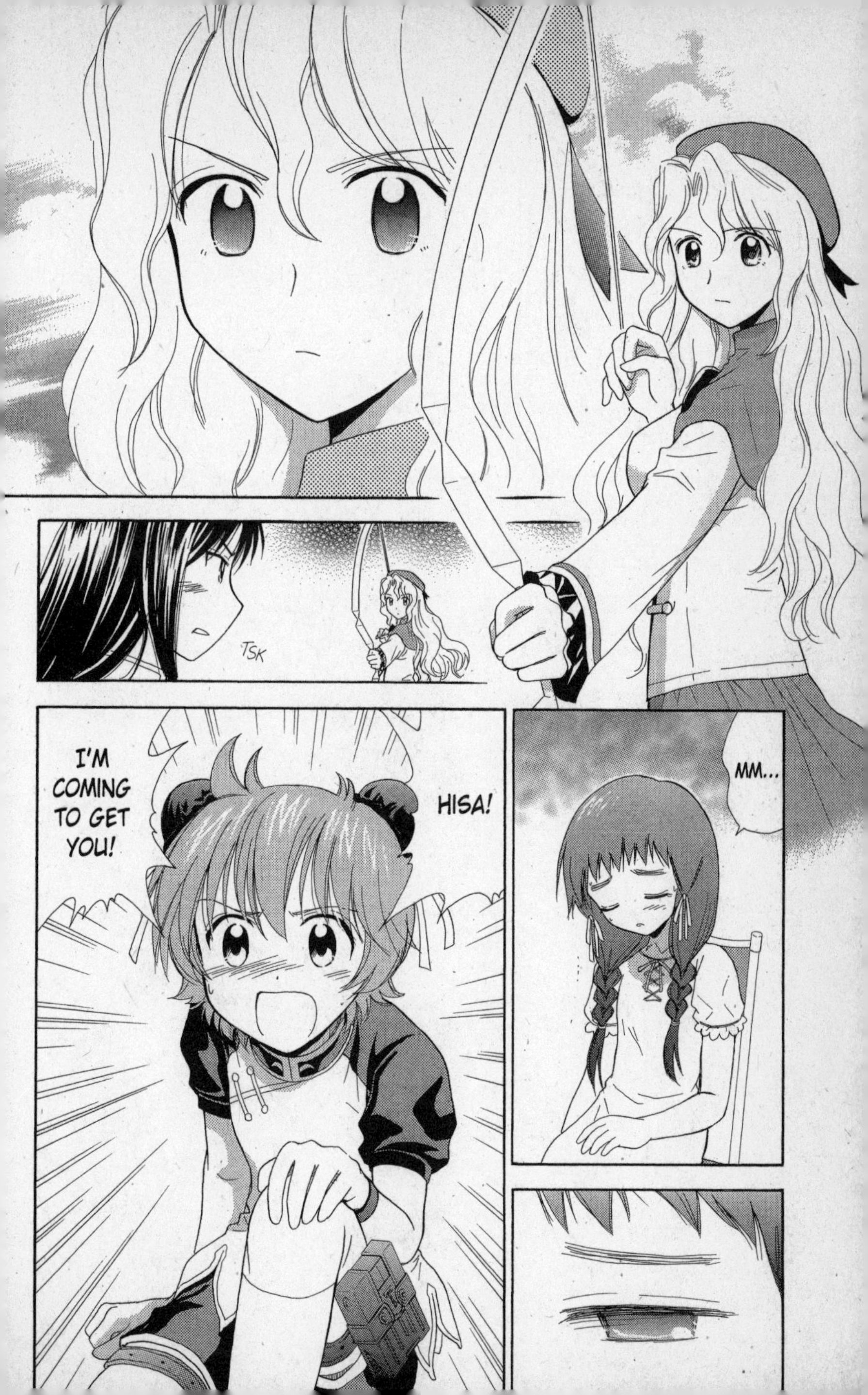
TSK
HISA!
I'M COMING TO GET YOU!
MM...

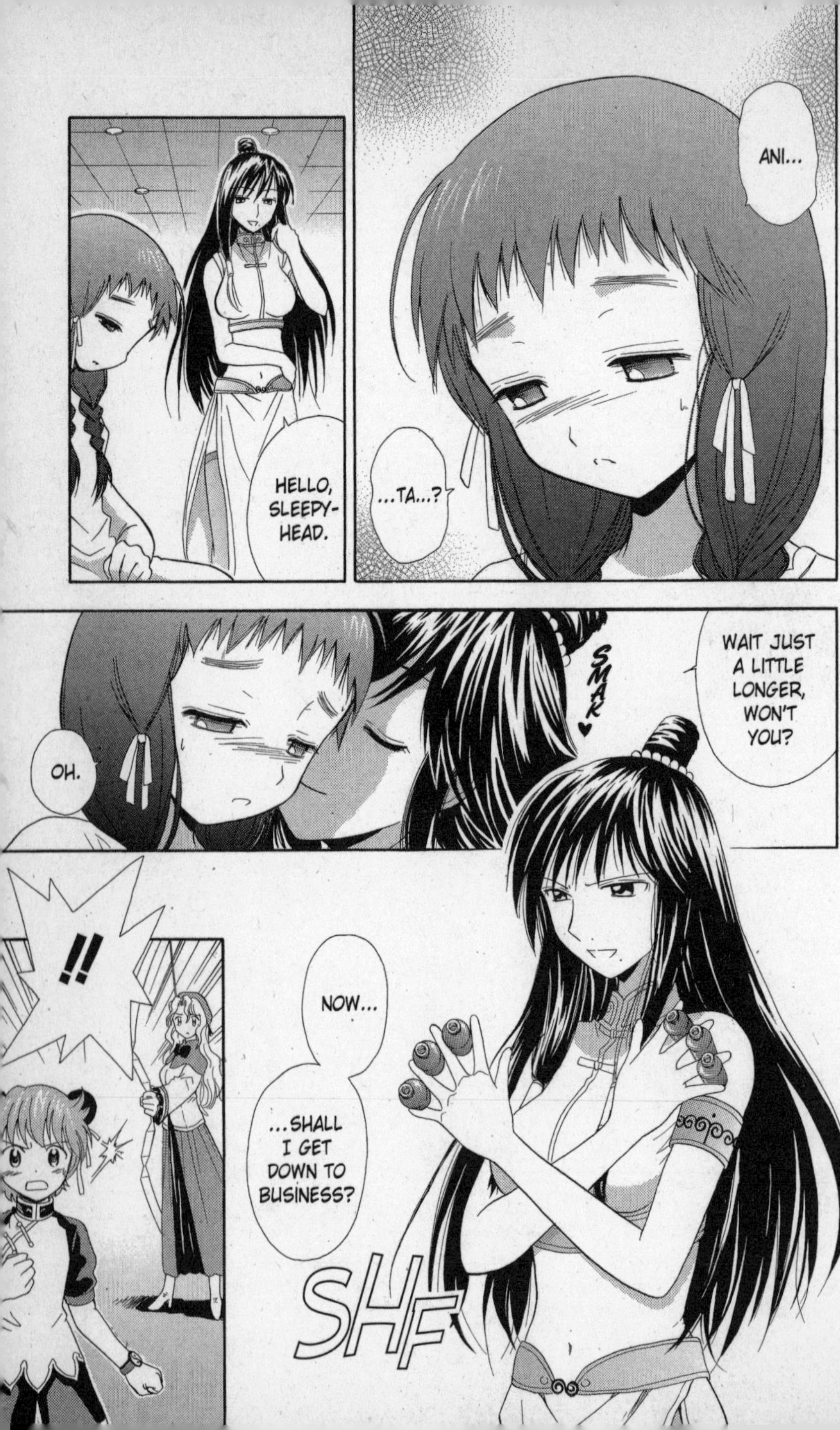
ANI...
...TA...?
HELLO, SLEEPY-HEAD.
WAIT JUST A LITTLE LONGER, WON'T YOU?
SMAK♥
OH.
NOW...
...SHALL I GET DOWN TO BUSINESS?
SHF
!!

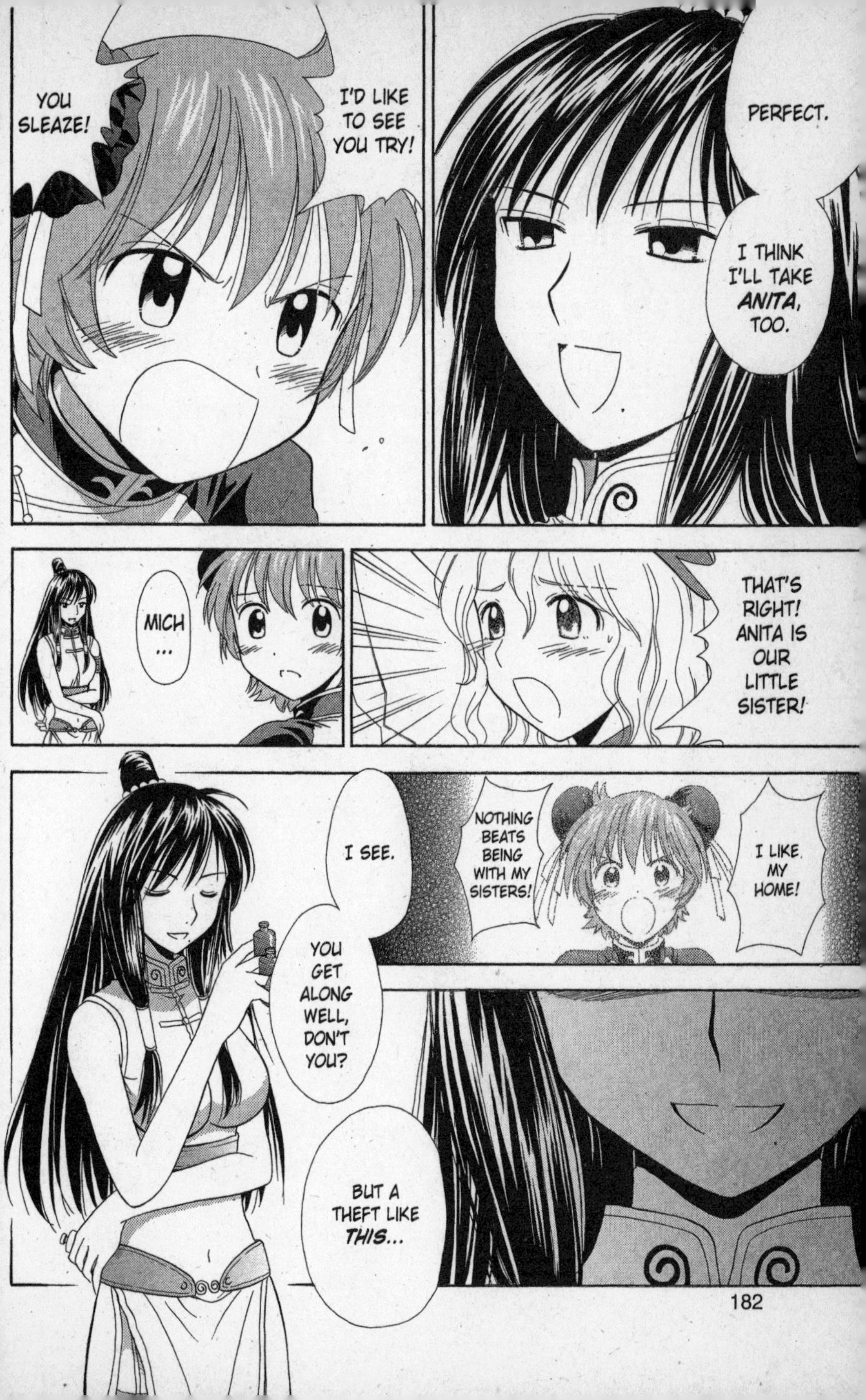
PERFECT.
I THINK I'LL TAKE *ANITA*, TOO.
I'D LIKE TO SEE YOU TRY!
YOU SLEAZE!
THAT'S RIGHT! ANITA IS OUR LITTLE SISTER!
MICH...
I LIKE MY HOME!
NOTHING BEATS BEING WITH MY SISTERS!
I SEE.
YOU GET ALONG WELL, DON'T YOU?
BUT A THEFT LIKE *THIS*...

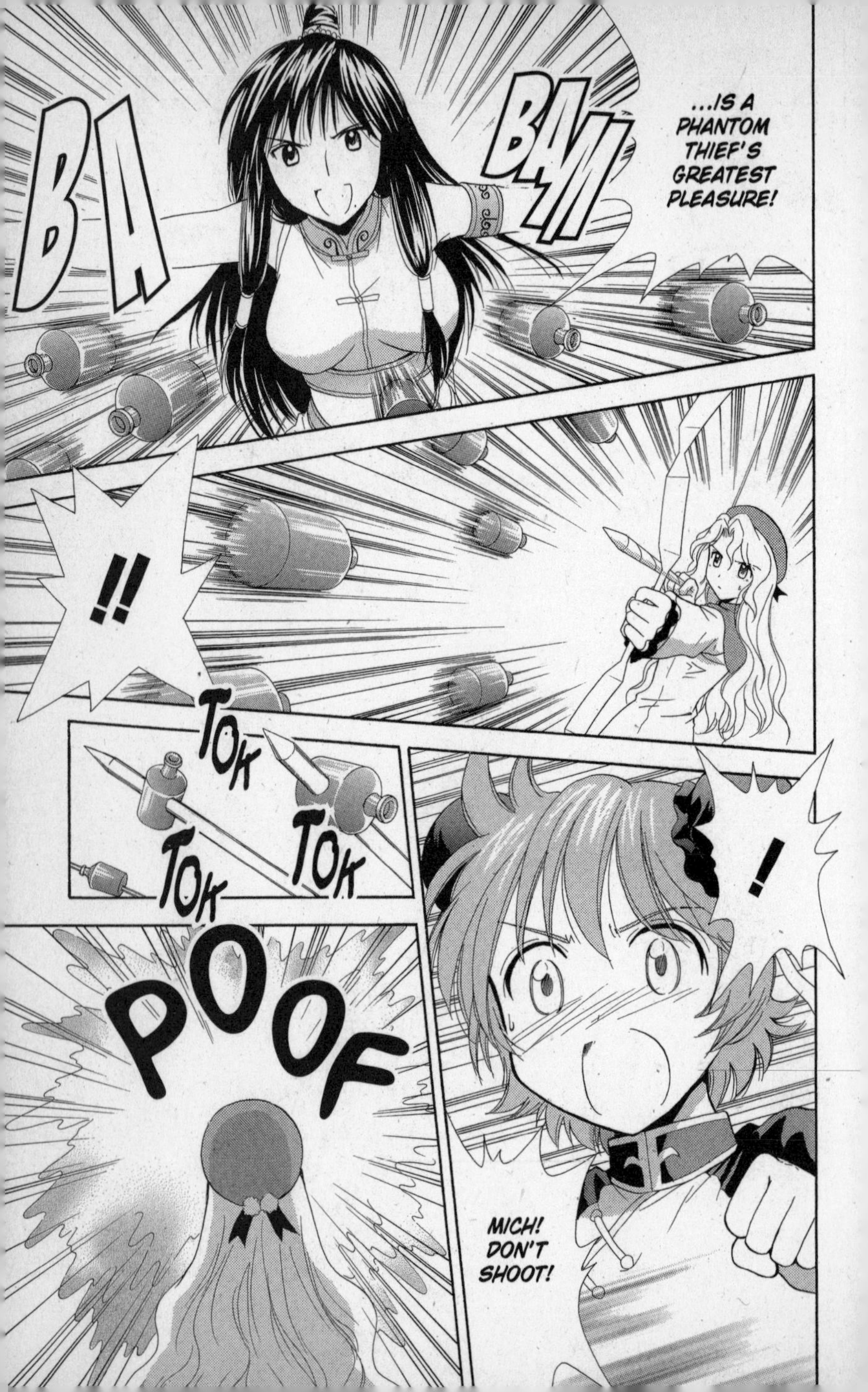
...IS A PHANTOM THIEF'S GREATEST PLEASURE!
BAM
BA
!!
!
MICH! DON'T SHOOT!
TOK
TOK
TOK
POOF

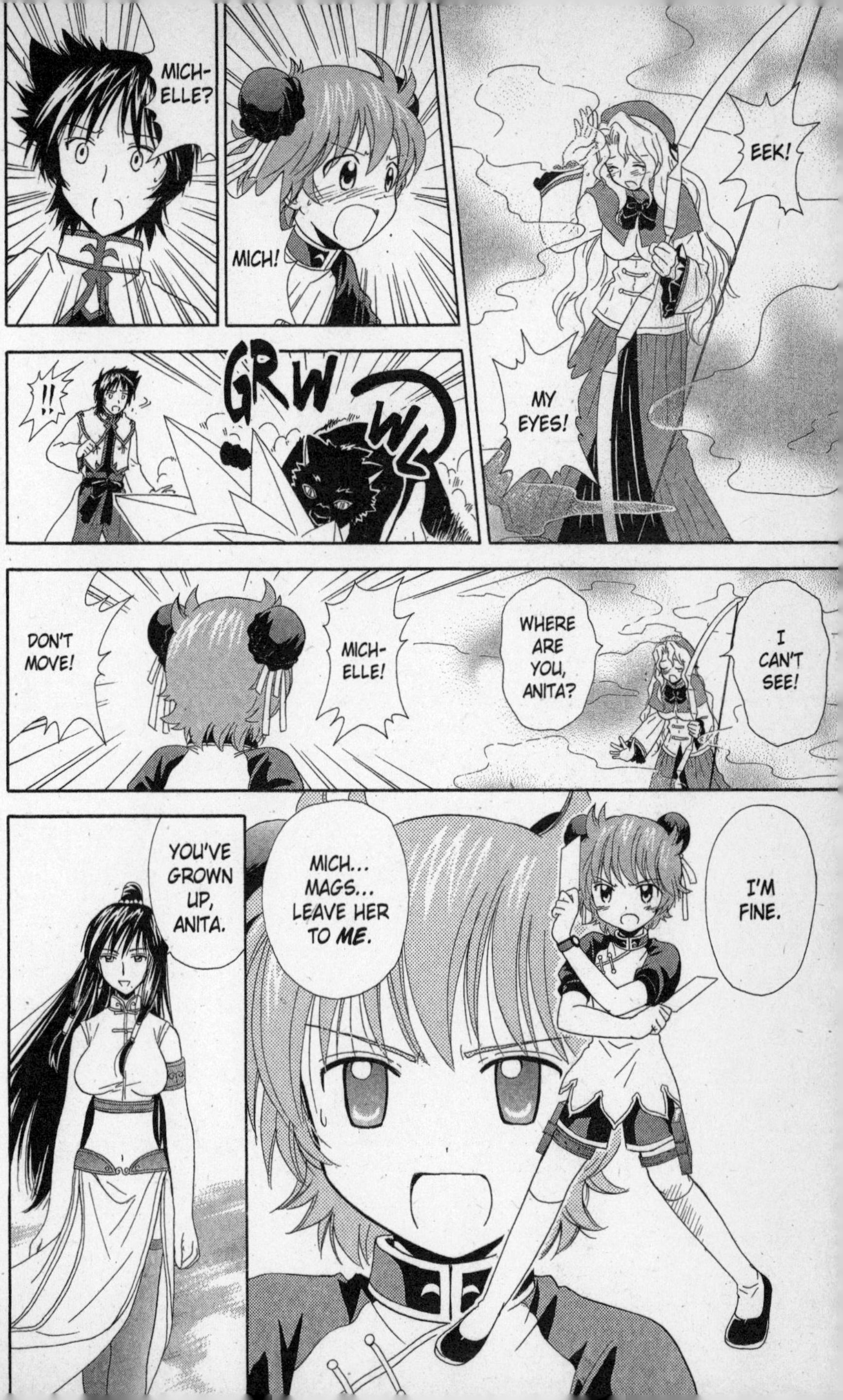
EEK!
MY EYES!
MICH!
MICH-ELLE?
GRWWL
!!
I CAN'T SEE!
WHERE ARE YOU, ANITA?
MICH-ELLE!
DON'T MOVE!
I'M FINE.
MICH... MAGS... LEAVE HER TO *ME*.
YOU'VE GROWN UP, ANITA.

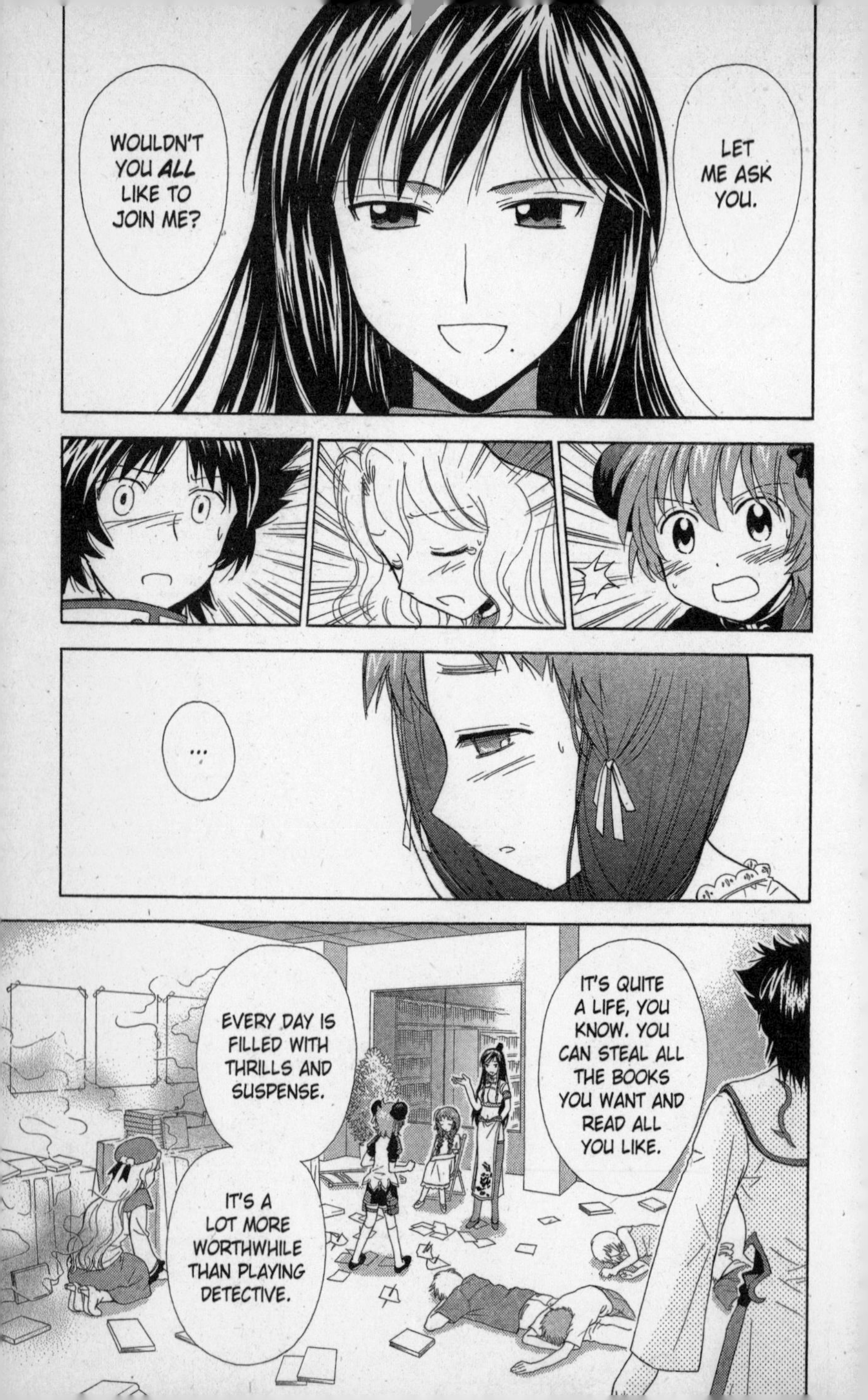
LET ME ASK YOU.
WOULDN'T YOU ALL LIKE TO JOIN ME?
...
IT'S QUITE A LIFE, YOU KNOW. YOU CAN STEAL ALL THE BOOKS YOU WANT AND READ ALL YOU LIKE.
EVERY DAY IS FILLED WITH THRILLS AND SUSPENSE.
IT'S A LOT MORE WORTHWHILE THAN PLAYING DETECTIVE.

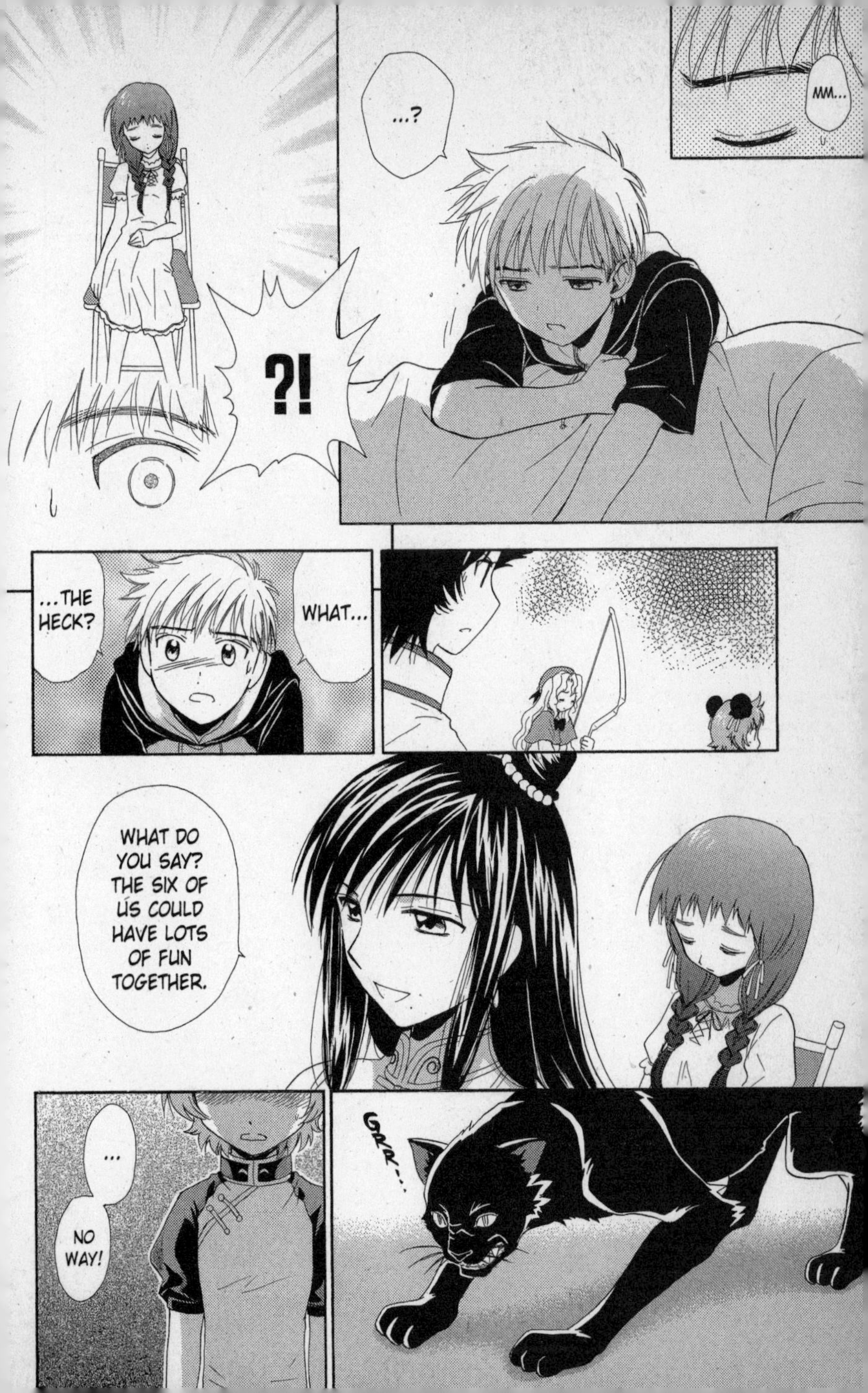
MM...
...?
?!
WHAT...
...THE HECK?
WHAT DO YOU SAY? THE SIX OF US COULD HAVE LOTS OF FUN TOGETHER.
GRRR...
...
NO WAY!

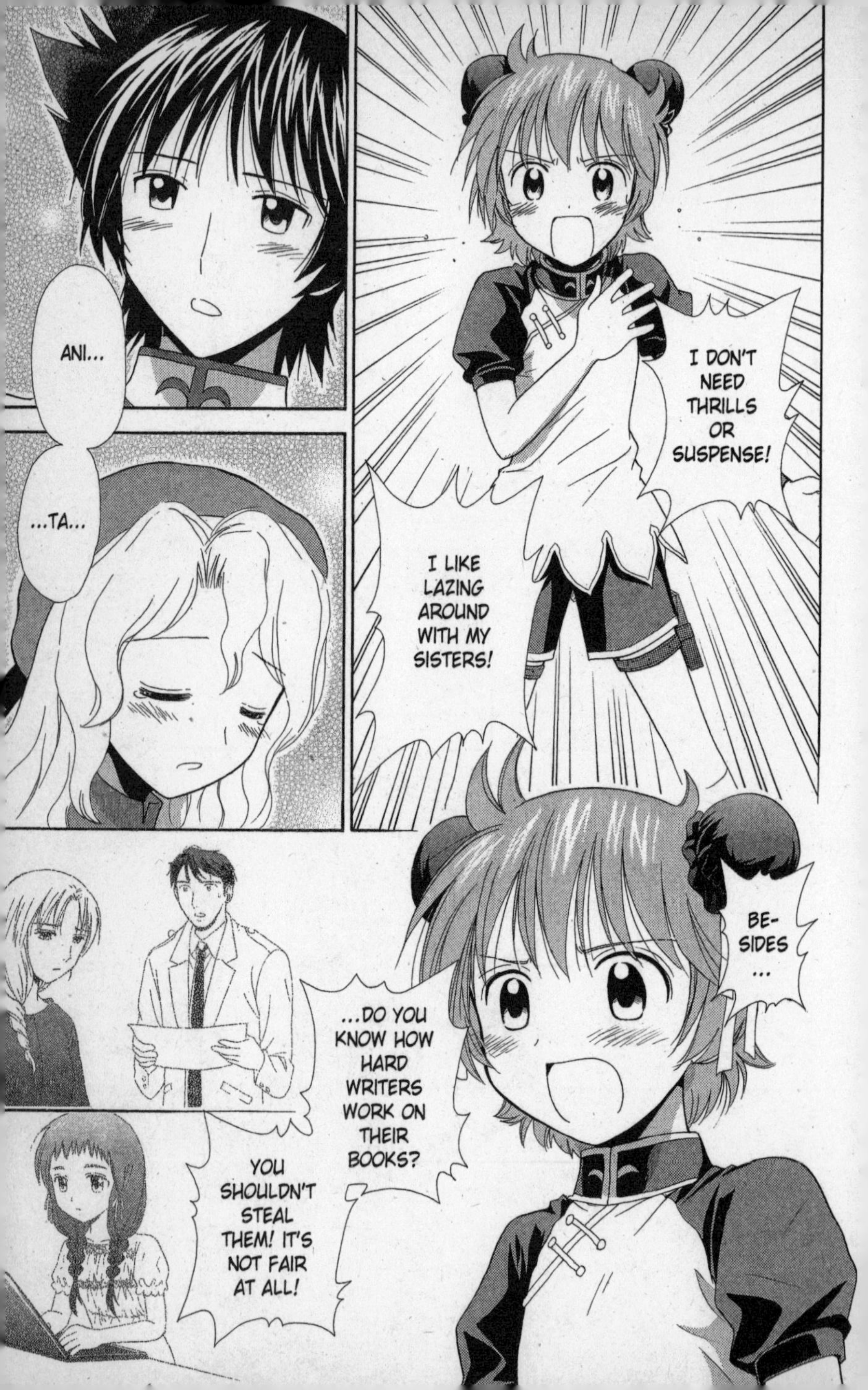
I DON'T NEED THRILLS OR SUSPENSE!
I LIKE LAZING AROUND WITH MY SISTERS!
ANI...
...TA...
BE-SIDES...
...DO YOU KNOW HOW HARD WRITERS WORK ON THEIR BOOKS?
YOU SHOULDN'T STEAL THEM! IT'S NOT FAIR AT ALL!

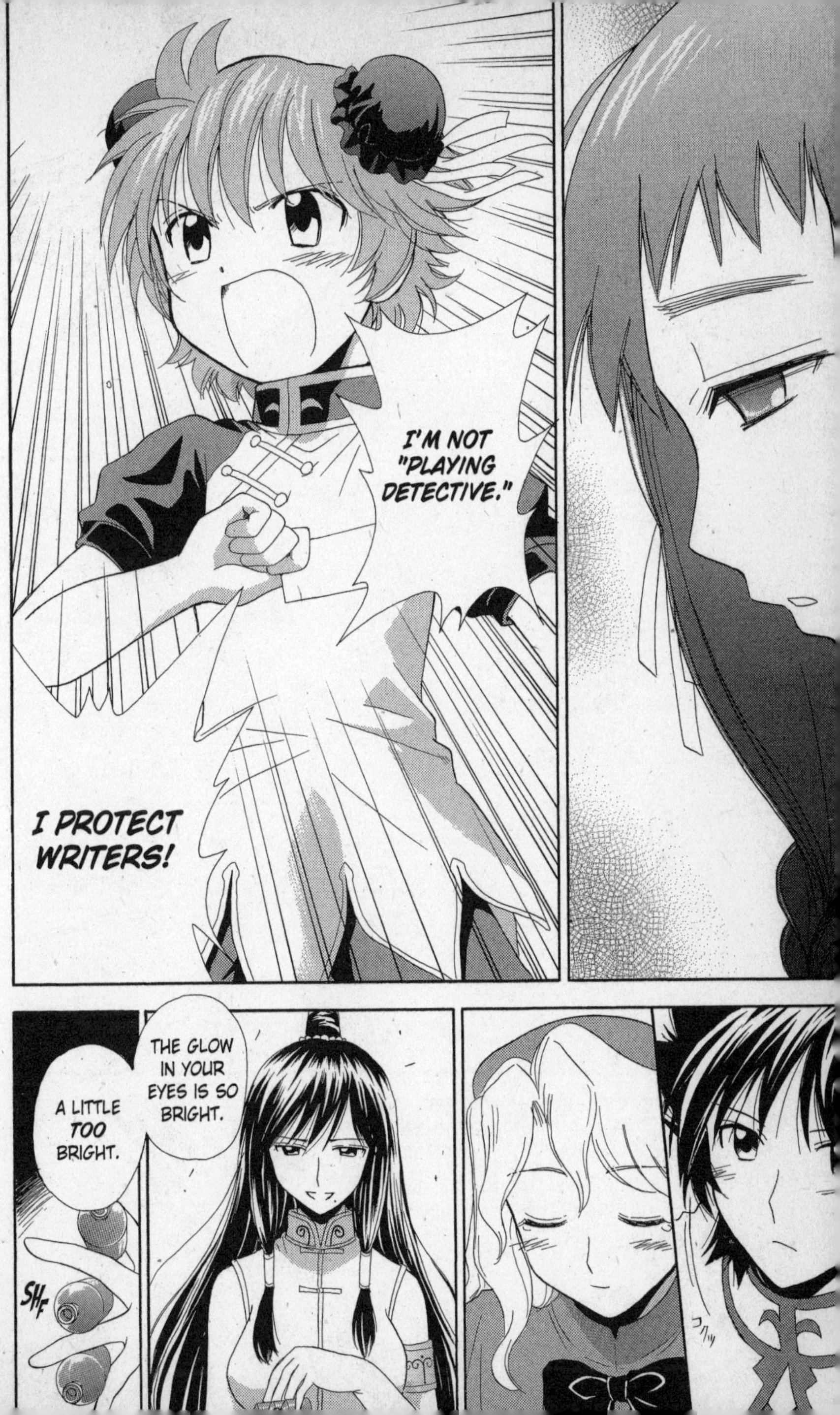
I'M NOT "PLAYING DETECTIVE."
I PROTECT WRITERS!
THE GLOW IN YOUR EYES IS SO BRIGHT.
A LITTLE TOO BRIGHT.
SHF

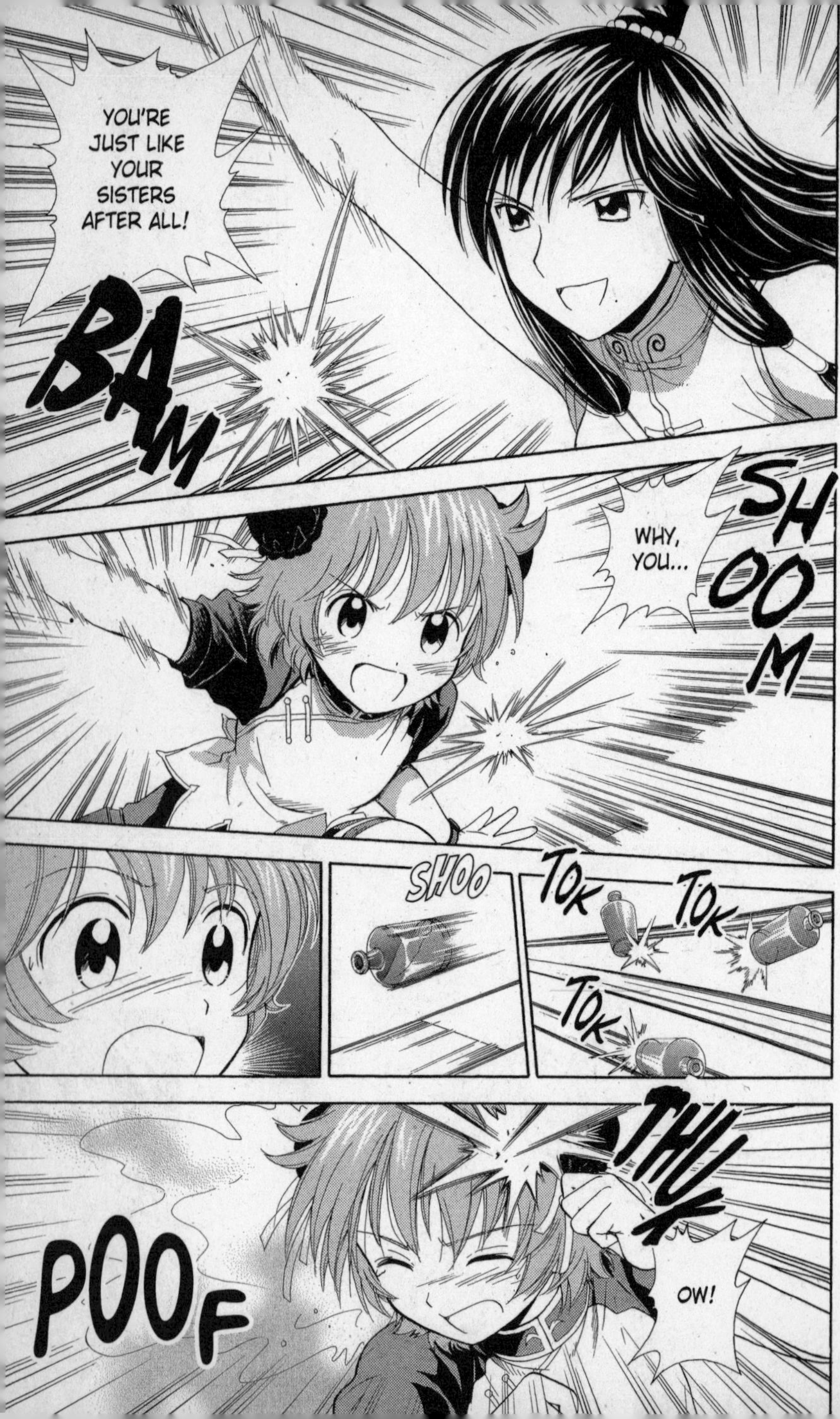
YOU'RE JUST LIKE YOUR SISTERS AFTER ALL!
BAM
WHY, YOU...
SHOOOM
TOK
TOK
TOK
SHOO
THUK
OW!
POOF

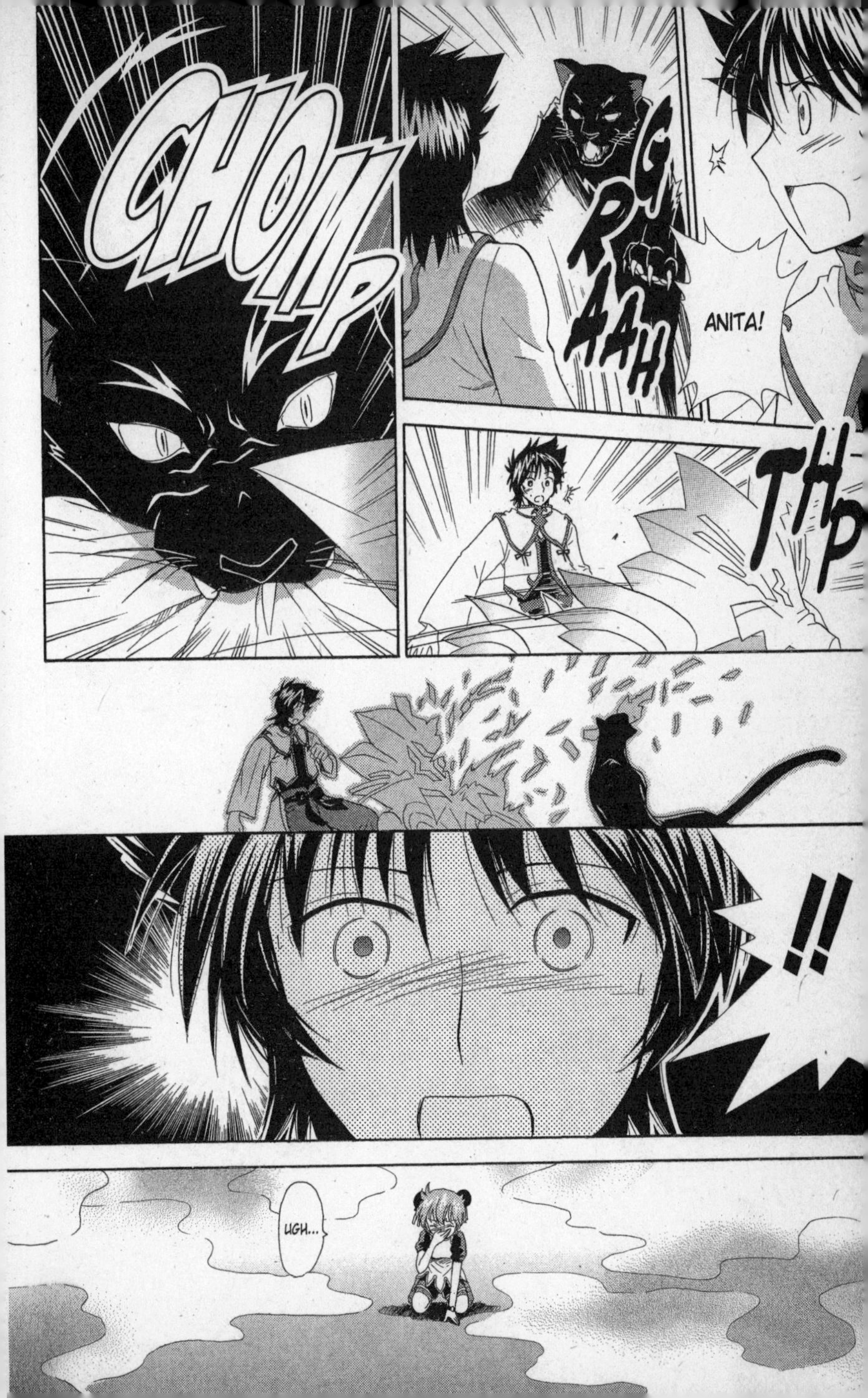
ANITA!
GRAAH
THP
CHOMP
!!
UGH...

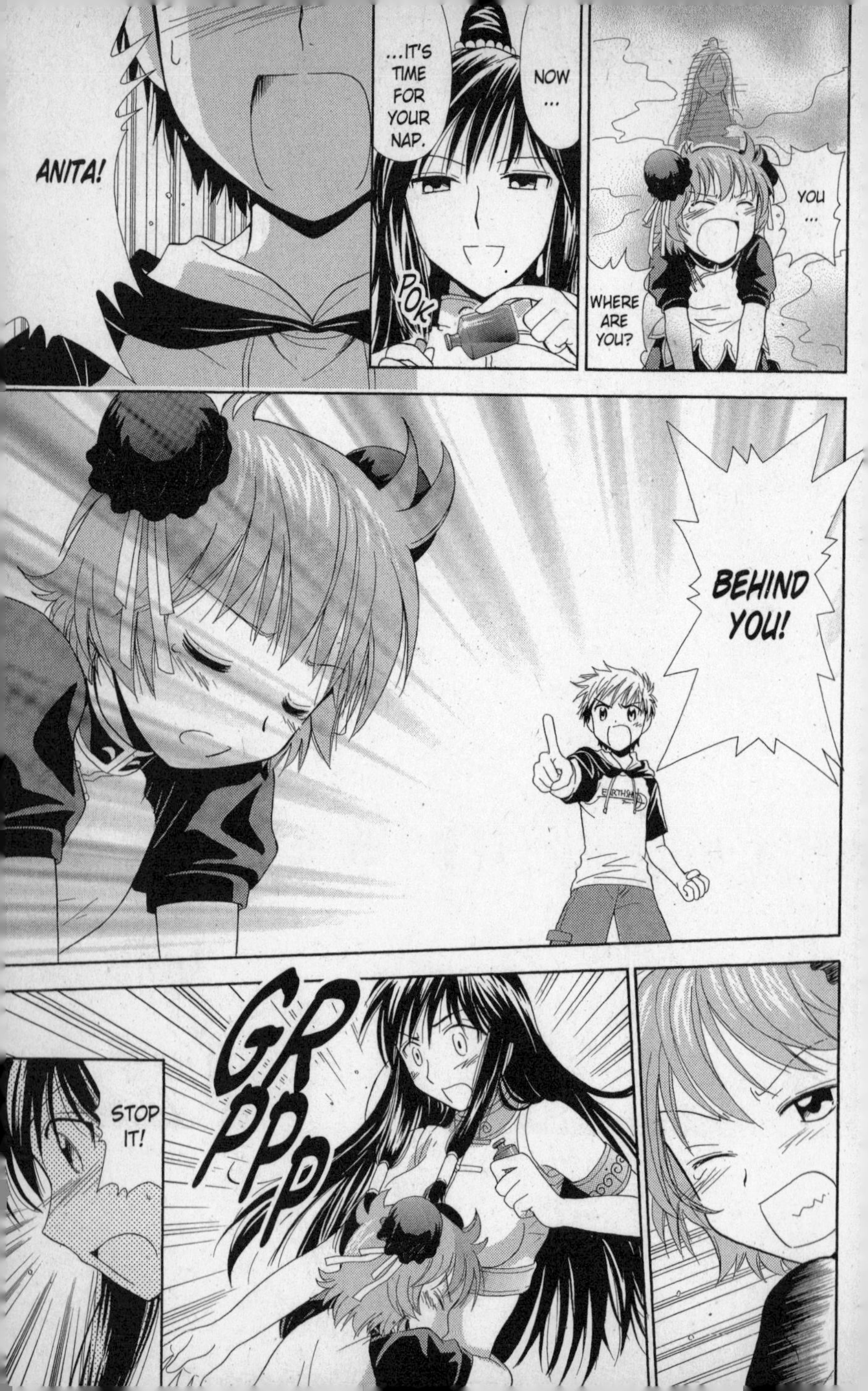
YOU ...
WHERE ARE YOU?
NOW ...
...IT'S TIME FOR YOUR NAP.
POK
ANITA!
BEHIND YOU!
GRPPP
STOP IT!

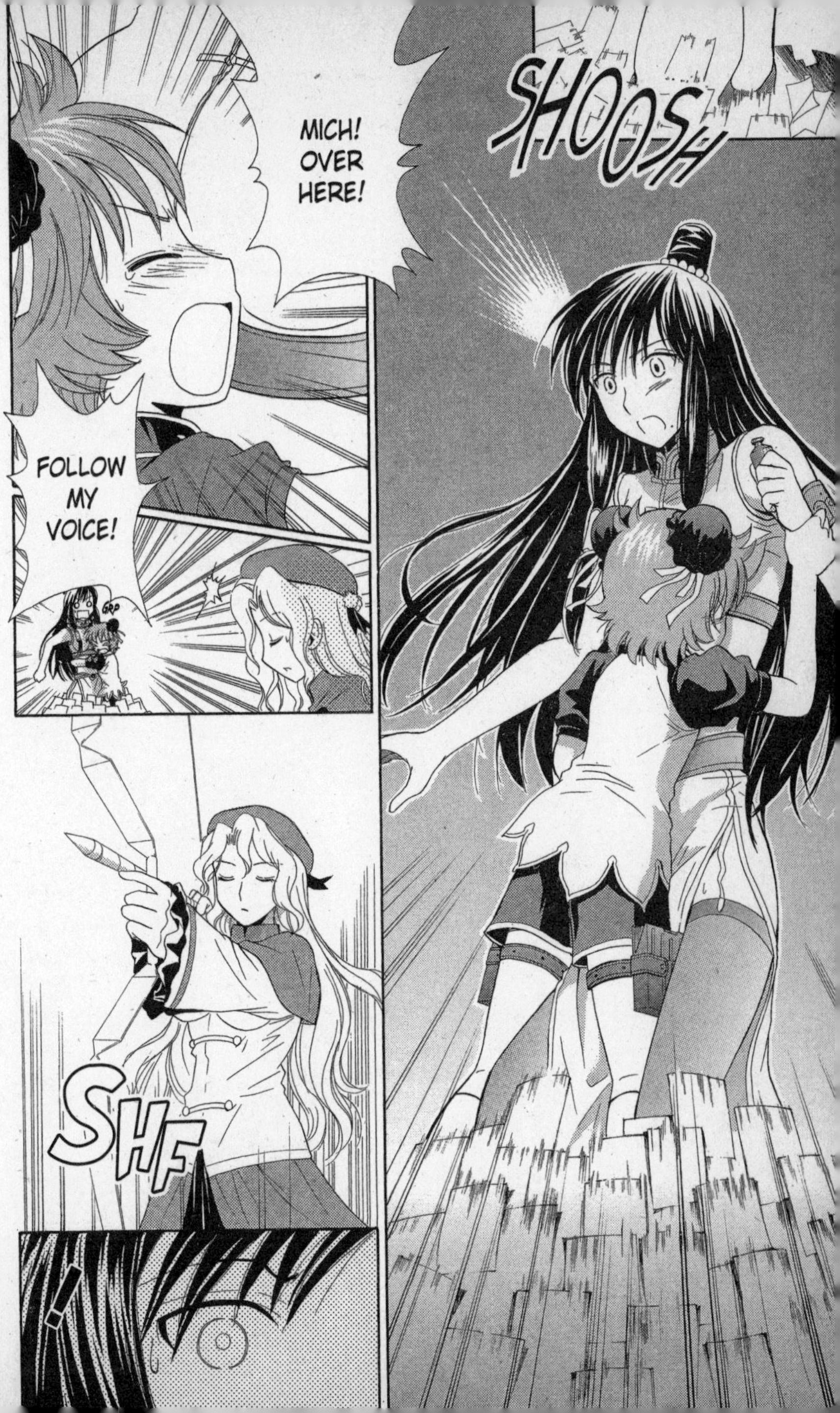
SHOOSH
MICH! OVER HERE!
FOLLOW MY VOICE!
GRP
SHF
!

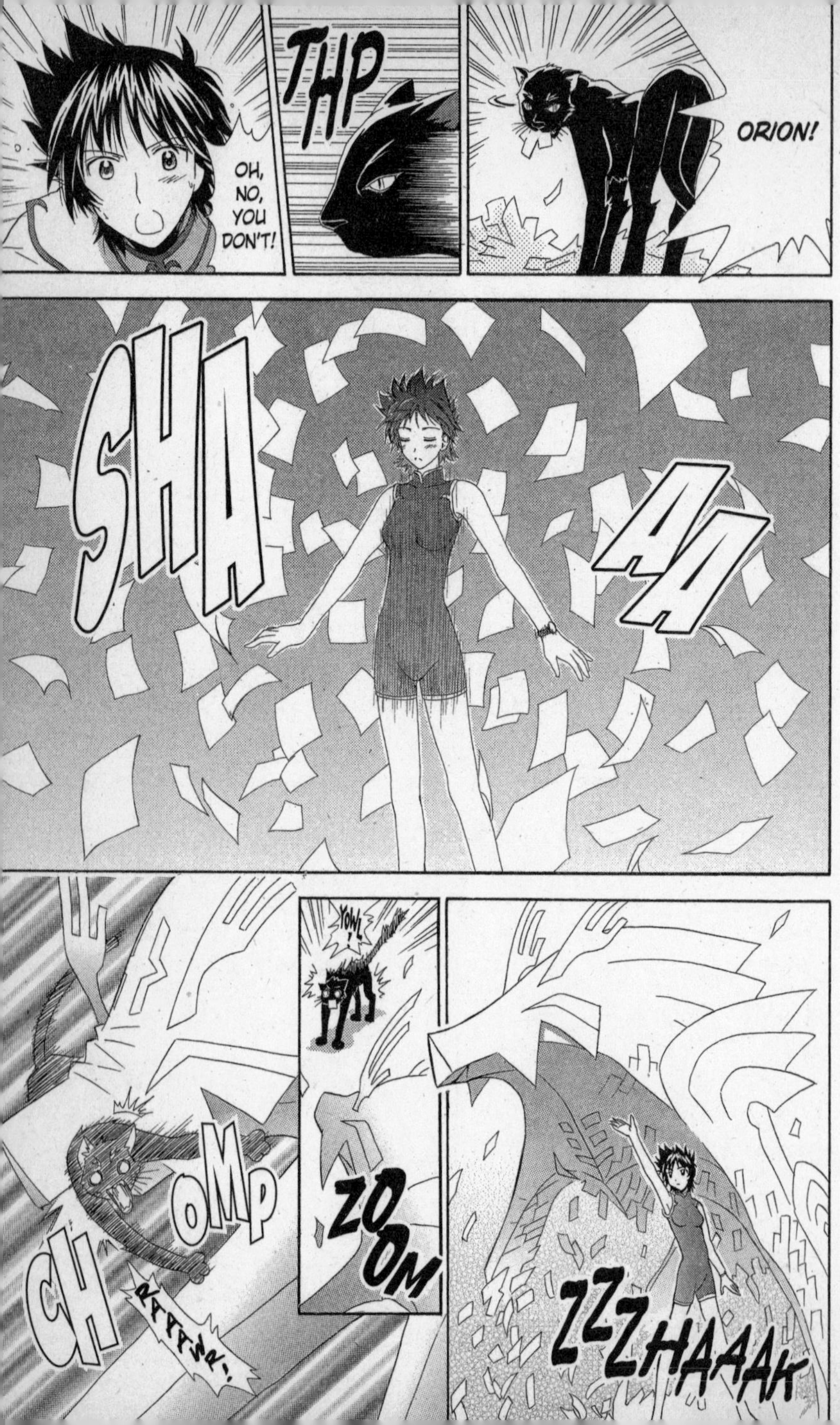
ORION!
THP
OH, NO, YOU DON'T!
SHA
AA
ZZZHAAAK
YOWL!
ZOOM
CHOMP
RAAAWR!

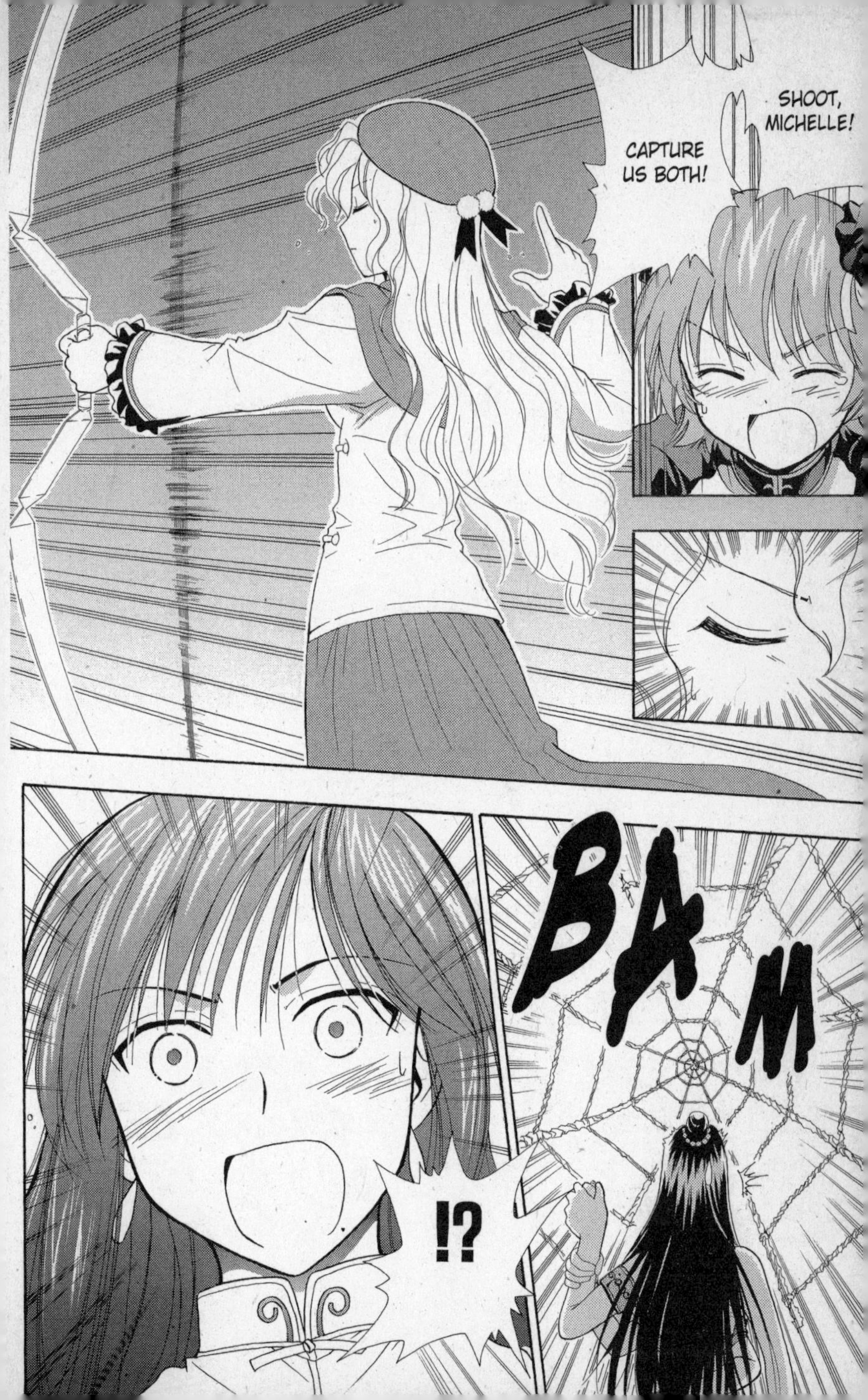
SHOOT, MICHELLE!
CAPTURE US BOTH!
BAM
!?

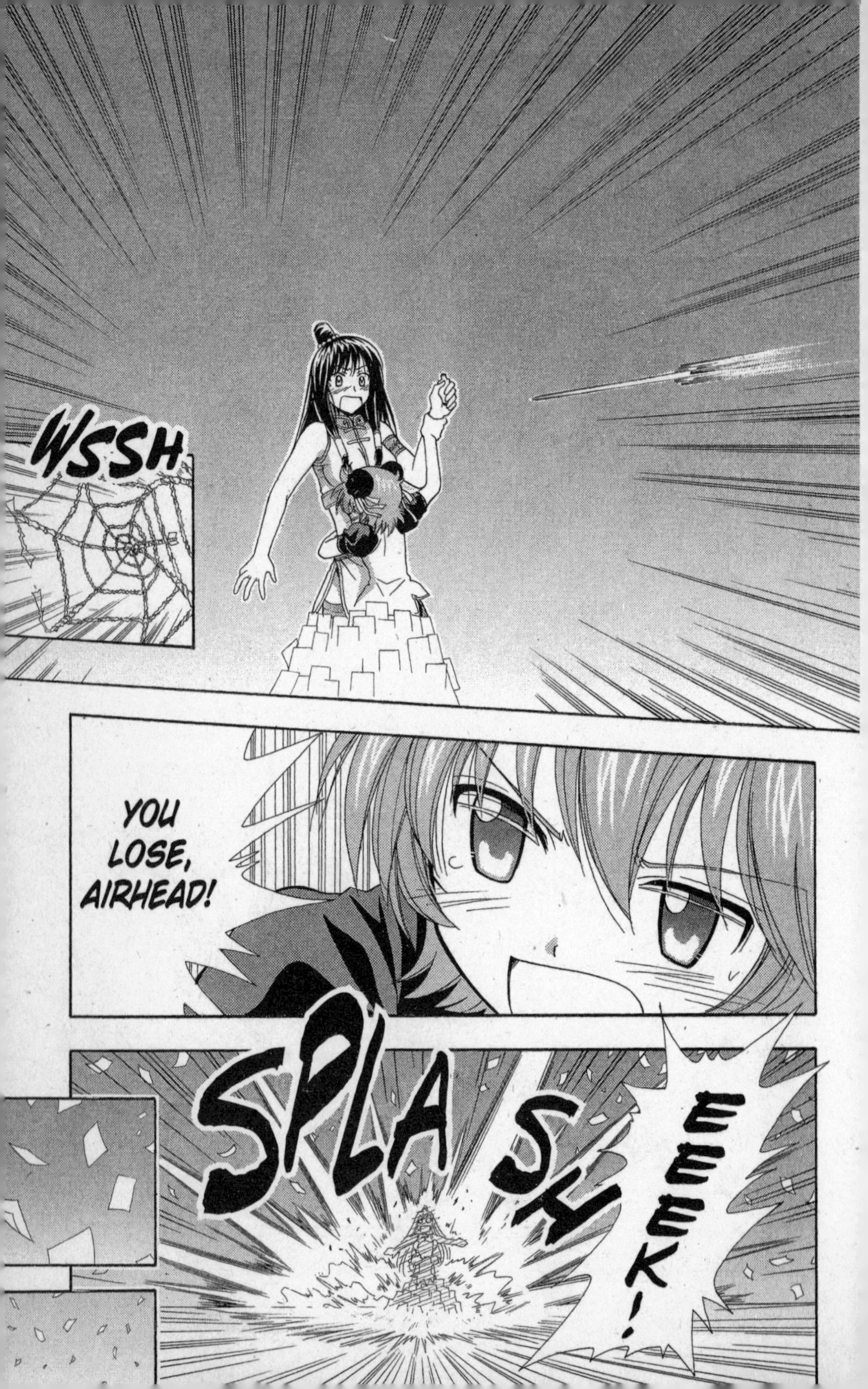
WSSH
YOU LOSE, AIRHEAD!
SPLASH
EEEEK!

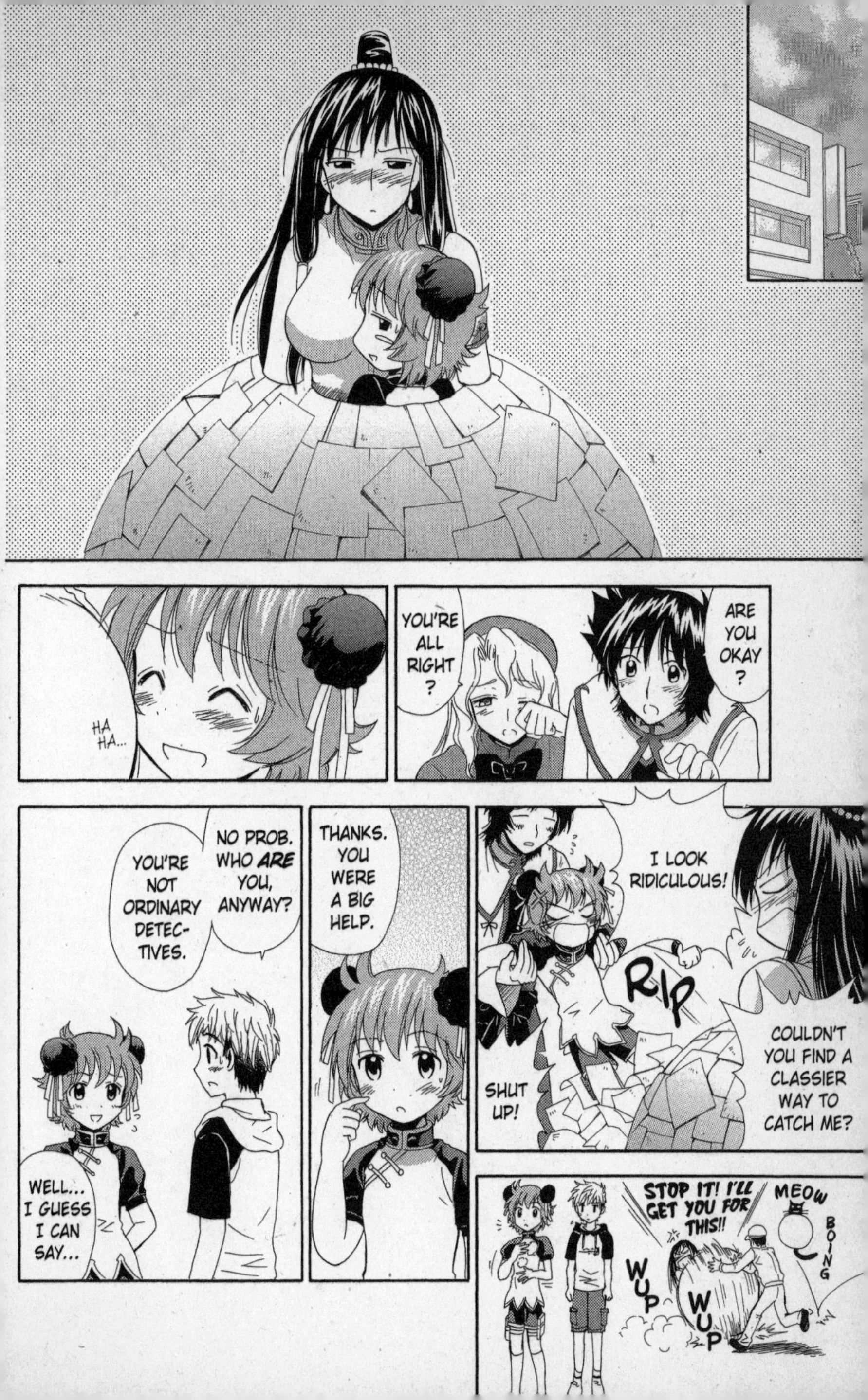
ARE YOU OKAY?
YOU'RE ALL RIGHT?
HA HA...
I LOOK RIDICULOUS!
COULDN'T YOU FIND A CLASSIER WAY TO CATCH ME?
RIP
SHUT UP!
MEOW
BOING
STOP IT! I'LL GET YOU FOR THIS!!
WUP
WUP
THANKS. YOU WERE A BIG HELP.
NO PROB. WHO *ARE* YOU, ANYWAY?
YOU'RE NOT ORDINARY DETEC-TIVES.
WELL... I GUESS I CAN SAY...

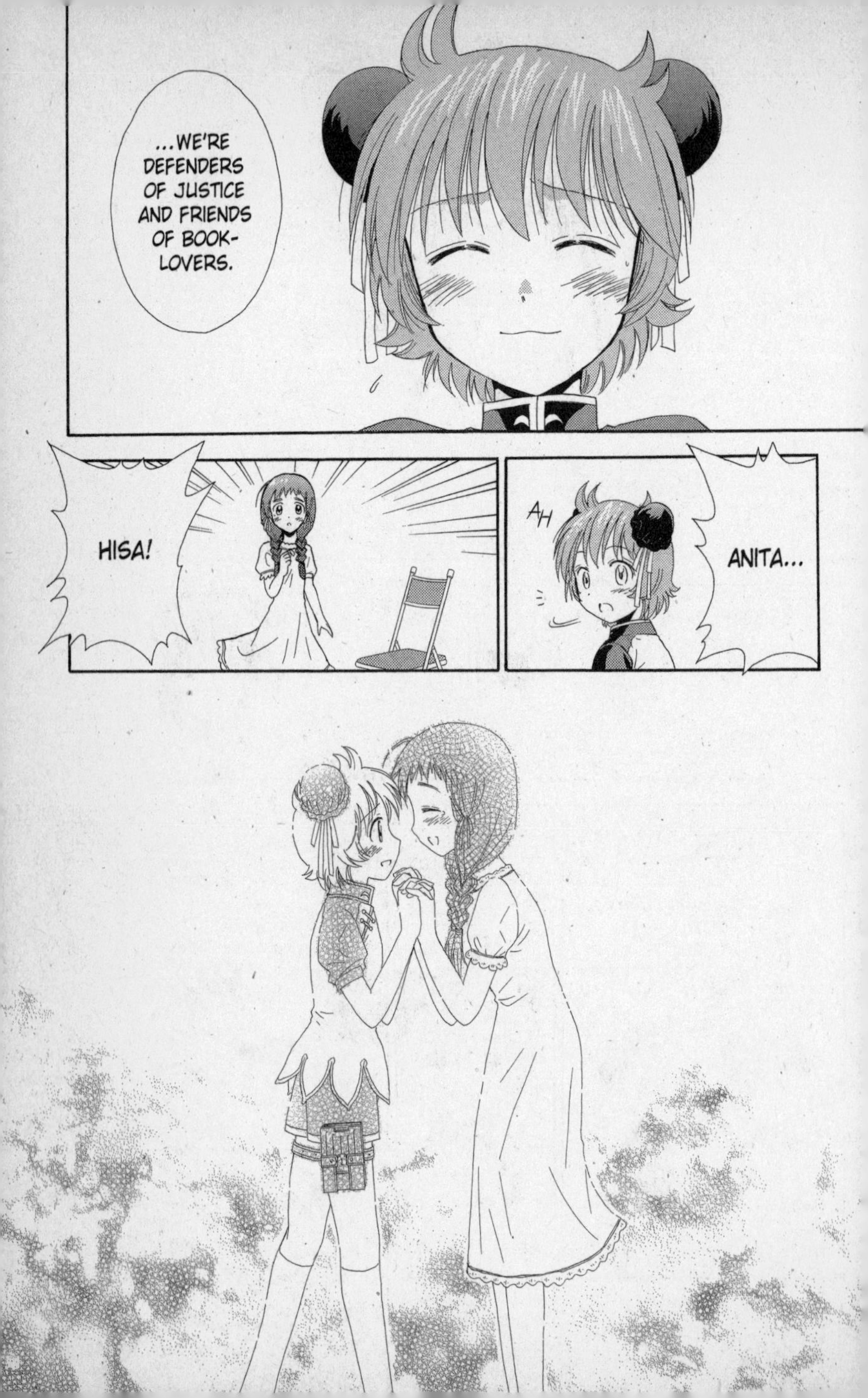
...WE'RE DEFENDERS OF JUSTICE AND FRIENDS OF BOOK-LOVERS.
ANITA...
AH
HISA!

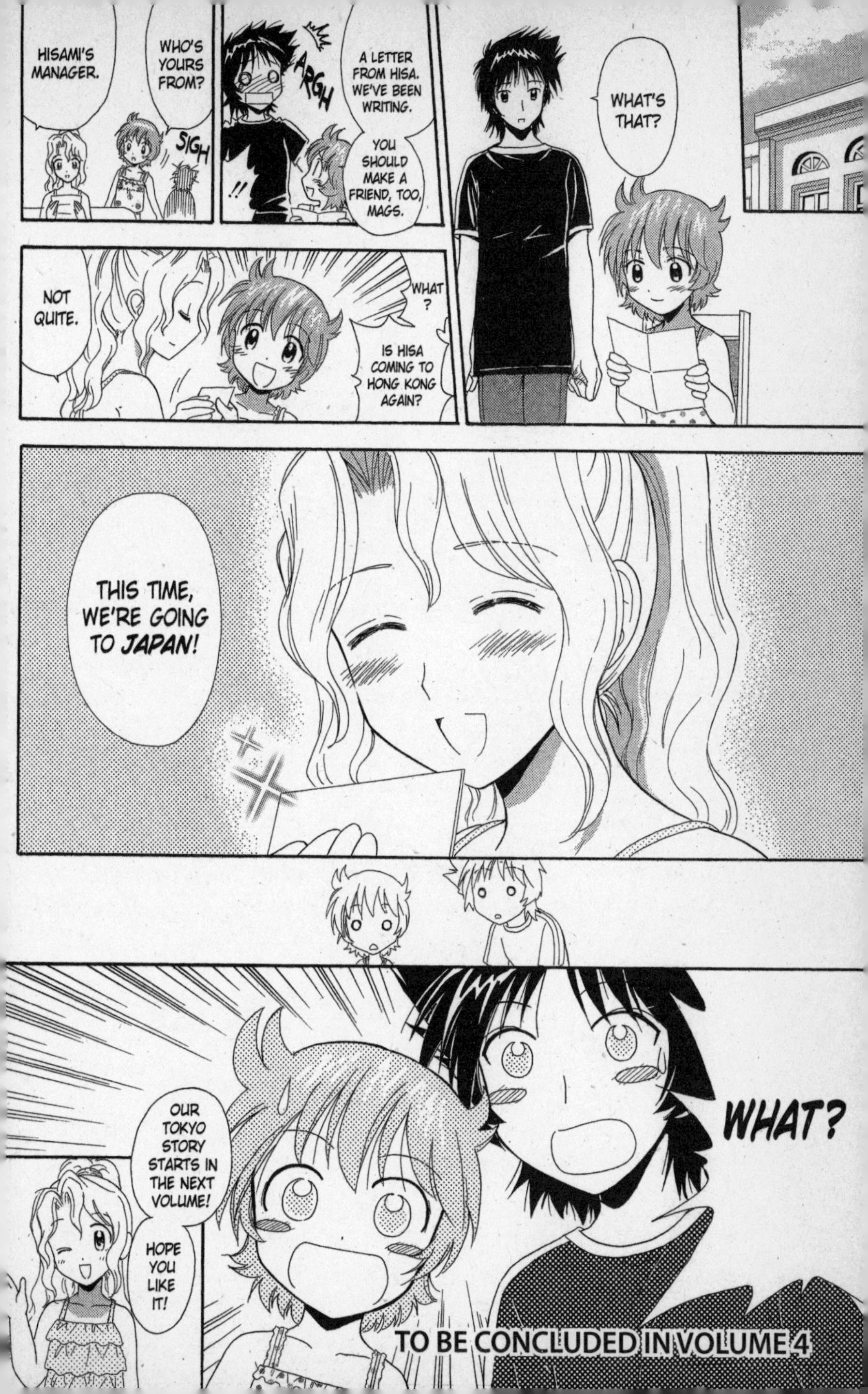
WHAT'S THAT?
A LETTER FROM HISA. WE'VE BEEN WRITING.
ARGH
YOU SHOULD MAKE A FRIEND, TOO, MAGS.
!!
WHO'S YOURS FROM?
SIGH
HISAMI'S MANAGER.
WHAT?
IS HISA COMING TO HONG KONG AGAIN?
NOT QUITE.
THIS TIME, WE'RE GOING TO JAPAN!
WHAT?
OUR TOKYO STORY STARTS IN THE NEXT VOLUME!
HOPE YOU LIKE IT!
TO BE CONCLUDED IN VOLUME 4

STAFF

Yasuyo Hirokane
Ai Udagawa
Taichi Sotoyama
Miki Sugiura
Satomi Hishinuma

EDITOR
Kunio Kondo

SPECIAL THANKS
Akihiro Yamada
MAGI

(Acknowledgements deleted...)

Ran Ayanaga

http://members.jcom.home.ne.jp/0724236901/

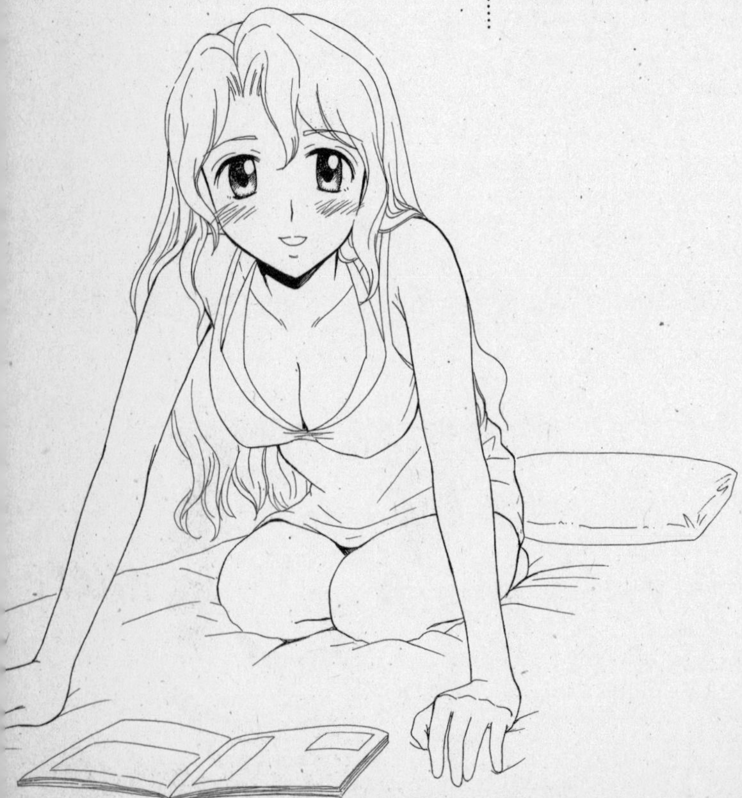

READER KING

HANDWRITTEN INTERVIEW!

A = RAN AYANAGA
K = HIDEYUKI KURATA

Ⓐ: Hope you're doing well! Mr. Kurata, we're up to Volume 3. Volume 3! When I started, I didn't think I'd be allowed to draw so many volumes, so I'm very, very happy.

Ⓚ: THAT'S RIGHT. AT FIRST, I THOUGHT THIS SERIES WOULD ONLY LAST FOR TWO VOLUMES. IT MAKES ME HAPPY, BUT I WONDER IF WE CAN KEEP COMING UP WITH STORYLINES.

Ⓐ: I only have to draw the pictures, but you have the **R.O.D** novels, anime and manga going on at the same time. I'm always amazed you can do it.

Ⓚ: SO AM I. I WAS HOPING TO GET EXTENSIONS ON MY DEADLINES, BUT NO SUCH LUCK. BECAUSE OF THAT, I THINK I CAUSED EVERYONE A LOT OF TROUBLE. DO I WORRY TOO MUCH?

Ⓐ: As far as I'm concerned, you've never caused me any trouble. In fact, I feel very grateful to you for taking care of me. In the manga, the gags seem to be getting funnier. Michelle seems to be wackier than ever. I'm especially frightened to think about what might have happened after that "7,600 Faces of Michelle" scene.

Ⓚ: DON'T WORRY. NO MATTER HOW MANY FACES SHE HAS, MICHELLE IS JUST ONE CHARACTER. SHE'D JUST BUY 7,600 TIMES MORE BOOKS. COME TO THINK OF IT, THAT'S A SCARY THOUGHT. I THINK THIS VOLUME IS FUNNIER, BUT IS THAT KIND OF THING EASIER FOR YOU TO DRAW?

A: We've gotten off track. Let's drop this for now.

K: ALL RIGHT. SHALL WE TALK ABOUT VOLUME 4? THE STORY SUDDENLY JUMPS TO TOKYO. HOW ABOUT WE HAVE THE SISTERS CAUSE AN UPROAR IN JINBOCHO[1]?

A: Yes. That's fine. You're really going all-out, doing everything you want, aren't you? We've had some pretty shocking scenes with the three sisters.

K: AND YET THE FINAL SCENE WILL BE VERY MOVING. WE'LL SQUEEZE TEARS OUT OF EVERY EYE. ER... THAT'S A LIE. I HAVEN'T DECIDED HOW TO END IT YET.

A: I'll do the best I can to the bitter end, so I hope you all give me your support. Now, shall we go out for drinks? Beer! Beer!

K: LET'S CALL SHUTARO YAMADA[2] AND CONTINUE THE INTERVIEW!

THE END

1. Jinbocho: a neighborhood in Tokyo known for its bookstores and publishing companies. It's one of the best places in Japan to find rare books and manga.

2. Shutaro Yamada was the artist on Kurata's previous manga series, **Read or Die**.

A: That's right. It's easier to draw funny, warmhearted gag material. And while I'm writing this, the men are suddenly speaking very seriously about girls with glasses.

K: YES. I WAS TALKING TO THE EDITOR, AND WE GOT ALL EXCITED AND BEGAN CONSIDERING ALL SORTS OF POSSIBLE TOPICS: GIRLS WITH GLASSES, MARRIED WOMEN, CRADLE-ROBBING, LESBIANS. WHICH WOULD YOU LIKE TO SEE WORKED INTO FUTURE STORIES?

A: Of those four... I'd say any of them would work. (Uh-oh, he and the editor are going on and on about sex. Kurata's laughing...)

K: AND WHILE I'M WRITING **THIS**, MISS AYANAGA AND OUR EDITOR WILL PROBABLY KEEP TALKING ABOUT SEX. WORDS LIKE "BUSINESSMEN," "HOUSEWIVES" AND "SEXUAL HARASSMENT" ARE FLYING AROUND.

BONUS STORY:
CLEANING UP DEMONS WITH ANITA THE CLEANER

THE INCANTATION FROZE MAGGIE IN HER TRACKS. "CURSES! WHAT'S HAPPENING?"

"HOW DO YOU LIKE THAT?" CHUCKLED ANITA.

"ANITA," SAID MICHELLE, "THIS IS JUST THE BEGINNING! YOU'VE GOT TO CLEAN OUT THE DEMON THAT'S INSIDE MAGGIE."

"OH, RIGHT! OKAY, TIME TO USE MY BRUSH."

ANITA FLUTTERED TO THE FLOOR AND BRANDISHED A CHIMNEY BRUSH—HER STOCK IN TRADE.

"NO, DON'T!" CRIED MAGGIE. "IF YOU SCRUB ME WITH THAT BRUSH, I'LL GET EVEN DIRTIER!"

"HMPH!" SAID ANITA. "I'LL SHOW YOU JUST WHAT I CAN DO!"

"GO, GO, ANITA!" MICHELLE CRIED.

SPURRED ON BY THE FAIRY'S CHEERS, ANITA BEGAN SCRUBBING MAGGIE WITH HER BRUSH.

SCRUB, SCRUB...

"OUCH! ST-STOP THAT!"

SCRUB, SCRUB...

THE BLACK BEGAN TO RUB OFF OF MAGGIE.

"OKAY, NOW FOR THE FINISH!" ANITA SCRUBBED MERCILESSLY AT MAGGIE'S FACE. TO HER SURPRISE, MAGGIE'S BODY BEGAN TO GLITTER AND GLOW.

"OH!" CRIED ANITA AS THE LIGHT GREW. "WHAT'S HAPPENING?"

"MAGGIE'S DEMON HAS DISAPPEARED COMPLETELY," EXPLAINED MICHELLE.

WHEN THE BLINDING GLOW FADED, THERE STOOD MAGGIE IN A WEDDING GOWN.

"I GUESS I'M DONE CLEANING," SAID ANITA.

"NO...SOMETHING'S WRONG," MICHELLE FROWNED. "WITH THE EVIL ERADICATED, MAGGIE SHOULD HAVE RETURNED TO HER USUAL SWEATSHIRT-AND-JEANS SELF."

"YOU MEAN MY CLEANING FAILED? YOU'VE GOTTA BE KIDDING!"

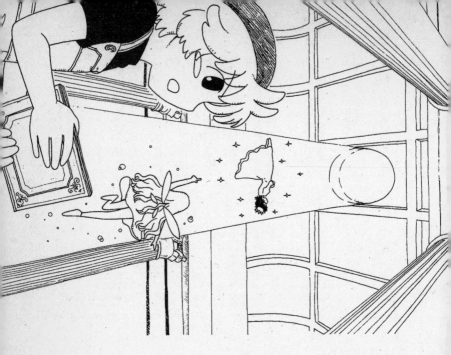

HER PRIDE AS A CHIMNEY-SWEEP. HUH, I, ANITA, RETURNED TO STUDYING THE BOOK.

SUDDENLY...

"HA HA HA HA HA!"

A VOICE SOUNDED FROM HIGH ABOVE. A LIGHT SHONE DOWN UPON MAGGIE.

"OH...IT'S SO BRIGHT!"

"WHO IN THE WORLD COULD IT BE?"

LOOKING UP, ANITA AND MICHELLE SAW A FLYING SAUCER IN THE NIGHT SKY. THE LIGHT WAS BEAMING DOWN FROM THE SAUCER.

A VOICE SOUNDED FROM THE SAUCER. "I AM AN ALIEN FROM OUTER SPACE. I AM TAKING MAGGIE WITH ME."

MAGGIE FAINTED. HER BODY LIMP, SHE ROSE IN THE BEAM.

AN ANGRY GLEAM GLOWED IN ANITA'S EYE. "AFTER EVERYTHING I DID TO RETURN HER TO NORMAL!" ALL HER OVERTIME WORK HAD GONE TO WASTE.

MICHELLE POINTED TO THE SKY. "THIS WON'T DO. LET'S FOLLOW THEM INTO SPACE!"

TO BE CONTINIIED...

R.O.D-THE TV- AYANAGA WORKS

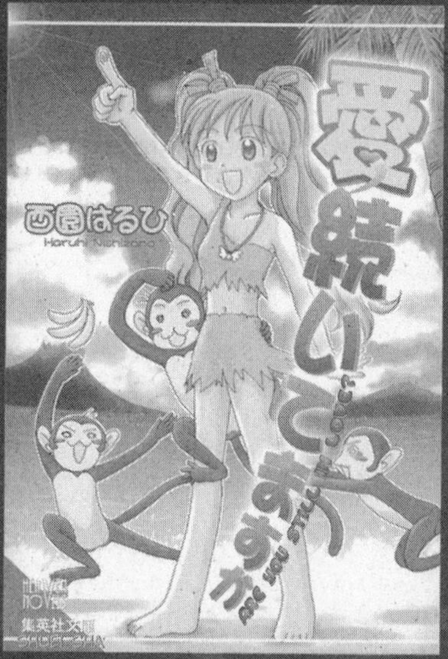
愛
続いてますか
西園はるひ
Haruhi Nishizono
集英社文庫

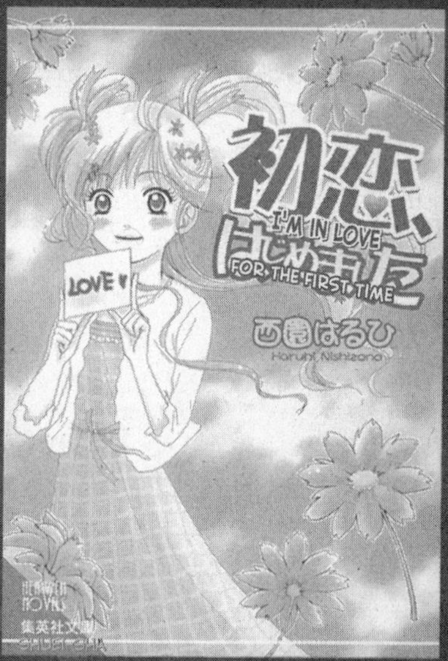
初恋、はじめました
I'M IN LOVE
FOR THE FIRST TIME
LOVE♥
西園はるひ
Haruhi Nishizono
集英社文庫

*

○ cover illustration by AYANAGA RAN
○ cover design & art direction by NORIYUKI ZINGUZI+ZiN STUDIO

R.O.D-THE TV-
AYANAGA WORKS

● THESE ILLUSTRATIONS BY RAN AYANAGA WERE USED AS THE COVERS OF NOVELS IN THE R.O.D ANIMATED TV SERIES. THERE ARE SLIGHT DIFFERENCES IN THE ANIME AND MANGA VERSIONS OF R.O.D, SO IT MIGHT BE INTERESTING TO TRY TO COMPARE THOSE DIFFERENCES.

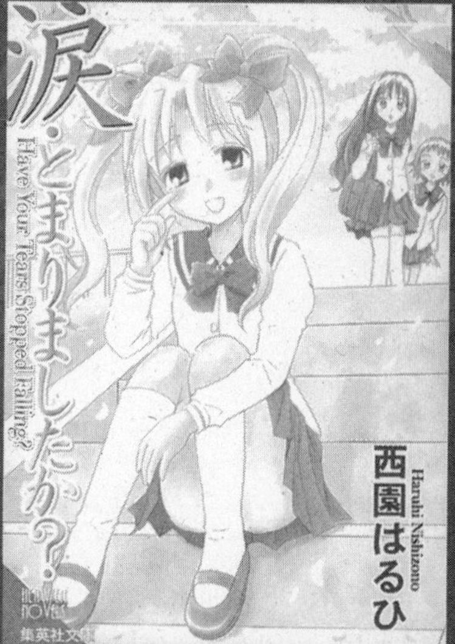
涙、とまりましたか？
Have Your Tears Stopped Falling?
西園はるひ
Haruhi Nishizono
集英社文庫

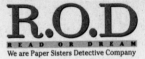

R.O.D
READ OR DREAM
We are Paper Sisters Detective Company

VIZ Media Edition
Vol. 3

STORY BY HIDEYUKI KURATA
ART BY RAN AYANAGA

Translation/JN Productions
Touch-up Art & Lettering/Mark McMurray
Design/Amy Martin
Editor/Shaenon K. Garrity

Managing Editor/Annette Roman
Editorial Director/Elizabeth Kawasaki
Editor in Chief/Alvin Lu
Sr. Director of Acquisitions/Rika Inouye
Sr. VP of Marketing/Liza Coppola
Exec. VP of Sales & Marketing/John Easum
Publisher/Hyoe Narita

Printed in the U.S.A.

Published by VIZ Media, LLC
P.O. Box 77010
San Francisco, CA 94107

10 9 8 7 6 5 4 3 2 1
First printing, March 2007

www.viz.com

store.viz.com

PARENTAL ADVISORY
READ OR DREAM is rated T+ for Older Teen and is recommended for ages 16 and up. This volume contains sexual themes.

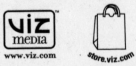

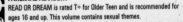

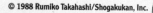

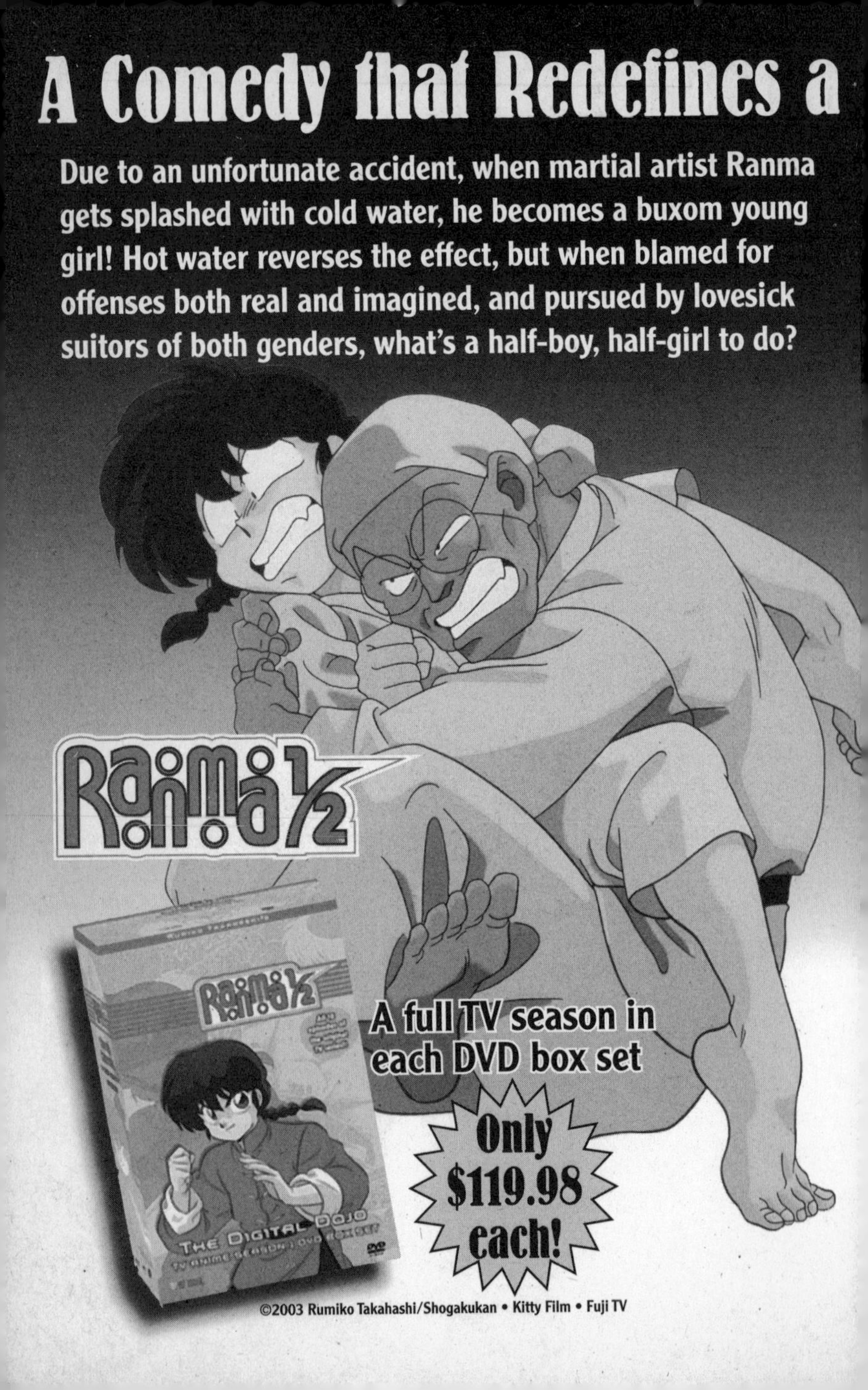
A Comedy that Redefines a
Due to an unfortunate accident, when martial artist Ranma gets splashed with cold water, he becomes a buxom young girl! Hot water reverses the effect, but when blamed for offenses both real and imagined, and pursued by lovesick suitors of both genders, what's a half-boy, half-girl to do?
Ranma 1/2
Ranma 1/2
THE DIGITAL DOJO
DVD
A full TV season in each DVD box set
Only $119.98 each!
©2003 Rumiko Takahashi/Shogakukan • Kitty Film • Fuji TV

LOVE MANGA?
LET US KNOW WHAT YOU THINK!

OUR MANGA SURVEY IS NOW AVAILABLE ONLINE. PLEASE VISIT: VIZ.COM/MANGASURVEY

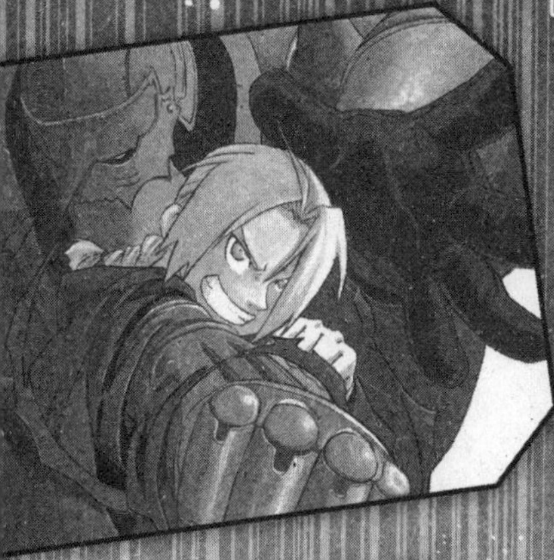

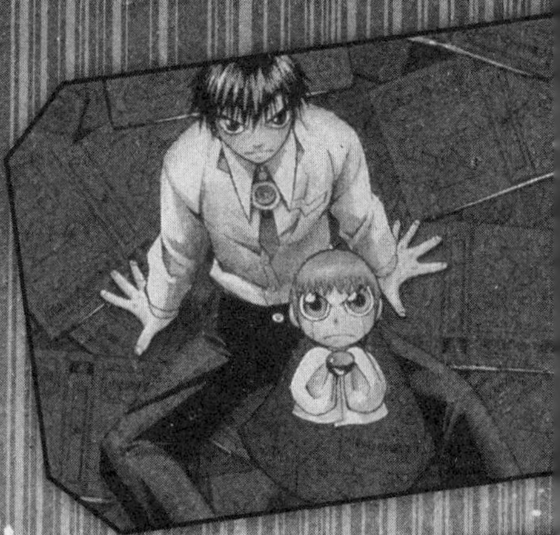

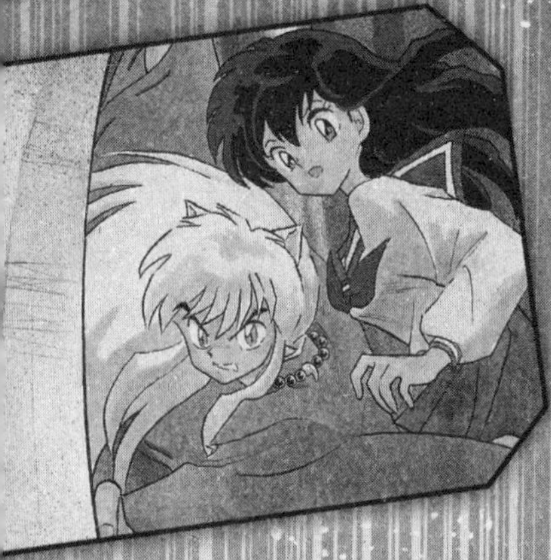

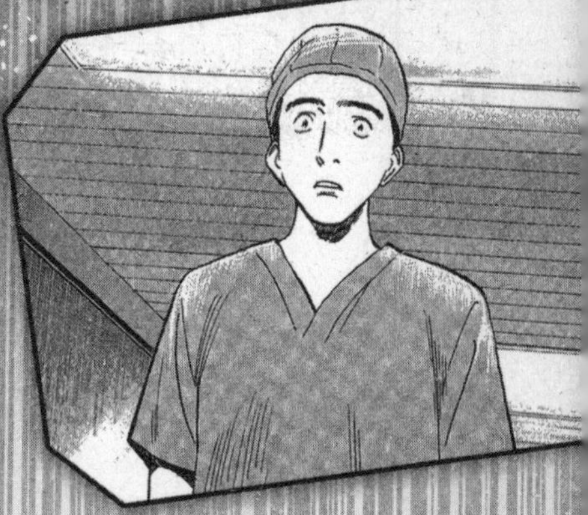

HELP US MAKE THE MANGA YOU LOVE BETTER!

viz media